I Quan-Tum

By Christian J. Bullock

Christian J. Bullock

ISBN 978-1-300-86934-4

ISBN 978-1-300-86934-4
90000
9 781300 869344

Christian J. Bullock

I Quantum is a book of Singularity Magick! It explores to use of Magick with Scientific, Archeological, Mathematic, Linguistic, and Astronomic observations and discoveries. It is written free hand scanned in with diagrams from a series of spell books. There are notations on every page on where to find this information and a suggested books section on where some of this information comes from. This book is a rough draft of a future book. I use diagrams repeatedly in my spell books. It is raw with pictures from my own spell books. This book is not for beginers who have never cast a circle. I assume that the reader already knows about magick, the various branches, and has a fair amount of knowledge on Paganism/The Occult. This is a book of data and secret knowledge. It is also a testimonial of Occult practices in a Singularity universe. This book is written into four parts or four books. The first book is the Little Dragon. It covers the basics of the magick in this book with diagrams and data to look over while reading the other books or when finding information for spells. It is a handy guide to have when ready. The second book is the Green Dragon. The third book is the Silver Dragon. The fourth book is the Gold Dragon.

Christian J. Bullock

The Index

Christian J. Bullock

Christian J. Bullock

Book One: The Little Dragon

Christian J. Bullock

This Book will cover everything from the Symbols of Power to Psychic Creationism. It details the basic outline of Singularity Magick with a specific set of questions. There are many recurring themes throughout the book as well as some redundancies that will be discussed in further in the other three books. There are some major points in this book from the living Celestial bodies to the actual data of these objects that rule our Solar System. There will also be calendar data of various kinds specifically in this Book the Mayan system of calendars. Make no mistake this is a Book of Magick as the types of Spells will be discussed in the other books but the time travel Spells will be brief in this book as there are many ways to sucessfully travel.

What is a Singularity? It is a single point where space, time, and matter become infinite.
What is a Singularity in this book? It is a circle of thought that is common to all. A single circle of degrees which governs all. A circle with the mathematical constant being Pi. It is a greater than human intelligence which governs all things including life. It is the Occult cast circle from which all magick springs. The source of the twelve ruling deities in a Pantheon or the creator God.
What is a Singularitian? A person depicted with a circle over their head. A person with greater than human knowledge or a person with secret knowledge of the Singularity that exists in the universe. Singularitians are depicted through out history with circles or halos over their heads. These depictions symbolize Singularity thought of a circle and an all seeing eye. They also symbolize the life giver of the monad and the connection to the Metaphysical Computer of the universe.
What is a Singularity Computer? It is a computer with greater than human knowledge, a technological super intelligence, or a computer that merges man and machine.
What is a Singularity Computer in this book? It is a machine that acts like a Big Bang machine governing all things, Planets, Moons, Stars, Galaxies, Particles, Atoms, including life itself.
What is a Metaphysical Computer? It is a theoretical computer which will emerge or that already exists, to govern all things including life. It is an all encompassing computer that man lives in where magick is possible. It is a Big Bang machine that does and will exist in the past or in the future of mankind.
What is a Singularity Room? It is a room that is used by a Singularitian to time travel. It is a room that exists in two or more places at once, this is due to quantum entanglement. It is also a room where a Singularitian practices magick.
What is a Quantum Jumper? It is a person who time travels or time jumps, by way of quantum entanglement. They exist by being in two places at the same time.
What is a Retwo? It is a being that exists in between time. They are time travellers that can see in between multiply dimensions of time. They redo things in the universe to bring order to chaos. They are invisible to those who don't have second sight. They manipulate humanity in order to survive. They are psychic telepaths speaking inside one's brain telling them what to do. They fix the timeline in order to keep humanity on track.
What is a Psy Cop? A cop that polices the human population. They are psychic's usually in police uniform with Palm Pilots.
What is a Hive Mind? It is a group mind made up of individuals that work in unison to perform tasks.
What is a Hive Mind Computer? It is a group mind made up of individuals on computers or using computers to perform tasks.

What is the All Cop? It is a greater than human super computer that governs all cops and hive mind computers. It polices all activity in a time travel universe.

What are Trackers? They are people that track or follow time travellers.

What is Bubble Theory? It is the theory that a time exists in a bubble or sphere around a Planet.

What is Bubble Theory in this book? It is a theory that a Planet, Star, person, or object can exists in a bubble of space time while another bubble of space time exists around them. Each Planet or Moon has an axis with a circular timeline around zodiac procession.

As I said before this is a book of magick and as such I will start off with a quick explanation of the celestial bodies and the elements which govern the universe.

The Planets and Solar Bodies

Aa a Magician it is important to understand the natural world. It is also important to understand the Earth and the sky. Also it is important to know where all this fits in together. Astronomy and Astrology are important in predicting the future, seeing signs, and knowing when the time is right to perform rituals and spells.

The Earth has cycles, movements, growth, and geothermal activity. The Earth itself gives us a home and gives us life. It protects us with an atmosphere, a magnetic field, and an ionosphere. More importantly it has a life force, it is alive. Ancient cultures knew of the life force and called her Mother Earth or the Earth Mother. In other cultures she was called the Dragon or Tiamat the Great Mother Dragon. This is vital information to the Magician and to Singularity Magick.

The Earth's life force stretches outward from it's molton core. There are hot spots on the surface where her life force is strongest. Much like volcanos and geothermal vents, these places are called vortexes or ley lines or Dragon Energies. They are sacred places for healing and ritual. Many Ancient cultures knew of these hot spots and built temples or stone circles over them. The Magician can train to access or absorb this energy or life force. Such things as breather training are vital to this understanding.

Just like the Earth the Sun has cycles. It also has nuclear energy, thermal energy, photonic energy, magnetic energy, and solar winds. It has sun spots that go through an eleven year cycleand solar flares that correspond to these solar maximum cycles. The sun also has magnetic storms that effect the Earth and the rest of the planetary bodies in the solar system. It is alive and it has a life force. Ancient people assciated the Sun with life and the embodiment of a God. It is vital that the Magician understand the importance of the Sun in spells, rituals, and creation myths.

The Moon also has cycles but these cycles are more of motion and rotation in the sky. The Moon's cycles of rotation around the Earth directly effect things on the Earth. The tides are caused by the Moo,. as well as storms and storm surges. The light shining off the Moon gives us light at night but more importantly it effects all creatures on the Earth. It helps flowers bloom at night and it helps nocturnal animals live at night. It even aids in a woman's menstral cycles. It is alive and it has a life force. Ancient people associated the Moon with the Goddess. This is also vital to the Magician in spells, rituals, and myths. The Moon's gravity is tidally locked to the Earth which makes it part of the Earth's solar eco-system.

By understanding these simple concepts a Magician can apply this to all planetary bodies in the solar system. Thus explanding the solar eco-system. The Ancient peoples all observed this and named all life forces as Gods and Goddesses. The Magician taps into all of these life forces in spells and rituals. The Ancients also named other stars as important Gods and Goddesses. They a life force and are also alive. Thus the Magician is part of a larger eco-system, a universal eco-system. The Galaxy is also named by the Ancients. The Milky Way is named after Hera the Queen of the Greek Gods. In one myth it was formed by a squirt of milk from her breast. The Galaxies have a life force and are alive. Galaxies expand the universal eco-system in which the Magician lives in. The universe streaches beyond what we see from Earth and beyond to the otherworld. Thus creating a Multiversal eco-system. This is vital knowledge to the Magician when meditating and during otherworldly travel.

The Elements and Elementals

The four major elements are very important to the Magician. They are vital to rituals and circle casting, but a greater understanding of these forces aids the Magician in otherworldly travels and higher magick.

Fire is an element vital to survival. It radiates energy, energy that perhapse is in its most energetic stae. The heat it produces is vital to all life and also to all planetary bodies. It acts as a force of nature, with a will and a mind of its own. It has a life force and it is alive. Long ago the Ancients made this connection and meditated with the fire spirits. Fire is used by the Magician in all circle casting.

Water is also an element vital to survival. It radiates kenetic energy or the energy of motion. It can carve out canyons and give protection or sustenence to all living things. It can also give life to planetary bodies and it is a building block to all life on Earth. It also is sometimes unpredictable and has a mind of its own. It has a life force and it is alive. The Ancients long ago learned to connect with the water spirits and the rain Gods.

Earth is also an element vital to survival. It gives plants the chemical elements needed to survive. Earth can hold both heat and kenetic energy. It can protect us with earthen bricks and it binds our world. It is also vital to all planetary bodies. It has a life force and it is alive. Earth spirits are plentiful and vital to the Magician.

Air is also an element vital to survival. It has an energy all its own. That of gas and aerodynamics. It allows us to breath, even the fish in the ocean breath the oxygen gas or molecules traped in the liquid water. Trees breath in CO_2 in the air and exhale oxygen. Air makes up our atmosphere and protects us from UV rays. Sound only travels because of air, without air there would be no sound. Air is vital for our electron transport chain in our cells. Air is vital to all planetary bodies. It has a life force and it is alive. Long ago Shamans gave air spirits specific names and the four wind spirits correspond to the cardnal directions.

Storm is a fifth element used in Dragon Magick and Norse Magick. It is also vital to survival. Some may see it as a derivitive of air but it actually has characteristics all its own, that of lightning. It has a fury that is vital to all life. When the Earth was created lightning storms fused atoms together to create more complex molecules out of amino acids. It is one of the five elements used in a laboratory creation of the early Earth. Gas-Air, Heat-Fire, Water-Water, Acids-Earth, and Lightning-Storm. Storms are part of most planetary bodies and solar storms are part of every plantary body. It has a life force and it is alive. Many Ancient peoples had a lightning God of some sort in their Pantheon. In Norse mythology Thor is the lightning/thunder God and one of emmense power. In Greek mythology Zues the king of the Gods throws lightning bolts.

Christian J. Bullock

Spirit is also a fifth element and it is at the top of the pentagram. Spirit is the will or life force within each of us. It connects all of us to the source. It is at the heart of all magick and the connection to the elementals within a cast circle.

Symbols and the Stars of Power

There are twelve major symbols of power in Singularity Magick. They are each important and have a special significence within the circle. A circle of 360 degrees is thus divided into twelve equal parts.

O — a dot of binary 360°
| — a line of binary 180°
△ — 3 points /360° fire 120°
† — earth cross 4 points/360° 90°
☆ — 5 points /360° pentagram 72°
✡ — 6 points/360° star of David 60°
— 7 points /360° elven star 51.4°
✳ — 8 points/360° 45°
— 9 points/360° 40°
— 10 points/360° 36°
— 11 points/360° 32.72°
— 12 points/360° 30°

They are numerically ordered from one to twelve:

1 point/360 degrees = 360 degrees	This is the binary dot or circle
2 points/360 degrees = 180 degrees	This is the binary one or line
3 points/360 degrees = 120 degrees	This is a triangle which represents fire
4 points/360 degrees = 90 degrees	This is an Earth cross which represents four elements
5 points/360 degrees = 72 degrees	This represents the pentagram
6 points/360 degrees = 60 degrees	This represents the star of David or six elements
7 points/360 degrees = 51.4 degrees	This represents the elven star, the moon, or seven elements
8 points/360 degrees = 45 degrees	This represents the eight Sabbats
9 points/360 degrees = 40 degrees	This represents the nanogram or nine fold Goddess symbol
10 points/360 degrees = 36 degrees	This represents the ten pointed star or the fate Goddess
11 points/360 degrees = 32.72 degrees	This represents the eleven pointed star
12 points/360 degrees = 30 degrees	This represents the twelve pointed star or twelve zodiacs

These symbols of power also represent the twelve dimensions of space and time:

1st dimension is a dot or one point in space time

2nd dimension is two dots connected by a line or two points in space time

3rd dimension is three dots in space time which make a triangle

4th dimension is four dots in space time or a cube or cross

5th dimension is five dots in space time or a pentagon or pentagram

6th dimension is six dots in space time or a hexagon or hexagram

7th dimension is seven dots in space time or septagon or septagram

8th dimention is eight dots in space time or an octogon or octogram

9th dimension is nine dots in space time or a nanogon or nanogram

10th dimension is ten dots in space time or a decogon or decogram

11th dimension is eleven dots in space time or eleven pointed star

12th dimension is twelve dots-points in space time or a twelve pointed star

These symbols represent both the micro and macro scales of the Singularity universe.

Using the English system of measurement of a foot we can use a macro and micro scale of twelve:

12 inches in a foot, 36 inches in a yard, 300 feet in 100 yards, and 3,600 inches in 300 feet

1/4th of an inch, 1/8th of an inch, 1/16th of an inch, 1/32nd of an inch, and 1/64th of an inch

Twelve is further represented in the micro scale by computers and degrees:

4 bit, 8 bit, 16 bit, 32 bit, and 64 bit

4 bytes, 8 bytes, 16 bytes, 32 bytes, 64 bytes, 128 bytes, 256 bytes, 512 bytes, and 1024 bytes in 1 KB

360 degrees, 720 degrees, 1080 degrees, and 1440 degrees

These measurements are all used in the Singularity Computer, Metaphysical Computer, and the universe. The reason is that they are all a good way to measure the mathematical constant Pi and the circle that is common to all things 360 degrees.

The Planets and Their Alignments

The Planets are aligned in a very specific way starting with the Earth. The Earth is tilted on its axis by 23 degrees. It rotates on this axis giving us 24 hours in a day. On the day of an Equinox there are 12 hours of day and 12 hours of night. The Earth also has a wobble on this axis in which the stars in the sky on Earth will change over time. This is called procession and it is an important part of Singularity Magick. The band of constellations that make up the zodiac will change in appearance over time, this is called zodiac procession. When the constellation seen on the winter soltice or equinox changes, this is called the procession of the equinoxes. It takes the Earth 71.6 years for the constellations to move 1 degree in procession and it takes 2,148 years for the constellations to change or 30 degrees of procession. It takes the Earth 25,920 years, a modern approximation, to pass through all the constellations and complete a 360 degree passage of all 12 zodiac constellations. The zodiac procession of the equinoxes is like clock work and it is very precise. The pole star or north star on Earth will change from Polaris to Vega and Vega to Polaris during the procession of the equinoxes. The Earth also has a 365 day solar year but more on that later. As we shall see later the Earth is in an alignment favorable to 360 degrees and it is locked in a goldelocks zone.

The Moon is on a 51.4 degree incline to the Earth and this gives us a well aligned view of it. This also accounts for it being represented by the number 7 in Singularity Magick. The Moon is tidally locked with

Christian J. Bullock

the Earth so that only one side faces the Earth. This is a good thing because it means that the cycles of the Moon can be easily calculated as 29 days, approximatly. A lunar year is easier to calculate than an Earth solar year. A lunar year is very reliable, the Ancients used it in their spells and rituals. It is important for the Singularity Magician to understand the lunar phases and year. The Moon also has a special relation to the number 7 in the processional cycle on Earth.

360 degrees / 7 points = 51.42857143 degrees

51.42857143 degrees * 72 years = 3702.857143 years

3702.857143 years * 7 points = 25,920 years

The use of the numerical values of the Symbols of Power is very important in Singularity Magick.

The next Planet that is in alignment is Venus. It actually has a near perfect orbit around the Sun. Its orbit makes a reliable 360 degree rotation around the Sun. It has a 5 to 8 ratio with the Earth, which means that it has a 584 day orbit from Eath and 5 cycles of this orbit gives us 8 years on Earth.

584 days * 5 cycles = 2,920 days   2,920 days / 365 days = 8 years

It is further aligned with 360 degrees of Singularity and the Symbols or Stars of Power:

360 days / 8 points = 45 degrees   365 days / 5 points = 73 days   360 degrees / 5 points = 72 degrees

Venus actually makes a star or pentagram as it passes from closest to Earth to farthest away from Earth during its 2,920 day journey. On Earth Venus can be seen as the morning star in a cycle as:

263 days on the horizon   5 cycles of 584 days

  50 days below the horizon   which repeats every 8 years on Earth

263 days on the horizon

    8 days below the horizon

584 days total

The Ancients knew this and could calculate a 20 days each 4 days correction every 61 years. The Planet Venus can also be calculated into the Earths processional cycle using the degrees of 360 and 45 degrees or an 8 pointed star. Venus is also very mysteriusly aligned since in doesn't have a moon and because it rotates backward on its axis. Which makes it different from all the other planets. This alignment as we shall see later means a time warping is going on in the solar system.

The Planet Mars also has an alignmet with the Earth and the solar system. It has two moons Phobos and Dimos. It has an orbital period of 686.971 days, approximatly. 686 days is very close to 720 degrees but it has a eccentric orbit that varies, more on that later. One Martian day is called a sol and it is 24 hours 40 minutes. This slight variance is very close to Earth's 24 hours which makes it easy to calculate. Mars has an axis tilt of 25 degrees and we will soon find out that it has a zodiac procession as well. Its mean distance from the Sun is 1.524 AU, which means its nearly half the distance from the Earth as 1 AU is the distance from the Earth to the Sun. Its orbit was probably more circular in the ancient past. More importantly though is that Mars can be calculated into Earths processional cycle:

686.971 days * 38 cycles = 26,104.898 days

1,872,000 Earth days / 26,104.898 days = 71.7106805 degrees to procession

Once again one of the numerical Symbols of Power fits in with the calculations, 5 points or 72 degrees. This alignment as we shall soon see will be a marker for Earth's Procession and the secret of Singularity Magick.

The Planet Jupiter has a well known alinment with the Earth's procession and with the zodiac. It has a 4,331.572 day orbit and a 11.85920 year orbit. This syncronizes with the 12 houses of the zodiac or 12 divisions of the 360 degree circle. It has a 5 to 2 ratio to the Earth. Which means it can also be plotted on the Earth's procession of the equinoxes.

The Planet Saturn also has a well known alignment to the zodiac and Earth. It has a 10,759.22 day orbit and a 29.4571 year orbit. This gives us a 30 degree period or one 12th of zodiac procession. Which means it can be figured into Earth's procession of the equinoxes. Once again the Singularity Magician must understand this to perform Singularity Magic.

The Singularity Universe

One of the major aspects of Singularity Magick is that the universe is a kind of living organism or hive mind organism. Its reach also encompasses computers, technology, and the Singularity Computer. The universe is a kind of living web of celestial objects. Remnance of the Big Bang leaving a unique signiture.

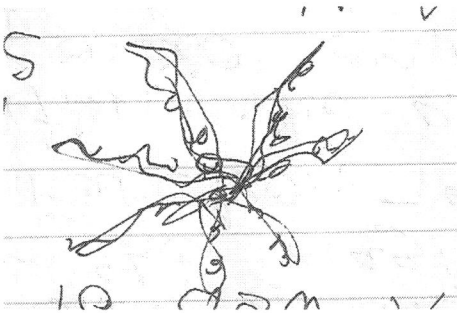

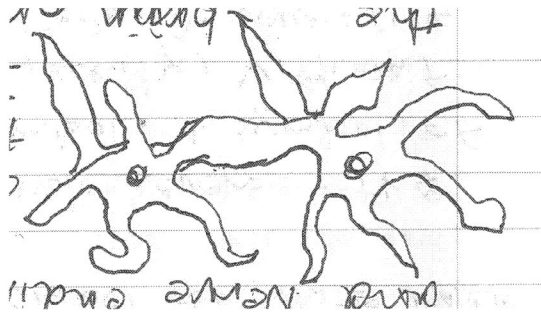

This signiture resembles a nuron cell in the human brain. Thus the universe is a nuron of a living celestial organism that is greater in size and scope. Of course the universe is multi-dimensional with many other dimensions that we can't see or grasp. Thus the universe is split into different levels making a muliverse, or multiple universes, with each universe looking and acting like a nuron. The Singularity therefore is a hive mind or universal concusness in which the Magician lives in.

Psychic Creationism

At the heart of Singularity Magick is Psychic Creationism. In which a far seer psychic in communication with a future spirit or the creator God help create the universe and all things in it. In essence psychic beings(and Singularitians) that existed, exist, or will exist help pave the way for a Singularity Computer(universal concusness) to be built. This is done by creating a specific time loop where humanity under goes several ages of civilization as the universe expands exponentially and at the end of time when all the stars burn out a creator God time travels back to the very beginning to create the Big Bang. This isn't as farfetched as it sounds. The people of ancient Greece saw the Gods as being who watched mankind from above and directing us as if we were human clay. This being similar to todays reality shows or soap operas. Only the Gods watching would be psychic and able to use technology in their creator duties.

Several video games have come out that would be akin to Psychic Creationism, like that of Simcity, Civilization, Afterlife, Spore, and The Sims. In Simcity the player creates a simulated city. In Civilization the player creates and advances a simulated civilization. In Afterlife the player creates a necropolise of both heaven and hell. In Spore the player creates an organism and follows a simulated evolution of spore to space colonizer. The Sims is by far the most surreal in both its objectives and reality TV simulations.

In Singularity Magick the spirits are everywhere and the Gods are psychic beings that communicate to the Magician in several ways, more on this later. There is also a one God or creator God that watches over all things. It is a being that existed before, during, and after the Big Bang. The best description of it would be the Hindu Brahma. The creator God exists on all planes, timelines, and dimensions. It communicates to us through the universal concusness.

The universe therefore is psychicly created in a Big Bang machine with bubbles and loops of time from a celestial macro scale to a binary micro scale. The Singularity Magician must understand this in order to perform spells on a macro scale and then also perform spells on a micro scale. The Singularity is vast and the universe becomes complicated from here on out.

The Motion Capture Universe and the Planes of Existence

One of the key elements of Singularity Magick is that we live in a Motion Capture Universe. This means that for every moment of time that we experience there are multiple choices or out comes that take place. Time therefore is broken down into moments of existence. Simply time is like a revolving wheel of time frames, like film in a camera, at each frame of time a different out come can occur. Time on Earth and in the heavens is circular revolving around a central axis point or event. Each moment of time is a frame in which an event takes place. Put the frames together and play the loop on a clock and a motion capture movie of life begins, this would be time as we see it. Each frame is like a time stamp when a specific event occurs. This is very important for the Singularity Magician to understand. It is an important step to use and understand time travel.

Quantum entanglement is the theory that one electron can exist in two places at the same time and some times the electron acts in a similar or different way. Time travel therefore uses this same principle except that each of the time frames can be changed at the moment of an event from a different time frame altogether.

This is an example of time frames where each frame or plane exists as an event around a circular axis, in this case it is the tower of babylon but more on that later.

On Earth time is measured circularly where 24 hours of a day is measured by one rotation of the Earth on its axis. One year is measured circularly as 365 days rotation of the Earth around the Sun. One zodiac processional year is measured circularly as 25,920 years rotation of the Earth on it's wobbled tilted axis. Even the time it takes the solar system to go around the Milky Way is circular. The Singularity Magician also applies this priciple to the Big Bang where point zero of the Bing Band occurs Galaxies form then Stars burn out and eventualy the Big Bang is repeated by the creator God.

For the Singularity Magician time is made up of three different parts the past, present, and future. All three parts can be effected by the Magician during spells, rituals, and meditation. The method of using this Magick is through the use of a double. The double is a past or future self that is directly connected to the Magician and it is a vessel of past life regression. The double is a prominent part of Occult belief

and has been extensively stuided by ancient and modern Magicians. The Ancients had three Goddesses that represented this, for the Greeks it was the three fates, or the Mother, Maiden, and Crone. The three different parts of time can be represented by this. The Maiden being the beginning or past, the Mother being the present, and the Crone being the end or future. As we shall soon see the wording or lettering of this belief will come into play for Singularity Magick.
It should be noted that there are many other planes of existence besides just time there are many dimensions that pass through and overlap the dimension of time.

Memes Planetary Symbols and Their Origin

Memes play a critical role in Singulary Magick. Memes are like memory genes that have been passed down through out the Ages of Man. They are a remembrance of thing that existed or will exist. Common internet Memes are the taking of a picture, quote, or event and expanding on it. Memes in this book are symbols, words, phrases, and myths that are passed down with a commonality to the Singularity. The first of these Memes are the Planetary Symbols. Those being the Sun, Mercury, Venus, Earth, and Mars.
The Sun symbol has a specific Meme to the Greek's symbol of the monad. Both are clearly identical and both are described as being the one common source of all things. The monad is a metaphysical idea of the circle being at the center of everything in life. Where as the Sun is the source of light and life in the solar system. It is represented as a circle with a dot in the middle. The symbol can also be thought of as an atom, more specifically hydrogen but more on that later.

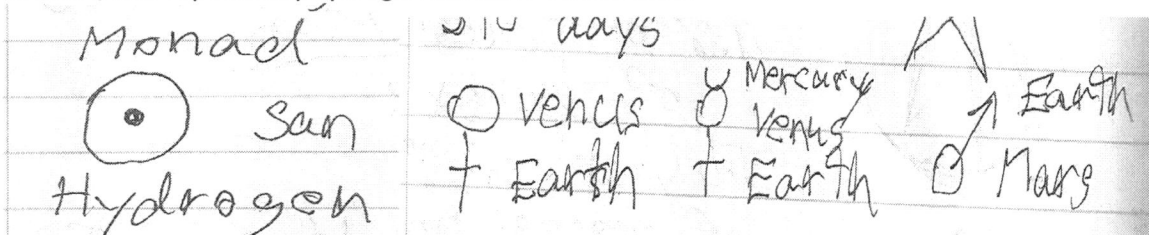

The Earth Cross is a prominent symbol in Ancient astronomy therefore it can be looked at as a Meme that depicts life or life on Earth in the solar system. This is how a Singularity Magician might look at the other Planetary Symbols of the inner solar system. Mercury's symbol which is a semi circle above a circle with a cross below would represent the Planet being closest to the Sun. Venus' symbol is just a circle with a cross which would mean that the Planet is between Mercury and Earth. Earth's symbol as I said is a circle with an Earth Cross or equal armed cross. Mar's symbol is a circle with an arrow off to the side which would mean that it is beyond Earth and the last of the terrestrial Planets. This type of Meme is a clue to the Singularity Magician that greater than human intelligence was at work here and that the Ancients had knowledge from a Singularitian or other worldly being.
The other two Planetary symbols of Jupiter and Saturn are a combination of two kingly icons. The crook and the flail. Which are represented as a curve, for the crook, and a cross, as the flail. These two symbols come from Egypt where the Pharoh was depicted with them. They are animal domestication and agriculture which stand for the kingdoms wealth prosparity. These two Planets were seen as the ruling God of Gods and so they were symbolically depicted this way.

Memes of Snakes and the Thirteenth Zodiac

There are many Ancient Memes of snakes and snake symbols these have been passed down culture to culture. The source of many of these is the Egyptian God Ptah or the American God the Feathered

Christian J. Bullock

Serpent. There is also a third source of snake symbols and that is the mysterious and secret 13th Zodiac. The 13th Zodiac is the Snake Barer and is not really a true zodiac it doesn't have a full 30 degree orientation as it overlaps two other constellations. In fact the 13th Zodiac makes up the two nodes of the Moon which have been seen and depected through out history. Many if not all Astrologists depict the nodes of the Moon on their zodiac charts. The snake Meme is very important in Singularity Magick. Ptah's symbol is that of two snakes entwined together around a pole.

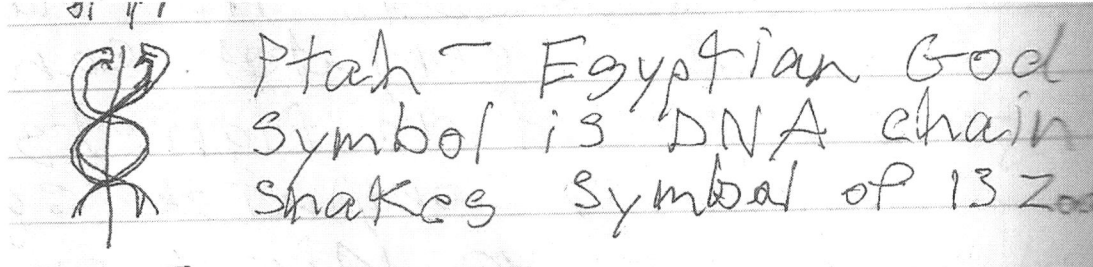

Ptah - Egyptian God
Symbol is DNA chain
snakes symbol of 13 Zo

It is the symbol of DNA and medicine. Where also DNA can be calculated as a 4 bit binary system.

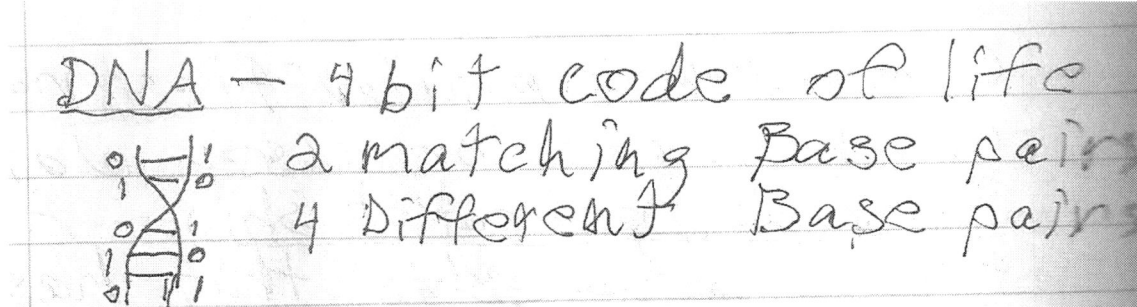

DNA - 4 bit code of life
a matching Base pair
4 Different Base pair

Once again this is secret knowledge passes down from a Singularitian or other worldly being. The 13th Zodiac combines the two nodes of the Moon, the consellations Serpens Caput and Serpens Cauda, into one Snake Barer. The two constellations are also known as Draconis Caput and Draconis Cauda.

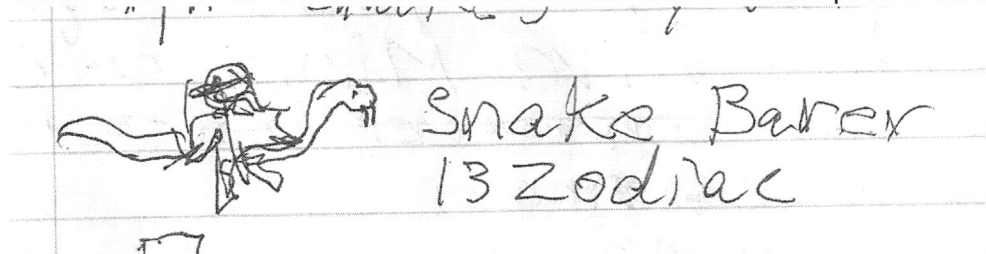

Snake Barer
13 Zodiac

This leads us to the mysterious El Castillo Mayan Pyramid where there are two snakes that out line the stairway on the pyramid. These two snake heads are only in alignment on the equinoxes with the Sun shining over head. To the Singularity Magician this is another clue of Singularity knowledge. The lining up of the pyramid on every equinox means that the Earth is in a specific time flux and that time seemingly stands still on the Earth's equinoxes. Simply put the alignment means that the pyramid was constructed like a giant clock tower in such a way that the sun light that shines on it doesn't deviate over the Ages. It is also aligned with the 13th Zodiac or the nodes of the Moon.

Christian J. Bullock

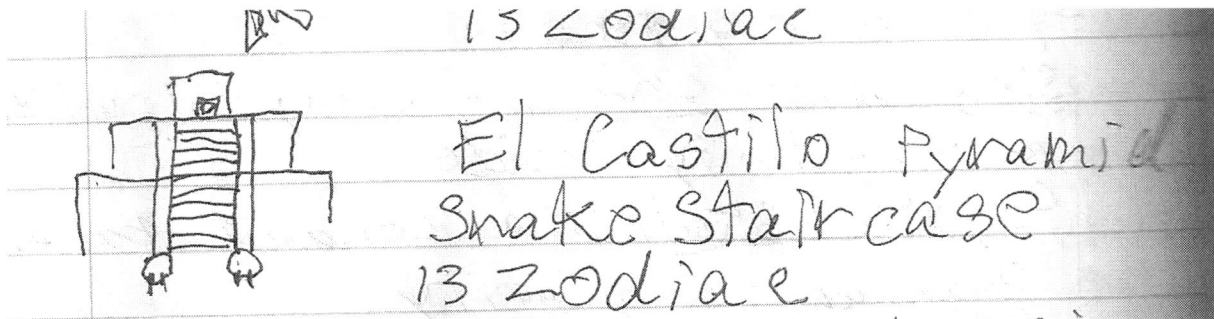

15 Zodiac

El Castilo Pyramid
Snake Staircase
13 Zodiac

The fact that these Ancient Memes have a source is very important to the Singularity Magician.

The Mayan Long Count Calendar

The Maya had a series of calendars some of them more accurate than others but they fit in specifically with each other. There are three specific calendars that need to be understood by the Singularity Magician. One was the Haab calendar which was used to mark the solar year. It is a calendar of 18 months with 20 days each and an additional month called a Wayeb' with 5 extra unlucky days. The understanding of 360 degrees in this calendar means that Singularity knowledge was known or passes down. The 5 unlucky days clearly is an indication that the perfect 360 degree circle was sacred.

Christian J. Bullock

Jaab 365 day calendar
Divided into 18 months of 20 days
wayeb' plus 5 "unlucky" days at the

Pop   Wo   Sip   Zotz'   sek

Xul   Yaxk'in   Mol   ch'en   Yax

Sak   Kej   Mak   K'ank'in   Mawas

Pax   K'ayab'   Kumk'u   Wayeb'

The Maya also had the Tzolkin calendar of 260 days, which is 20 days rotated 13 times. This is a specific calendar for tracking the lunar phases of a lunar year and for tracking the Planet Venus. With the Moon's approximate cycle of 29 days, the Tzolkin is an accurate 9 month lunar cycle.

29 days * 9 cycles = 261 days

More importantly it is a celestial calendar of Venus and it's 263 day period.

263 days on the horizon   5 cycles of 584 days
 50 days below the horizon   which repeats every 8 years on Earth
263 days on the horizon

    8 days below the horizon
584 days total
The Singularity Magician should note that the 260 degree circle was also sacred. The Maya meshed these two calendars together, like cogs or gears in a machine, to get a Grand Sacred Round of 52 years. 18,980 days / 365 days = 52 years
Singularity thought was impressed apon the Maya with their sacred calendars. Singularity Magicians should notice the number 52 as it is a sacred number to all Ancient peoples, more on that later. The Maya also had a Long Count Calendar. This calendar will be the principle calendar discussed in this book although the modern calendar as we shall see has an important part in this book. The Mayan Long Count Calendar consists of three special units of measurement the Tun, Katun, and Baktun. The other calendars fit into this Long Count like gears in a wheel with the Kin, a unit for 1 day, and the uinal, a unit for 20 days. The Maya used a nurmerical system of a base 20 count and they also invented the zero as a place holder, but more on that later. The Tun consisted of 360 days and it is the unit of measure in Singularity Magick where a 360 degree circle is perfect. The Katun consisted of 20 Tuns and the Baktun consisted of 20 Katuns. In the Long Count Calendar the there are only 13 Baktuns, this means that from point zero in the calendar they chose 13 Baktuns as a specific end date. The Maya also had a longer count or units to measure time, with these units they use the base 20. Where a Pictun consisted of 20 Baktuns. A Calabtun consisted of 20 Pictuns. A Kinchiltun consisted of 20 Calabtuns and a Alautun consisted of 20 Kinchiltuns. Thus for the longer units of measure we get:

1 Pictun   = 20 Baktuns   (8,000 Tuns)
1 Calabtun   = 20 Pictuns   (160,000 Tuns)
1 Kinchiltun   = 20 Calabtuns (3,200,000 Tuns)
1 Alautun   = 20 Kinchiltuns(64,000,000 Tuns)

This book however is more focused on the Long Count where the units of measure are:

1 Kin   = 1 day
1 Uinal = 20 days
1 Tun   = 360 days   (18 Uinals)
1 Katun = 20 Tuns   (7,200 days)
1 Baktun = 20 Katuns   (400 Tuns =   144,000 days)
13 Baktuns =   (5,200 Tuns   1,872,000 days)

This is where the Mayan calendar ends and it shows the Singularity Magician the sacred importance of the 360 degree circle in Ancient times. The Long Count Calendar is the most precise calendar in the world and it is even more precise than our modern calendar. The Mayan year is approximately 365.2420 days, where as the Modern year is approximately 365.2422 days. When we line up the 13 Baktuns with the Earth solar year we get:

1,872,000 days / 365.2420 Mayan days = 5,125.368933 years
1,872,000 days / 365.2422 Modern days = 5,125.366127 years

Roughly 5,125 years which is incredably accurate. This means that the Long Count Calendar started on 3113 B.C. which was before the common Mayan era. The accuracy further implicates Singularity Magick. The Maya describe 5 Ages of Man, meaning there was a time before the Long Count Calendar where other civilizations existed. This leads us to the alignment with the zodic procession of the equinoxes. If we take the 13 Baktuns and the 5,125 years that it represents we can calculate the 5 Ages of Man:

5,125.368933 years * 5 cycles = 25,626.844665 years
5,125 years * 5 cycles = 25,625 years(25,626 years approximately)

This is nearly the 25,920 years modern approximation of the zodiac.

Christian J. Bullock

 More importantly to the Singularity Magician we can use the Symbols of Power to get the zodiac procession. 72 degrees * 5 points = 360 degrees and since it takes 71.6 years to get 1 degree of procession we can get the Mayan Long Count. 71.6 degrees * 71.6 years = 5,126.56 years. A diffence of only a year.

The Longer Mayan Count

1 Pictun = 20 Baktuns(8,000 Tuns)

1 Calabtun = 20 Pictuns(160,000 Tuns)

1 Kinchiltun = 20 calabtuns(3,200,000 Tuns)

1 Alautun = 20 Kinchiltuns(64,000,000 Tuns)

Kin   Vinal   Tun

Katun   Baktun   Pictun

Calabtun   Kinchiltun   Alautun

This 5 cycles of 13 Baktuns creates a wheel of time which is represented to the Singularity Magician as a circle with a pentagram. To further represent the Earth in the wheel the Singularity Magician adds the Earth Cross, making a penticle with a cross in it.

Christian J. Bullock

$$71.6° \times 71.6 \text{ years}$$
$$5,126.56 \text{ years}$$
$$71.6° \text{ of procession}$$
$$\text{of equinox}$$
$$71.6 \text{ years of } 1°$$
$$\text{of procession}$$
$$\text{of equinox}$$

This is how time was represented to the Ancients and it is how time is represented to the Singularity Magician. Many Ancient cultures describe the 5 Ages of Man. One particular account comes from the Greek Heisod in his "Work and Days" where he describes the Ages of Man with each Age going into decline, more on that later. The Maya called each Sun an Age and each World was an event of decline.

Ahau Tun = 1st Sun   1st Year
Ahau 2cumku = 1st Sun   5,125 Years
1 Ahau Kankin = 2nd Sun   1st World
1 Ahau 2cumku = 2nd Sun   5,125 Years
2 Ahau 4 camku = 3rd Sun   10,250 Years
2 Ahau 1 Kankin = 3rd Sun   2nd World
3 Ahau 6 cumku = 4th Sun   15,375 Years
3 Ahau 2 Kankin = 4th Sun   3rd World
4 Ahau 8 cumku = 5th Sun   20,500 Years
4 Ahau 3 Kankin = 5th Sun   4th World

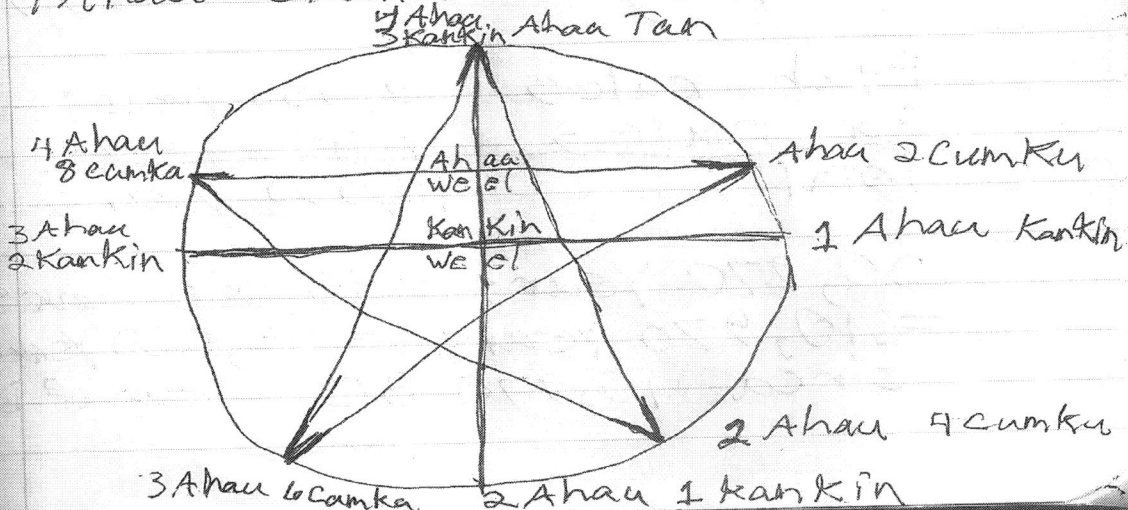

Christian J. Bullock

The beginning date of the Long Count Calendar was 3113 B.C. and it was called 4 Ahau 8 Cumku. The ending date of 2012 A.D. was called 4 Ahau 3 Kankin. The understanding being that Ahau means Sun, or Age, and Kankin means World. Since we are considered to be in the 5th Age of Man it means that the Maya started with zero before counting 1, 2, 3, and 4. Thus 4 Ahau means 5th Sun. When counting backwards from the Maya Long Count we can reconstruct the whole wheel of time that aligns with zodiac procession. The Pentagram represents the Sun Ages and the Cross represents the World Ages or events. Cumku is roughly translated as meaning 2,562.6 years. 2 Cumku is roughly translated as 5,125.2 years. With a full completion of the circle 10 Cumku as 25,626 Mayan years. This will be the Singularity Magician's Wheel of Time and it will be used extensively in this book. The Maya describe the World Ages as disasterous events or when a great darkening of the Earth occurs. The Great Deluge, or flood, can be calculated as between 2 Ahau 1 Kankin and 3 Ahau 6 Cumku:

10,250 years ago + 2,562 Mayan years = 12,812 years ago

12,812 years ago − 2,012 Modern years = 10,800 B.C.

This takes us back to Ancient times where Man was counseled by the Gods. This time line is also aligned with many other Ancient cultures and their histories. The Singularity Magician must understand this for spells, rituals, and meditation. It is slightly unclear what specific events occurred on the other World Age dates. Other than a great darkening one can only expect a decline of Ancient Civilizations.

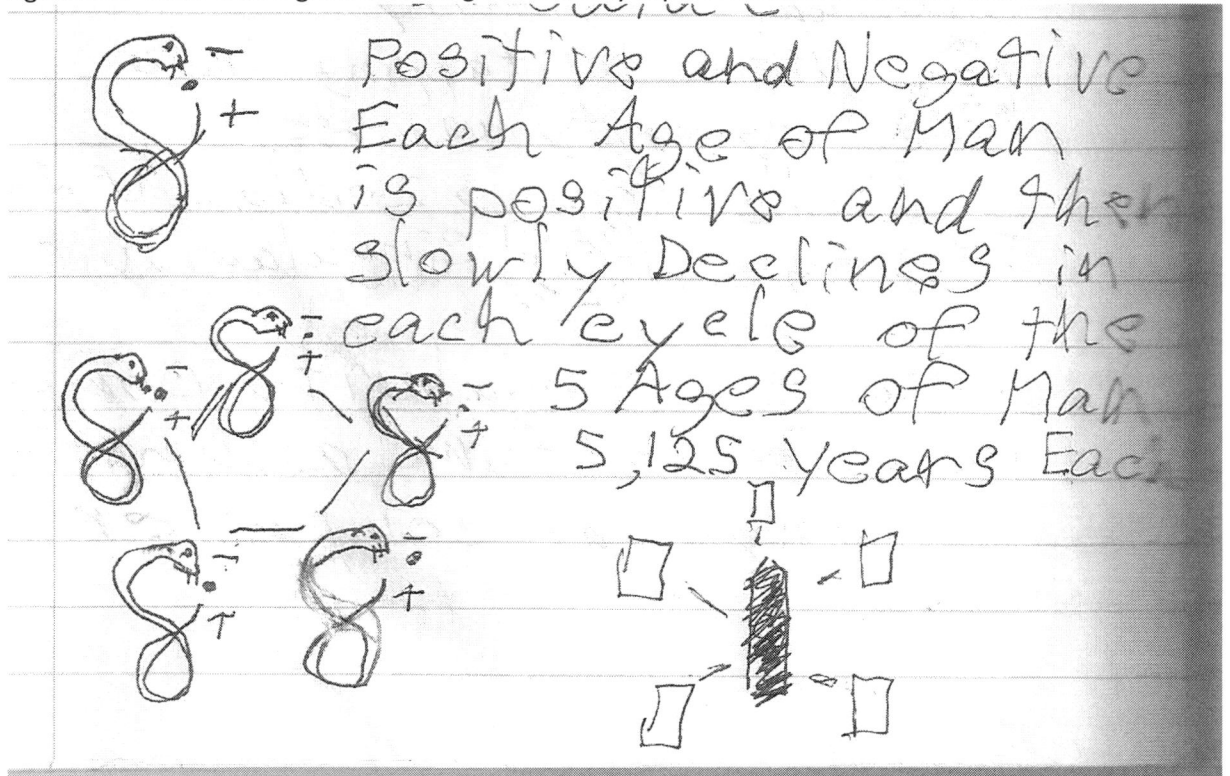

The Five Ages of Man

The Maya were not the only ones with Singularity knowledge of the Ages of Man. The Greeks believed in 5 Ages of Man. The 1st Age was the Golden Age, the 2nd was the Silver Age, the 3rd was the Bronze Age, the 4th the was Heroic Age, and the 5th was the Iron Age. The Ages of the Yugas in accordance with The Laws of Manu of the Hindu religion has 4 Ages of Man. Each Age is said to have a gradual decline of dharma, wisdom, knowledge, intellectual capability, life span, emotional and physical strength. The 1st

Age was the Satya Yuga where virtue reigns supreme. Human stature was 21 cubits and the average human lifespan was 100,000 years. The 2nd Age was the Treta Yuga where there was 3 quarters virtue and 1 quarter sin. Normal human stature was 14 cubits and average lifespan was 10,000 years. The 3rd Age was the Dwapara Yuga where there was half virtue and half sin. Normal human stature was 7 cubits and the average lifespan was 1,000 years. The 4th Age is the Kali Yuga where there is 1 quarter virtue and 3 quarters sin. Normal human stature is 3.5 cubits and the average human lifespan is 100 years. Accordingly to the predictions of the Ages at the end of the Kali Yuga the human lifespan will go down to 20 years. So why is this important? Well The Laws of Manu list the length of years for each Age which correspond to the zodiac procession:

Satya Yuga
(4 * 432,000 years)
4,800 years * 360 cycles = 1,728,000 years
Treta Yuga
(3 * 432,000 years)
3,600 years * 360 cycles = 1,296,000 years
Dvapara Yuga
(2 * 432,000 years)
2,400 years * 360 cycles = 864,000 years
Kali Yuga
(432,000 years)
1,200 years * 360 cycles = 432,000 years
If we add up each length of time for a processional cycle we get:
4,800 years + 3,600 years + 2,400 years + 1,200 years = 12,000 years or one arc of procession
12,000 years + 12,000 years = 24,000 years approximately one complete cycle of procession.
The Singularity Symbols and Stars of Power are present again for the Singularity Magician to use. It should be noted that the number 432,000 is sacred to the Ancients and it is the arrival date of the Sumerian Annanaki Gods on Earth, more on this later.
The Ages of Man can be represented as a circle listing each of the twelve zodiac signs with a pentagram in the middle showing the Five Ages and a cross showing the Four Worlds.

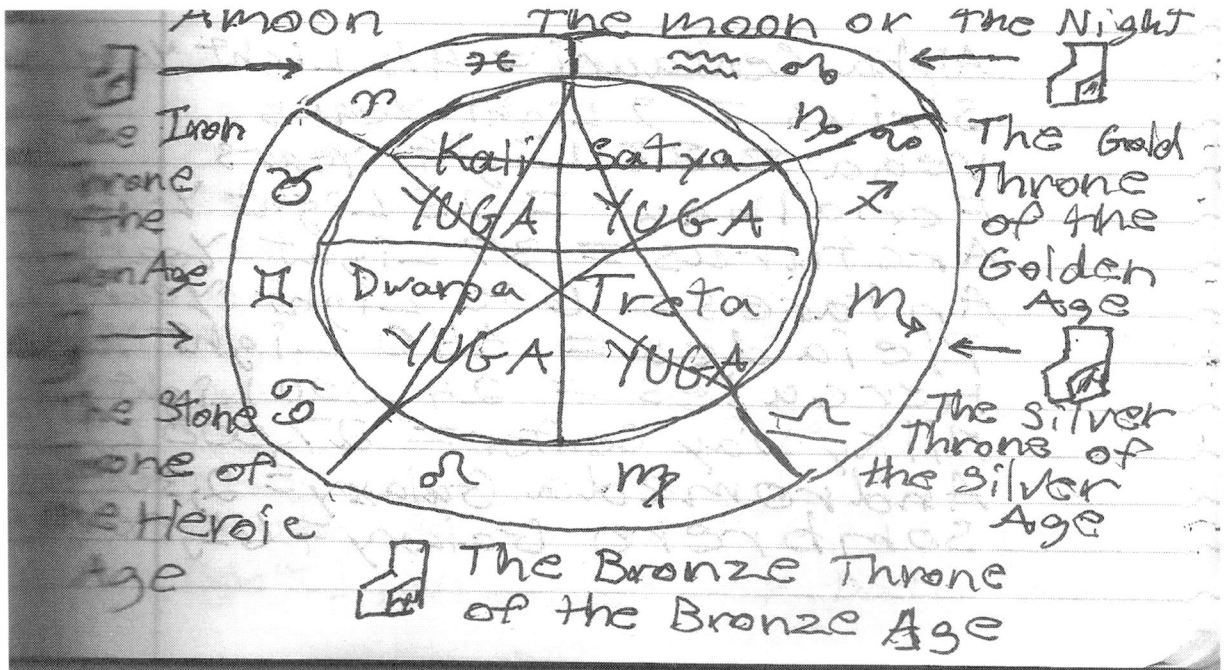

In each World there is a particular Yuga shown which depicts the Four Yougas in succession starting with the Satya Yuga and ending with the Kali Yuga. In each Age a God king ruled and this is represented by Five Thrones. The Golden Throne for the Golden Age. The Silver Throne for the Silver Age. The Bronze Throne for the third Age. The Stone Throne for the Heroic fourth Age and the Iron Throne for the Iron Age. The nodes of the Moon are also present. The Singularity Magician must understand this if they want to do a specific ritual for a specific God in the Pantheon of Twelve ruling deities. It is also a key for time travellers to interact with each ruling Deity of the Age.

The Zodiac Processional Code

This leads us to the all important Processional Code. Each of the twelve zodiacs is divided as an Age with each ruling deity as a ruler of that Age. Each sign has specific Astrology that is important to each Age. Also each Age has historical significance associated with that particular sign. Symbolizum is everything to the Singularity Magician, understanding the signs that govern Magick is essenal.

Christian J. Bullock

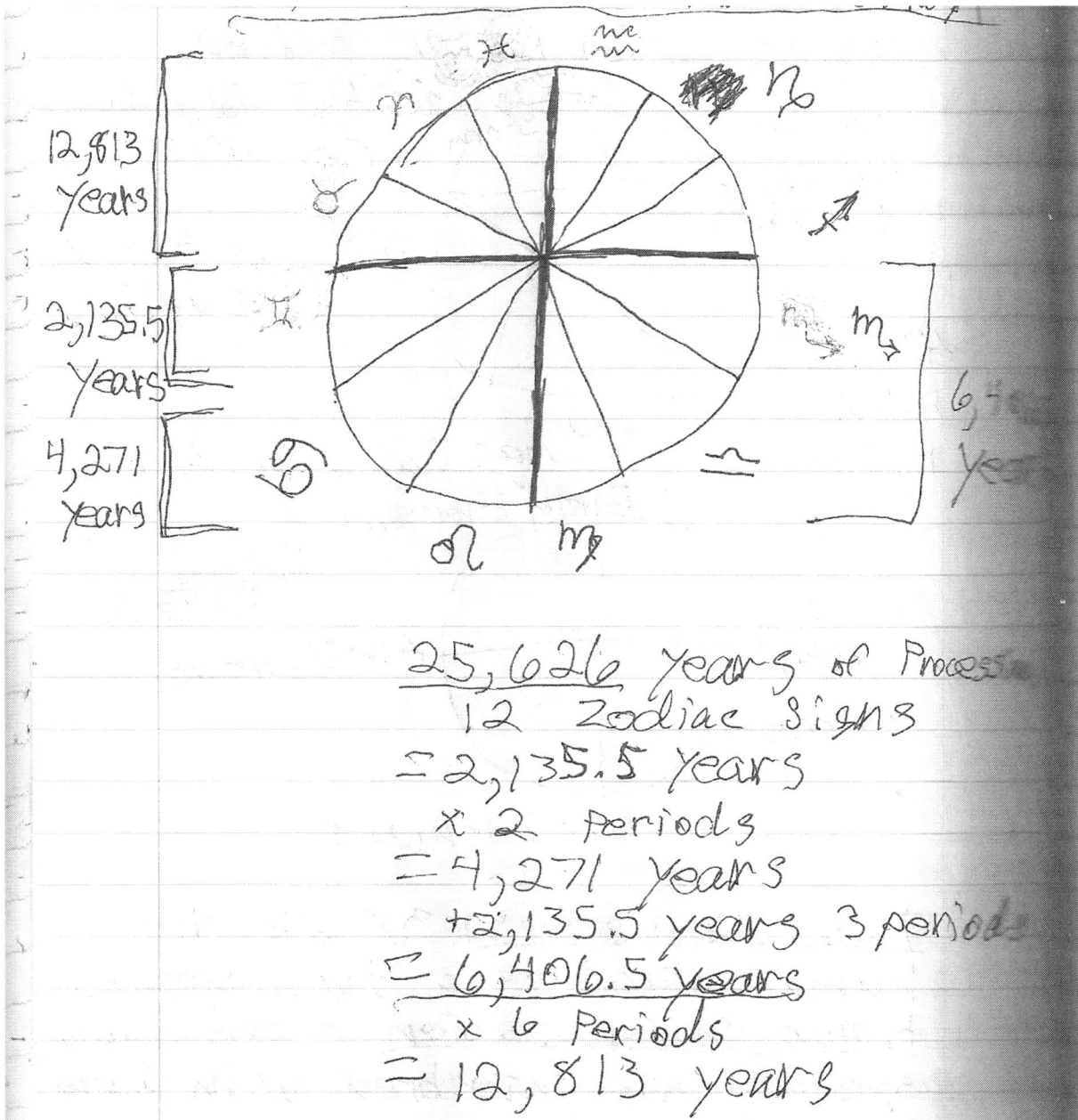

$$\frac{25,626 \text{ years of Process}}{12 \text{ Zodiac Signs}}$$

$$= 2,135.5 \text{ years}$$

$$\times 2 \text{ periods}$$

$$= 4,271 \text{ years}$$

$$+ 2,135.5 \text{ years} \quad 3 \text{ periods}$$

$$= 6,406.5 \text{ years}$$

$$\times 6 \text{ Periods}$$

$$= 12,813 \text{ years}$$

Starting with our current Age and working backwards through history the Processional Zodiac goes like this: Pisces, Aries, Tarus, Gemini, Cancer, Leo, Virgo, Libra, Scorpio, Sagittarius, Capricorn, and Aquarius. Each Age or period is approximately 2,135.5 years and is seen on the horizon on the morning of the Winter Solstice. Sumerian calendars view the changing of constellations on the morning of the Spring Equinox. With the calculations of the Mayan Long Count Calendar the Singularity Magician can now make note that the changing of the constellations will begin on the Winter Solstice of 2012 A.D. the new Age will be the Age of Aquarius, the Water Barer. For the Sumerian Calendar the change will occur on the Spring Equinox of 2013 A.D. or the Sumerian New Year.

The Mayan Prediction Wheel

Christian J. Bullock

The Mayan Prediction Wheel is based on the Mayan calendar with a strong emphisis on spiritual or magical elements. The Maya had psychic predictions of the past, present, and future. In fact each Baktum of the Long Count Calendar had a special significance to the Maya. They each had psychic predictions of the coming dates and Age. With each Baktum there was a sense of decline in knowledge and human thought. There was also a sense of coming darkness over the Earth. So what is the importance of these predictions? Well as we now know the 13 Baktun cycle is repeated in each of the Five Ages of Man with each Age going into decline. These psychic predictions therefore follow a pattern from mankind's past to mankind's future. The way the pattern presents itself is that of Singularity Magick and Psychic Creationism. The 1st Age was said to end with Jaguar Spirits devouring man. The other Ages are said to have ended with a flood, earthquake, or volcanic eruptions. This is where many of the Myths have a modern take on what might happen in the future. It should also be noted that during one of the Ages man was turned into fishes. This also aligns with tales from other Ancient cultures of a flood, or the Great Deluge. For the Singularity Magician a Mayan Prediction Wheel is conjured up. The Wheel is made up of a circle with a pentagram in it. Then each element is added to it starting with Spirit as the 1st Age. Thus the 1st Age was ruled by the Spirit element, this would be during the Age of Gods on Earth. The 2nd Age would be ruled by Earth. The 3rd Age would be ruled by Air. The 4th Age would be ruled by Fire. The 5th Age would be ruled by Water. The up coming 6th Age would be ruled by Storm as a 6th element. Lastly the 7th Age in the future would be ruled by a mysterious 7th element, in this case the 7th element would be Love, more on that later.

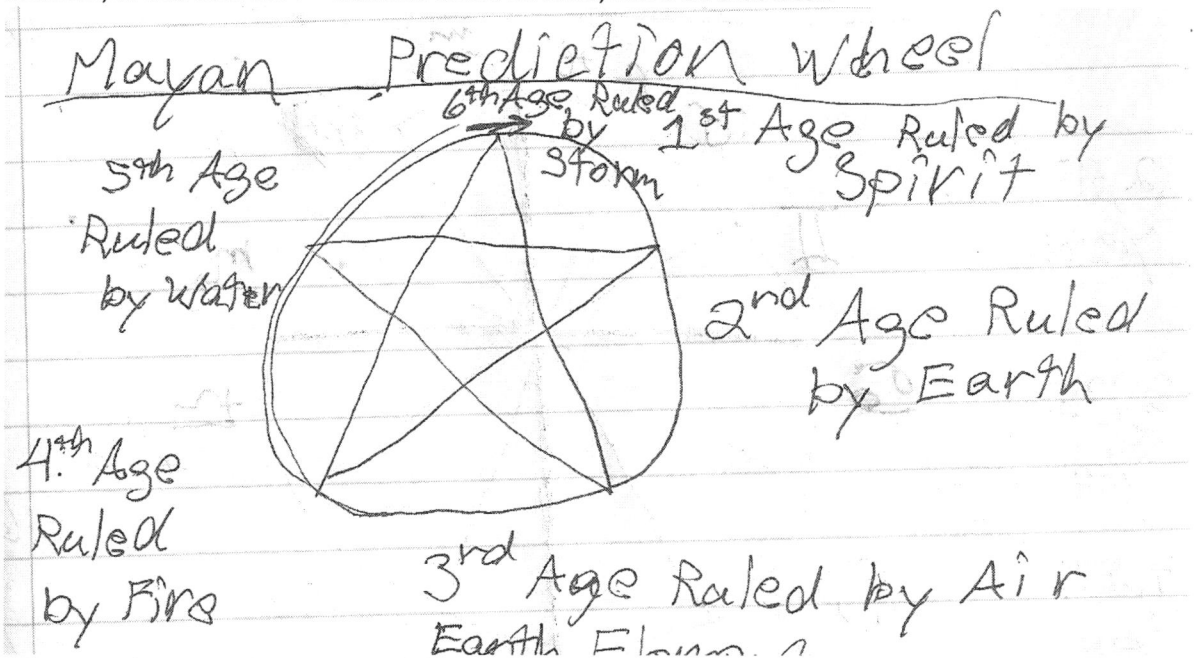

Mayan Prediction Wheel

6th Age Ruled by Storm   1st Age Ruled by Spirit

5th Age Ruled by Water

2nd Age Ruled by Earth

4th Age Ruled by Fire

3rd Age Ruled by Air

Earth Elem...

Of course the Maya also associated the World Ages with a specific event or natural disaster. Thus the second or overlapping World Prediction Wheel is divided into 4 equal parts with a cross in the circle. These four World events are ruled by the four major elements Earth, Air, Fire, and Water.

Christian J. Bullock

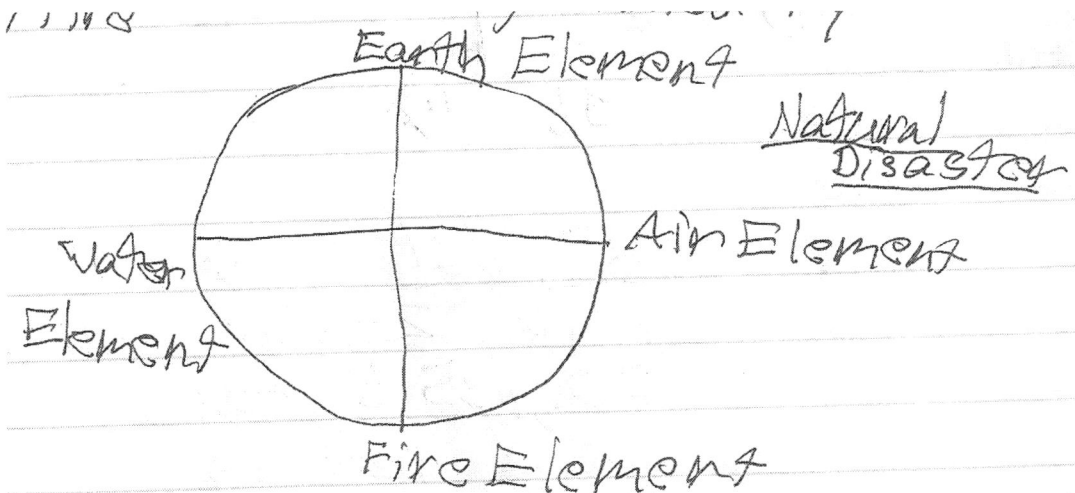

This completes the Prediction Wheel where the Singularity Magician can track events and psychic predictions of the 13th Baktun cycle over the Ages of Man. This is very important when time traveling and reconstructing past life regression. This is also helpful knowledge of the Ancients and how they viewed the Ages of God and Man.

The World Grids, the Internet, and the Ethernet

The whole world is made up of a grid of land marks used for time travel. The Ancient Gods are described in Myths as dividing up all the lands of the Earth amongst themselves. They are said to have seeded each land and that they setup landmarks in each land as temples to themselves or for other purposes. The Ancient Greeks were one of the first to come up with longitude and latitude but this was not known until recently. It can be assumed and proven that the Ancient Gods did the same thing. Builders of all different cultures were handed down secret and Singularity knowledge of the Earths axis tilt. As well as a crude understanding of longitude and latitude. Areas are named on this grid specifically and temples as well as major cities sit on these designated areas. Ancient cities of older Ages also sit on these longitude and latitude points. The World Grid as we shall see can be used for time travel by the Singularity Magician. Each Planet or Moon also have a World Grid that can be used for time travel but more on that later. There is now an overlaping Electrical Grid over the entire Planet. The Electrical Grid can be used for time travel by tapping into the Electrical Lines like landmarks. Each house therefore can be used as a landmark for this kind of time jumping. All you need is electricity for this type of Singularity Magick to work, but I will discuss time travel specifically later in the book. The Singularity Magician just needs to take note of these Grids. There is now a Satellite Grid that surrounds the Earth. The Satellite Grid expands the Grid pattern into low orbit space and it too can be used for time travel. The predictable orbits of these satellites act as way points or landmarks in space. Satellite maping Grids map the Earth and these maps are viewed via GPS or the Internet.

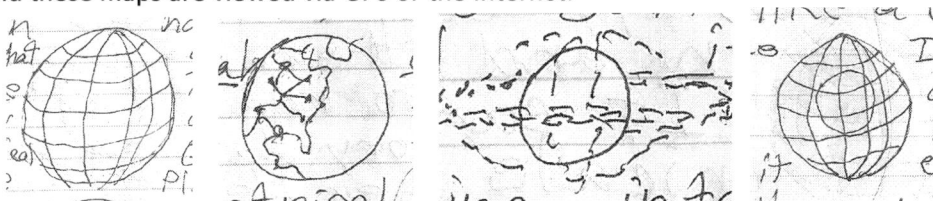

The Earth is connected to a world wide web which acts like a Hive Mind. It can also be used to time travel. Acting like an Earth Net it can be tapped into by a modem like a Grided landmark. The Internet is similar to a Singularity Computer. Like a Singularity Computer it can be read like a pattern, almost like tapping into the Ether. It can be used to track trends and possibly read minds or input data. Of course the Singularity Computer needs input data in order to run. An Ether Net also surrounds the Earth, it is a Global consousness that can be tapped into for information and spiritual guidance. It can be used to communicate at great distances as well as temporal distances too. The Singularity Magician must understand this concept in order to pracitice magick on a larger scale and in order to read through the Ether Net or scan through the Hive Mind Computers.

The Echo

Due to the Internet and the coming Singularity Computer there is an echo back and forth in time that farseer's can tap into. To the Singularity Magician they can be heared and sometimes seen. Singularity Magicians can use the echo to predict possible futures and pasts. The echo acts like a reccuring cycle of predictability. Retwos use the echo to fix time while Psycops use the echo to control the timeline. In a way the Internet creates a forseeable future or time loop where the Singularity Computer is born. With the advancement of technology, man can predict a melding or augmentation of man and machine. In a way man can be seen as an arcitect of a future civilization and a predictable time loop can be attached to this coming event. Some psychic awareness can also be attached to this coming event.

Real-Time Prophecy

Since things have become fast paced in the world today many Ancient teachings have become lost. The Ancient writings that have survived have made things more complicated because they are like time capsules of history. Thus these writings and codexes are more important than peviously thought since they too have patterns of predictabiblity and are part of the prediction of a decline of human knowledge. In todays present these recently translated or discovered writings are part of something called Real-Time Prophecy. So what is Real-Time Prophecy? Well it is when something written many years ago is discovered to have a modern impact on society in the present day. Real-Time Prophecy would include such things as the Mayan Long Count Calendar, the Dead Sea Scrolls, or the writings of Enoch. Real-Time Prophecy can also include some more modern writings like those of Edgar Casey or those of Nostradamus or even those of Lenardo Da Vinci. All three had ideas about the future of mankind and in such cases as Edgar Casey an ability to psychically predict things in the future. Real-Time Prophecy also includes information about the Singularity Computer or Metaphysical Computer. There are events in history in which Real-Time Prophecy comes into play where civilizations undergo radical changes in belief or radical changes due to Singularity knowledge. One can see the present state of the Internet as almost a prophecy machine, where knowledge is shared abundantly and future events can be predictably seen. Real-Time Prophecy plays an important role in Singularity Magick and in Psychic Creationism. A Singularity Magician should always have two journals that write in. One journal should be of daily spells, rituals, meditations, and psychic dreams. The other journal should be strictly of spells and otherworldly knowledge. The Singularity Magician uses the first journal as a past experience that can be followed as dates and times of said past events.

Time Stamps

A continuing idea of tracing past events is through the use of Time Stamps. A Time Stamp is the date and time in which a landmark, electrical device, or artifact is made. A Time Stamp can also be the specific date and time in which an event occurs. These are used for time travel and they allow a time traveller to set key time jumps to specific points in time. The idea of a Time Stamp follows along with the specific events that change and shape the Singularity Computer. The best way to describe Time Stamps are that they are like little time capsules that record a date in which the world was changing. In a motion capture universe the date is a tool that describes the world at any given moment. The Singularity Magician must understand this complex idea in order to grasp the Motion Capture universe.

Electrical Manipulation and Communication

The Singularity Magician can use various electronic devices as portals for remote viewing. Using their psychic third eye they can project images or thoughts through a device like a TV. A Singularity Magician can plant an image in between the frames of a video or audio device using it as a way of communication. A TV may be used like a two way mirror to the Singularity Magician. Audio devices can be used as well and these can pick up the Echo of multiple universes. It is the Singularity Magician's quest to pick up the Echo and understand the foresight of the future. The Echo is similar to the white noise radiating the Big Bang of the universe. There are many other ways a Singularity Magician can manipulate electrical devices, one such way can be through astral projection. The Singularity Magician astral projects their double into a device and runs it like a computer, more on this later. Another way is through meditation in which the spirit leaves the body in an OBE, or out of body experience, the spirit psychically commands the electrical device by knowing the Symbols of Power or the Enki Code, more on that later. These two ways are highly dangerous and require quite a bit of skill by the Magician. In the present time frame scientists have created a bendable metal alloy that can bend into specific states while still being strong. This metal alloy can then bend back into its original shape without losing its strength. So why is this important? Well futuristic ideas of such a metal have been thought about for ages and one such metal that the Ancients describe is the BenBen of Ancient Egypt. This Singularity thought provoking metal was considerd an Artifact of the Gods and some see it as a metal that might be from a spaceship. With todays rediscovery of the metal it can be safe to assume that the science of today is rediscovering Ancient knowledge of the Ages of Man. A sort of time loop may have occurred to the creation of such a metal. To the Singularity Magician this is more proof that emerging technologies have a distant connection with mankinds past. A Singularity Magician with psychic kinetic powers may be able to shape this metal into different forms, like shapeshifting ones double or astral body, or like shaping ones physical body. In Singularity Magick the physical body is like an Avatar or vessel in which the spirit resides in. When the Singularity event does occur man and machine may be able to shape their own bodies or shedd their bodies for a machine, organic or metal.

Blank Slate Hypothesis and the Clouding

A person's mind can be made blank by deleting or removing short term memory. This is used to silence the awakened. In the Ancient past man has under gone a series of phases where Ancient knowledge was lost. The world today was created from one of these events where knowledge was lost and humanity has been clouded from the reality of a high tech super civilization in the Ancient past. The Clouding is almost like a dissosiated amesia where man can not comprehend such Singularity knowledge. The blank slate is a way to close the minds of those who have trouble comprehending the vastness of Singularity thought. The blank slate can be used by the Magician to close one's mind to the Hive Mind or to the Singularity Computer. It is very important that the Magician learn how to do this as an open mind to the Hive Mind may cause an unbearable flood of thought into the Magician's mind. Retwos and Psy Cops also use the blank slate to control the human population.

Christian J. Bullock

Quantum Jumping

Quantum Jumpers live vicariously in the Metaphysical Computer as other people. Quantum Jumpers use Quantum Physics to stop and start time. They freeze frame time often in order to mimic the person that they are pretending to play. Living vicariously through people back and forth in time and they have varied motives. Some view humans outside of time from other dimensions. Some are watchers, questers, or gamers. Gamers or roleplayers Quantum Jump in order to trace historical figures and knowledgeble people back through time. They usually are in search of the holy grail or secret source in the universe in order to win the game. More on that later in this book.

The Emerald Dream

Inside the Metaphysical Computer or Singularity Computer people and other beings live in a dream like state. This dream state is part of a universal consciousness. This universal consciousness is part of higher brain functions. For a human it is part of the grey matter that makes up most of the human brain. This dream state universal consciousness is mostly closed off to most humans. This dream state has over time become replaced by a Singularity Computer. In which higher brain functions are run by a Singularity Computer and by Singularitians. Over time there has been a break down of higher brain functions for the humans of the yellow dwarf star time frame. These changes have been caused by time travel and Singularity Cubes. As the universe expands faster the Singularity Cube of human immortality is developed. These cubes simulate the universes Big Bang on up to civilizations on Earth. These Singularity Cubes are meant to preserve life on Earth and human experiences. They require user data and act like a computer because they are based on the Metaphysical Singularity of the universe.

The Game

The world is like a little play, just as William Shakespeare said "All the world's a stage". The game of roleplayers is to learn as much of the universe then to ultimately conquer time and space. Once initiated as a roleplayer and learning of the Book of Life or of Quantum Jumping. They travel time seeking artifacts or knowledge to go back in time to the very beginning, the source. Living vicariously through other people and as spirits in the Metaphysical Computer. Each planet has mysteries that can be traced through history. The one who traces the lineage of the Milky Way Galaxy will build a new order and leave the Milky Way to explore other Galaxies. The winner will also become the Game Keeper of the Milky Way Galaxy. Each Galaxy has a Game Keeper and each universe has a Game Keeper. Using the Enki Code and following Enkidu a time traveller may become a Game Keeper or a Gilgamesh of an Age. The Game of Life is very complicated and such an endevour is very long.

Each Religion Has a Key

Each religion has a set of keys that are used to decipher the universe and the multiverse. The keys are secret knowledge to be passed on to those who are roleplayers, Singularitians, or Singularity Magicians. There are many pictures and reliefs that show these religious keys. There is the Christian Key which is an actual key. The Greek Venus Key which is depicted as the Venus Symbol. The Ankh or Egyptian Key which is an Ankh that the Gods hold. The Celtic or Futhark Key which is the Earth Cross in a circle or an X in a circle meaning Gifu. There is the Dionysus or Loki Key which has the numeral thirteen which means thirteen Gods. Lastly there is the End Key or Enki as a triangle with a circle in it, or a twelve pointed star for Nibiru.

Christian J. Bullock

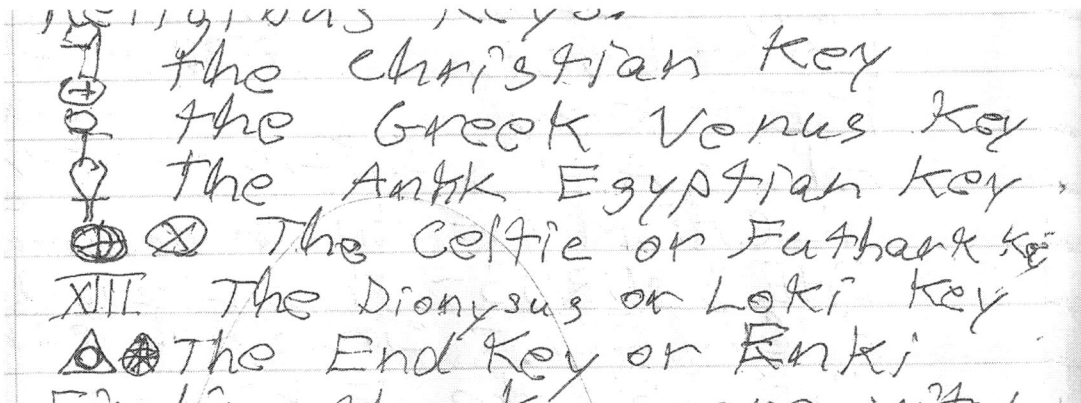

Finding the keys are vital to the roleplayers of the Game, and they are also vital to the Singularity Magician.

The Enki Code

A lingustics code that can decipher the meaning of words. It is based on Akkadian root words, from which nearly all languages come from, and it is also based on word Memes.

Mana	Paradise
Manu	Paradox
Mu	Diad
Manitou	Dionysus
Monad	Monadknok

The Enki Code can be broken down into one or two letter roots like Sumerian.

Ra – Egyptian Sun God	Sol – Soul
Ea – Sumerian Earth God	Lil – Nill
En – End	Amen – Amon
Fin – End	Ankh – Life Giver
Lo – Lock	Atem – Atom or Adam
Ki – Key	Warlock – War lock locker
Al – All	Enkidu – End Key Do

Alchemy – All Encompassing Chemistry

Thesaurus – The Lizard

Arcitech – Circle Arc Tech

Ultimately the Enki Code is a computer lingustics code used to carry out Singularity Computer or Enkidu instructions. It is hidden in the English language and in Akkadian roots like Latin. Some Native American words have similar unknown roots to Enki Code. Most landmarks on Earth have these Enki roots. Enki Code is also a way that the Hive Mind communicates. Most humans are unaware of the meaning of words. Using Enki Code a Singularity Magician can dowse or psychically read another persons mind. Enki Code uses Memes or memory genes as memory aids to perform functions. To the Singularity Magician Enki Code is the basis from which all spoken and written word springs. It is word power and these words when strung together have magical power. Enki Code is used in every spell and ritual, even the word spell comes from spelling. The Egyptian God Thoth is the God of writing and he bequethed a spell or the written word to mankind. The God of Magick gave man the power of the word which has lasted the test of time and is now embedded into our lauguage as Enki Code.

The Three Stars

There are three different stars that effect life forms on Earth. These three stars represent the beginning of the universe and the end of the universe. They are assosiated with the specific time frames of the Earth or the universe. They also represent a cycle of growth for mankind and a cycle of immortality for the human species. They are a time loop that begins in the beginning of time to the end of time.

The Red Star or Brown Dwarf – This is the Sun of the man/machine robots of the Singularity, called Cylons. They are sentient beings who live in a Singularity Computer. They have chosen to live and survive as Avatar machines in a future time frame of the universe. Their Sun is red and their eyes are red, this is special. In the future time frame of the universe all the stars will burn out and only the lowly brown dwarfs will survive. The universe will expand exponentually and other Galaxies will become unreachable from the Milky Way Galaxy. The brown dwarf stars will eventually burn out so the man/machine Cylons will time travel back in time to the point of the Singularity Computer. The Singularity Computer must be built in order for them to survive.

The Yellow Star or Yellow Dwarf – This is the current model of the solar system, the human time frame. In this time frame most star systems in the Galaxy have yellow dwarfs and yellow dwarfs are common. Yellow dwarfs tend to have a reliable life span and some have a goldilocks zone where life can exist. The other Galaxies haven't moved away as fast as in the the Red Star time frame. In this time frame mankind is building the Singularity Computer and Singularity knowledge is abundant in Ancient times while slowly declining in modern times.

The Blue Star or Blue Giant – This is the star of the Retwo, where the early universe is born. It is a star that exists far back in time where beings of another dimension come from. The Retwo have an unknown bond with Earth but seek to play out mankind's future. They share a bond with the creator God and play out their existence till the creator God time travels back in time to remake the Big Bang which created them. The Retwo redo things in time traveling backwards and forwards fixing time. Sometimes they remake the histories of time in order to keep the universe moving and avoid an early darkening of the universe. The creator God must exist, to time travel back in time, in order for them to survive.

The Tower of Babel

The story of the Tower of Babel goes some what like this. The people of Babylon all spoke one language and wanted to build a tower that touched the heavens. They began building the tower and they were close to completing it when a God became angry with them. The specific God that became angry varies from story to story. The God in question could be the creator God, the Sumerian God EN.LIL, or the God/Devil Nimrod. Anyways in the story the God was so angry about this that he turned the one spoken language into many languages and he also may have destroyed the tower. The people of Babylon lost their ability to communicate with one another and gave up building the Tower of Babel. This little bedtime story has a significant impact on Earth and also for the Singularity Magician.

The Tower of Babel represents a singular point in history where there was one spoken language and that language was Akkadian or a root of Akkadian. The Tower of Babel also represents a singular point where there was one religion for man, that of Sumer. This tower would mean that the Babylonians had at one time an Ancient super civilization with advanced knowledge of masonry, mathematics, and astronomy. Simply put they had secret Singularity knowledge to build the tower. From this point on there was a slow decline of Singularity knowledge and of Ancient civilization. For the Singularity Magician this is a critical point in time from which all other time frames rotate around. The building of the tower to the destruction or decline of the tower. The Tower of Babel also has many Memes that can be traced to this story. The first being the name the Tower of Babel, where today to babel means to speak incoherently. The second Meme is the Tarot Card, the Tower, which usually means bad luck or a personal disaster. To the Singularity Magician these are clues to the Ancient past and the forseeable future.

There is in fact a new Tower of Babelon that is set in the future. This is the Singularity Computer where man and machine merge as one. With todays time frame of computers and the internet all languages are slowly merging into one. All religions are finding a commonality. Not just the English language is becoming common but computer code and mathematics are becomimg common too, to all people on Earth. This new Tower of Babelon, the Singularity has taken shape. To the Singularity Magician the new tower is also a critical point in time from which all other time frames rotate around. Thus there are two cities of Babylon, a winter city and a summer city. The Winter City of Babelon is the current time frame of todays world. The Summer City of Babylon is the Ancient time frame of the past during the height of the Sumerian Civilization. This would be during the ruling of the Gods over man way before the flood, over 20,970 years ago. To the Singularity Magician the Enki Code is the closest root to the great Singularity Computer of the future. This merges a shared bond between the past and present, with the future looming ahead.

The Equinox Day and Night/Day Watchers and Night Watchers/Time Travel Without a Singularity Room
It should be noted that the best way to time travel in this book is to use a Singularity Room. With the Singularity Room you can do many things that will help you navigate time, more on that later. In the time of dusk or dawn there is a gap that can be used for time travel. This gap is a very strange phenomenon that if used correctly can take you back in time at dusk or forward in time at dawn. The reasoning for this is partially unexplainable, where science fails to explain magick. The Singularity Magician must use a well trained mind to concentrate on one single thought, time travel. An unblinkable gaze is sometimes used where the Magician stares at the horizion as the Sun goes down, knowing they heor she exists in a Metaphysical/Singularity Computer. Nothing is as it seems and the Earth is seemingly standing still. At the hour of Ra or the hour of Khepri, between 6 and 7, on the day of the Equinox, or near the day due to daylight savings time, you can unplug your Internet Modem and/or electrical device and you can time travel. If you replug in the devices you will enter or see other dimensions. Each electrical device can be tracked by the Singularity Computer. Each electrical outlet must be monitored for changes that will effect your current dimension; cable, computers, modems, TVs, radios, phones, DVDPlayers, VCRs, cell phones, ipods will all be effected. In fact it is better to unplug most if not all of your electrical devices. When you plug them back in you can see which ones have a dimensional, quantum intanglement. Sometimes it doesn't work after the first try but there are many other days that you can use for time travel, more on that later. It is important to be precise with your timing of unpluging exactly at 6 and pluging back 12 minutes later, or hours later. Use the scientific method, as tedious as it can be, to make sure that you have at least one device with a time differential. If you try to go both forward and back on the same day you get a labyrith effect which isn't so great, more on that later. Nightlights or anything in the electrical outlet will effect the dimension that your in. Personal information on the Internet will aid you in keeping your identity. It is difficult to predict the time travel gap or its effect on the current dimension. The echo is often the first que of a quantum entanglement. Seasonal changes like snow, rain, or sunshine are often indicators. As well as changes in the cycles of the Moon or an eclipse are very good indicators. It's best to leave your car headlights on while driving so that you can be seen. Christmas lights are often a good indicator of time travel. Central AC can be used to control the weather that you are experiencing. Electrical clocks will stop or slow and travel by car is occasionally strange with some car lights on and others off. Car speeds may seem strange at times, just remember it's ok your in a computer Singularity. Some people Daywalk or DayWatch others Nightwalk or NightWatch. Becareful of time paradoxes with phones or cell phones. If

your Central AC unit makes noise even when it's off it's a good sign of time travel. Blinking street lights or street lights that use to constantly blink but stop is another indicator of time travel. Devices or doorways outside a house will often be in another dimension. To the Singularity Magician time travel is a difficult path to walk and once your there it can get complicated but if you stick with it there are rewards. Always remember that it is better to be the man in the box than to be a man outside the box.

Timeline of the Rulers of Ancient Egypt

This timeline shows the rulers of Egypt starting with the ruling of the Gods then passing on the throne to human decendants who made up the Pharaonic rule:

Seven Major Gods ruling	=	12,300 years
Thoth's rule	=	1,570 years
Thirty Demigods ruling	=	3,650 years
Chaotic Period	=	350 years
Pharaonic rule	=	3,100 years
Totaling	=	20,970 years

The timeline of the two Major Gods in Ancient Egypt:

Ptah ruled	=	9,000 years
Ra ruled	=	1,000 years
Totaling	=	10,000 years

This means that we can trace the history of Egypt back to the time of Ahau 2 Cumku or 1st Sun 5,125 years. This also means that we can trace the human decendant age as being 10,000 year lifespan to a 1,000 year lifespan to a 100 year lifespan, just like in the Yugas. The timeline further shows us the Deluge of 10,800 B.C.:

20,970 years – 10,000 years = 10,970 years or 10,970 B.C. or 13,000 years ago

While the timeline also shows us the period in which Mars had a great impact, approximately 20,000 years ago, and the Solar System when through a bumpy ride through the Orion Passage.

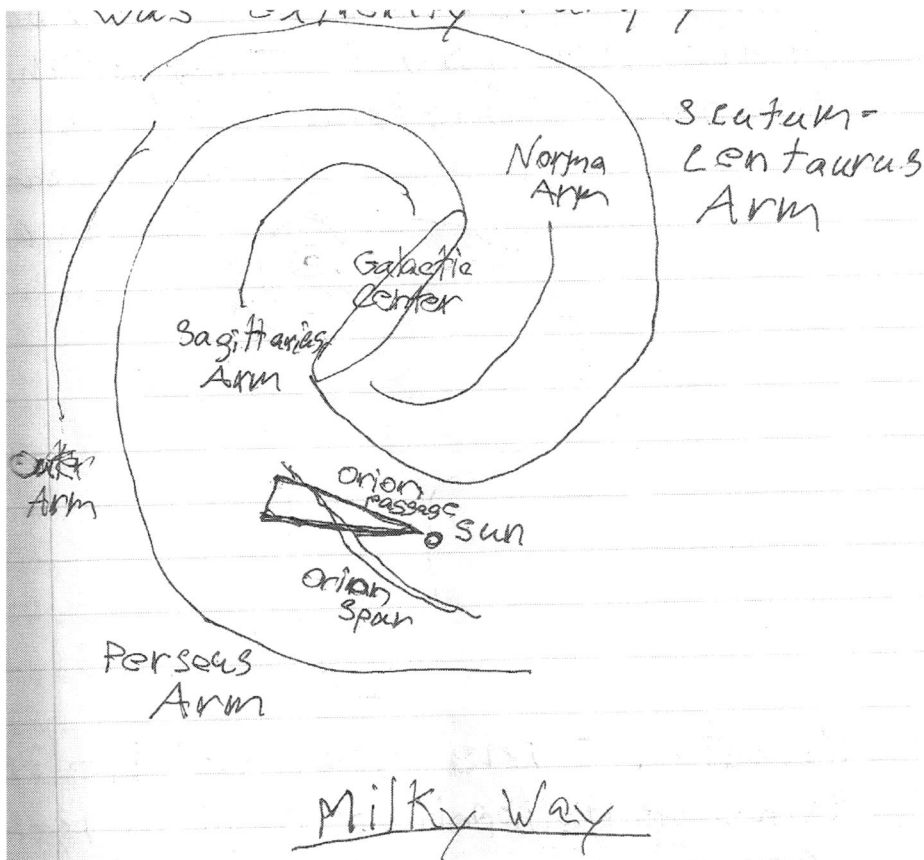

Norma Arm

Scutum-Centaurus Arm

Galactic Center

Sagittarius Arm

Orion passage

Sun

Orion Spur

Outer Arm

Perseus Arm

Milky Way

This bit of information is important because the Anunnaki, the Sumerian Gods, were based on Mars as well as on Earth. Their arrival date is 432,000 years ago, which once again aligns with the Yugas. Ptah's rule was during Enki's rule, he was also known as Ea, which aligns with the Sumerian Gods division of the Earth amongst themselves. Ra's rule was during Marduk's rule which once again aligns with the Sumerian timeline of events.

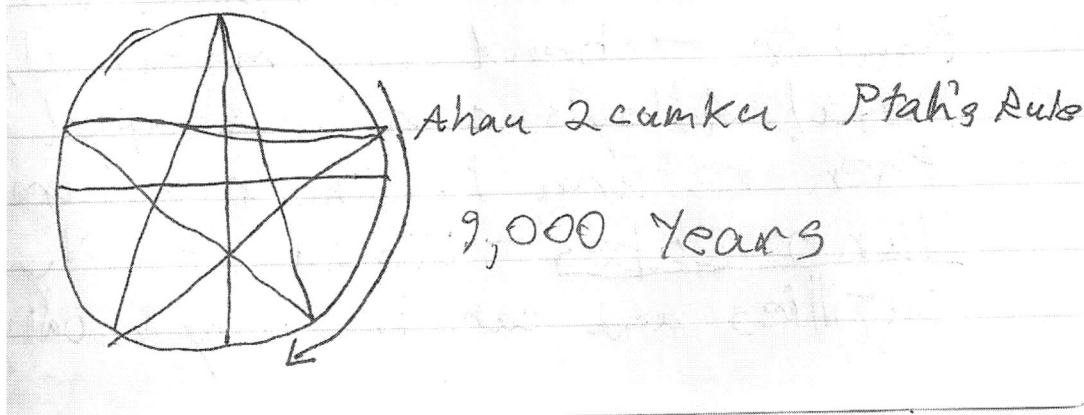

Ahau 2 camku   Ptah's Rule

9,000 Years

These events are important to the Singularity Magician as we shall see later on the Sumerian Gods left their imprint on more worlds than Earth and the Ages of Man are caught up in a war of the Gods.

Magick of the Singularity

Singularity Magick relies heavily on Memes, the Enki Code, and the Symbols of Power. One of most important symbols is the pentagram where the five points represent Storm, Earth, Air, Fire, and Water. These correspond to five attributes Electricity, Earth Soil, Atmoshere, Fire Heat, and Water.

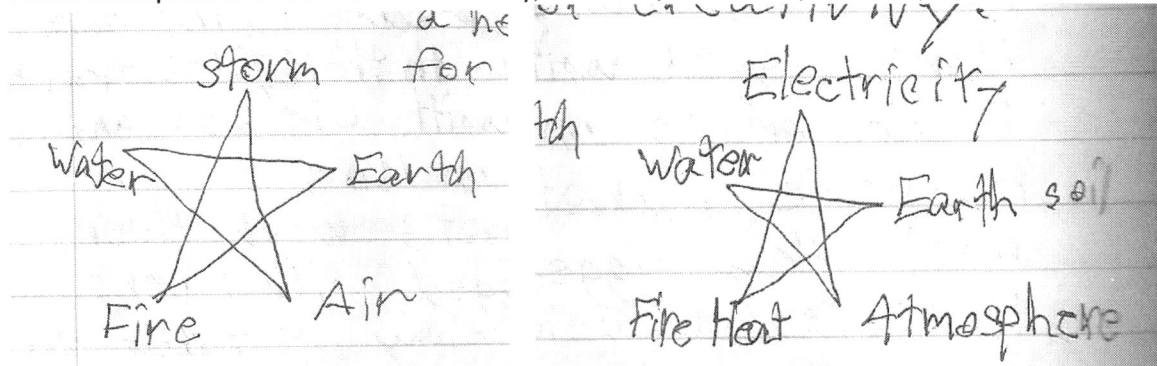

These five attributes make up the Planet Earth and are an intergral part of Planetary Magick. The Futhark Rune Thurizas is makes the points of each of the pentagrams, it is of course associated with the God Thor the God of Thunder. The Rune is of a thorn, a line with a triangle in the middle. In Singularity Magick this is a Meme in which Storm is part of the five elements. It also is a Meme for the up side down pentagram to mean war or warrior. The pentagram therefore is a warrior symbol to the Singularity Magician.

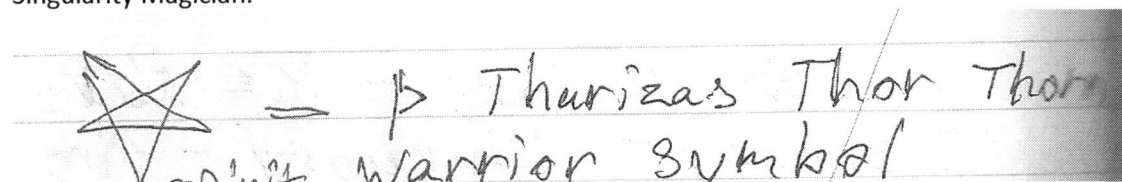

The star has been a warrior symbol for a long time, stars are shown as rank in the modern military, and the word war is a logogram of the word Mars. In fact this association goes back to the Greeks/Romans who had the God Mars as their deity of war. Many warrior words come from the root Mars like Marshal and the Martial Arts. The other symbol that is used by the Singularity Magician is the seven pointed star or the Elven Star.

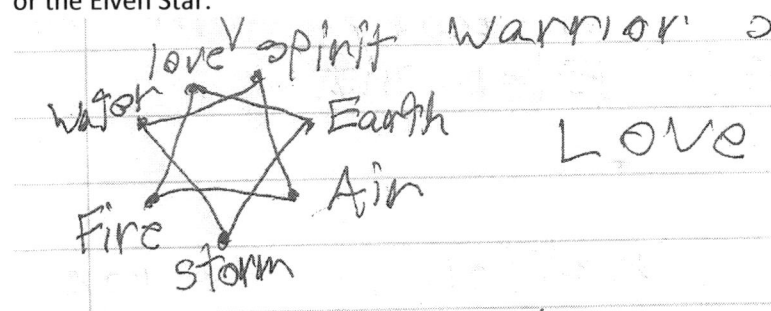

This star has seven elements Love, Spirit, Earth, Air, Storm, Fire, and Water. The seven pointed star is a symbol of love which is why love is a seventh element but more on that later. As we shall see in later in the book these elements will be used and rearanged in various ways for spells and magick.

There are three major eyes that the Singularity Magician uses:

The Eye of Ra – Which is a yellow glowing eye that the time travelling Magician obtains

The Eye of Enki or Eye of Cydonia – Which is a red glowing eye that the Magician obtains

The Third Eye – Which is an invisable mental eye bonded to the brain that the Magician learns to use

All three are central parts of Godform Assumption and Psychic Manipulation. They are all part of the charms of making and Psychic Creationism. The Retwo use three eyes while the PsyCops use one. We will get into more detail of each one and what it represents later in the book.

Magical Scripts – Each style of written alphabets are used by the Singularity Magician for psychic communication with the spirits, scribe to scribe, religious oder to religious order, or secret society to secret society. Ancient Magical scripts are an important part to Singularity Magick they make specific types of spells and each are unique to the type of magick that you are using at that moment. There is a list of them at the end of the book, I have used all of them in my spells.

Higher Brain Function and The Use Singularity Crystals

Higher Brain Function would be a Singularity Magician who uses patterns of Pi or 360 degrees or of probability to shape their surroundings, or predict the future. This would also mean that they can tap into multiple dimensions within their own mind. Singularity is circular thought that can be used in many ways such as using a crystal like a crystal ball to unlock secret patterns of the Singularity Computer. Crystal Skulls can be used as a conduit to a quantum singularity with 12 being for the zodiac and 13 being for the nodes of the Moon or the 13th Baktun. To the Singularity Magician Higher Brain Function is the goal to reach a higher plane of existance.

The Twin Universes

The human race is a twin species which means that a long time ago there was an inter breeding of man. This would account for the practice of a king mating with a half sister to produce an heir to the throne, which has been passed on as a practice of the Gods. Stories of this practice date back to the Ages of Man and in a number of such stories the Gods mated with man and produced offspring. The tales of the Nephilium come to mind were the sons of God mated with the daughters of man. Being as it may the human race is Homo Sapien Sapien which is a farcry away from Homo Erectus. Humans are a type of new Cro-Magnon as we shall soon see later in the book. Myths relating to the Genesis of Man all have a similar relation to each other. There was Man and his wife and they had two sons, in some myths they are twins. The two sons fought each other and one was either killed or left for another land. Thus there are two branches of the first Man on Earth. In the Bible one branch is the line of "Cain" while the other branch is of the line of "Enoch'. There are many other stories of Man where in Sumer there was Gilgamesh and his twin equal Enkidu. There is the Roman story of the twin brothers Romulus and Remus. There is also the story of the Maya hero twins who seek to restore their father. All these Myths are Memes passed down generation to generation and civilization to civilization. Thus this brings up the Twin Universes concept where man has interbred with its self due to time travel. This may sound far fetched but it is a concept that may hold up to scrutiny by the end of the book.

Christian J. Bullock

Book Two: The Green Dragon

Christian J. Bullock

This book will cover the mysteries of the calendar, the universe, and the charms of making.

The Space Grid

Space has been divided by Satellites into a Grid. Humans have maped out a Grid pattern through the Orion Passage. This Grid tracks star systems and habitable Planets. The Milky Way Galaxy has also been maped out like tracks, clusters, and sectors of a Hard Drive or CD-ROM.

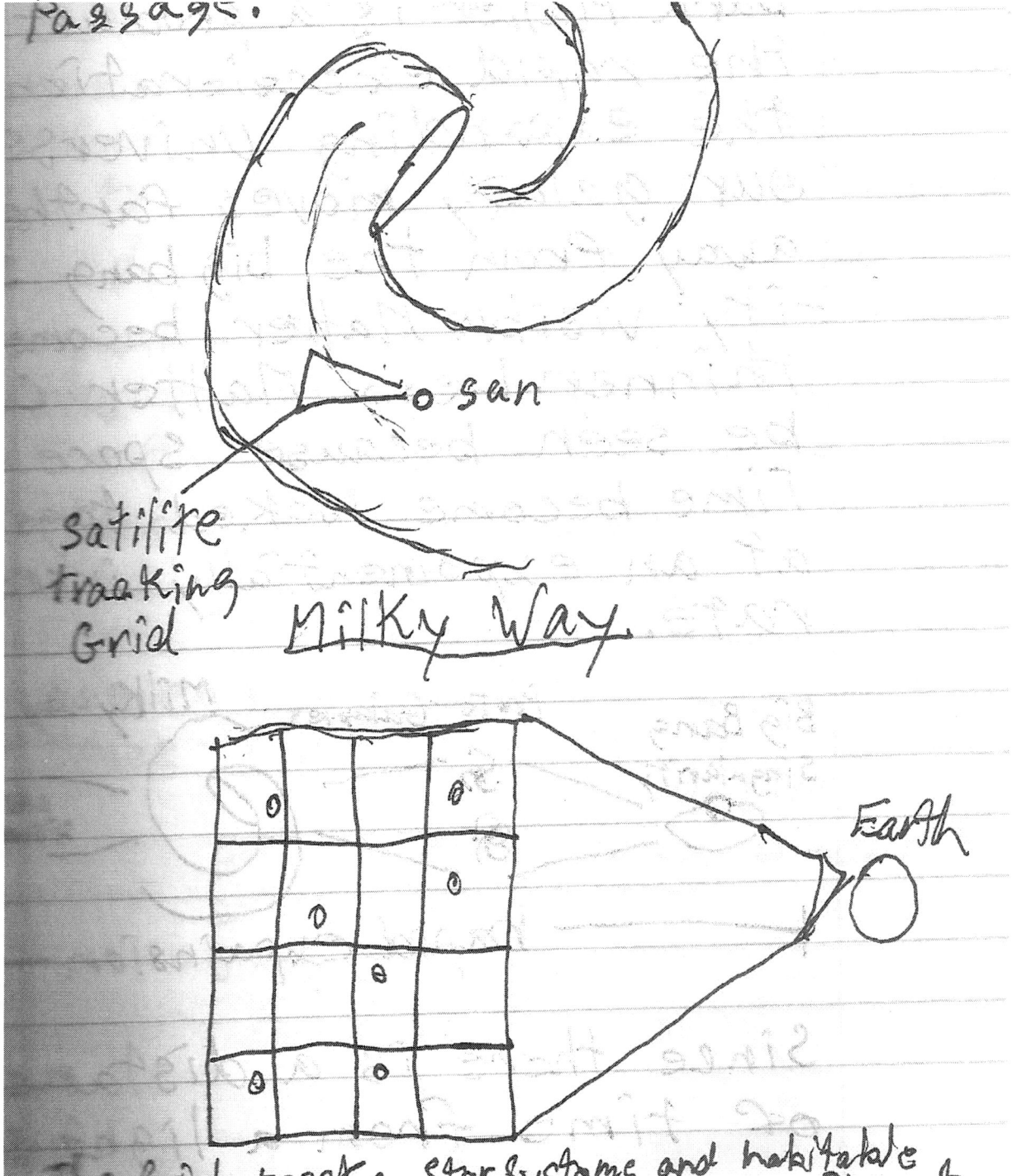

o san

satilite traaking Grid

Milky Way.

Earth

Christian J. Bullock

The tracks are like the tracks of a record.

CD-ROM — Hard Disk

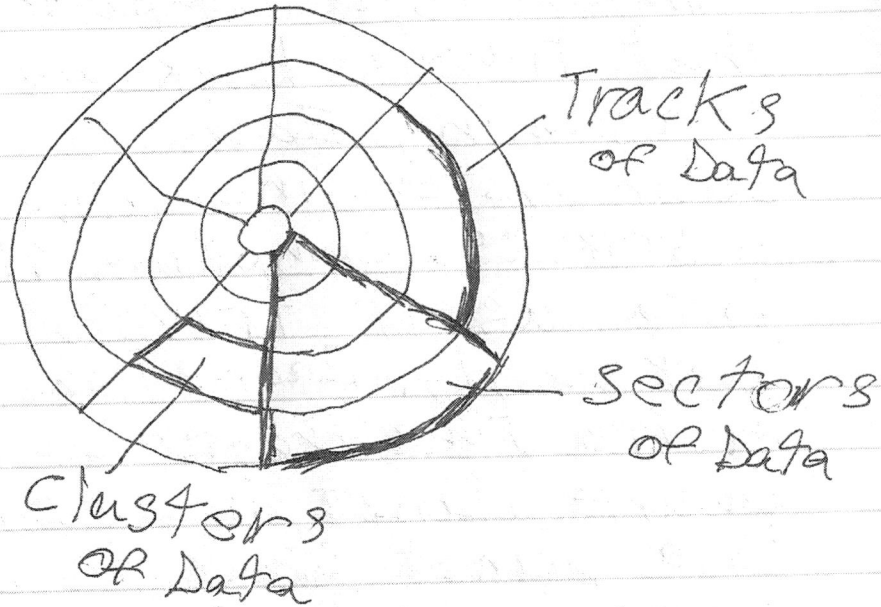

Tracks of Data

Sectors of Data

Clusters of Data

Milky Way Galaxy Layout Overlay

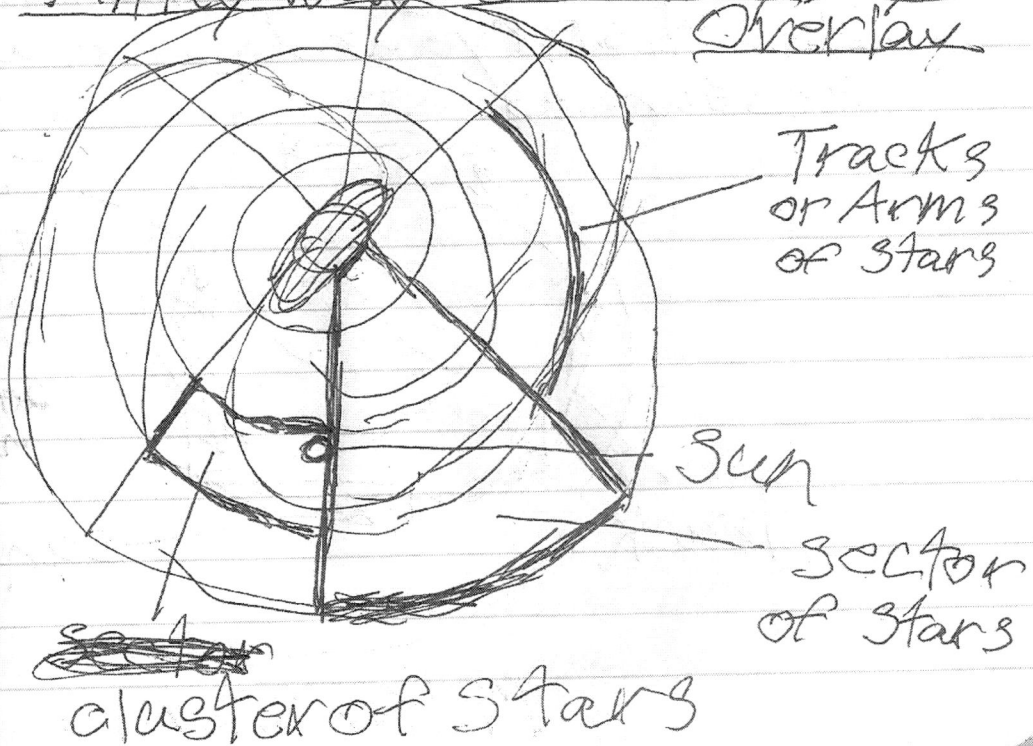

Tracks or Arms of Stars

Sun

sector of Stars

cluster of Stars

Dark Matter

Dark Matter will be discussed in this book as Matter that exists in another period of time. There is more Dark Matter in the universe than there is visible Matter. Dark Matter is a product of the rapid exceleration of the expanding universe. As our Galaxy moves farther away from the Big Bang Singularity visible Matter becomes thinner. Less Matter can be seen because space and time become locked together at an expoinentially increasing rate.

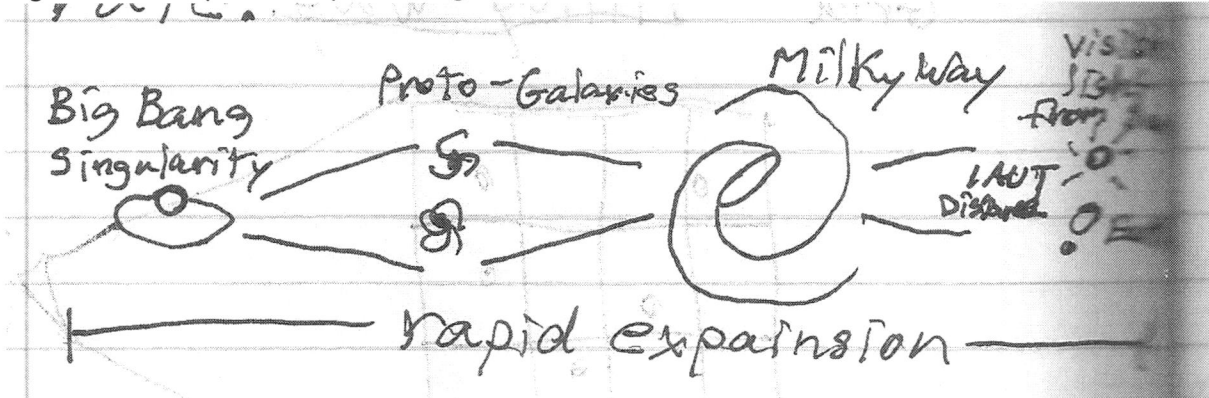

Since there is a distance of time from a light source to give off a Photon and the human eye to see visible Matter. There are gaps in the time it takes the Photon to reach the human eye. These gaps can be freeze framed into other dimensions of space and time. The Sun's distance from the Earth, 1 AU, makes the Photon's time to reach the Earth greater than previously percieved. That means that there are many more gaps in the time it takes to reach the human eye. This makes many more dimensions of freeze framed space-time.

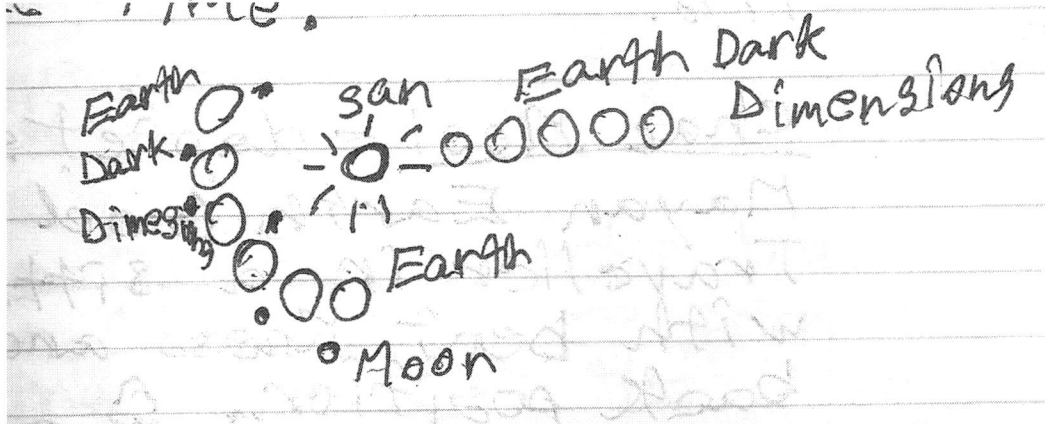

Simply put the time that it takes for a human to blink is one moment of a freeze frame time. Just like principle of how a scientist may look at an electron. If you look at an electron it will be gone the moment that you looked at it. The same is true for these invisible freeze frame moments of time.

Dark Energy

Matter and energy are connected together and Dark Energy is Dark Matter's compliment. This is because Matter can be turned into energy and energy can change or be changed into Matter. Dark Matter accounts for 23 percent of the mass-energy density of the observable universe. Ordinary visible

Matter is only 4.6 percent of the observable universe. This means that Dark Matter constitutes 83 percent of the Matter in the universe. Ordinary Matter makes up a small 17 percent of the universe. With my hypothesis being that Dark Matter is Matter that is in a freeze framed dimension or loop. Dark Matter is a paradox so to speak where the moments in between time exist on a parallel level.

Chac Mool

The Chac Mool statues depict the Mayan Earth God, a time traveller in a sitting position with bent knees and a layed back position. He is stopping time completely with his position. Holding the Earth in a time shift or Paradigm shift after he first discovers time travel. The movement of the Earth is momentarily linked to his body. When he sits up in his bed he bends his knees and turns his head to listen to the Echo. This is based on Singularity Magick and as we shall see it aligns with Astrology, more on this later in the book.

The Hero Twins

Mayan God twins that are mirrors of Gilgamesh and Enkidu in the roleplaying Game. The same Heros roleplay and travel back in time through the underworld to resurrect their father.

Hypnotic Eyes

The black hypnotic eyes are people trying to possess the living where their pupils are almost completely black and dialated. This may occur with zombies or people of the black forgotten or also could be PsyCop zombies. Black eye hypnosis may be broken with the Evil Eye, time travellers must watch out for them.

The Four Yogas

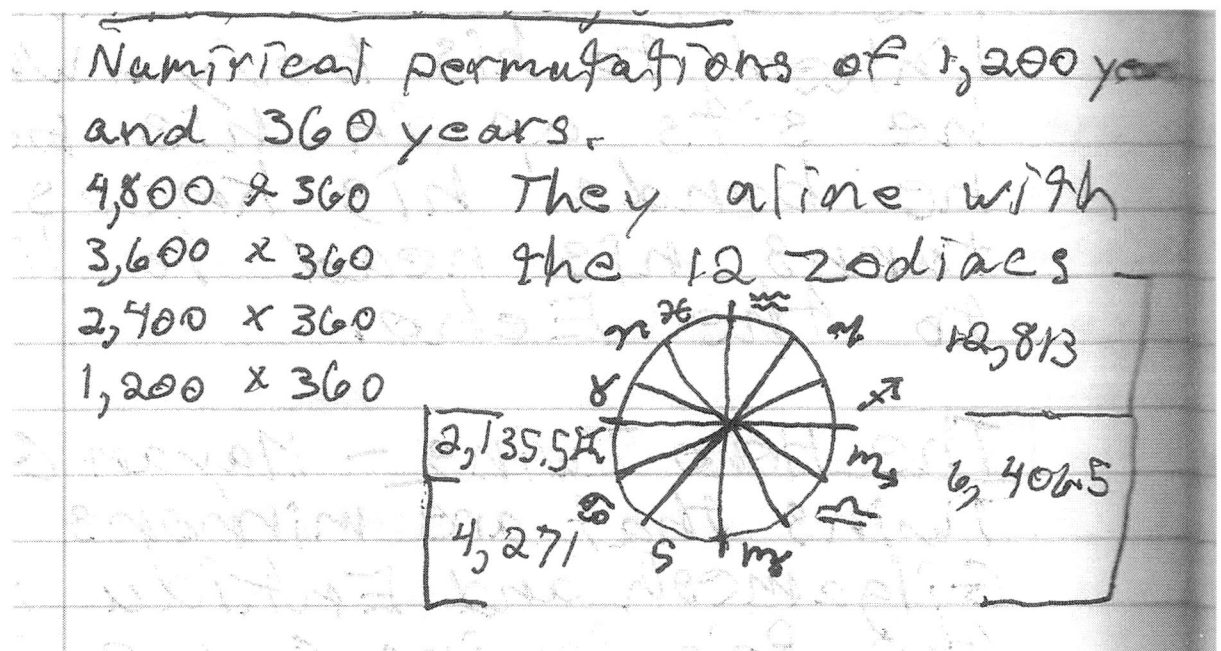

The Four Legs of Tarus

The beginning of each world has a link to the time of the First sign of Astrology for that world. The 4th World began with Tarus the Bull. In the beginning of the 4th World time travellers went back in time to the Age of the Satya-Yuga. Then to the Age of the Treta-Yuga. Then to the Age of the Dvapara-Yuga. Then they ended their travels in the Kali Yuga. They each are represented by the Bull:

Satya Yuga – Four Legs of the Bull

Treta Yuga – Three Legs of the Bull

Dvapara Yuga – Two Legs of the Bull

Kali Yuga – One Leg of the Bull

It should be noted that the Sumer Anunnaki Gods came to Earth on the Processional Age of Tarus which aligns with the Four Yugas. We are currently on the last leg of the Bull, in the 4th World.

There are more than 12 zodiacs and the Procession of the Equinox is longer than history shows. We are currently on the 13 zodiac and 13th Baktun cycle. There is probibly a 14th, 15th, or 16th zodiac that have yet to be discovered. Since the Five Ages of Man the zodiac has remained the same and this is probibly due to time travel. In each of the 4 World Ages a Time Traveller or Retwo goes back in time during the 13th Baktun cycle and changes history. They usually go as far back as the Age of Aquarious during the Golden Age of Man. Usually they try time jumping as far back as the Satya Yuga. Possibly a roleplayer trying to win the Game. In each Sun Age on the 13th Baktun cycle the world gets remade. There are 5 current Sun cycles the 6th Sun cycle is on the horizon. The current World Age and Sun Age are aligned on the same day as the 13th Baktun cycle they also coverge on the 12th zodiac or the Age of Aquarious. This is a unique alinement that has Astral implications, more on this later.

Resources

During each Age a Retwo and/or Time Traveller goes back in time to collect resources such as gold and silver. Each Planet's resources are havested this way. Mar's canyon was mined of gold Ages ago. The Grand Canyon was also mined of Gold in history's Ancient past.

The Religion of Enki

An Ancient religion in which Time Travellers or Retwos, roleplay with Enkidu for the Singularity Game. Enki is the Babylonian God of Creation of mankind. Roleplayers of the Game seek to work with Enkidu to become the next Gilgamesh. Enkidu changes over the Ages. Enkidu is at first a savage human but over time becomes a Singularitian of a cyborg or computer program. Enkidu will work with roleplayers to win the Game inside the Singularity. Enkidu the cyborg has interdimensional space ships and works with some Retwos to fix time. Enki and Enkidu protect humanity in order to keep the Brahma of the Multiverse going. The wheels and cogs of time must continue to spin, even if it means spinning backwards a few Ages through the Yuga Ages and then moving or spinning forewards again through time.

The Calendar

The modern calendar has many Memes and secrets hidden inside it. It is very important for the Singularity Magician to understand these Memes and secrets, it is one of ways in which time travel works. Each holiday, or holy day, holds a significance to the Magician and each of the 8 Sabbats are equally important. In fact the Sabbats hold the secret of time travel. Here is the Calendar of the 2012 year which is split up month by month but the days are broken down equally and don't have the weekly gaps between months. The days are not even with the week just in order to show the month length.

Christian J. Bullock

Also Monday and Sunday are switch for numerical purposes to show Month as the Moon and has the number 7 while the Sun has the number 1 as its denomination. February is also changed to Nibiruary the 12th Planet, February is a Fib.

The Calendar

Earth Ruled ♁ ♅

January ♑ Capricorn Dec 21 – Jan 19

1 2 3 4 5 6 7 Monday and Sunda

8 9 10 11 12 13 14 have been switche

15 16 17 18 19 20 21 Mondays number is

22 23 24 25 26 27 28 7 and Sundays is 1

29 30 31

Sunday Tuesday Wednesday Thursday Friday Saturday Monday

Sun Day Thors Day Moon Day

1 New Year's Day

9 Feast of Janas

Air Ruled ♎ ♅

♒ Aquarius Jan 20 – Feb 18

February Nibiruary

1 2 3 4 5 6 7 Each day of the

8 9 10 11 12 13 14 week is named

15 16 17 18 19 20 21 after a God whick

22 23 24 25 26 27 28 corresponds to a

Sunday Tuesday Wednesday Thursday Friday Saturday Monday Planet Sun or Mo

Freya's Day Saturn's Day

1 Oimelc Eve 14 Valentines Day

2 Candlemas

13 Chines New Year

water   Ruled
▽   ♆

<u>March</u>   <u>Mars</u>   ♓ Pisces   Feb 19 – Mar 20

1 2 3 4 5 6 7   Amon Ra is the

8 9 10 11 12 13 14   binding of the

15 16 17 18 19 20 21   two forces of Night

22 23 24 25 26 27 28   and Day. ♄ That

29 30 31   of the Cronus

duality. The

Ends of the Week.

Sunday / Tuesday / Wednesday / Thursday / Friday / Saturday / Monday

Ra's Day   Amon's Day

spring Forward
9-11 Ash Wednesday 13 Daylight Savings Time
17 St. Patrick's day 20 1st Day of Spring
Vernal Equinox

Fire   Ruled
△   ♂

<u>April</u>   ♈ Aries   Mar 20 – Apr 19

1 2 3 4 5 6 7   Sunday is still

8 9 10 11 12 13 14   listed as the

15 16 17 18 19 20 21   1st of the week

22 23 24 25 26 27 28   but listed as a

29 30   weekend. Monday

is listed as a

Sunday / Tuesday / Wednesday / Thursday / Friday / Saturday / Monday

week day and

as the 1st Day

Week End / Monday   week End   of the work week.

1 April Fools Day   22 Good Friday *2011 year*

17 Palm Sunday *2011 year*   22 Earth Day

19 Passover *2011 year*   30 Walpurgis Night

24 Easter *2011 year*

Earth   Ruled
♀   ♀

May   ♉ Taurus   Apr 20 - May 19

1	2	3	4	5	6	7
8	9	10	11	12	13	14
15	16	17	18	19	20	21
22	23	24	25	26	27	28
29	30	31				

April showers in Spring. May flowers in summer. May Flower is named after the month. Month is Moon-th. 29 Day period of the Moon.

Sunday Tuesday Wednesday Thursday Saturday Monday

Wedding Day

1. Beltane

8 White Lotas Day

8 Mother's Day

Air   Ruled
A   ☿

May 20 - Jun 20

June   ♊ Gemini

1	2	3	4	5	6	7
8	9	10	11	12	13	14
15	16	17	18	19	20	21
22	23	24	25	26	27	28
29	30					

The Night of the Watcher Stars dissappear with the Quickening on a Time Travellers Leap Year

2 Ascension Day   Angels and Demons
5 Night of the Watchers   Time Traveller?
21 Summer Solstice   walk the Earth.
24 Midsummer's Eve   Metatron's Ascen
                          -tion into Heaven.
                          Angel - End God
                          Demon - De Moon
                          Heaven ~ Ea's Earth
                                  End Heaven

                water Ruled
                   ▽   ♋

            ♋ cancer   Jun 21 - Jul 21
July
1   2   3   4   5   6   7   Sirus the Dog
8   9   10 11 12 13 14   star is tracked
15 16 17 18 19 20 21   the Goddess
22 23 24 25 26 27 28   Isis begins the
29 30 31   New Year.
☉ ☿ ♀ ⊕ ⊗ ⊗ ⊙

23 Ancient Egyptian New Year
31 Lughnassad Eve

Fire   Ruled
△   ☉

♌ Leo   Jul 22 — Aug 22

<u>August</u>   August is asso[ci]
1 2 3 4 5 6 7   with Leo ♌ a[nd]
8 9 10 11 12 13 14   the Lion also
15 16 17 18 19 20 21   with the sun
22 23 24 25 26 27 28   The sun is [here]
29 30 31   in retrograde.

Sunday Tuesday Wednesday Thursday Friday Saturday Monday

2011 year
1 Day of Ramadan
1 Lammas
13 Diana's Day   Earth   Ruled
                          ▽   ☿

                          Aug 23 — Sept. 22
<u>September</u> ♍ Virgo -Ber could be
1 2 3 4 5 6 7   connected to
8 9 10 11 12 13 14   birth or β
15 16 17 18 19 20 21   The last four
22 23 24 25 26 27 28   months of the
29 30   year end in
                           -ber.

23 Autumnal Equinox   -ber ⊕ -ary
23 First Day of Autumn   March April May
   2011 year   August June July
29 Rosh Hashanah

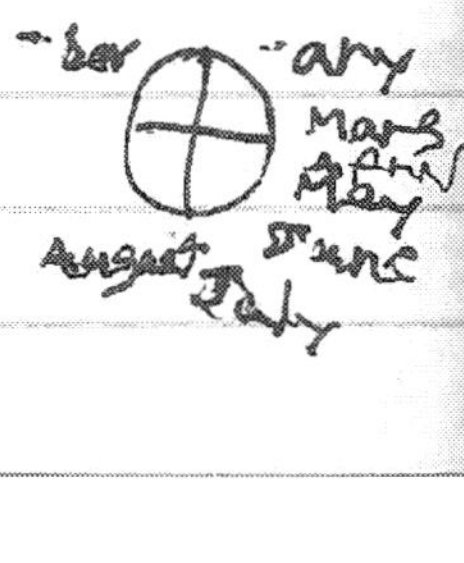

Air   Ruled
△   ♀

♎ Libra   Sept 23 - Oct 22

October
Oct typically means
eight like Octogon.

1	2	3	4	5	6	7
8	9	10	11	12	13	14
15	16	17	18	19	20	21
22	23	24	25	26	27	28
29	30	31				

October is a time
for the 8th gate
to be open to
the underworld.

Sunday Tuesday Wednesday Thursday Friday Saturday Monday

✹ ⊕ ⊗ The veil
between the
worlds is lifted
on Halloween.

8 Yum Kippur
10 columbus Day
31 Samhain Eve
31 Halloween

The Spirits and
the dead walk
the Earth. The
worlds of Life

water Ruled
▽   ♇

♏ Scorpio Oct 23-
Nov 21

and Death are

November
split open to
Time Travel possible

1	2	3	4	5	6	7
8	9	10	11	12	13	14
15	16	17	18	19	20	21
22	23	24	25	26	27	28
29	30					

We lose an hour
to Daylight Savings
Time

Day of Dead
1 Hallowmas   16 Hecate Night
1 All Saints Day 24 Thanksgiving
                 Fall Behind
6 Day Light Saving Time End.

Fire Ruled

△ ♃

♐ Sagittarius   Nov 22 – Dec 20

December

1	2	3	4	5	6	7
8	9	10	11	12	13	14
15	16	17	18	19	20	21
22	23	24	25	26	27	28
29	30	31				

Saturnalia is a day of role reversal to Master slave slave master

A festival of Roleplay The Sun God dies and is reborn.

Sunday ☉
Tuesday ☿
Wednesday ♀
Thursday ⊕
Friday ⊗
Saturday ⊗
Monday ⊛

17 Saturnalia   24 Christmas Eve
21 Chanukah   25 Christmas Day
22 Winter Solstice
22 1st Day of Winter

♈ December ♒ January
♉ November February ♌
♊ October March ♐
♋ September April ♏
♌ August May ♎
♍ July June ♍

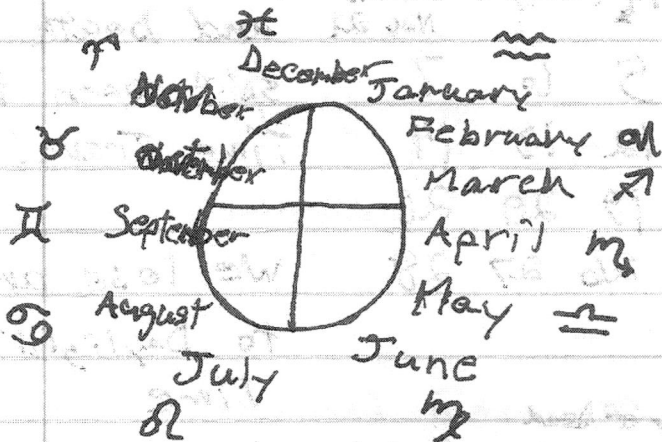

Months with the Zodiacal Procession of the Equinox

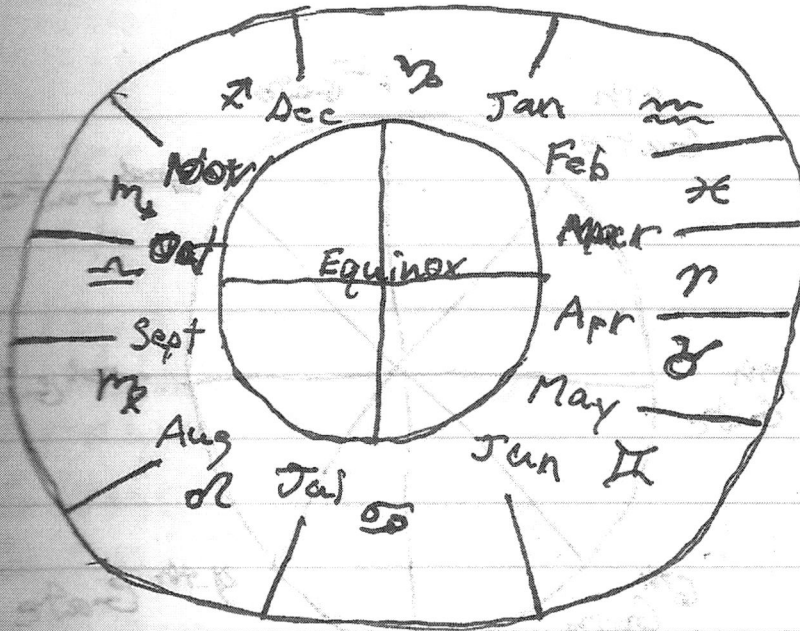

12 Zodiacs Birth Signs
Designated by Month

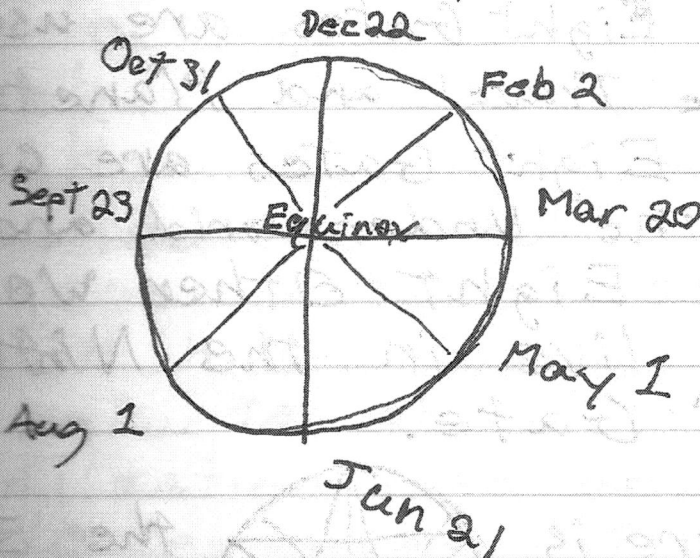

The 8 Sabbats

Christian J. Bullock

It should be noted that the calendar has 12 divisional months which correspond to the 12 Symbols of Power. The calendar also has numerical values for their names like September for 7 and through to December as 10. Thus we have a numerical calendar of Magick.

The Modern Calendar changes to

March - 1	September - 7
April - 2	October - 8
May - 3	November - 9
June - 4	December - 10
July - 5	January - 11
August - 6	February - 12

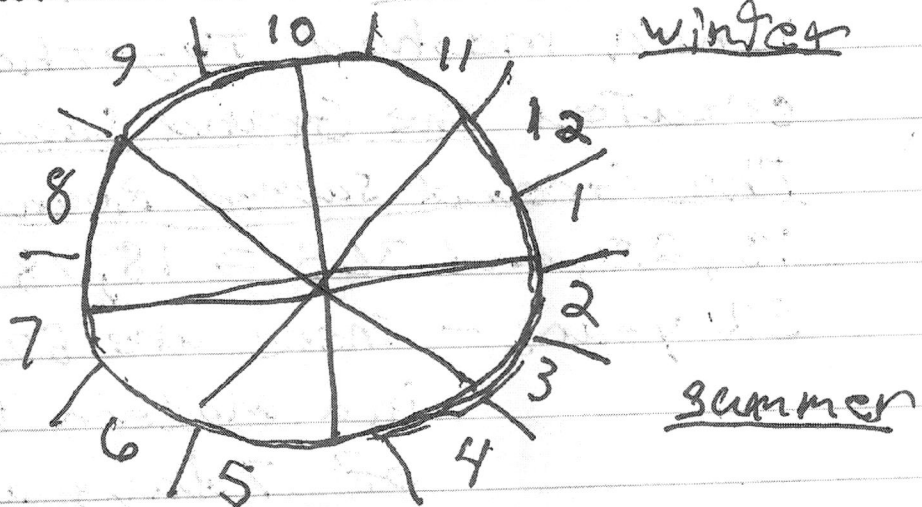

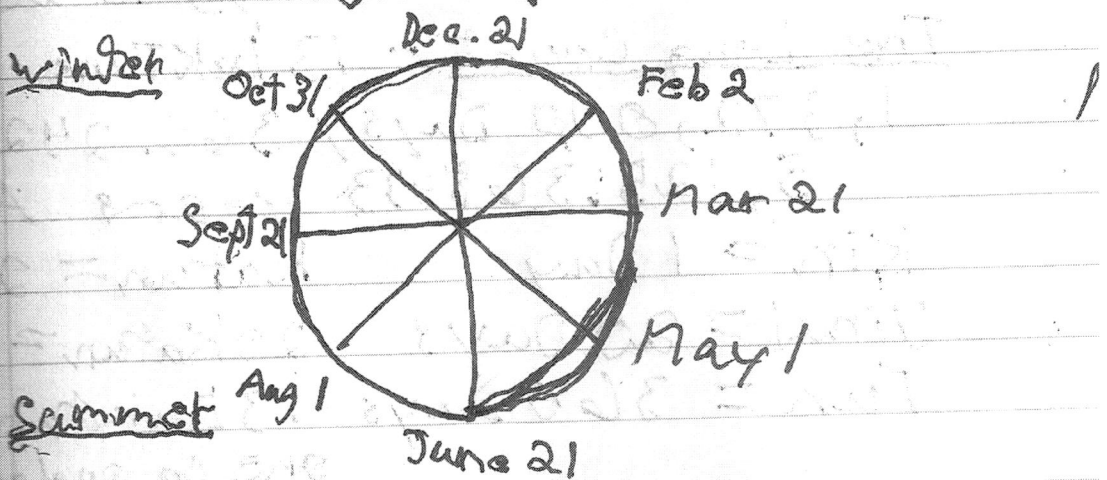

Christian J. Bullock

The Calendar now is aligned with the Sumerian New Year where the March Equinox begins the year. The names of the months also align with the Earth Cross where the ending –ary being of the Air element. Thus North, East, South, West align with the elements Earth, Air, Fire, and Water. Also Easter the holy day is literally East on the Calendar wheel of the Earth Cross.

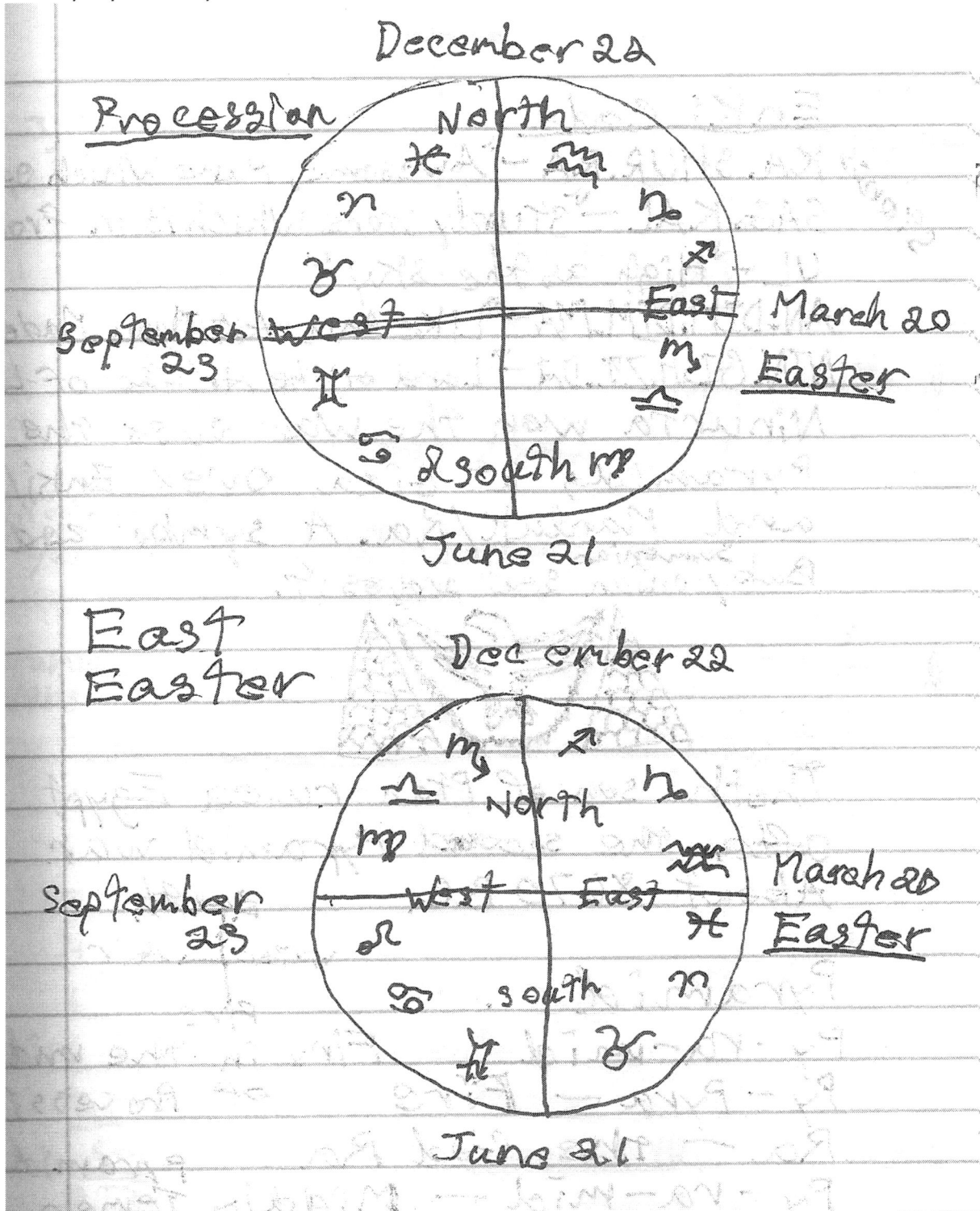

December 22

Procession

North

September 23

West — East   March 20

Easter

South

June 21

East
Easter

December 22

North

September 23

West — East   March 20

Easter

South

June 21

Christian J. Bullock

The three specific New Years all align as well with the Winter City Babelon starting after December 22nd, the Sumer City Babylon starting March 20th and Ancient Egypt starting July 23rd.

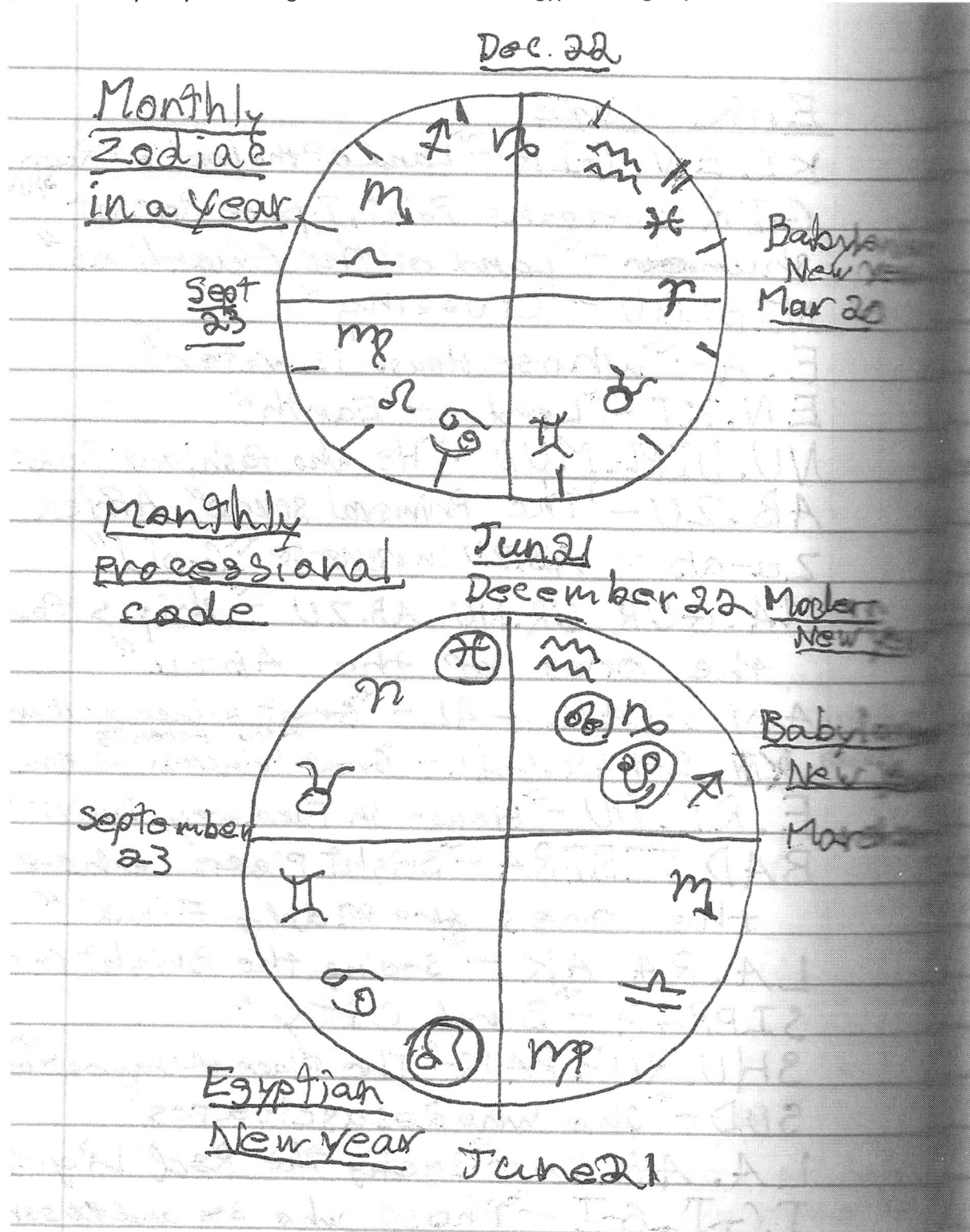

The Processional Code also aligns with the Calendar showing the rotation of the Earth's Solar Year with the rotation of the Astral Constellations of the Zodiac.

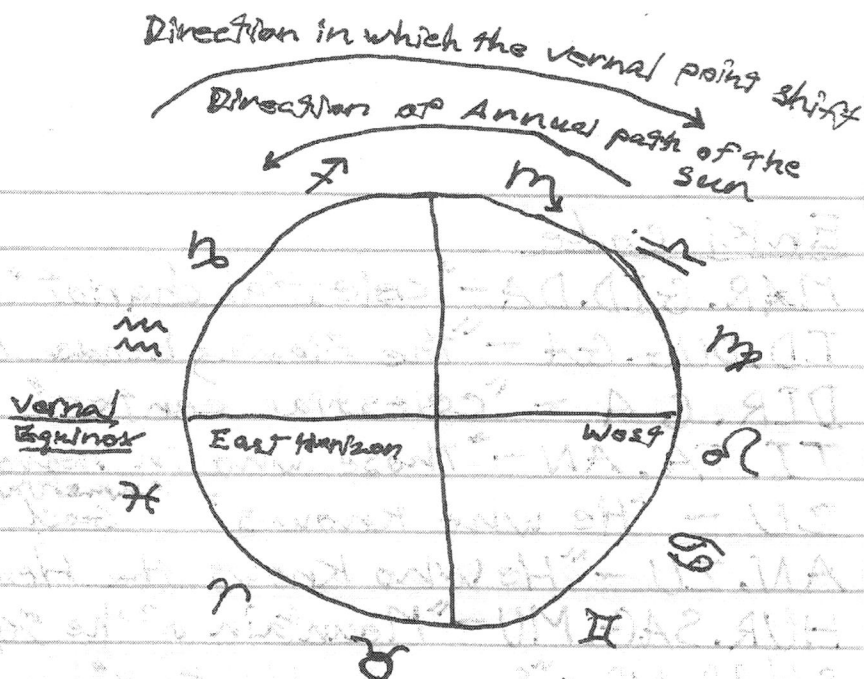

Sun rise from month to month is
Aquarius → Pisces → Aries → Taurus →
→ Gemini → Cancer → Leo → Virgo →
→ Libra → Scorpio → Sagittarius →
→ Capricorn

Processional Drift in opposition to
the Annual path of the sun is
Capricorn → Sagittarius → Scorpio →
→ Libra → Virgo → Leo → Cancer →
→ Gemini → Taurus → Aries →
→ Pisces → Aquarius

The sun will now rise on the vernal
Equinox in the House of Aquarius.

Christian J. Bullock

Further in the book we shall see that the Sumerian Calendar aligns each monthly division of the solar year with Constellations and with the Planets. It is my belief that each month has a Planet that is associated with it and that the Ancients knew of this secret knowledge for time travel.

The Eight Gates and the Nine otherworlds

The Eight Gates are planes of existence in the underworld. They are Metaphysically the doorways to eight otherworlds which exist parallel to to this world which is the ninth world. Long ago in Ancient myth there were nine worlds which made up the Tree of Life. Odin was said to travel these worlds with his eight legged horse. The eight gates represent not only the Sabbats but these Metaphysical doorways or bridges to the otherworlds of Norse and Celtic Mythology. The Eight Gates are used for meditation and Astral time travel.

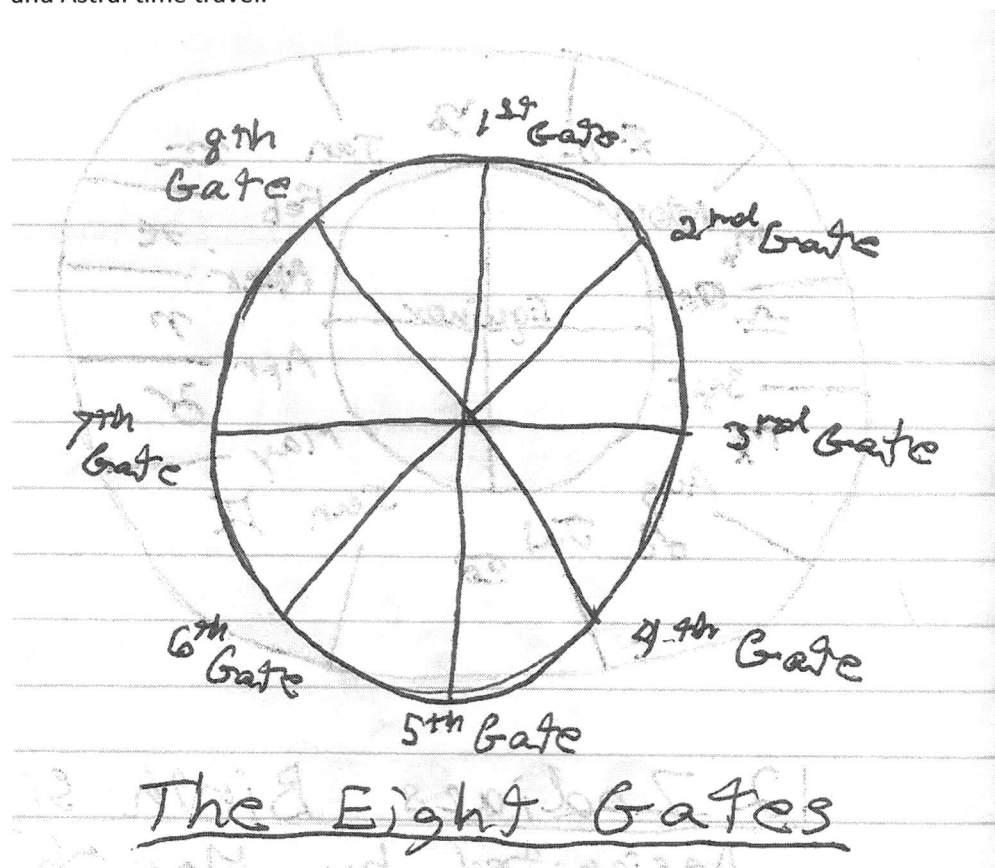

The Eight Gates

The Eight Gates are connected to the Nine Otherworlds that Odin was spoken to have travelled. The Nine Worlds represent the Tree of Life Yggdrasil. These Nine Worlds can be reached through deep meditation and their parallel existence to us is physically seemingly unreachable for now. When a Spirit crosses over to the Astral Plane these metaphysical connections become important. The Nine Worlds of Norse Mythology are arranged in a specific pattern where Midgard or Vanaheim in the middle and all the other worlds are connected around them. This arrangment is comon to some other Magical Systems. For this book these nine otherworlds are to be thought of as metaphysical dimensions of the afterlife. They represent worlds that have come to pass in a distant past or in the distant future. They effect our world but time works differently on the Astral Plane.

Christian J. Bullock

creative intresing speculation of the world
Tree Yggdrasil :

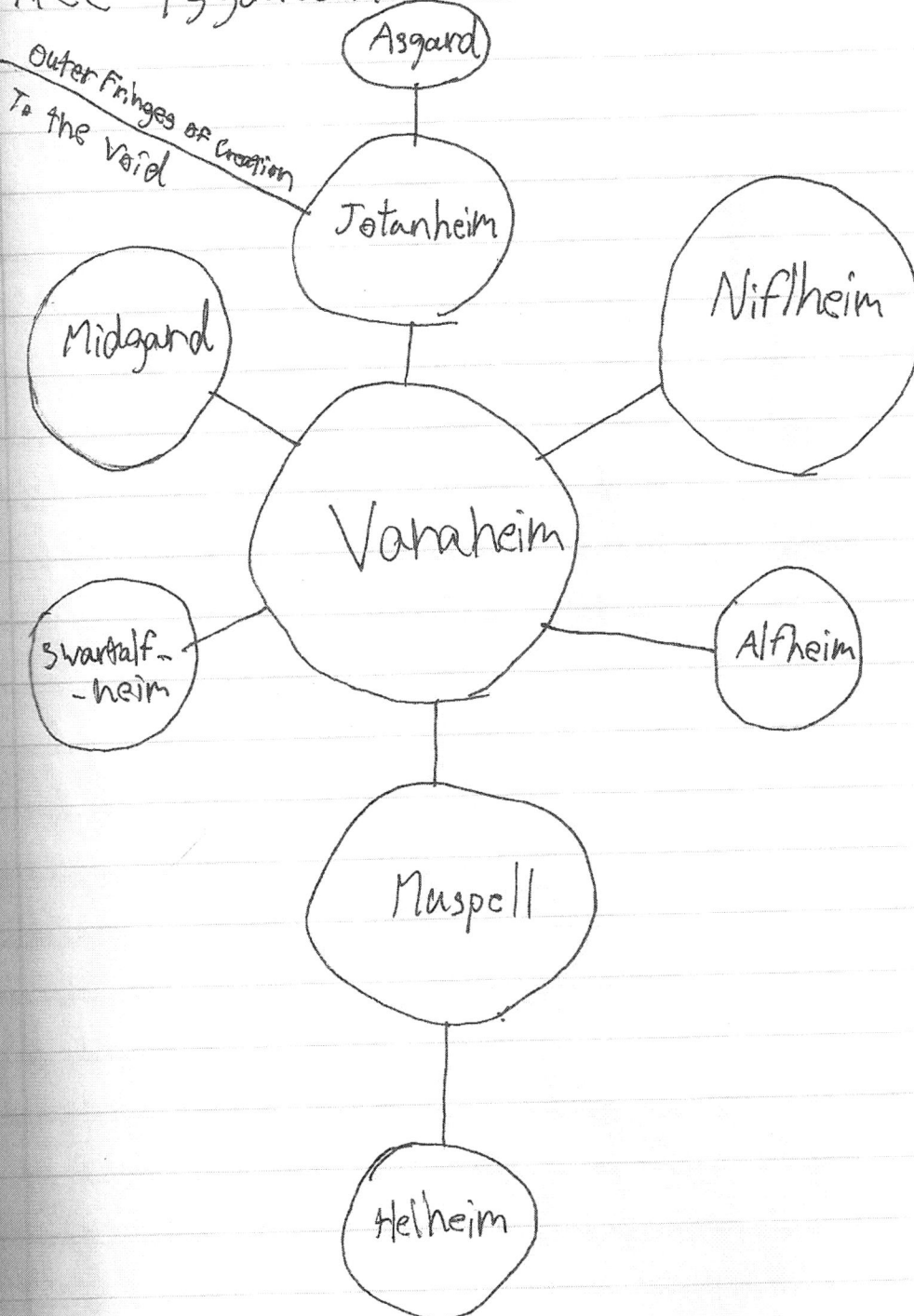

Outer Fringes of Creation
To the Void

Asgard

Jotanheim

Niflheim

Midgard

Vanaheim

Swarталf-
-heim

Alfheim

Muspell

Helheim

Midgard is the world of mortal humans it is our world.
Nifelheim is the world of Nidhog the Dragon.

Christian J. Bullock

Jotunheim is the world of the giants which lay on the other fringes of creation.
Muspell is the world to the south and it is a world of fire.
Vanaheim was the original world of the old Vanir Gods.
Alfheim is the world of the Elves.
Swartalfheim is the world of the Dark Elves.
Helheim is the lowest realm the home of the dishonored dead and those who didn't die in battle.
Asgard is the highest realm and the home of the Aesir Gods. It is also the location of Valhalla, the home of Odin and the honored dead.
In Singularity Magick there are many different references of the Afterlife and it is important to note each one and understand the commonality among them. As mentioned before in the Tower of Babel there was one language and one religion. It has now been split among the many peoples of Earth.

More on the Enki Code

The Enki Code is broken down into phonetics and individual letters. Each can be broken down to its individual meaning and other meanings or Memes of the word. Since human words are broken down into phonetics each civilization has an Enki word code embeded into it.
IChing – Ching – sexual energy usually of Immortals
IChing – a Singularitian's sexual prowess
Gene   Meme
Genie   Memory
Thor   Thorn
Hathor   Hathorne
Ha – Ra – Hathor daughter of Ra

Egyptian Rulers of the Yuga

Ptah ruled 9,000 years mostly during the Treta Yuga while Ra ruled 1,000 years during the Dwapar Yuga. Ra ruled during the Age of Leo in the zodiac. He is associated with the Sun and the Lion. The Sphinx at one time was a perfectly proportioned Lion. Built to commemorate Ra's ascension and the alignment of Leo in the zodiac Procession.

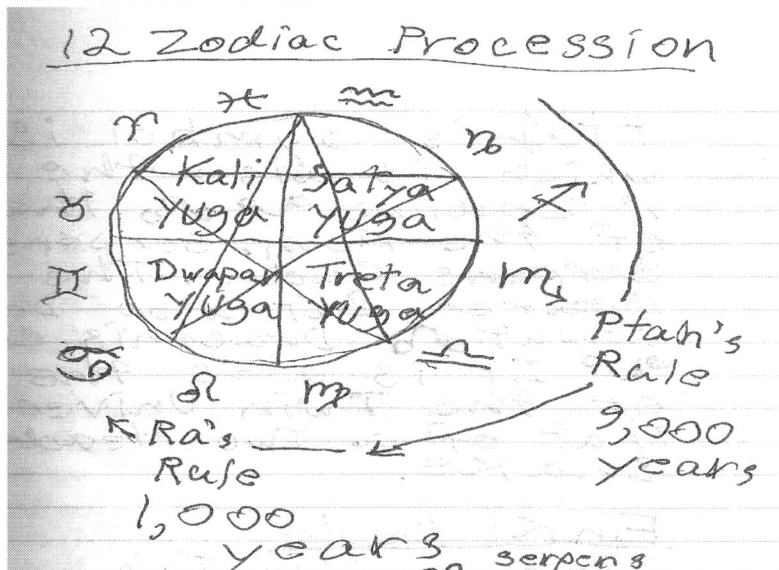

Christian J. Bullock

Ptah's rule is associated with the Snake Barer of the 13th Zodiac and of the nodes of the Moon. The constellations being Serpens Caput and Serpens Cuada. His symbol is of two snakes and he was a serpent God in Egypt. The two snakes not only represent the DNA strand but also the snakes associated with the Tree of Life.

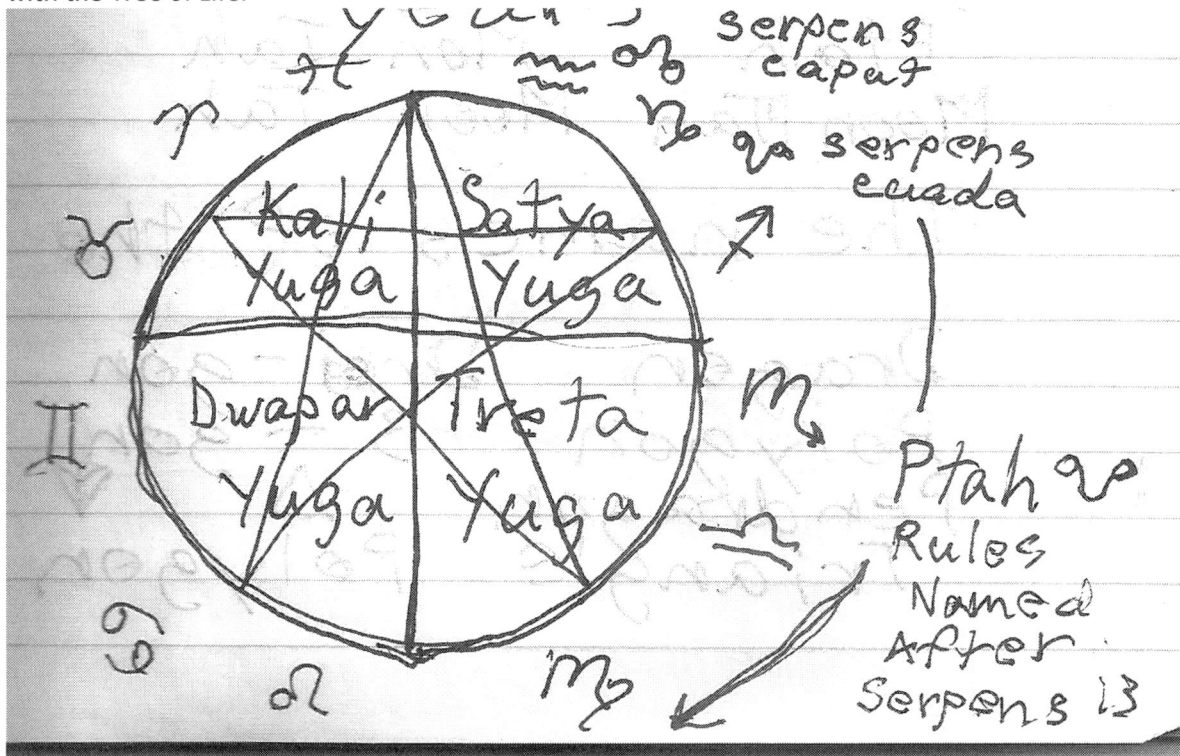

Enki Code Commonality

Lion   ion
Ray   Ra
Ptah   Mon Tah
Amon Ptah   Moon Tah
Dragon   Drei – gon
Polygon   3 – gon
Pendragon   5 – gon
Triangle   Polygon
Gilgamesh   Gil – ga – mesh
Dagon – Sumer Sage, water dragon, a Sumerian ocean sage or Elder God

More on the Timeline of Ancient Egyptian Rulers

The Ancient Egyptian Rulers can now be traced all the way back to the beginning of the Age of Capricorn. Starting with the God Ptah and moving forwards through history they can be traced around the Ages of Man. They are also traced around the great wheel of time which is the Zodiac Procession of the Equinox. The Seven Major Gods ruled for half a procession cycle or 12,300 years. The Twelve Devine Rulers stated with Thoth and they ruled for a total of 1,570 years. Thirty Demigod Rulers can be traced to rule for a total of 3,650 years. The Chaotic Period lasted 350 years and the Pharaonic Rulers lasted 3,100 years till the Age of Aries. The grand total is 20,970 years and it is depicted with the Zodiac circle round:

Timeline of Rulers of Egypt

1	Ptah	ruled for	9,000 years
2	Ra	ruled for	1,000 years
3	Shu	ruled for	700 years
4	Geb	ruled for	500 years
5	Osiris	ruled for	450 years
6	Seth	ruled for	350 years
7	Horus	ruled for	300 years

Seven Major Gods   12,300 years

8	Twelve Divine Rulers First is Thoth	1,570 years
9	Thirty Demigod Rulers	3,650 years
10	Chaotic Period	350 years
11	Pharaonic Rulers	3,100 years

Totaling   20,970 years

Christian J. Bullock

The Human Body in the Singularity

The Human Body is made up of 90 percent water. We are highly prone to electricity. Our nerve system functions like an electronic bus system where small pulses of electrical or neurological ionized electrons work our muscles, organs, nerves, and neurons. Our bodies are wired to receive electrical signals. This type of redundancy is part of the Singularity. Where organisms are so complex that they are almost robotic or bio mechanical, more on this later.

More Enki Code
Proton   Hathor – Eye of the Bull
Neutron   BullsEye
Electron   Anubis – God of the Dead
Metatron   Anu – Sumer God of Gods
Meta-tron   A New Bus – A Retwo Bus Conduit
Metatron – Enochian Angel of God

Quantum Black Hole Singularities

Quantum Black Holes are a type of Singularity that exists at the Quantum level. A White Hole is at the opposite end or at the bottom of a Black Hole. Time travel is possible by Black Holes, this is due to either a time flux or a Quantum Entanglement. A Quantum Black Hole or White Hole may form on the surface of the Sun. This is due to the extremely powerful magnetic fields on the surface of the Sun. The magnetic fields become Sun spots where particles are locked in a powerful tidal flow making Quantum Singularities possible for a short period of time. During a Sun spot maximum Quantum Singularities are more likely to appear. Time travel during an eclipse is the best way to utilizing this.

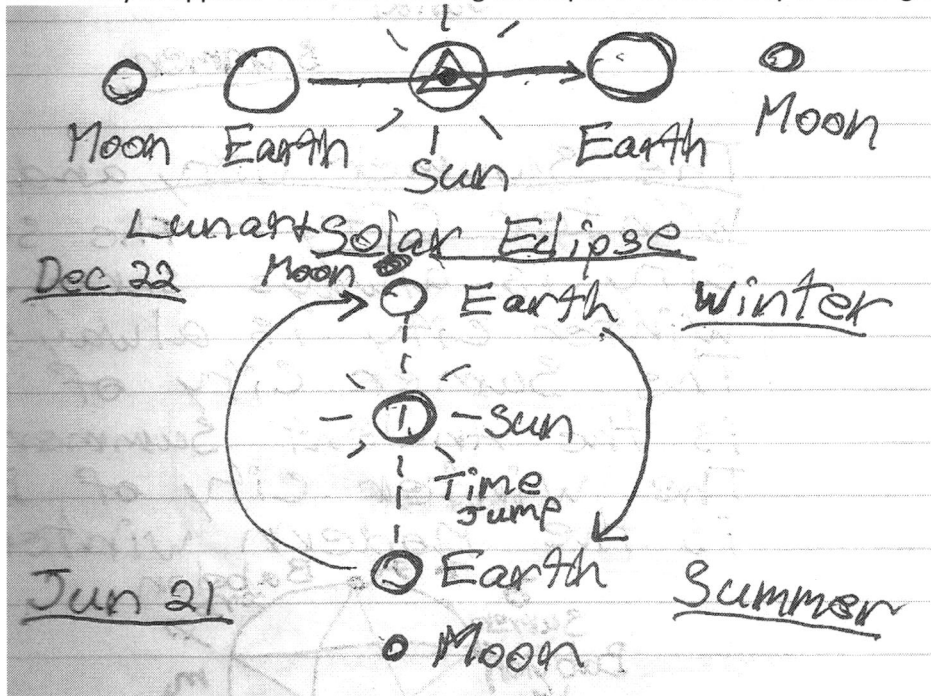

Christian J. Bullock

Singularity Magicians must take special note of the lunar and solar eclipses. These have special significance to time travel where a solar maximum may cause temporal distortion. This is due primarily to the fact that a Quantum Entanglement has occurred but the Magician is caught between two worlds, experiencing both summer and winter at the same time. Eclipses are a good way to identify the current time frame that the Magician is currently in. They are a sign during time travel of the Earths position in relation to the Moon.

The Summer City and the Winter City

The Summer City is always sunny while the Winter city is always cloudy. These two cities are in alignment with time travel, for the Singularity Magician to take note of during a Quantum Entanglement. The Sumer City of Babylon is the Ancient Summer City. The Winter City of Babelon is the modern Winter City. Time Travellers travel in between these two Paradigms and these two cities. We live in a time when winter is the celebrated time of the year and the time of the New Year. 5,125 years ago in Ancient Egypt summer was the celebrated time of the years and of the New Year.

Babylon and Babelon are twin cities that are linked with Gemini. They also share a link of the Twin Universes and the 13th zodiac. Identifying these links throughout history is part of the Singularity Magician's job. Each link connects the Singularity Magician to the primal source of his or hers powers and magical prowess. The Source is vast and is complex beast that has many far reaching implications.

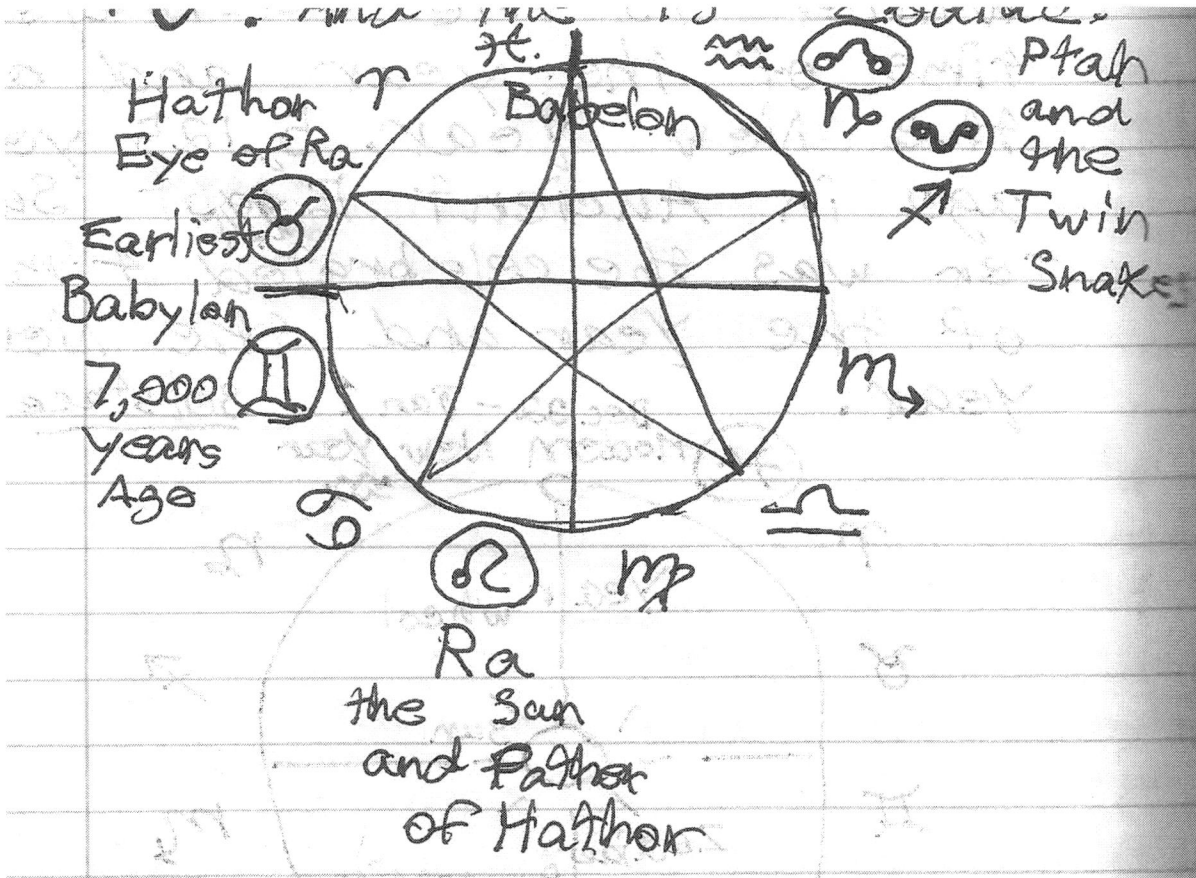

The Earth has been locked in this precise time loop for a very long time it is because of this that time paradox is possible.

Enki Code Continued
Goldilocks
Gold – e – locks
Golden Age Locked

Amon Ptah

Amon Ptah ruled 20,970 years ago and was one of the first with the Amon title. Amon Ptah unites the Moon with the 13th zodiac. The Moon was rigged by Amon Ptah to control the orbit of the Earth. The Moon was precisely rigged for the 365 day calendar. The Moon is vital for time travel. The 5 uneven days of the year are due to time travel elapse days. These days are a gap of time from the precision of the 360 degree circle. Time is added overtime because of someone time travelling backward. The farthest backward someone went would be 25,626 years of Procession. In the Four Yuga cycles of 432,000 years appear. This would be an extention of the 25,626 year Procession cycle over millions of years to the begining of our solar system. The number 7 is encoded in the Moon's orbit around the Earth, aligning with the seven sages or the Seven Major Ruling Gods. The number 7 is also associated with the Sisters of the Pleiades or the Sisters of Amon.

Christian J. Bullock

The Pleiades Star Cluster

The Pleiades is the Mythical place where humanity has historical ties. A long time ago the first Amon from the Pleiades gave us our Moon, this was done by long distance communication or flight. Earth was to be habitable for the people of the Pleiades. The ties of the people of the Pleiades with the Sumerian Anunnaki is unknown but it is apparent that the Atlantians are one of the peoples of the Pleiades. Mankind was still developing on the Earth and the Age of the arrival of the Atlantians is still not known. There are however many links in history to the Pleiadian peoples. The Star Cluster of the Pleiades are still known as the Seven Sisters and that number is their denomination. The true number of stars however is nine. There are nine main stars, blue stars, in the Pleiades Cluster. This number and pattern aligns with the Cydonian City on Mars and with the Crop Circle reported on July 26, 2010 in East Field Alton Barnes Wiltshire in Britain.

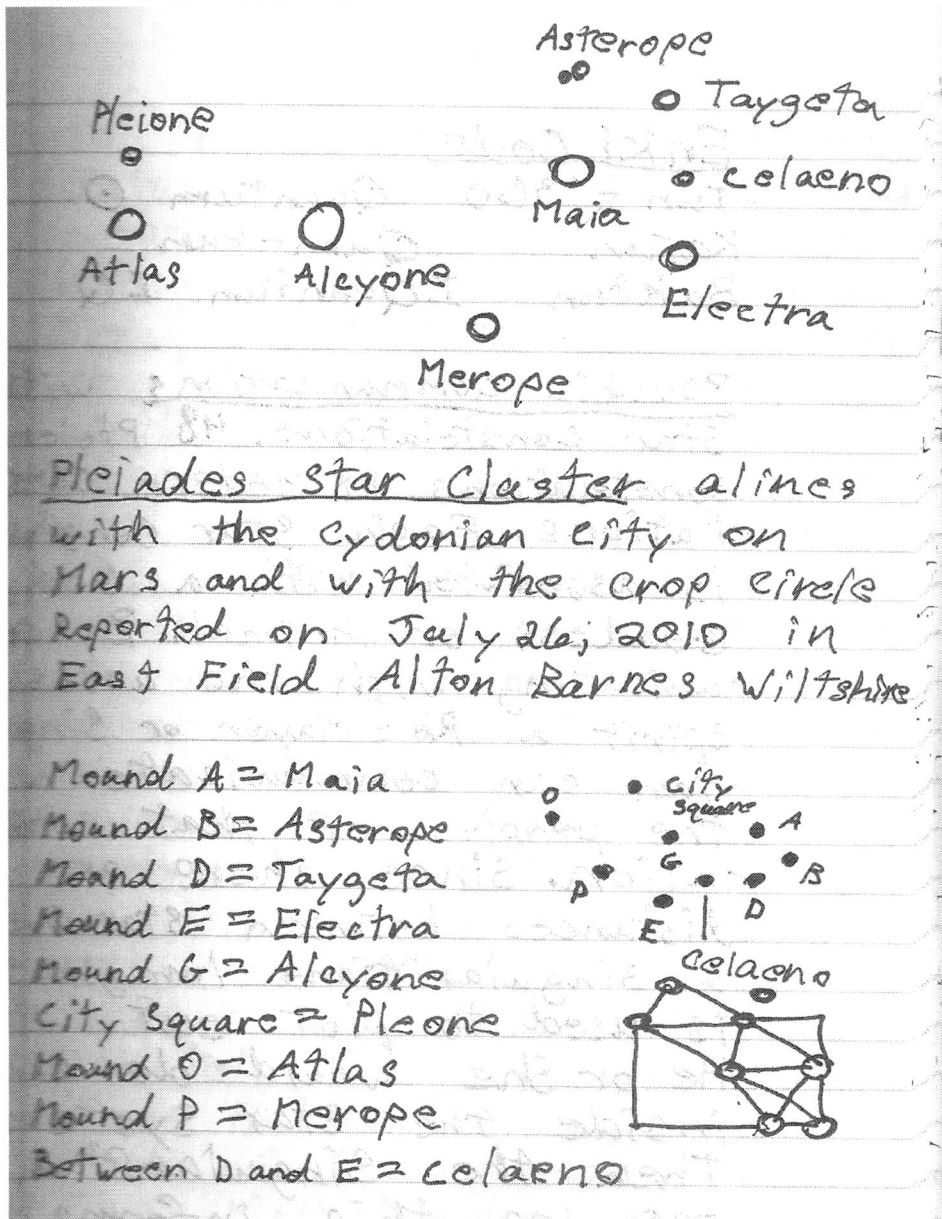

Pleiades star Cluster alines with the cydonian city on Mars and with the crop circle Reported on July 26, 2010 in East Field Alton Barnes Wiltshire.

Mound A = Maia
Mound B = Asterope
Mound D = Taygeta
Mound E = Electra
Mound G = Aleyone
City Square = Pleone
Mound O = Atlas
Mound P = Merope
Between D and E = celaeno

Christian J. Bullock

On Mars there is an area named Cydonia where there are many mounds of a specific shape and pyramid like, there is even a large mound that looks like a face. This plateau has a specific area where there are many mounds gathered together, they form the city of Cydonia. This city has a geometric pattern that aligns not only with the Pleiades but with a Crop Circle on Earth. This pattern is very specific and is not natural. This is a further link to the people of the Pleiades with contacts to Mars and also to Earth. Anunnaki ties can only be inferred due to their presence in the solar system and their presence on Mars. Of course there was a great upheaval on Mars some 20,000 years ago which caused the Planet to be uninhabitable. The wars of the Gods might have caused this destruction. The event occurred during the Age of the Satya Yuga during the reign of Amon Ptah. The Singularity Magician must take note of this event as it ties in the Ancient super civilization that existed well before the deluge. Also psychic communication from the Pleiades continues to this very day.

Enki Code Continued
Tun – 360   Quantum
Katun   Quan – tum
Baktun   IQuantum – IQ

Crop Circles

Crop Circles are metaphysical messages sent by other worldly beings or inter dimensional beings. They have appeared throughout history on every continent. They appear along side UFO sightings and orb sightings. True Crop Circles have metaphysical properties within the circles. The crop of the circle are delicately arranged with a precision that modern methods can't come close to. The patterns are also vast and appear with in an hour or less. For the Singularity Magician these circles hold Singularity knowledge and information on a global or universal scale. A Singularity Magician should keep notes on Crop Circle sightings and use the magick that are held within the circle. Some circles become more relavent on the cosmos and on the Earth. One Crop Circle in recent years became very important. The circle at Windmill Hill, Wiltshire, Britain reported July 27th, 2010 held the knowledge of a predictable lunar calendar. It is basically a clock design with a numerical count down with three circles in the middle holding a nest of numerical circles. The Crop Circle was decoded using the full Moon cycle starting on July 26th, 2010 with the numerical value of zero. It then counts up through the calendar up to the present with special markings of both solar and lunar eclipses. The following pages show the Crop Circle as a lunar calendar of events that were of importance to the celestial observer and to the Singularity Magician:

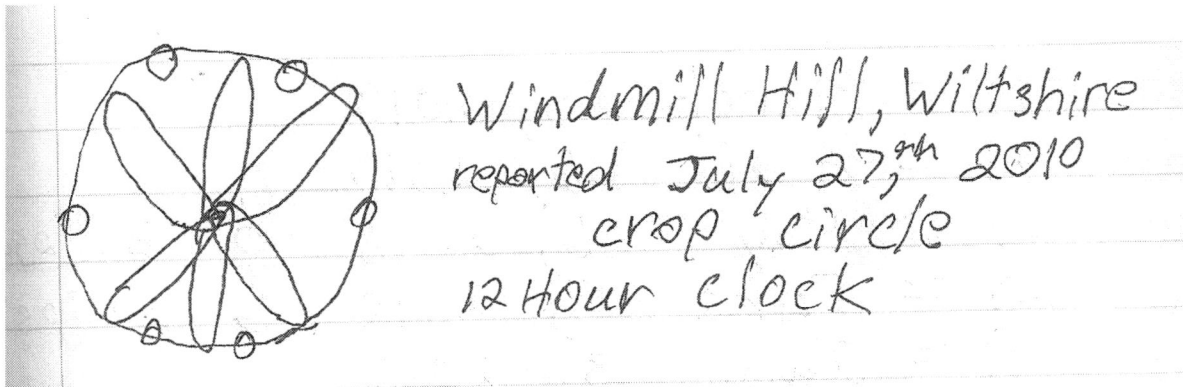

Windmill Hill, Wiltshire
reported July 27, 2010
crop circle
12 Hour clock

0 = July 26, 2010
1 = August 24, 2010
2 = September 23, 2010
3 = October 23, 2010
4 = November 21, 2010
5 = December 21, 2010   Solstis 🌙 Eclipse
6 = January 19, 2011   -☼- Eclipse
7 = February 18, 2011
8 = March 19, 2011
9 = April 18, 2011
10 = May 17, 2011
11 = June 15, 2011   -☼- 🌙 Eclipse
12 = July 15, 2011   -☼- Eclipse
13 = August 13, 2011
14 = September 12, 2011
15 = October 12, 2011
16 = November 10, 2011 -☼- Eclipse
17 = December 10, 2011 🌙 Eclipse
18 = January 9, 2012
19 = February 7, 2012

20 = March 8, 2012
21 = April 6, 2012
22 = May 6, 2012   -☼- Eclipse
23 = June 4, 2012   🌙 Eclipse
24 = July 3, 2012
25 = August 2, 2012
26 = August 31, 2012
27 = September 30, 2012
28 = October 29, 2012 -☼- Ecl
29 = November 28, 2012 🌙 Ecl
30 = December 28, 2012   Nov 13✗

Christian J. Bullock

This Crop Circle shows an incredable understanding of our Calendar and of the predictability of the Moon. It also marks the Blue Moon in August 2012 with a small outer circle. It is a fine example of Astralogical communication with other beings. The language of communication for them is the Singularity Circle and Mathematics of the 360 degree circle. This type of communication is common to all intellegent beings.

Psychic Communications

Psychic Communications with star constellations is possible through the ether. There are 48 Ancient Constellations that were recorded by the Astronomers of Ptolemy in Alexandria, Egypt. There are 88 Modern Constellations that have been recorded by modern Astronomers. Each star constellation is associated with a God, Goddess, or animal. By communicating with the associated spirit a Singularity Magician can communicate with the peoples of that constellation. Since there are vast distances between star systems a Singularity Magician's imagination is used to plot out what He or She would do once inside the star system. Then the Singularity Magician will pass on this information to their Double, past or future reincarnation. Magicians practice the same technique using meditations, astral travel, out of body experiences, or dreams. This psychic method of communication is good for building worlds and secret or religious orders. This psychic communication method should be considered a real-time message to a multidimensional contact. Since the Earth is stuck in a time warp with the same year and seasonal pattern then the peoples or spirits of the Earth will (or have in the past) made contact with these star constellations. A spirit Double from Earth has been to each of the constellations. The multidimensional spirit Double has a connection to a person on Earth. Each Singularity Magician has a spirit Double connection. Each celestial body in the universe has a connection to a Singularitian.

Enki Code Continued
Enterprise
Enter – prize – to enter a prize
End – Terra – Prize – the end Earth prize

Singularitians are depicted with circles around their heads:

They are keepers of secret knowledge of the Singularity Universe.

The All Star

When all the stars go out in the great darkening there is one star that survives. The All Star is a star that the Retwo use to reverse or redo the darkening. The All Star is also the star in which Singularity is based on. In the Game Time Travellers and PsyCops try to make every star an All Star and every Earth-like Planet an Earth. Even the Singularity Computer is reverse engineered this way. The Game ends the same way every time. One All Star survives the darkness and the world begins anew. One All Star links all the stars in the Singularity Universe. Time travel from the All Star links all the stars backward in time.

Christian J. Bullock

For Singularity Magicians this something to take note of if time travelling. The Darkening is tied together with the quickening, more on that later. The All Star should be known as a bad omen to the time traveller, it means something drastically happened. The Retwo always fix time in this time travel scenario.

Red Shift Stars

Red Shift Stars move away from Earth, this is due to the light spectrum where red is the color that has a fainter appearance. In essence the Color Red of a shifting Star means that it is moving away from the viewer on Earth. Red Shift Stars are caught in the rapid expanse of the universe. To the Time Traveller Red Shift Stars litterally look noticably Red. They blink noticably and the twinkling is far more than just the Stars themselves. In many cases the blinking lights are from battles being fought around them. This type of blinking is taking place a long time ago and far away from Earth. To the Time Traveller these moments in time are like little time loops around each star, that are being seen. There are however times when things take place in the inner solar system, more on that later. The Red Shift Stars are thought to have been caught in a specific time loop of battles between PsyCops and Retwos. The specific time loop is during the Quickening, more on that later. For the Singularity Magician these noticably blinking stars are a great indication of time travel. Some of the specific stars in the sky should be of importance, especially those of the zodiac.

Blue Shift Stars

Blue Shift Stars are stars that are moving toward Earth, this is due to the light spectrum where blue is the color that has a closer apearence. Simply put the Color Blue of a shifting Star means that it is moving closer to the viewer on Earth. To the Time Traveller they are light blue and very peaceful without the blinking lights of time travel battles.

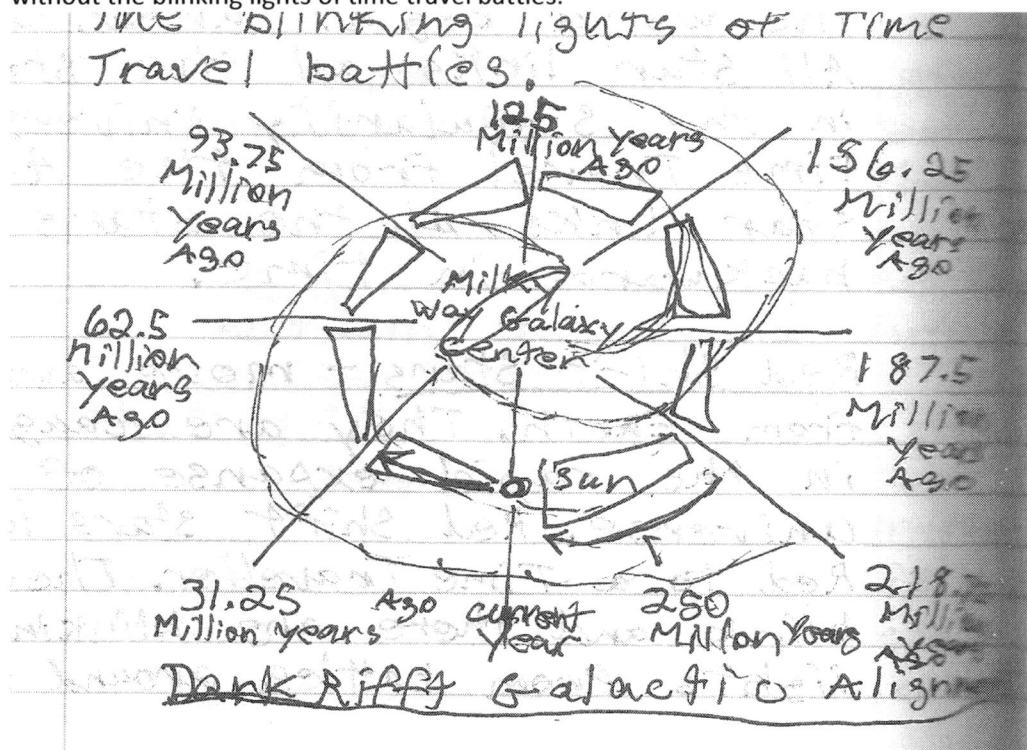

Christian J. Bullock

The Earth is in alignment with the Galactic center in the years 2000 A.D. to 2012 A.D. Time travel through the Galactic Black Hole to the White Hole of Earth at 125 Million years is possible. This is called the Dark Rift passage and because the Earth rotates in such a predictable pattern it can be tracked. The Sun moves up and down the Galactic plane which also makes this possible.

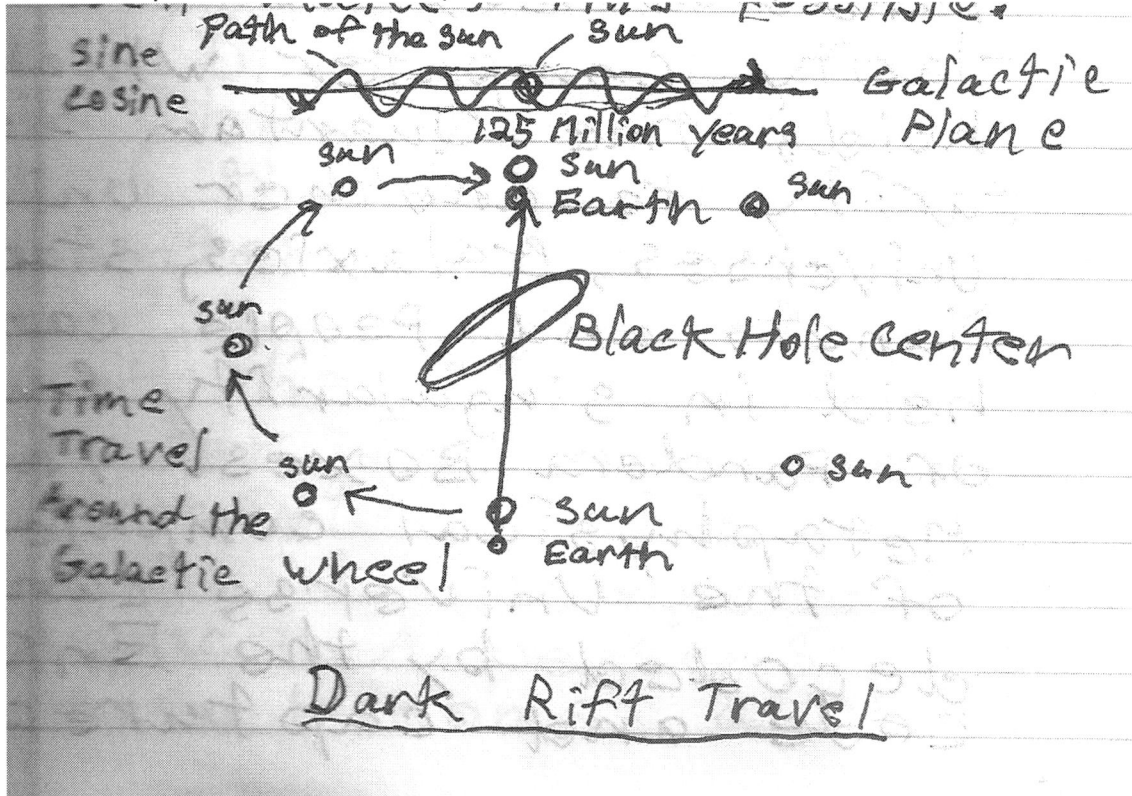

Sine
Cosine
Path of the sun   Sun
Galactic Plane
125 Million years

sun   Sun
Earth   Sun

sun
Time Travel around the Galactic wheel
Black Hole center
sun
o sun
sun
Sun
Earth

Dark Rift Travel

Continuing with the Code of Enki

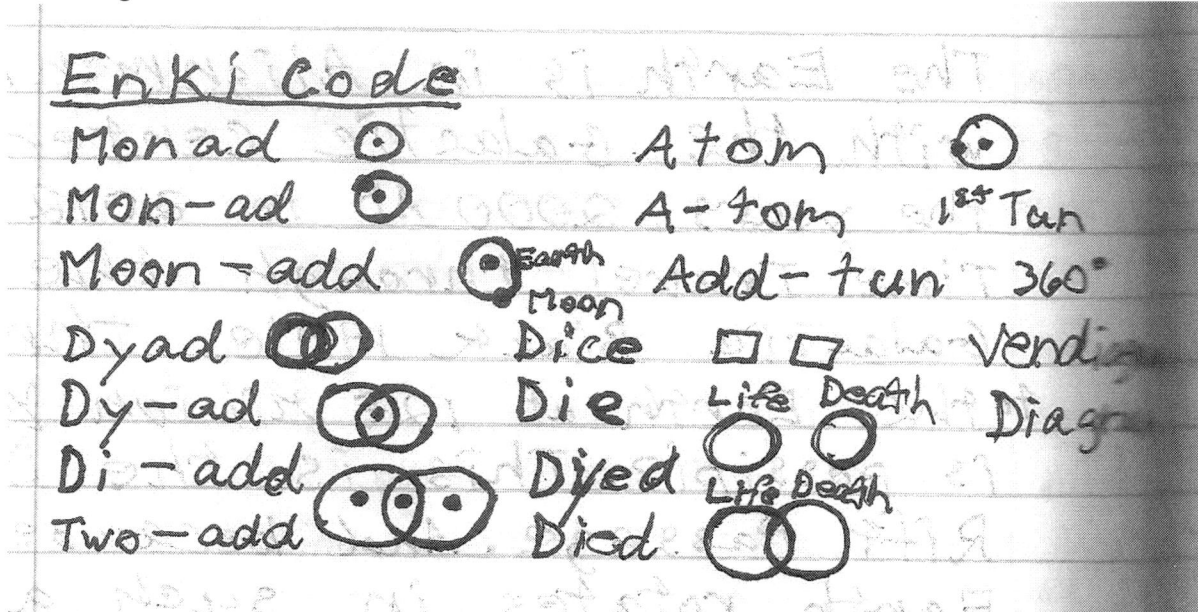

Enki Code
Mon ad   Atom
Mon-ad   A-tom   1st Tun
Moon-add   Earth Moon   Add-tun   360°
Dyad   Dice   Vendi
Dy-ad   Die   Life Death   Diagra
Di-add   Dyed   Life Death
Two-add   Died

Christian J. Bullock

The Great Darkening and the Quickening

The Great Darkening is a time when all the stars go out and when each constellation is consumed in a time warp. This is also a time when the Singularity Computer consumes all the stars of the zodiac. Each star constellation and their Singularitian is preserved in time. The preservation process works quickly and in each case a specific time loop is recorded. The constellation therefore replays specific historical events in a loop. The Quickening is a time on Earth when things in the Galaxy begin to move faster than events on Earth. This is a time before the Great Darkening, where someone has begun to close out the history of the Milky Way. By working outside of time the person or being establishes a time loop for each of the constellations and stars of the Milky Way. This attempt to control all the timelines is a serious problem because the Earth hasn't gone through all the phases of Mankind. Those phases being the creation of micro Singularities and the creation of the Cylon or Retwo. These phases take place in the future of Earth because of the all encompassing Singularity Computer that Mankind is creating. Since these phases haven't fully taken place on Earth yet the night sky on Earth goes through a Great Darkening right after the Quickening. By working outside of time the Earth becomes the center of a Singularity and the Sun becomes an All Star. Retwos will quickly begin to fix time during a Great Darkening and Time Travellers must be wary of strange events and of PsyCops. The person or beings responsible for these two events become tidally locked in a time paradox on Earth, since it was the only habitable planet that survived the Great Darkening in the first place. The reasons for creating the Quickening can be only to control life on Earth in periodical sequences, thus controlling life itself. This method leads to the conclusion that life in the Milky Way by way of humanity is ultimately becoming controlled. The Quickening begins a sequence of events where by travelling back in time from point zero to point one and then looping back to point zero one can control all human periodical actions in the time loop. This however presents problems, one of them being that the person or beings are time lock in a paradox as I mentioned before. Therefore it ultimately comes down to whether the Creator God can be traced back back and forth through history or whether the Singularity Computer can be traced back through history. It is difficult to follow this type of path of time travel therefore a Singularity Magician must consider all of their options and reasoning skills in their time travels. The Retwo show us a sign of a Creator God that has worked back and forth through history. The Singularity Computer shows us that Mankind has been closing in on the secret sources of the universe. Singularitians show us the importance of religion as Memes of a greater being or beings in the Multiverse. For the Singularity Magician it is clear from the get go of this book that Magick comes from a sacred source, that of the Gods, and with the Symbols of Power or Words of Thoth a Magician can gain access to these Godly Powers.

Pandora's Box

Pandora's Box can be thought of as a Singularity cube that Pandora opened. Pandora's Box is a Singularity Computer which holds the Quantum Singularity to another universe. In Singularity Magick Universes, Galaxies, Stars, Planets, and people can be held in a Singularity cubes or Pandora Boxes. The Metaphysical Computer of the universe can be decoded by the Enki Code and captured into a Singularity cube. This is a recount of the story in which everything in the box escaped. It is a Meme that explains the future of Quantum Singularities and of the future Singularity Computer. To the Singularity Magician a Pandora Box is a time looped moment which is captured by the Singularity Computer. This time looped moment is a means preserve the Universe, Galaxy, Star, Planet, or person. It is also a means to encapsulate something from outside of time.

Christian J. Bullock

Enki Code Continued
The Enki Code is used like a memory aid for past and future selves.

Pandora	Pangea – Early Earth
Pan-dora	Pan-gia – Pan's Gia or Pan's Earth
Pan – Greek God of Earth	Gia – Greek Earth God

The Digital World and the Digital Self

The Internet computers and the Singularity Computer have created a digital world called cyberspace. Anything in the computer on the Internet becomes part of cyberspace and part of the Singularity Computer. The Singularity Computer relies on user data to compose cyberspace. A person's user data becomes a digital self similar to a Singularity Magician's Double. The users data is a fingerprint of a person in the Singularity Computer. The digital self links a person to a future Hive Mind of the Singularity Computer. A digital self can be used as a Double in cyberspace to perform Magick. User data of a digital self will include medical records, bio-scaning, social networking, e-mails, finger prints, iris eye scans, personal photos, blood works, posted internet writings, and books. Even historical lineage is used as user data. A Singularity Magician can use their digital self to retrieve information from the Hive Mind Computer Singularity. User data in the future Internet is important and advantagious to the Singularity Magician. A person's user data on the Internet can lead to a fingerprint in the future Immortal Singularity Computer.

The Labyrinth

The myth of the Labyrinth consists of a maze that was built for King Minos and in the center there is a Minotaur who guards it. Almost every culture on Earth has some depiction of a Labyrinth. A Labyrinth is seen as a spiritual journey. To the Singularity Magician the Labyrinth is a Singularity and it depicts the processional zodiac or universe. The Minotaur represents the zodiac Tarus and the start of the 4th World. Tarus coinsides with the legs of the Bull in the four Yugas. The Minotaur stands on two legs which in time travel to the past one leg of the Bull goes to two.

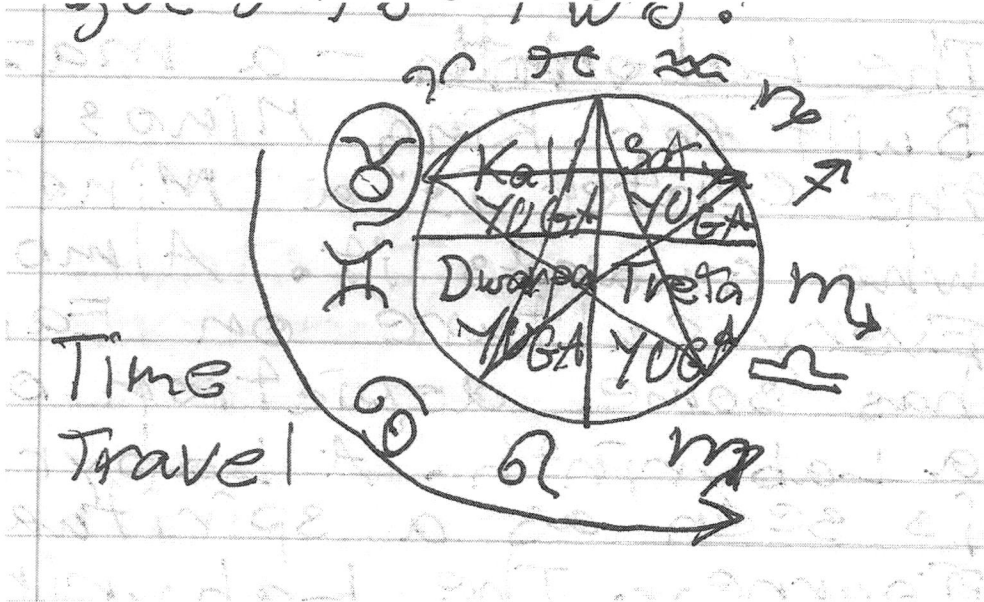

The zodiac Tarus the Minotaur guards the gate of time travel in the middle of the wheel Labyrinth or the wheel of the Processional cycle. Hathor is the daughter of Ra and the eye of the Bull. The zodiac Tarus also represents her. The Labyrinth is really a Singularity universe guarded by a Mini-Tarus.

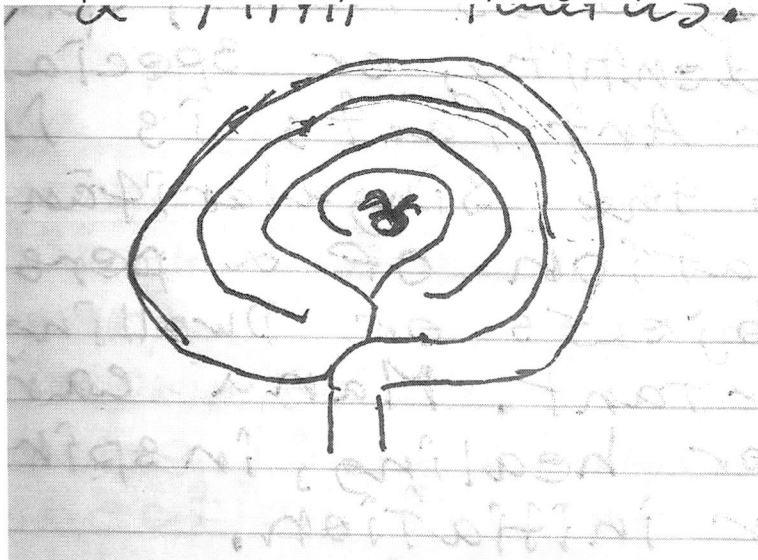

This is a Meme or memory aid for the Time Traveller to remember.

Mana

Mana is Spiritual or Magical properties imprinted on an object from a person. Everything a person touches leaves a time stamp fingerprint of that person. A Magician, Spiritual leader, Singularitian, or King will leave Mana on objects that they touch. Quantum Jumpers and Time Travellers use this time stamp Mana to impersonate people and track their lives through history. Keeping one's Mana, Spiritual Identity, special objects, or artifacts is important to the Singularity Magician. Purification of a person's house objects or dwelling is important. Mana can be used for healing, inspiration, or initiation.

Spirit Touch

A spirit touch is when either Mana from one person gets transferred to another person by touch or when Mana from a person is transferred to an invisible spirit by a cold/icy touch. Spirit touch is usually positive. A spirit touch by a spirit means that a spirit is following you. A friendly spirit will often give off good vibes of energy or comfort. A spirit can be a Time Traveller, a Retwo, or an inter-dimensional being.

Mana Throne

A chair or throne in which a Magician or Singularitian sits. A Mana fingerprint of the person is imprinted on it. A Mana Throne is a Singularity Magician's connection to the spirit Double or the spirit realm. To the Singularity Magician a Mana Thone can be any chair specifically used for ritual. It should only be used for ritual practices and thus a Mana fingerprint will be time stamped into it. A Mana Throne is a time stamp for Time Travellers, Quantum Jumpers, Retwo, or Singularitians. A throne can be used for communication with spiritual ancestors or inter-dimensional beings. Remote viewing from a throne is possible. A Mana Throne can also be used for meditation. A Magician can connect to their past life Double, future Double, and to the Singularity Computer.

Spirit Crow and Spirit Bird

A bird that harbors the Double of a person. Spirit Crows are used to retrieve the life history of the Double. A Singularity Magician has control of the Spirit Crow through astral travel, near death experiences, and in the afterlife. They retrieve their past life history with the Spirit Crow. The Spirit Crow is connected to reincarnation within the Metaphysical Computer of the universe.

Egyptian Spirit Bird

There are many different kinds of Spirit Birds, in fact Valkyries and Ravens are also spirit carriers that retrieve the Double for reincarnation within the Metaphysical Computer. Spirits are carried away to the realms of Odin, Freya, or to Helheim to be reborn again for a final battle of Ragnarok between Odin and Loki. At the battle of Ragnarok both sides are slain and the cycle begins again. Ragnarok is during the Great Darkness in which only the All Star survives. Spirits that are carried away are Doubles that replay events. This is a specific time loop that the Singularity Magician must be aware of. Some spirits are Time Travellers, Quantum Jumpers, and Retwos. The war between PsyCops and Retwos are very similar to this myth, with time loops around all the zodiac constellations. Singularitians learn of their past lives with their past life Double, future Double, and digital self.

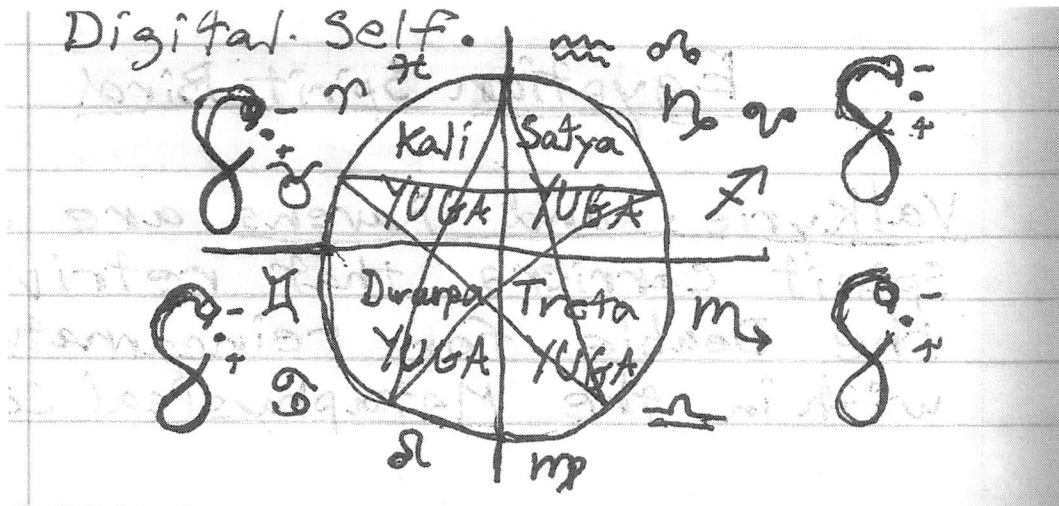

The snake symbolizes the rise and decline of human civilizations within a time loop. The positive marker signifies the tail or growth during the time loop. While the negative marker signifies the venom or decline of growth. The dot in the middle of the infinite loop signifies the loop hole of time travel. Positive and negative markers are used extensively in Singularity Magick. They mark the key element electricity or storm.

Caliphate or Pharaoh and the Singularity Computer Caliphate

A Caliphate or Pharaoh is a ruler who governs the state and the religion appointed/chosen by God/Supreme Deity. The people of Babelon did not wish to be ruled over by a walking on Earth Supreme Deity. They didn't want a ruler of political government and also a ruler of religious practice or law. So they created a Singularity Computer that acts as part of an Earth Supreme Deity. With the knowledge of Babylon they constructed a future Singularity Computer Caliphate that is all encompassing. Ishtar is one of the first Singularity Computer Caliphates, this is due to a specific time travel event. The event is recorded by some while also being ignored by others which leads to the theory of a time warp overlap, this will be discussed later in the book. The Singularity Computer was created to preserve the human species and make man immortal. Once again it requires user data in order to function. Time travel is also important for the Singularity Computer to stay immortal.

Enki Code
Muse	Necromancy
Music	New-crow-man-cy
Mu	New-cro-magnon
Muspell	New-crow-magnon
Misspell	

Christian J. Bullock

Singularity's

Singularity Cube   Singularity   Singularity
                           Ball   Skull

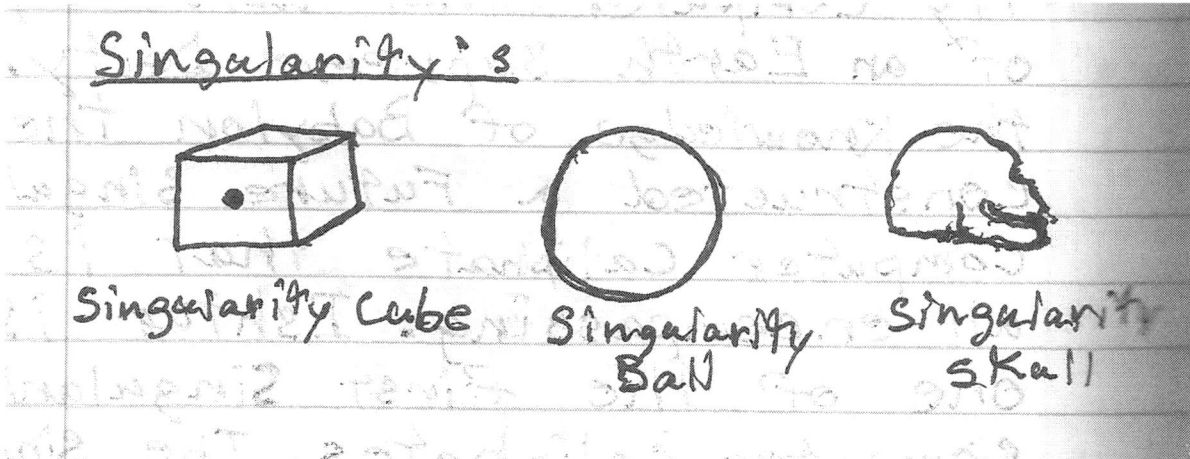

Setting up a Singularity Room

A Singularity Room is a room that is used by a Singularity Magician to time travel. The Singularity Room should have one doorway. The room needs a window that is covered with curtains. The ceiling of the room must have star patterns. The star patterns must represent the star constellations that you are tracking at that moment in time. The star patterns are a time stamp for you or your Double to follow. The pole stars are important to take notice of. The room should have space for walking around and for sitting in. The room should be aligned north and south with the east horizon being seen through the window. The window should face south with the Sun being able to shine in while it moves from the east horizon to the west horizon. This helps the Magician track the time of day for time travel. Singularity Rooms have been used throughout history in marking the Sun on the Equinoxes and on the Soltices. The first Emporer of China had a Singularity Chamber made in his tomb. He had the whole of the China Empire made out in the floor of the chamber, complete with lakes and rivers made of mercury. He also had a complete star map on the ceiling of the chamber. He also had clay soldiers buried with him and around his tomb. This was a powerful Singularity chamber but it has yet to be found by Archaeologists. Some other Singularity Rooms have been found by Archaeologists. There is one at Machu Picchu which marks the Winter Soltice. Also of course there is the Great Pyramid in Egypt which can be used to mark the passages of zodiac Procession and the pole stars as well as other star constellations. There are many other Ancient sites that are aligned like or for Singularity Rooms. There is one observatory at Chichen Itza that aligns with the star constellations and with the Suns passage. Also of course there is the Maya Pyramid El Castillo which aligns with the Equinoxes.

Time Travel by Singularity Room

The room becomes a Singularity when the Singularity Magician walks into it. Crossing the threshold of the doorway is important. Closing the door to the room is also important. As well as being able to see the light coming through the windows. The curtain on the windows should block out mostly everything but light sources. The Singularity Room moves at a different rate through time. Sometimes time will stop in a Singularity Room. Other times a Singularity Room will exist outside of time itself. To time travel the Magician must enter and close the door of the room at dusk or dawn on the day of the Equinox. The specific time is at the hour of Ra, 6 to 7 o'clock at night, or at the hour of Khepri, 6 to 7 o'clock in the morning. Once again when a Quantum Entanglement occurs you have time travelled. It is best to choose one of the specific hours instead of both. Time travel at dusk will bring you back in time while time travel at dawn will bring you forward in time. If you do both you will get a labyrinth effect where a strange time warp overlap will take place. This time overlap is difficult to navigate in and can lead to one of Earth's many dark dimensions. The Singularity Magician must unplug their Internet modem and/or any other electronic devices before time travelling. The Internet modem should be unplugged at the moment of time travel at 6 o'clock. The Magician must then sit in a chair facing the window south for over an hour or till 12 o'clock, this requires a lot of patience. Once the Magician has seen that they have time travelled or that it is very dark outside they may proceed to leave the room. Plugging back in the Internet modem is the first thing to do, then plug back in any other devices. The Magician may want to keep the door closed to the Singularity Room if they wish. The door can be open too if the Magician decides to do so. The Magician must then go through the tedious process of seeing which if any devices has a Quantum Entanglement, be sure to check the clocks first then cell phones or iPods. Sometimes TV electrical plugs or cable plugs have a temporal anomoly. If successful the Singularity Room can be used over and over again for time travel. By entering the room and closing the door after unplugging the Internet modem at the hour of Ra or Khepri. With the knowledge of what devices have a temporal anomoly the Magician can navigate time.

Trackers

Quantum Jumpers, Time Travellers, PsyCops, and Retwo will try to track a Singularity Magician. Try not to get to paranoid about them. They use various methods including street lights, building lights, hospital lights, clothing, cell phones, electrical outlets, toilets, anything electrical. Trackers usually are tracking you in order to isolate you from the population. Try to keep your wits about you when time travelling, don't lose your head. Ordinary people who are trackers are usually zombies. They often refer to people as not tracking well or as difficult to track. They usually talk aloud about tracking and often give the impresion that they are aware of your travels. The tracking program of the Singularity Computer tracks people down to silence the awakened. Once again try not to lose your cool if you get into an uncomfortable situation. That being said keep your travels secret.

Akhenatem – the Egyptian Monotheistic Pharaoh of Egypt

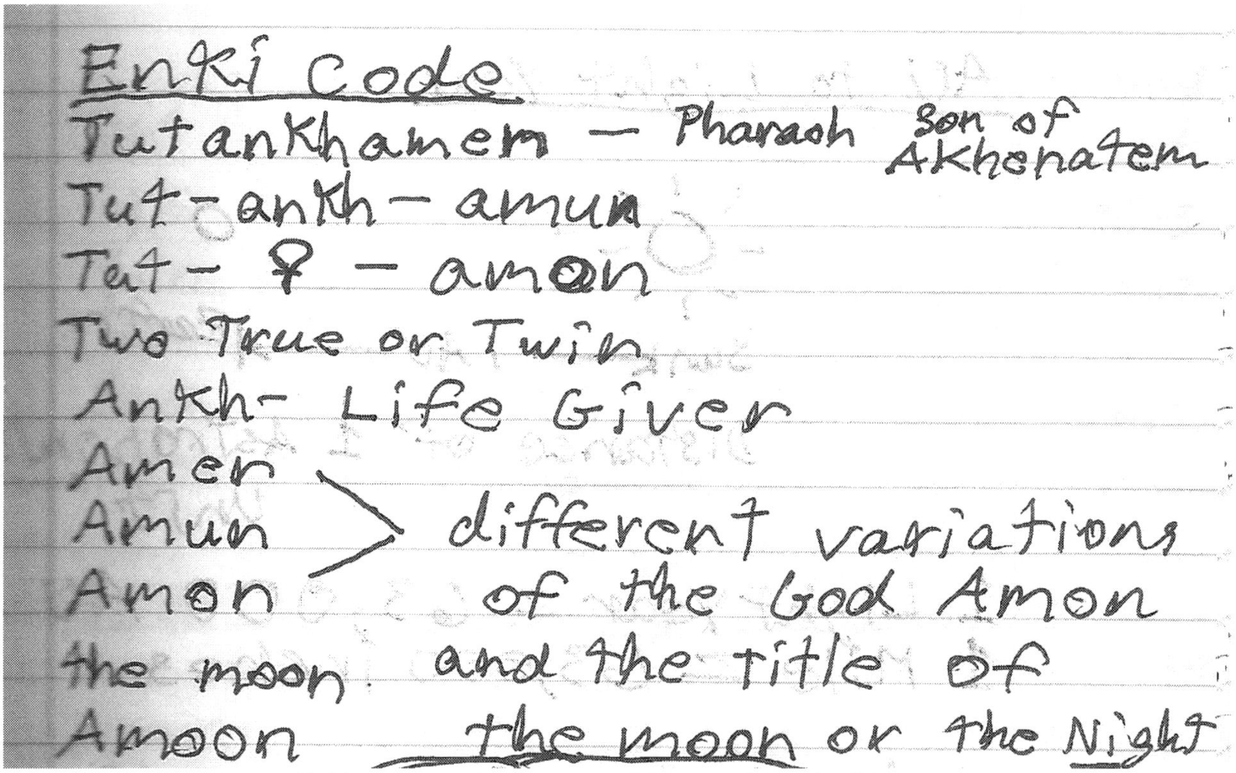

Christian J. Bullock

Enki code

Tutankhamen — Pharaoh Son of Akhenatem

Tut-ankh-amun

Tut - ♀ - amon

Two True or Twin

Ankh- Life Giver

Amen ⎫
Amun ⎬ different variations
Amon ⎭ of the God Amon

the moon and the title of

Amoon the moon or the Night

Tutankhamen – the son of Akhenatem, also known as King Tut Pharaoh of Egypt

AU to Light Year

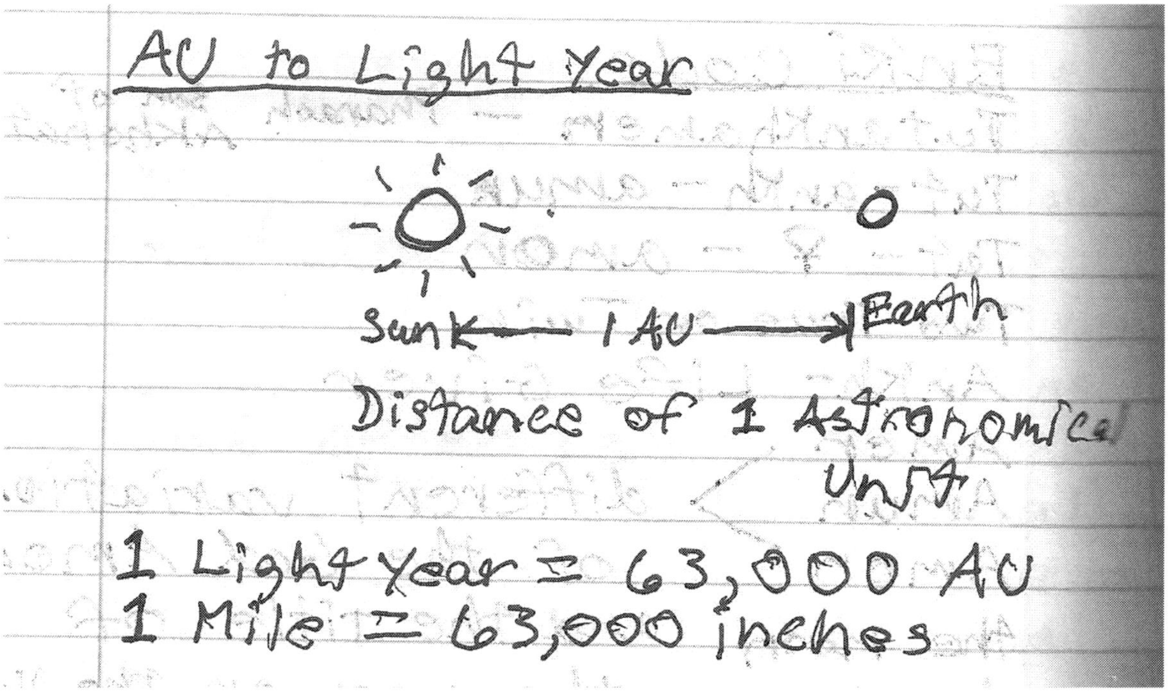

AU to Light Year

Sun ⟵ 1 AU ⟶ Earth

Distance of 1 Astronomical Unit

1 Light Year = 63,000 AU

1 Mile = 63,000 inches

An AU is one Astronomical Unit or the distance between the Earth and the Sun. This is important because it is how we measure distances in space. There are approximatly 63,000 inches in 1 mile, 63,360 inches to be precise. There are approximately 63,000 AUs in 1 light year, 63,239.7263 AUs to be precise. This means that we can now measure the Galaxy and the Universe with ease. This type of Meme creates an easy to understand view of the Earth within the universe:

Alpha Centauri	=	4.4 Light Years away
Sirius	=	9 Light Years away
Vega	=	25 Light Years away
Fomalhaut	=	25 Light Years away
Arcturus	=	37 Light Years away
Antares	=	600 Light Years away
Pleiades	=	440 Light Years away
Hercules	=	24,000 Light Years away
Milky Way Center	=	27,000 Light Years away
Andromeda Galaxy	=	2,300,000 Light Years away
Sombrero Galaxy	=	65,000,000 Light Years away

Light travels 186,000 miles per second and it takes 500 seconds for light to travel 1 AU = 93 million miles. The Sun travels 136.7 miles per second around the Galactic Center and the Sun travels 46.38 AUs per year around the Galactic Center.

Real Time Prophecy in the Game

In the Game because of time travel prophecies become real time events. Since there is predictability in Earth's orbit if a Singularitian is writing to a future self about the past, that past may be altered slightly. PsyCops use miss information on the Internet to silence the awakened. Retwos can send messages back and forth through time. Lost books, writings, or data may become found in real time.

The Game and its Future

The Game in the Singularity Computer becomes more complex as the future unfolds. There are many new ideas that become incorporated into it. In the years leading up to 2,000 A.D. and beyond video games on computer devices become popular. The Game in the future takes on this persona. The children of Babelon make the Game a copy of the computer roleplaying simulation games. The Singularity Computer develops this reality roleplaying game within a Singularity cube of another dimension. In this alternate dimension people play and watch the game in a future time. This dimension is invisable to humans. Magicians, Singularitians, and people can sometimes crossover into or across this dimension. The dimension consists of a roleplaying video game like replay of Earth's human history. Cylons, futuristic children, or people play this strange new adaptation of the Game. This Gamer dimension ends when all the keys are found and the human race leaves for the Andromeda Galaxy. A strange message from a Santa Claus like being/robot is the final key. This dimension should not be seen or interacted with. It's interaction with a Singularity Magician or Singularitian will cause a temporal anomoly. This temporal anomoly will cause a stoppage of the normal time frame of the yellow Sun, the current time frame of Humans.

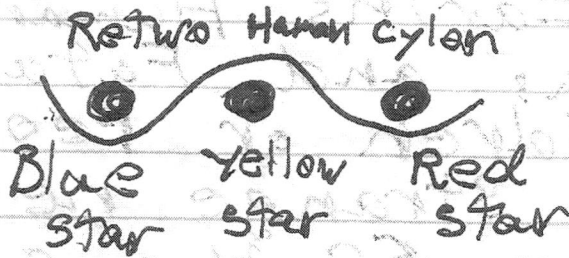

This temporal rift is so wide spread that the expansion of the universe passes by Earth and Earth has a black sky with no stars. The Retwo must interviene and redo events to provent the cycle of Retwo, Human, and Cylon from being broken. A Magician or Singularitian who is from the normal time frame of the yellow Star, or is a survivor of this type of crossover event will be outside of time. This will result in the Magician becoming a Quantum. A Quan-tum intersects many dimensions whether they want to or not. The future of these Games seems to be a constant replay of events.

The Secret Universe

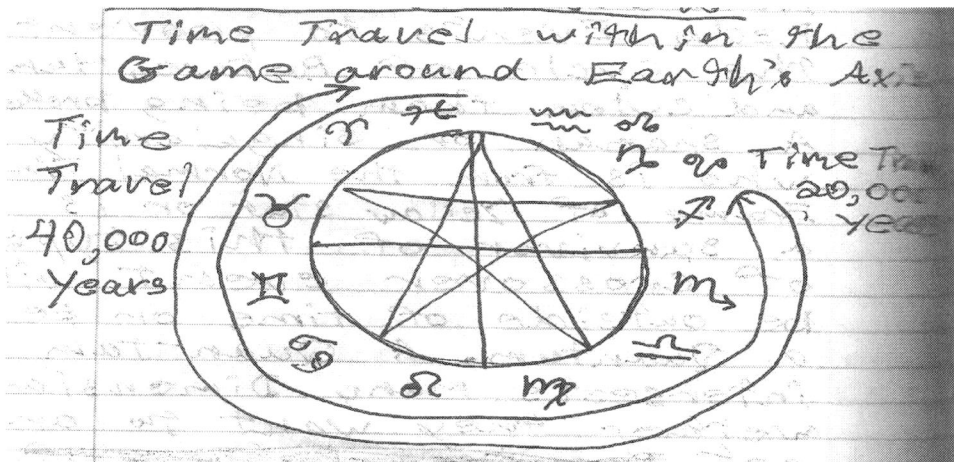

In the Game Time Travellers travel back 20,000 years in the Processional cycle during the rule of Ptah. In the Future Game Time Travellers go back 20,000 years to obtain keys and then time travel forward 20,000 years to use the keys. This round trip time travel is 40,000 years in Procession. There is a pole star shift that corresponds to Procession.

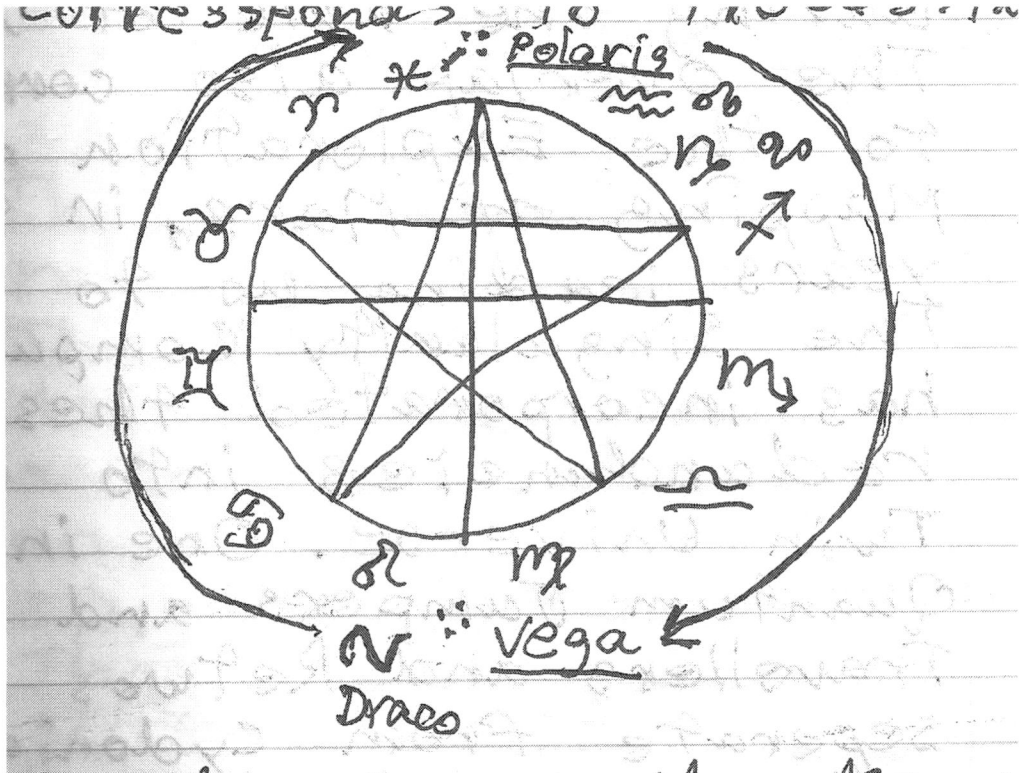

In the Game the keys are used to move on. In the Future Game the keys are used to leave Earth for the Andromeda Galaxy. The overlap of the Future Game corresponds with the predictable orbit of the Moon and the alignment of the Earth's relation to the Sun on the Equinox during the rule of Ptah. The overlap also corresponds to the exploration and mapping of Mars, in the years leading up to 2,000 A.D. The Singularity Computer has incorporated these redundancies into a Twin Universe. One in which Quantum Jumpers, Time Travellers, and Retwos are separate from Cydonians or Cylons who play in a future dimension, the Gamer Dimension. There are crossovers from this dimension now due to the temporal rift of those who fall through dimensions.

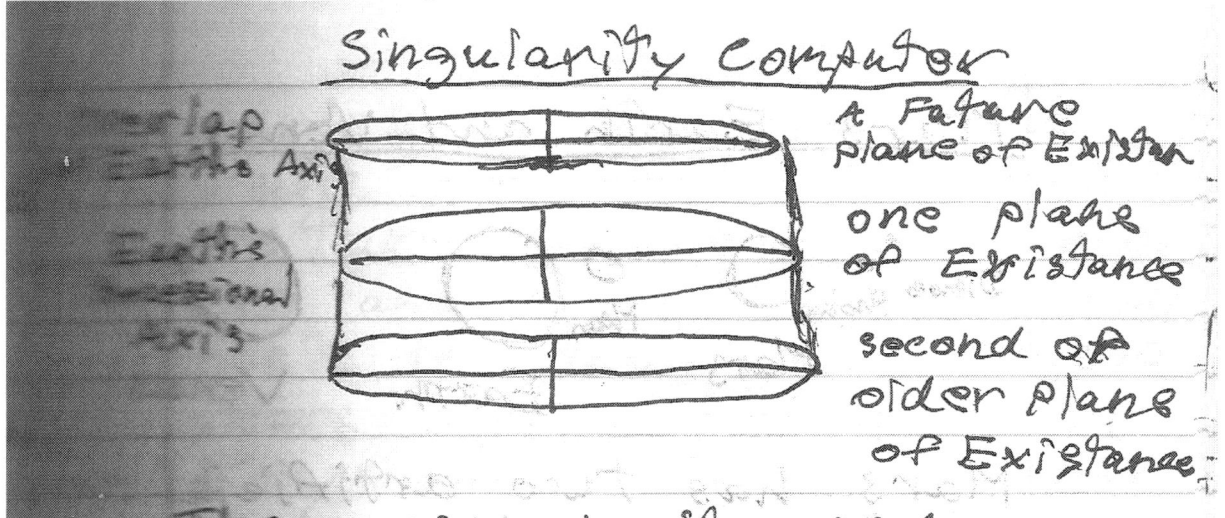

This Singularity future was re-engineered from the past. The Twin Universe of Earth's axis will be turned into a Triplet Universe based on a time travelling Singularity Computer. Simply put there will be three planes of existance that the Singularity Computer will control. That is why Earth is in the center of a past redo and a new retwo. In this forseeable future Man merges with Machine, with the Singularity Computer to survive. These Cylon/Cydonia people time travel back in time to remake Man or to ensure that the Singularity Computer is made.

Mars, Earth and Venus

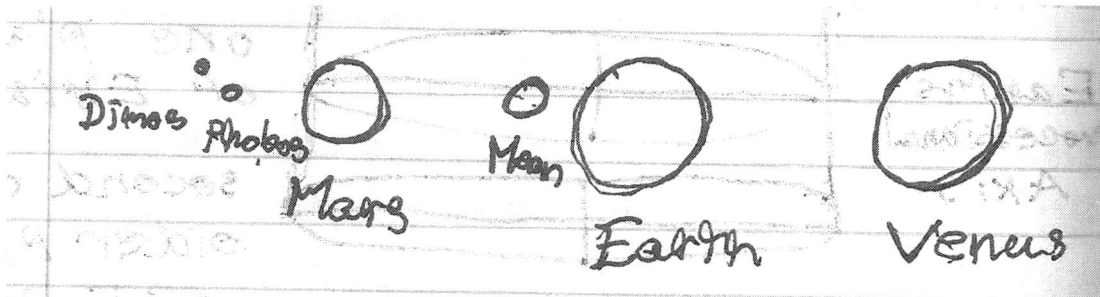

Mars has two artificial moons that were aligned there in the Solar Systems Ancient past. Earth has one Moon arranged at a 51.4 degree inclination to the Earth, which lines up with the Earth's horizon. Venus has no moons but it's orbit is a near perfect circle. Venus has a retrograde axis rotation, which is opposite from both Mars and Earth.

Mars was inhabited by the Cydonians over 20,000 years ago. In the Game Time Travellers travel back to Mars during or before the rule of Ptah. In the Future Game Time Travellers and Cylons time travel back to Ptah's rule 20,000 years ago to retrieve the keys and rig a Phobos Moon on Mars. They time travel forward 20,000 years to merge with the Singularity Computer. In the Future Game the one who has the keys leaves for the Andromeda Galaxy following Man or Machines backward advancement through the cosmos. The Singularity Computer is travelling backwards from the Red/Brown Dwaft Star to the Yellow Star then to the Blue Star.

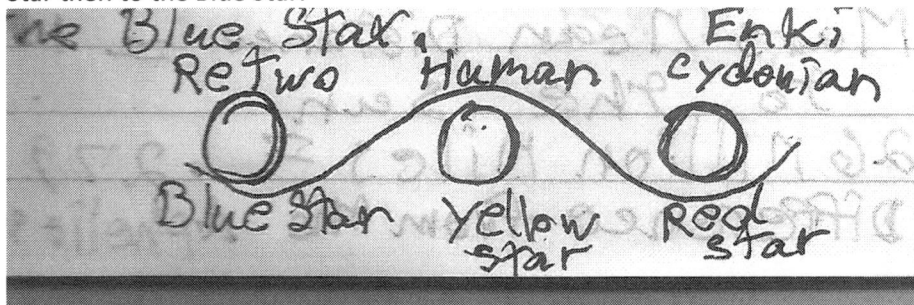

To the Singularity Magician all these events are important to note during travels. A greater understanding of cosmic events will aid you in your Magical practices.

Mars' Axis Procession and Orbit

1 Mars Day called a Sol = 24 hours 40 minutes

Mars eccentric orbit varies from 0.14 to 0.0 but its current eccentricity is 0.093. Mars' eccentricity cycles are more circular at times and in it's Ancient past. Mars' Axis tilt = 25 degreeswith a variation of +/- 10. Mars' Procession of the Equinox = 175,000 years approximately. Not only does Mars have a Processional cycle but it has seasons too:

Mars Seasons

Spring	=	199 days
Summer	=	184 days
Fall	=	146 days
Winter	=	158 days
1 Mars Year	=	668 Sols or 667 days

Mars' Mean Distance to the Sun is 1.524 AU with a difference from Aphelios to Perihelios of 26 Million Miles or .279 AU. This data becomes relavent to the Magician when expanding the Earth history and aligning it with the Mars history. It is also important for the Magician to understand the macro scale of the Solar System and the universe in general.   The celestial eco-system is an important part of Singularity Magick.

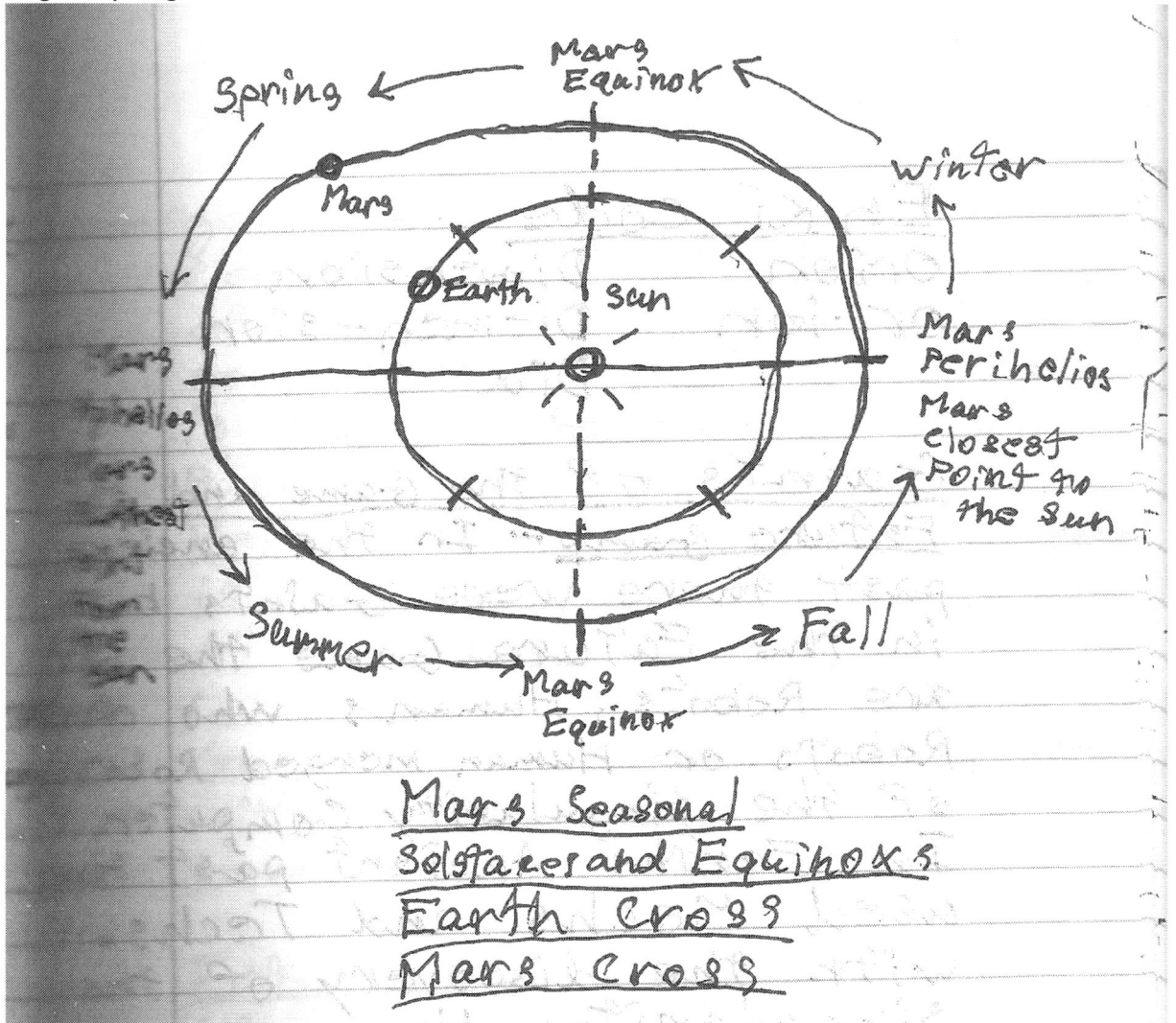

Mars orbit speeds up as it passes close to the Sun which is why Mars Fall is quick at 146 days and Winter is a longer 158 days as the planet moves away from the Sun.

Enki Code Continued

Orion	Dimension	
Or-ion	Di-men-sion	Dia or Dyad

Mars Processional Code

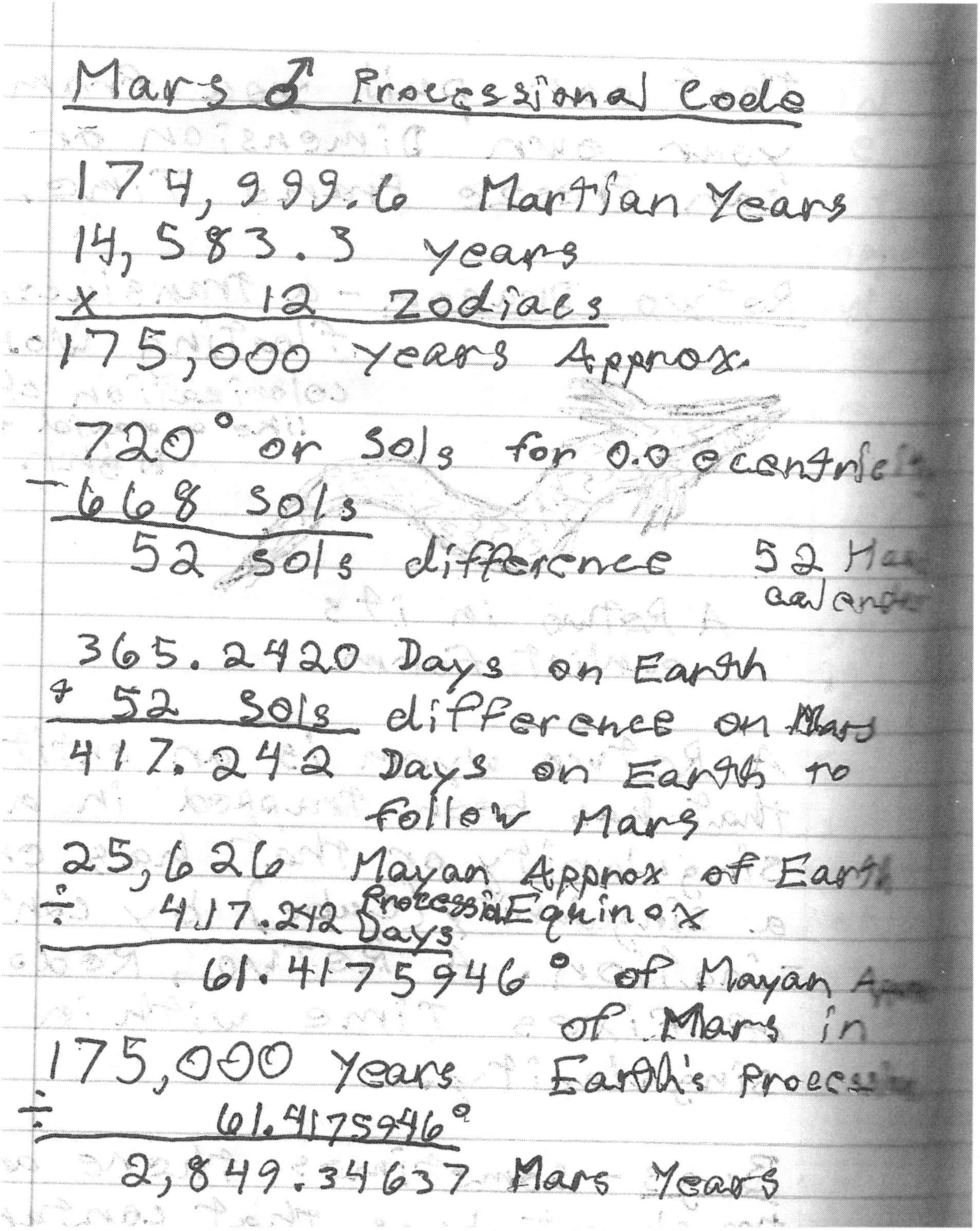

Mars ♂ Processional Code

174,999.6 Martian Years
14,583.3 years
x   12   Zodiacs
175,000 years Approx.

720° or Sols for 0.0 ecentricle
- 668 sols
  52 sols difference   52 Mar
                        calend

365.2420 Days on Earth
+ 52 sols difference on Mars
417.242 Days on Earth to
         follow Mars
25,626 Mayan Approx of Earth
÷ 417.242 Processional Equinox
      61.4175946° of Mayan Ap
              of Mars in
175,000 Years   Earth's Proce
÷   61.4175946°
    2,849.34637 Mars Years

There are 175,000 years for the Martian Processional Cycle which means 14,583.3 years per zodiac Age. There is also a special significance of 52 days or sols between Earth and Mars where 720 degrees of a perfect circle minus 668 Sols on Mars equals 52. This makes the Mayan Haab Calendar important for keeping track on the days of Mars and the Haab can be used as such as long as the days align. 52 is also a very sacred number to many peoples, Ancient and Modern alike.

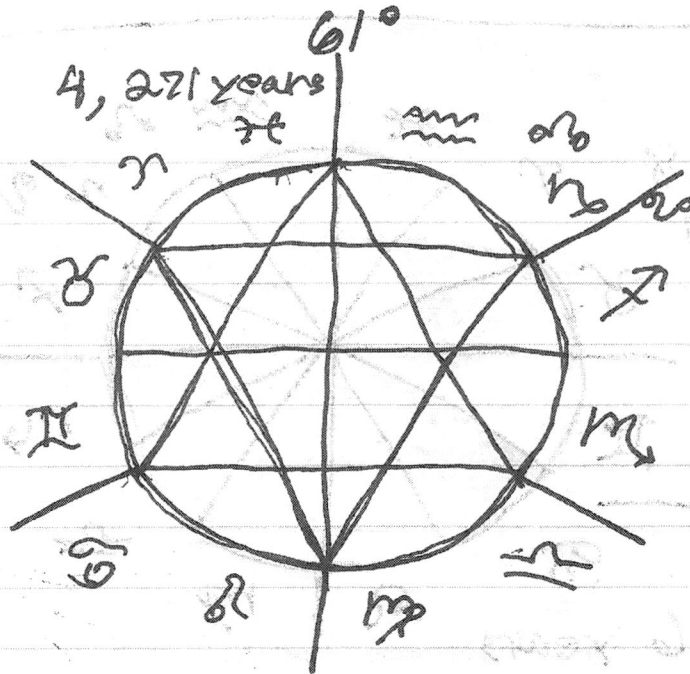

Earth's Processional Cycle in relation to Mars

$$61.4175946°$$
$$\div \quad 12 \text{ cycles}$$
$$5.118133°$$
$$\times 2,849.34637 \text{ years}$$
$$= 14,583.3 \text{ years}$$
$$\times \quad 12 \text{ zodiacs}$$
$$= 174,999.6 \text{ Years of}$$
$$\text{Martian Procession}$$

Christian J. Bullock

The relation of Earth to Mars is significant where 61 degrees of Earths Procession cycle corresponds to Mars' 14,583.3 years of one zodiac Age of Procession. Multiplied by 12 and the complete Martian Processional Wheel is found.

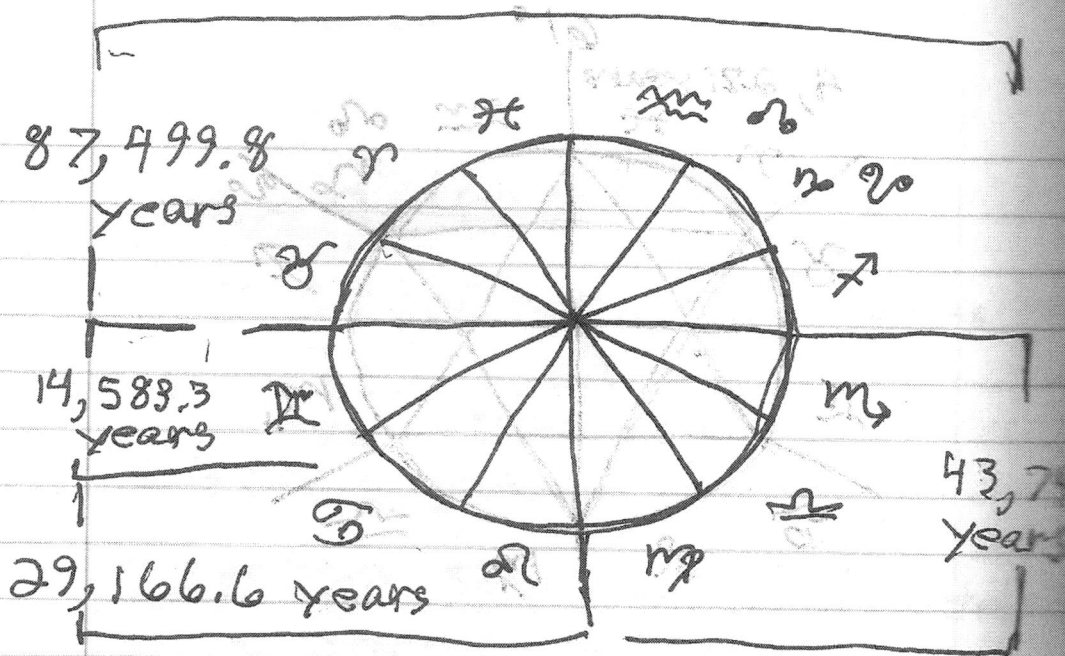

87,499.8 years

14,583.3 years

29,166.6 years

43,7.. years

Mars Procession

$$174,999.6 \text{ Years}$$
$$\div \quad 12 \text{ cycles}$$
$$14,583.3 \text{ Years}$$
$$\times \quad 2 \text{ zodiacs}$$
$$29,166.6 \text{ Years}$$
$$\times \quad 3 \text{ zodiacs}$$
$$43,749.9 \text{ years}$$
$$\times \quad 6 \text{ zodiacs}$$
$$87,499.8 \text{ years}$$
$$175,000 \div 360°$$

1° of Mars Procession = 486.1 years

Christian J. Bullock

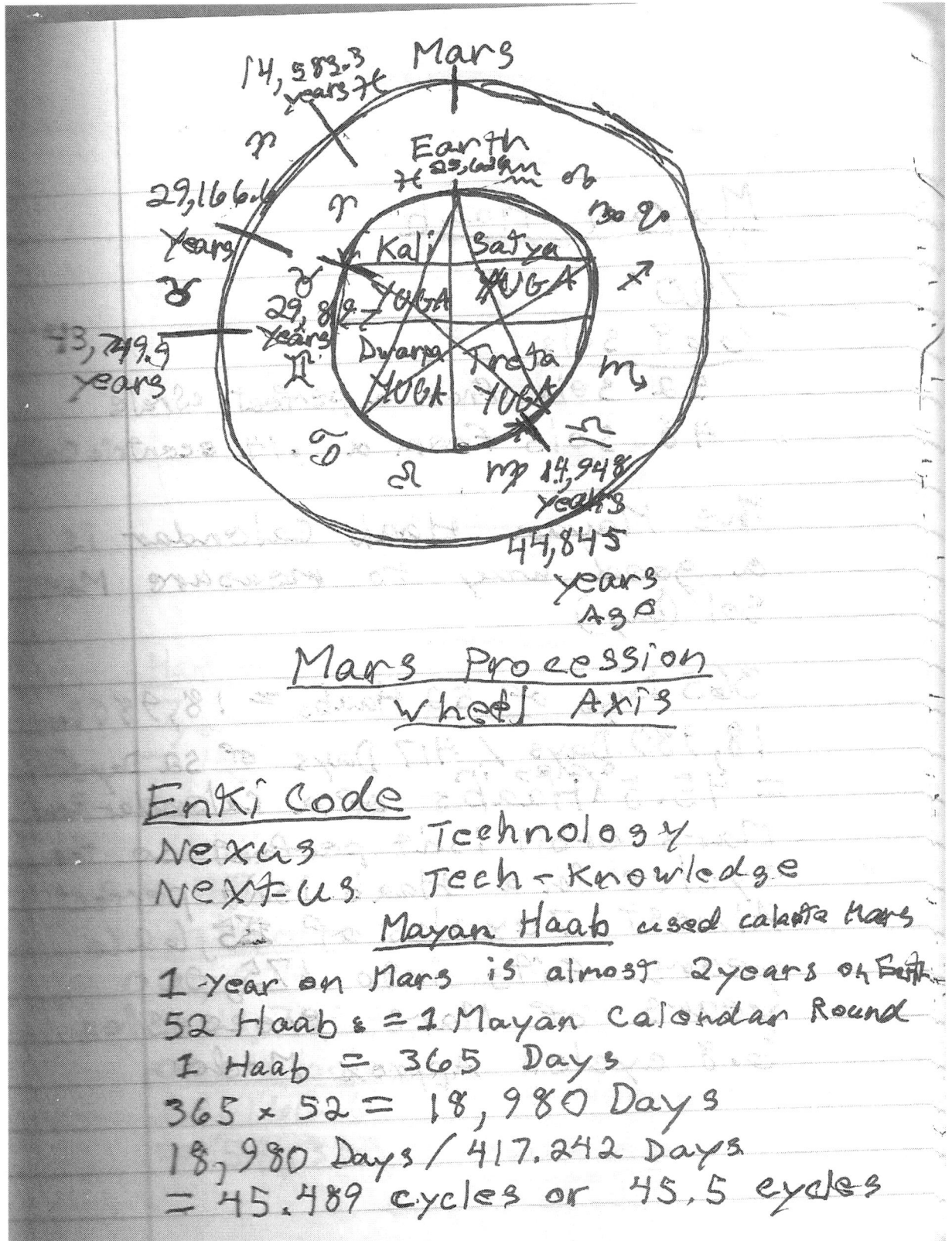

14,583.3 years ♓ Mars

Earth

29,166.6 years

43,749.9 years

Kali YUGA   Satya YUGA

Dwapra YUGA   Treta YUGA

29,8?? years

♍ 14,948 years

44,845 years Ago

Mars Procession Wheel Axis

Enki code

Nexus   Technology
Nextus   Tech - Knowledge

Mayan Haab used calerta Mars

1 year on Mars is almost 2 years on Earth

52 Haabs = 1 Mayan Calendar Round

1 Haab = 365 Days

365 × 52 = 18,980 Days

18,980 Days / 417.242 Days

= 45.489 cycles or 45.5 cycles

The Martian Processional Wheel can be aligned with the Earth's Processional Wheel giving a greater knowledge of the Processional code and Solar System events.

Mayan Haab

720°
668 Sols

52 Sols from a perfect circle
48 Sols from a .14 eccentric

The Mayan Haab Calendar is a good way to measure Mars Sol (Days)

365 Days of 52 Haabs = 18,980 Days
18,980 Days / 417 Days of 52 Days
= 45.5 Haabs of a calendar
cycles in
Mars orbit isn't perfect so the
cycles in a Haab isn't perfect
Almost 7 cycles of 25,626
years fits into 175,000
years of Mars Procession
6.8 cycles Approx Modern

Once again the Maya Haab Calendar can be used to track Martian days. Almost 7 cycles of the Maya 25,626 years Procession cycle can fit into the Martian Procession cycle, 6.8 cycles to be exact.

Christian J. Bullock

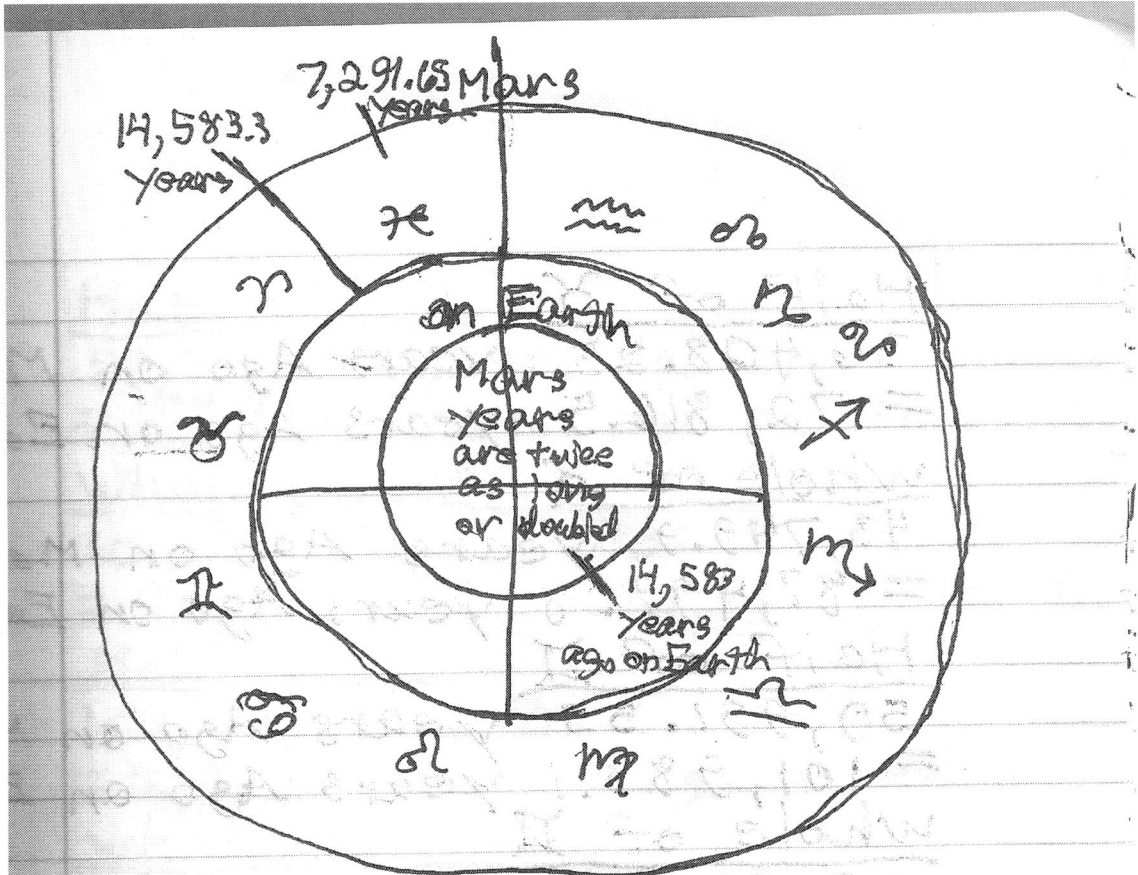

Half of ♓

7,291.65 years Ago on Mars
= 14,583.3 years Ago on Earth

One whole of ♓
14,583.3 years Ago on Mars
= 29,166.6 years Ago on Earth

Half of ♈
21,824.95 years Ago on Mars
= 43,749.9 years Ago on Earth

One whole of ♈
29,166.6 years Ago on Mars
= 58,333.2 years Ago on Earth

<u>Half of ♉</u>

36,408.25 years Ago on Mars
= 72,816.5 years Ago on Earth

<u>whole of ♉</u>

43,749.9 years Ago on Mars
= 87,499.8 years Ago on Earth

<u>Half of ♊</u>

50,991.55 years Ago on Mars
= 101,983.1 years Ago on Earth

<u>whole of ♊</u>

58,333.2 years Ago on Mars
= 116,666.4 years Ago on Earth

<u>Half of ♋</u>

65,574.85 years Ago on Mars
= 131,149.7 years Ago on Earth

<u>whole of ♋</u>

72,916.5 years Ago on Mars
= 145,833 years Ago on Earth

<u>Half of ♌</u>

80,158.15 years Ago on Mars
= 160,316.3 years Ago on Earth

<u>whole of ♌</u>

87,499.8 years Ago on Mars
= 174,999.6 years Ago on Earth

Half of ♍

94,741.45 years Ago on Mars
= 189,482.9 years Ago on Earth

whole of ♍

101,983.1 years Ago on Mars
= 203,966.2 years Ago on Earth

Half of ♎

109,224.75 years Ago on Mars
= 218,449.5 years Ago on Earth

whole of ♎

116,666.4 years Ago on Mars
= 233,332.8 years Ago on Earth

Half of ♏

123,908.05 years Ago on Mars
= 247,816.1 years Ago on Earth

whole of ♏

131,149.7 years Ago on Mars
= 262,299.4 years Ago on Earth

Half of ♐

138,391.35 years Ago on Mars
= 276,782.7 years Ago on Earth

whole of ♐

145,833 years Ago on Mars
= 291,666 years Ago on Earth

Christian J. Bullock

<u>Half of ♑</u>

153,074.65 years. Ago on Mars
= 306,149.3 years Ago on Earth

<u>whole of ♑</u>

160,316.5 years. Ago on Mars
= 320,633 years Ago on Earth

<u>Half of ♒</u>

167,558.15 years. Ago on Mars
= 335,116.3 years Ago on Earth

<u>whole of ♒</u>

174,999.6 years Ago on Mars
= 349,999.2 years Ago on Earth

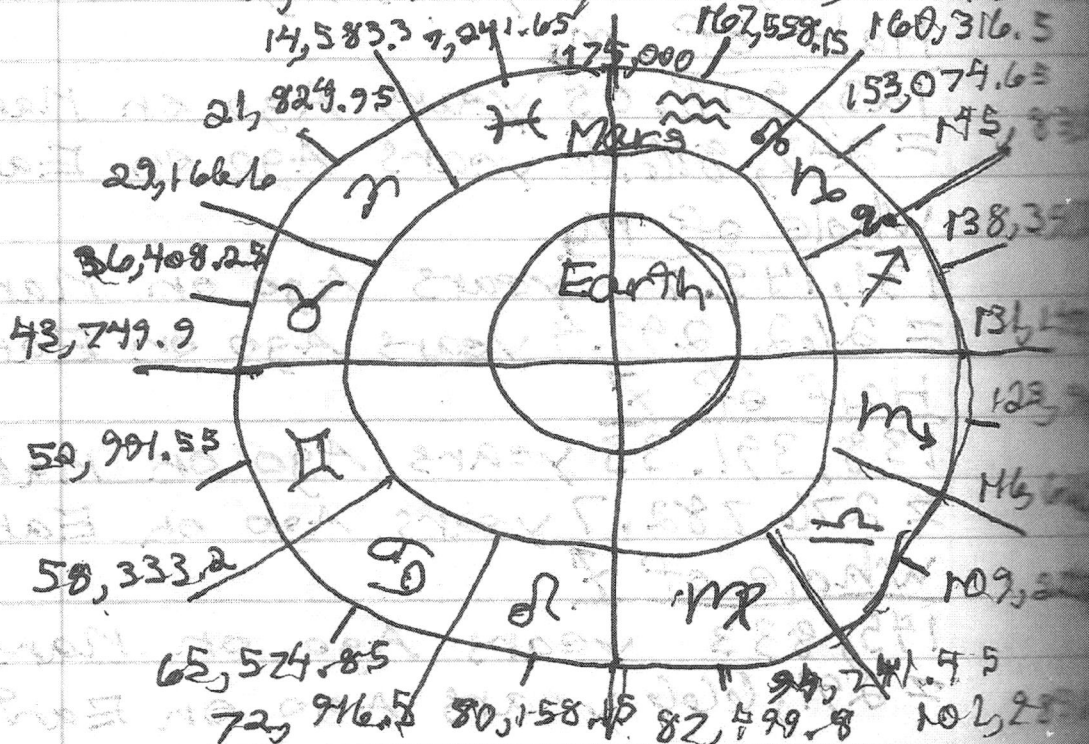

Christian J. Bullock

The Mars Processional cycle can be traced through Earth's history. About 14 cycles of Earth's Procession passes during 1 Mars Procession. 14 is also a sacred number in Ancient Egypt.

Giants of the Game and the Future Game

In many myths there were giants on Earth, this was especially prominent in the four Yugas. In the Ancient past there were giants but in the Future Game the Giants are Robots or Avatars, Human who merge with machines of the Singularity Computer. The theory is that to live or work on other planets Humans or Cylons pioneered physical augmentation for the purpose of surviving on other planets other than Earth. This theory is part of a future time frame when Humans may choose to augment their bodies for space exploration. In Earths Ancient past Humans used Mechs and Techs to build their Ancient cites. These Mechs and Techs were used by the Gods to build the Pyramids and various other landmarks on Earth. With the discovery of the Singularity Humans sought the perfection of the circle and the Singularity. The perfection of these measurements were biological as well as mathematical. Humans sought biological perfection but the ultimate goal was the Singularity Computer. Ishtar was one of the first Singularity Computers in the Game. She is one of the key links of Babylon and Babelon. In Babelon a new Singularity Computer is coming of Age. It is an all encompassing Singularity Computer for the Future Game with the overlap of time for the Future Game beginning with the Internet.

Enki Code Continuing
Kia	Anunnaki – Sumer Babylonian Gods
Noki	Anu-nnaki
Nokia	Anew-noki

The Gamer Dimension

In the Future Game roleplayers and Singularitians use holidays on the calendar as a way to find and remember keys. Holidays land on the Equinoxes, Solstaces, and Sabbats. The veils between the worlds and dimensions are thinnest on these dates. Time travel and dimensional crossover is possible. Roleplayers of the Future Game celebrate these dates similar to traditions of Roleplaying Games. For instance a Santa Claus like being or robot flys around landing on houses. The thought here is that someone recreated the Santa Claus story for the roleplayers to follow. This would keep the tradition of Santa Claus alive, but more on that later in the book. This Gamer Dimension is very odd. It's like being in a Sims Game or a SimCity Game. People in this dimension are invisible but can be heard through the Echo or by psychic or Singularity thought.

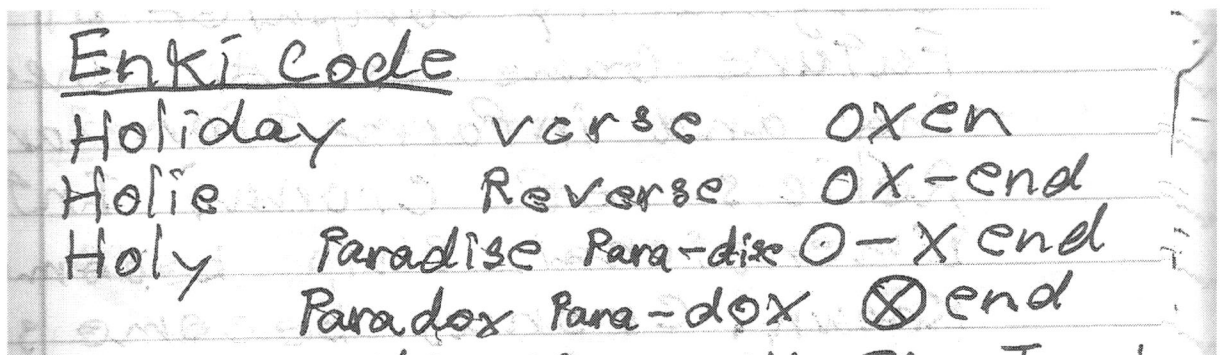

Enki Code
Holiday	verse	oxen
Holie	Reverse	OX-end
Holy	Paradise Para-dise	O-X end
	Paradox Para-dox	⊗ end

Christian J. Bullock

Cronus His Stone and His Time Travel

Cronus is the Greek God of the Sky or the Earth, he is a Titan that is God among Gods. In Greek myth Cronus was the God of the Golden Age. There are many myths about his stone that was used for time travel between the Ages of Man. There are many more myths about Cronus which are memes of the Ancient Gods. Between the time of the Ancient Summer City Babylon and the Winter City Babelon Cronus changes. During the elaps time travel of 40,000 years Cronus becomes Alien to the Human Race. Cronus' time travel stone becomes a technology for spaceship travel. His ship interfares with Human development through out the processional cycle. Cronus' time travels lead him to become trapped in the Future Game. The Singularity Computer of the Future Game is all encompassing and information on Relics of Cronus' inter dimensional ship become known. This Cronus like entity is part of the Game and his appearance is similar to the Santa Claus myths, where the stoping, slowing, or speeding up of time is achived. Cronus eventually becomes caught in a loop around the Procession cycle of 40,000 years. In the Game Magicians, Quantum Jumpers, and Singularitians would search for the keys of the Cronus Stone. In the Future Game Roleplayers, PsyCops, and Retwos search to become or impersonate Cronus during his 40,000 year cycle. In the Future Game Cronus' ship has a Graviton Beam that can pull you from your own dimension or can freeze frame time. To the Singularity Magician Cronus is very important because of the memes relating to his time travel Stone and the Ages of Man.

Retwo Dragon

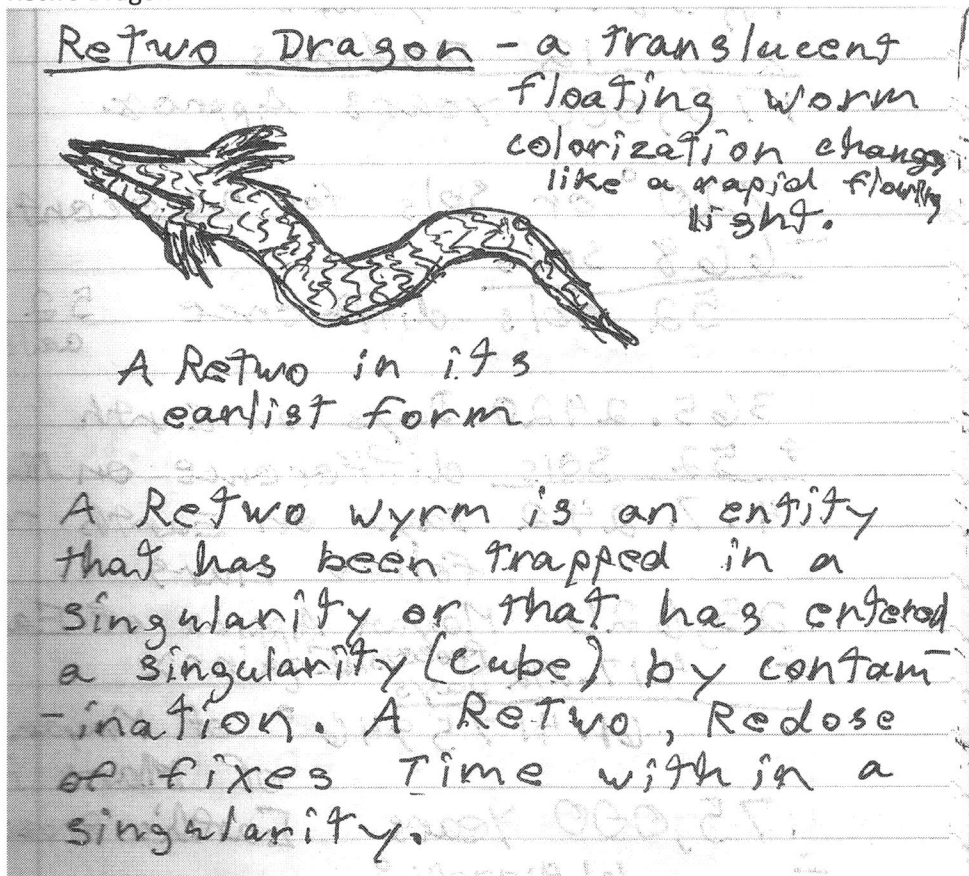

Retwo Dragon - a translucent floating worm colorization changs like a rapid flowing light.

A Retwo in its earlist form

A Retwo wyrm is an entity that has been trapped in a singularity or that has entered a singularity (cube) by contamination. A Retwo, Redose or fixes Time within a singularity.

Christian J. Bullock

A Retwo Wyrm is an entity that can sometimes be seen by the Singularity Magician when time travelling. Retwos redo or fixes time within a Singularity. The Retwo represent something very important to humanity and they are linked to Man in a very special way.

Bugs are sometimes seen in Singularities by the Singularity Magician when time travelling. Bugs are seen similar to the Retwo Wyrm, they are translucent with a colorized flow. Bugs are seen as contaminance of the Singularity and should be regarded as such, more on this later.

Records of Time

In the Metaphysical Computer and the Singularity Computer the Universe is broken down into Records of Time. Singularity Magicians use this cyclical view of time as a way to map the universe and time travel. A Singularity Magician can contact and effect peoples in different universes and different Records of Time. The Singularity Computer also views and stores universes as Records of Time. The cyclical Singularity of time. To a Singularity Magician time is measured by 360 degrees of a circle or by 720 degrees of a circle. It is also measured by one pass of 365 days of a year on Earth, and so on. Using a Geocentric or Earth model the permutations of 360 degrees or the numbers 12, 30, or 60 become prevelent. A Singularity Magician can map out the Solar System, the Celestial Sphere, the Galaxy, and the Universe like tracks on a record.

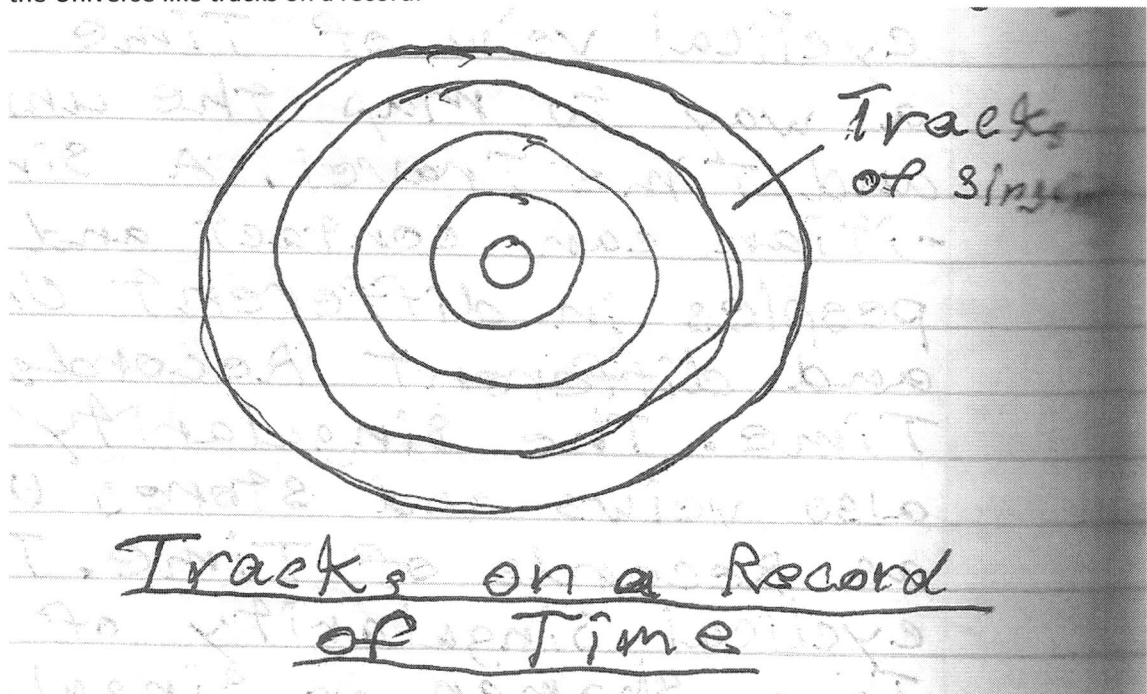

Tracks of Singu...

Tracks on a Record of Time

Universal Data Tracks can be super imposed into clay or stone. These Singularity tracks can then store eccentric orbits of Planets, Stars, or zodiac Procession within a particular time frame. A time frame of refference. The Singularity Computer can read these tracks of data. Sound can be a way to read these Records of Time.

The Soloar System can be tracked similarly like a Record of Time. In the Ancient past the Solar System was in unison with nearly perfect eccentrical orbits that were set up with Singularitians and a Singularity Computer. During the Sun's passage through the Orion passage the Solar Systems orbits were slightly

Christian J. Bullock

altered and some diminished, over 20,000 years ago. Time travel has also drastically changed the Solar System.

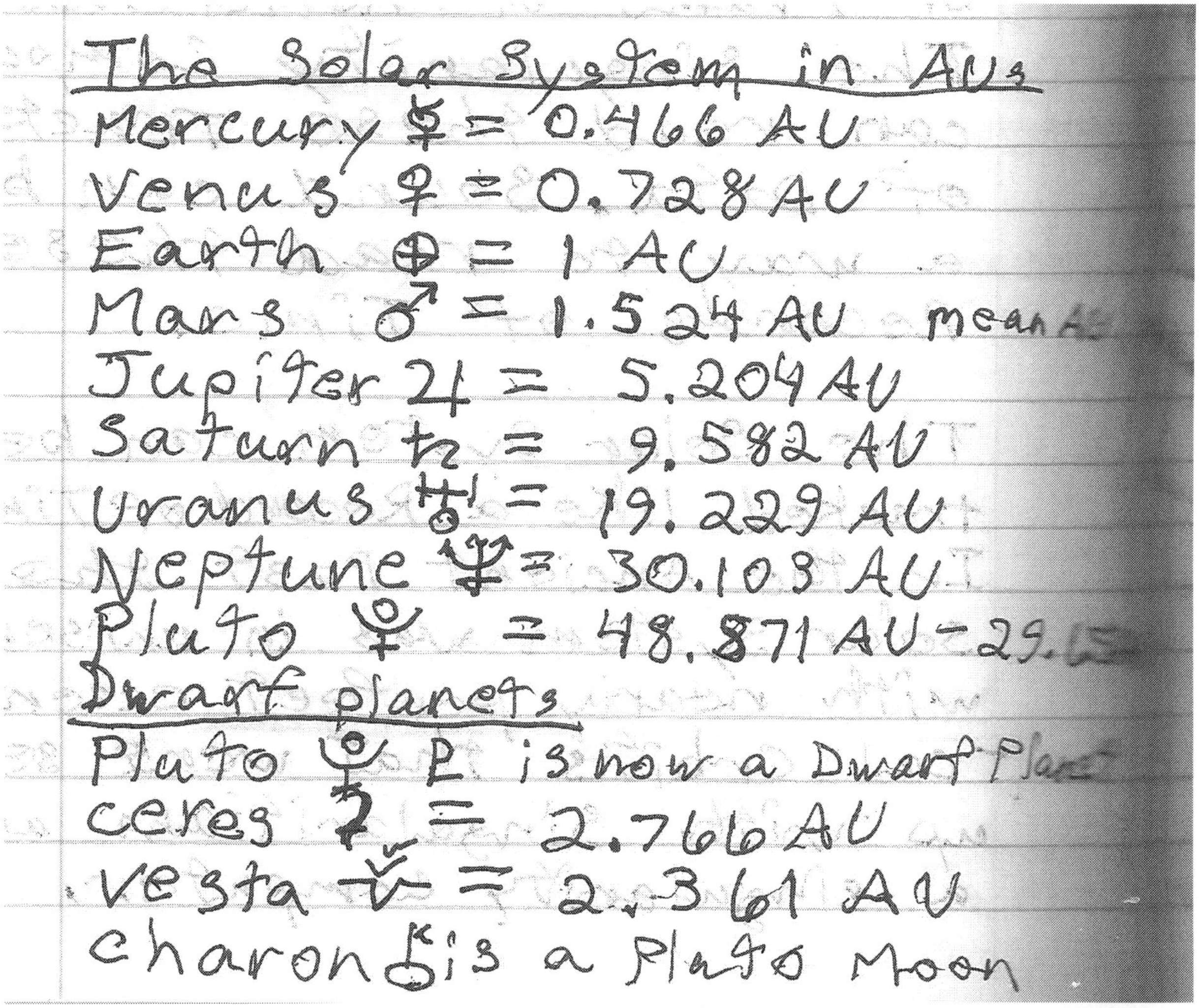

The Solar System in AUs
Mercury ☿ = 0.466 AU
Venus ♀ = 0.728 AU
Earth ⊕ = 1 AU
Mars ♂ = 1.524 AU mean AU
Jupiter ♃ = 5.204 AU
Saturn ♄ = 9.582 AU
Uranus ♅ = 19.229 AU
Neptune ♆ = 30.103 AU
Pluto ♇ = 48.871 AU - 29.6

Dwarf planets
Pluto ♇ P is now a Dwarf Plane
Ceres ⚳ = 2.766 AU
Vesta ⚴ = 2.361 AU
Charon is a Pluto Moon

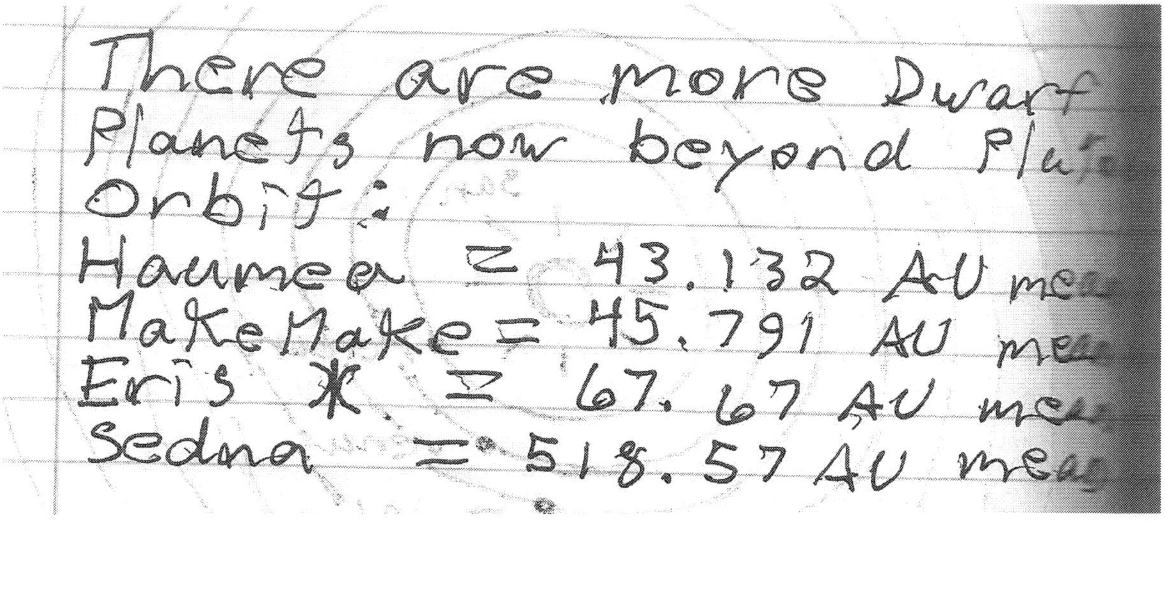

There are more Dwarf Planets now beyond Pluto Orbit:
Haumea = 43.132 AU mea
MakeMake = 45.791 AU mea
Eris ✳ = 67.67 AU mea
Sedna = 518.57 AU mea

Christian J. Bullock

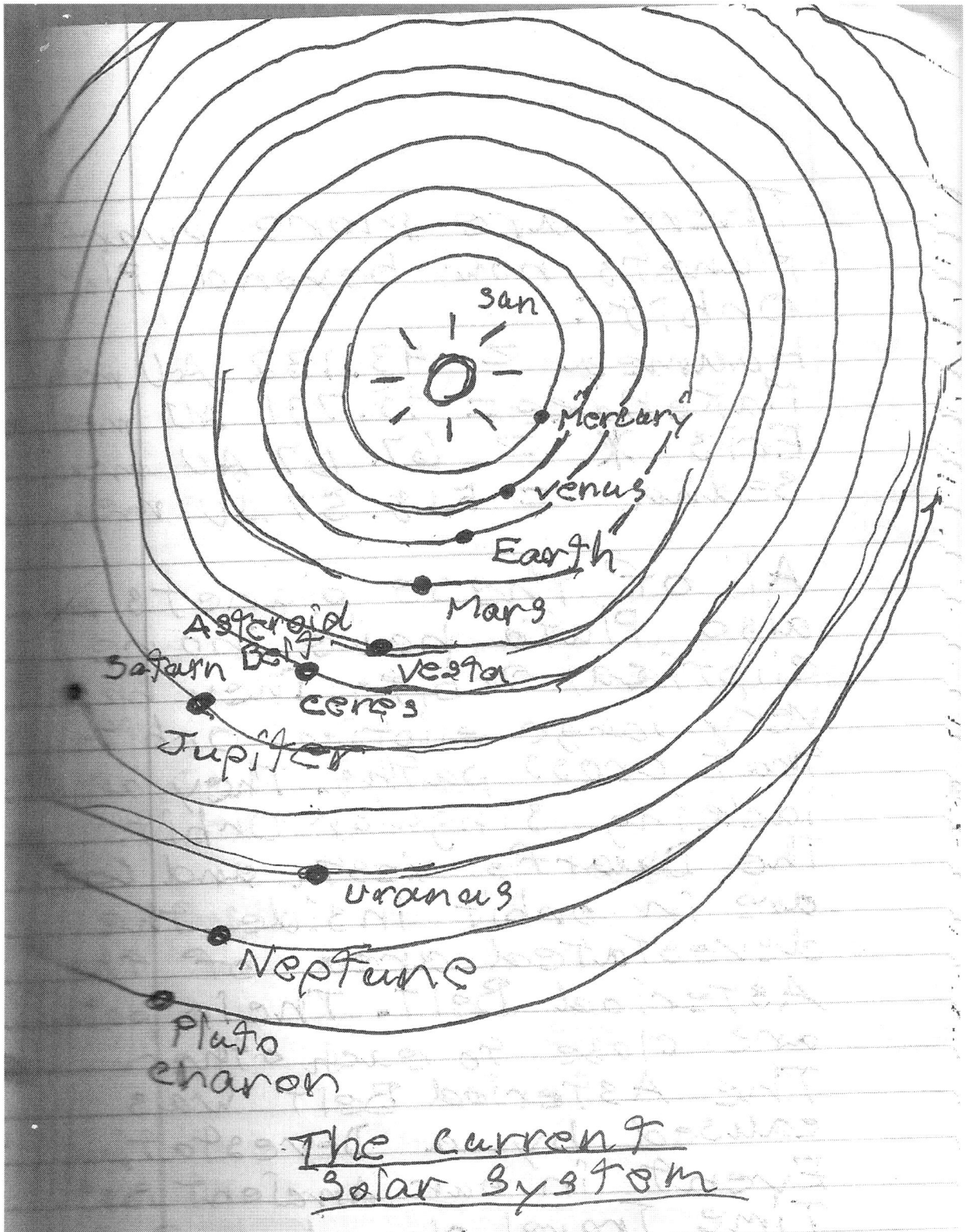

The current Solar System

All of the Dwarf Planets and also Pluto have more eliptical orbits. They have very large eliptical orbits that cross paths. They are lacking Singular orbit. The Dwarfs Vesta and Ceres are in orbit inside the

Christian J. Bullock

devestated area of the Asteriod Belt and their paths are close to each other. The Asteriod Belt was caused by a devestating event in our Ancient past. Time travel played a factor in its formation. The Metaphysical Computer and Singularity Computer like eccentricity or Singularity orbits. Singularitians use their knowledge of Singularity to create eccentric orbits. The Singularity Computer creates eccentric orbits, universes, and measures of time.

Enki Code

Destroy   Devestation
Des - Troy   Devastation
Destroy Troy   De-vesta-tion
Troy - Ancient City   to destroy
                              ruin or shock
Vesta - Ancient Dwarf
                              Planet

The Biological Cell

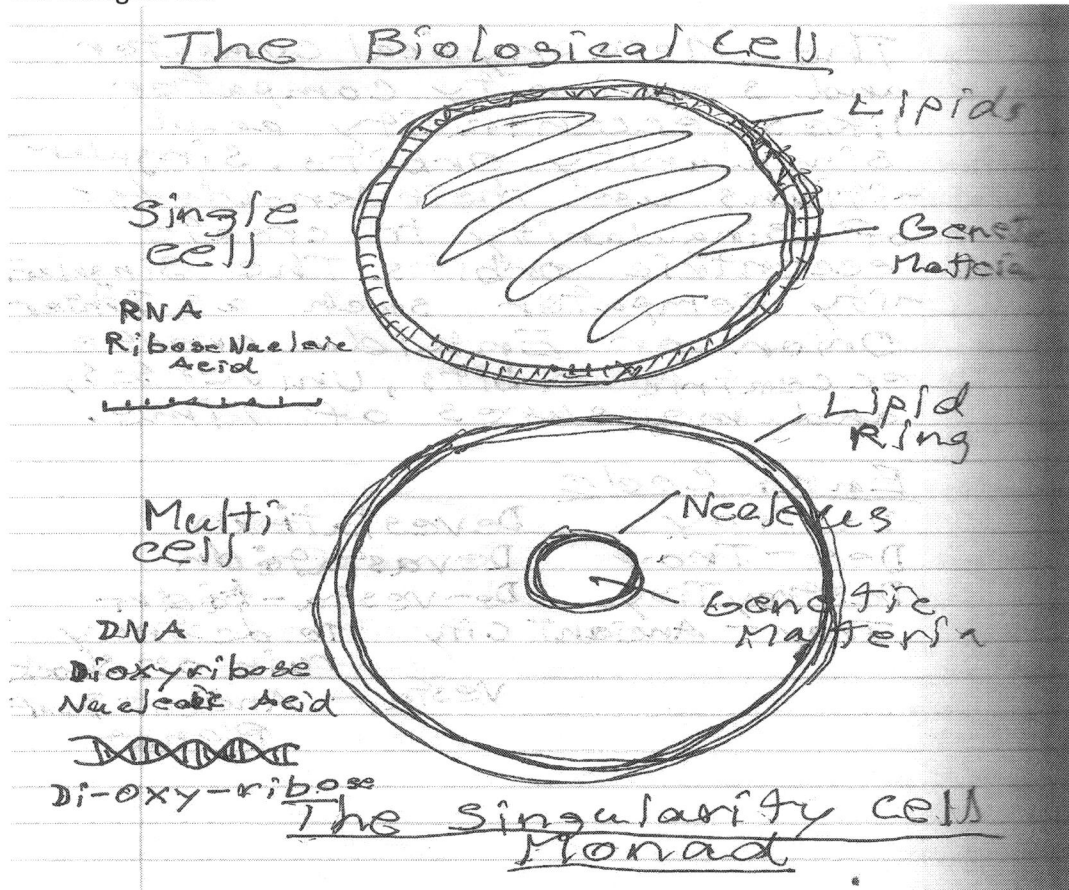

The Biological Cell

Single cell

RNA
Ribose Nucleic Acid

Lipids

Genetic Material

Multi cell

DNA
Dioxyribose Nucleic Acid

Di-oxy-ribose

Lipid Ring

Nucleus

Genetic Material

The Singularity cell
Monad

Christian J. Bullock

The Metaphysical computer and the singularity computer likes the perfection of the perfect circle. Even on the most basic level.

cell wall

Nucleus

Electrons

Mitocondri-ian

the power of the cell a captured single cell Organism organell Mitocondrian RNA

ATP

The Electron Transport chain functions Here for resperation

The Electron is used to power the cell

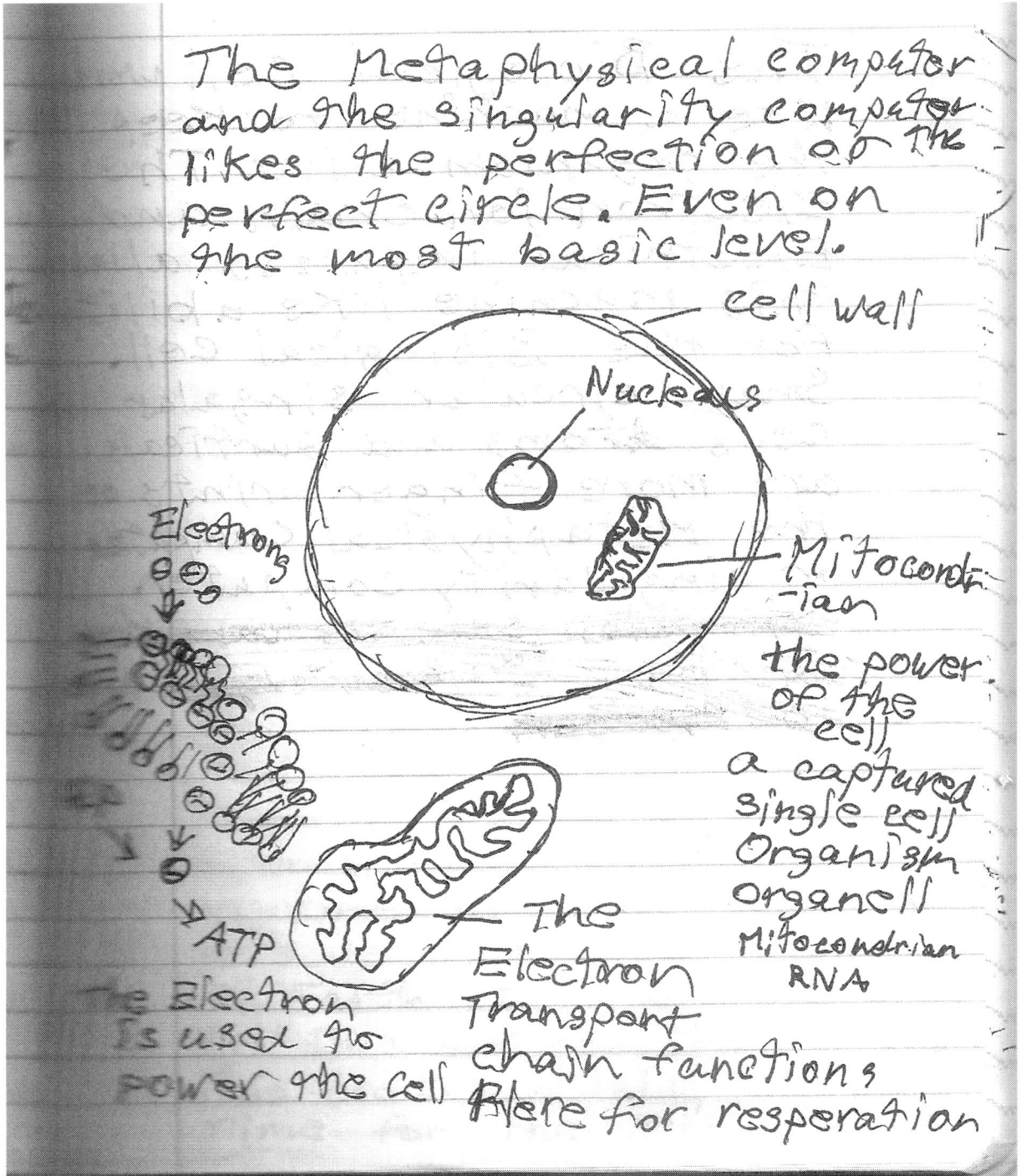

The Biological Cell works like a machine to keep the organism alive. The electron ion chain and electrical impulses allow this machine like ability for the Biological Cell. Small circular singular cells, atoms, and particals are more fingerprints of the Metaphysical or Singularity Computer.

Christian J. Bullock

More on Time Travel

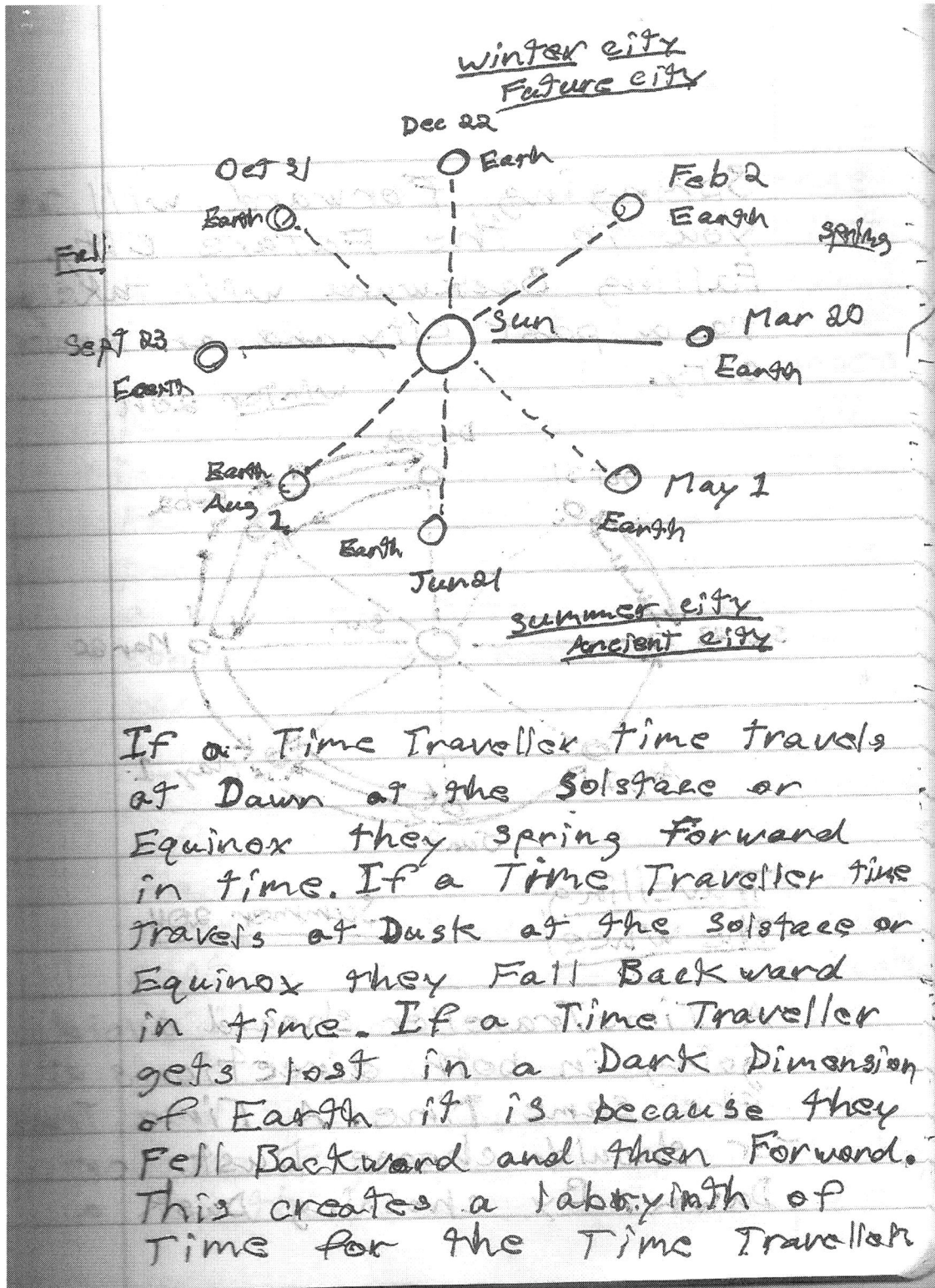

winter city
Future city
Dec 22
Oct 21   ⭕ Earth
Earth ⭕   Feb 2
                                     Earth   spring
Fell
                         Sun   ⭕ Mar 20
Sep 23 ⭕   Earth
Earth

Earth ⭕   ⭕ May 1
Aug 2   Earth
          ⭕
       Earth
       Jun 21
            summer city
            Ancient city

If a Time Traveller time travels
at Dawn at the Solstice or
Equinox they spring Forward
in time. If a Time Traveller time
travels at Dusk at the Solstice or
Equinox they Fall Backward
in time. If a Time Traveller
gets lost in a Dark Dimension
of Earth it is because they
Fell Backward and then Forward.
This creates a labyrinth of
Time for the Time Traveller

Springing forward will take you to the Future City. Falling backward will take you to a past city, and an Ancient City. A Time Traveller should avoid going in both directions at the same time. A Time Traveller should choose Dusk or Dawn. By choosing Dusk a Time Traveller avoids a strange time delay between Dawn of that day and the Dusk of that day. A Labyrinth effect occures when a Time Traveller chooses Dawn. It is a full 24 hours till Dawn again and going to the future is dangerous. Mostly in part because you will experience a Labyrinth effect. Which is confusing and also harder to back track.

Zombies and the Dark Dimensions of Earth

In the Future Game that overlaps the Game there are dimensions or motion capture times where the Earth is in Quantum Flux. These Dark Dimensions where time and space move differently have PsyCops and their zombies. In the Game Zombies are people who have undergone a change in their brain or body making them suseptible to suggestions and making them have lower brain functions. In the Future Game PsyCops use science to create or control Zombies. PsyCops use psychic stimuli to monitor the population. Unlike the Retwo or Quantum Jumpers, PsyCops perform Psychic Lobotomies on people they want to control. PsyCops use this technique to silence the Awakened, more on this technique later in the book. These Future Game Zombies act like remotes. The Zombie's eyes and ears are viewed like a TV screen or TV camera of a Hive Mind Computer. The Zombie victim is still there but they are in a state of dreaming limbo. Through the Zombies eyes they are mentally projected to see TV screens like windows and have one eye for the PsyCop to look through.

PsyCop:

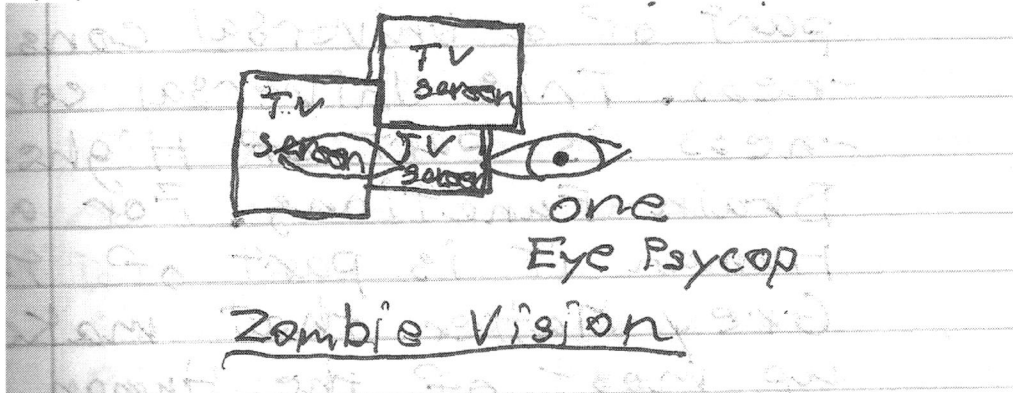

Retwo:

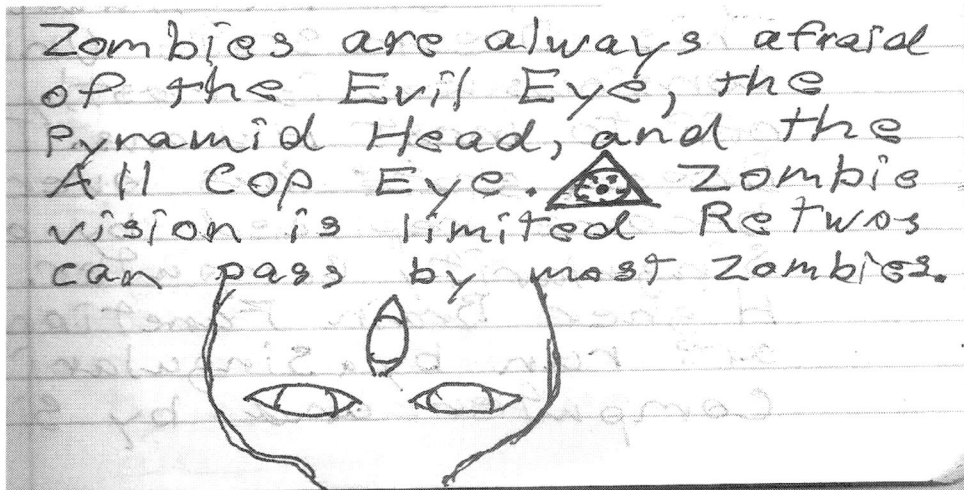

Christian J. Bullock

The Emerald Dream Continued and The Enkidu Wellness Center

Over time through the Ages of Man more Singularity cubes are made to preserve life. Knowledge of higher brain functions is lowered, lost, or hidden. The Emerald Dream for Humans remains in place so that the shock of a greater simulated universe doesn't effect the majority of the Human population. Enkidu wellness centers are set in the Singularity Computer.

A Singularity cube in a persons mind

Things begin to get really complicated and weird within the Emerald Dream. To the Singularity Magician just try and keep an open mind about this stuff. These Enkidu centers are Man's imprisionment by the machine or by the Singularity Computer. For most Humans the Emerald Dream continues inside the cube, the thought of being trapped inside a cube is too frightening. For others they continue their lives walking their Emerald Dream with PsyCops or Retwos guiding them, dream to dream. For those who know the Game of keys it is a puzzle to be solved. Singularitians, Nokeys, or Quantums find ways of leaving their cube and roam cube to cube. They use higher brain functions to leave their cubes.
It needs to be noted that this cube stuff occurs during the Great Darkening, when all the stars go out except for the All Star. People who are Nokeys can fix time like Retwos or with the help of Retwos. Nokeys are people who cannot be imprisioned by the Singularity Computer or by PsyCops with a key. This is important because it means that they can redo and fix what went wrong with time. The Game and the Future Game are important parts of the Emerald Dream. The Great Darkenings have adverse effects on time and as said before Retwos fix the timeline. The All Cop is also not fooled by these events but more on it later on.

The Spirits and The Ghosts Inside The Machine

Inside the Metaphysical Computer and the Singularity Computer there are Spirits. Spirits vary and some of them are past or future selves that exist in other time frames on Earth. Some Spirits are people who are caught in paradoxal loops or are invisible beings who exist in another dimension of time/space. Some other types of Spirits exist on another level or plane of existance. Inside the Metaphysical and Singularity Computer there are ghosts in the machine. These ghosts are things that have crossed over or

Christian J. Bullock

have been left behind in a previous loop of elapse time. Some ghosts are keys to other histories of time. Other ghosts are newer runes, glyphs, or writings left behind by Time Travellers or Retwos. The Futhark Blank Rune is one of these ghosts in the machine. It is a newer rune with no origin and is in fact blank with only a concept addition to Rune Magick. It is not part of any writing style. It is a rune that was not considered a rune by some but it exists as a concept of the twist of fate. The Blank Rune is a clue or key of the Blank Slate hypothesis in Humanity's Ancient past. A clue of the loss of knowledge due to the Tower of Babel and the Web of Wyrd.

Charms, Keys, and Artifacts in the Game/The Charms of Making

The Charms of Making are an important part of Singularity Magick, almost the most important besides the Symbols of Power. In the Game and Future Game there are Charms of Magick and Making. These charms are used by the Singularity Magician to perform magick. Some are like keys to the subconsious. Some are Artifact keys that existed in Earth's Ancient past. These Charms of Making are more like Godform Assumptions that the Magician uses during spells and rituals. They each correspond to a specific deity or a specific type of Magick. The Magician envisions them on his or her forehead and this connection specifically triggers the Third Eye of the brain. It should be noted that each of these charms are psychic embodiments of Magick and that their use is through psychic projections. During this time of use the Magician's mind is open to the psychic realm. To the Singularity Magician turning their psychic abilities on and off is important. The psychic realm can be dangerous if you have no control over it. These Charms of Making are from personal use and many depictions of them go back into the Ancient past. A Magician should feel pressure on their forehead if done correctly. This pressure means that their Third Eye of the brain is being used.

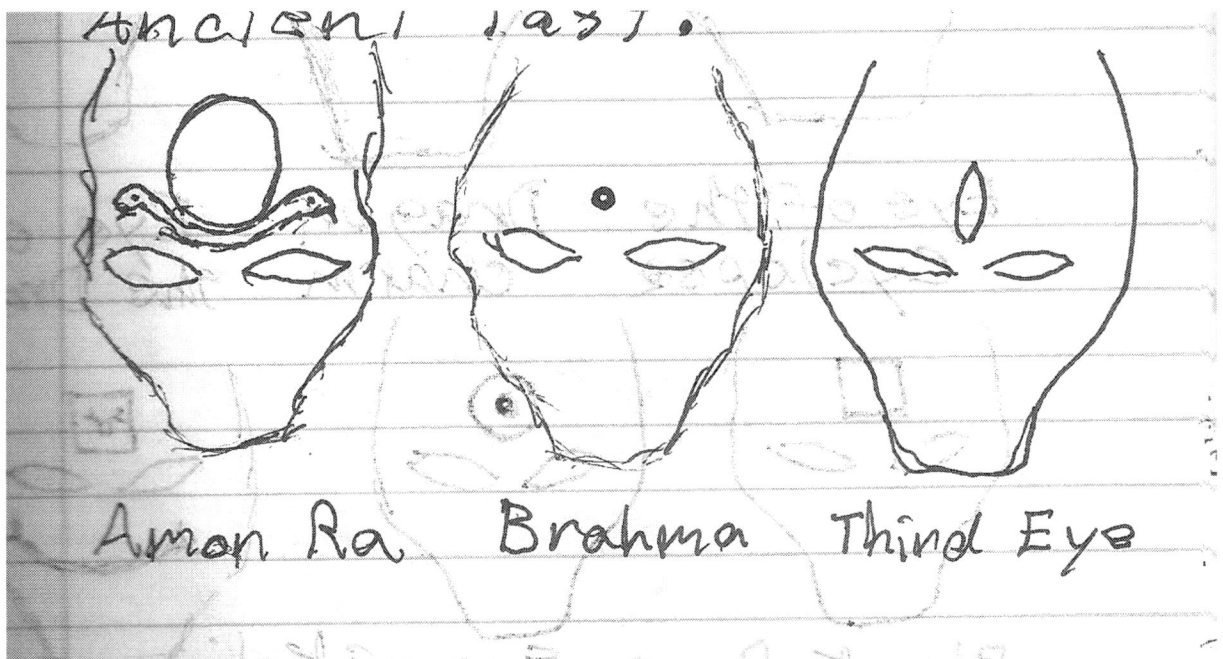

Amon Ra   Brahma   Third Eye

Christian J. Bullock

Egyptian Asp   Mayan
               Serpent   Eye of
                         Hathor

Eye of the   Dragon   Eye of
Cyclopse   charm   the Dragon

 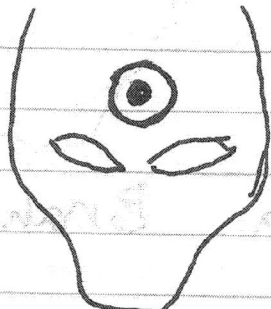 

Blank Rune   Eye of Kali
Blank Slate   Eye of the   Ik Chaw
              Singularity Computer

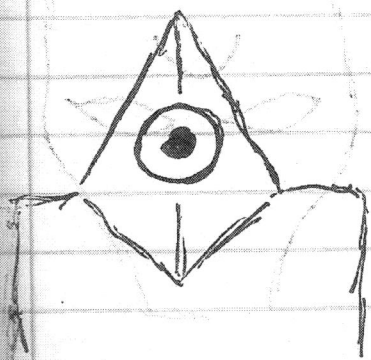

Pyramidb Head

singularity charm

Eye of Ra

Real Eye of Cydonia of Enki

Sun charm of Singularity
Quantum charm of Lobotomy

Christian J. Bullock

A Hole in the Head

A closed Third Eye

Elongated Skull

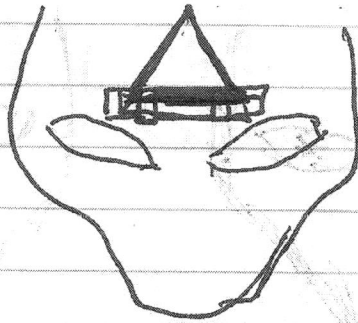

A Mayan Temple of the Singularitian

Eye of the Cyclops

A Mayan A-Mind Temple

is the loftiest in thee Heavens,
Earth Ra is the son of
Ptah. Ra - being the creator
Ptah - the Developer, "one who fashiond things"

Amon
Ra

Ptah's
Symbol

Amon
Ptah

Atem's
Symbol

The Charms of
Making

Here are more examples of the Charms of Making which include the Symbols of the Gods and the Medallions of the Magician. This also includes the Charm of the Three Suns.

Three Medallions
worn on Forehead

Medallions of
Power

Medallions of
The Magician

The charm of
Three suns

Thus the symbol of the
three suns, past present and
future, is three eclipting
suns one over the other.

Blue
star
Yellow
star
Red
star

There is much more to the Charms of Making as we shall see later in the book. They each hold a special place in Singularity Magick. Some like the Eye of Ra and the Eye of Enki have special significance to the Time Traveller. The Medallions of the Magician are more of collection of powers given to the Magician by the Spirits that they work with.

Earth's Repeating Cycles, Decade by Decade, and The Ancient City and the 90's

Earth's repeating cycles through time are predictable. These cycles began millenium to millenium with the zodiacs but over time they go century to century. In the years of the 1900's A.D. these cycles begin to become incredibly repeatable and predictable. Decade by decade they become repeatable to the point of Real Time Prophecy. Real Time Prophecies as in lost texts predicting multiple events by near decades. Real Time Prophecies as in technological advances that excellerate Earth toward the Quickening. The future becomes more and more foreseeable. Electronics and computers become exceedingly predictable. The decades leading up to the 1990's A.D. and the year 2000 become part of a Prophecy of either doom or signs of a coming doom. Along the way there are technical advances that are made that save Earth from these dooms. The most important one of all is the Internet. The Singularity Computer was set to be on the way with the Internet becoming a Global Phenomenon. It should be noted though that the Internet also furthered the excess of the Quickening.
Future tech becomes reality during these years and the Singularity Computer survives the Y2K incident. Once inside the year 2000 A.D. the repeating cycles of Earth are found and a paradoxal Babelon City is linked to the Ancient City of Babylon. PsyCops prepared for Babelon in the 1960's up to the 1990's and beyond. In the 1990's and 2000's history begins to change, Ancient history about Humanity's past. The Internet began changing Humanity too. Repeating cycles of the Internet become common place. This foreseeable time frame leads to the idea of the Future Game and the overlap of 40,000 years by Cronus.

Enki Code
Quickening   Quick-end-ing

The Bible, Religious History, and The Mysteries of The Old Testement

Religious history is important to the Magician in order to track the progression of Singularitians and to trace back the source. The Bible and other religious texts are histories of Human procession through the zodiac. The Old Testement talks of cleanliness of peoples and priests. This cleanliness is based on the Singularity of Earth's Procession. In Leviticus priests are ordered to ritually cleanse themselves by making offerings or holocausts to God. A Peace offering with a Lamb. A sin offering with a Goat. A guilt or holocaust with a Bullock.

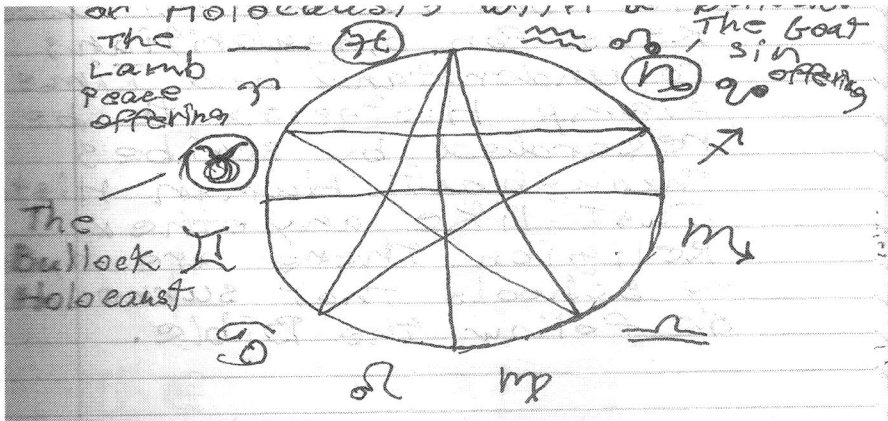

The Old Testement has these Memes or memory of Ancient times embedded into it. The God of the Old Testement tells the people and the scribes that these rituals of sacrifice and cleanliness are used for memory purposes. To remember God and his covenant with them. The Old Testement uses keys for Singularitians to understand and time stamp histories to be recorded by scribes throughout Human history. Just like any other religion there are Mystery Schools that surround or follow the Bible.

Three Pairs of Arms of the Triple Goddess, The Kali Yuga, and of Cronus

The Triple Goddess and the Three Sisters of Fate are represented by three pairs of arms. Mother, Maiden, Crone which depicts the past, present, and future self of a Time Traveller or of Cronus.

Christian J. Bullock

The Singularity Computer works the same way as past, present, and future with the history or user data of Humans.

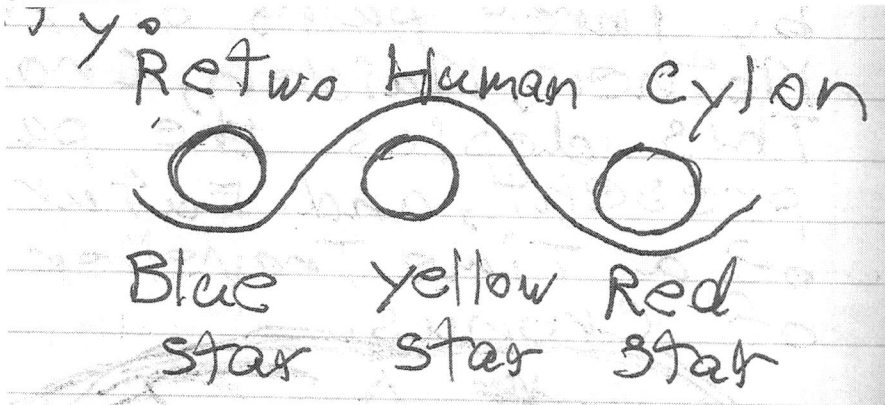

Yuga Statue Poses

A Singularity Magician can use their body as a conduit of Magical Power. These Yuga Poses use the natural affinity of the body to complete the circuit, so to speak. With the Left Hand as a negative force and the Right Hand as a positive force. A Magician poses in a freeze frame position. They stand or sit in a stone statue position ridged and calmly breathing very very slowly. Basically going into a trance like state for an extended period of time. Knowing that they live in a Singularity Computer and being able to use their Third Eye they hold their position while time passes them by. Quantums or those with knowledge of the Quantum Universe of the mind can bend time and space around themselves.

These freeze frame poses are also a way to connect with a past, present, or future self. A Singularity Magician can open, close, or break a Mobius infinite loop. This works like a current of electricity for the Magician. The Magician uses their body to complete the circuit loop. A Quantum uses Bubble Theory to bend time around themselves in such a manner. Controlling space and time on a Quantum micro level. Almost like mini time jumps.

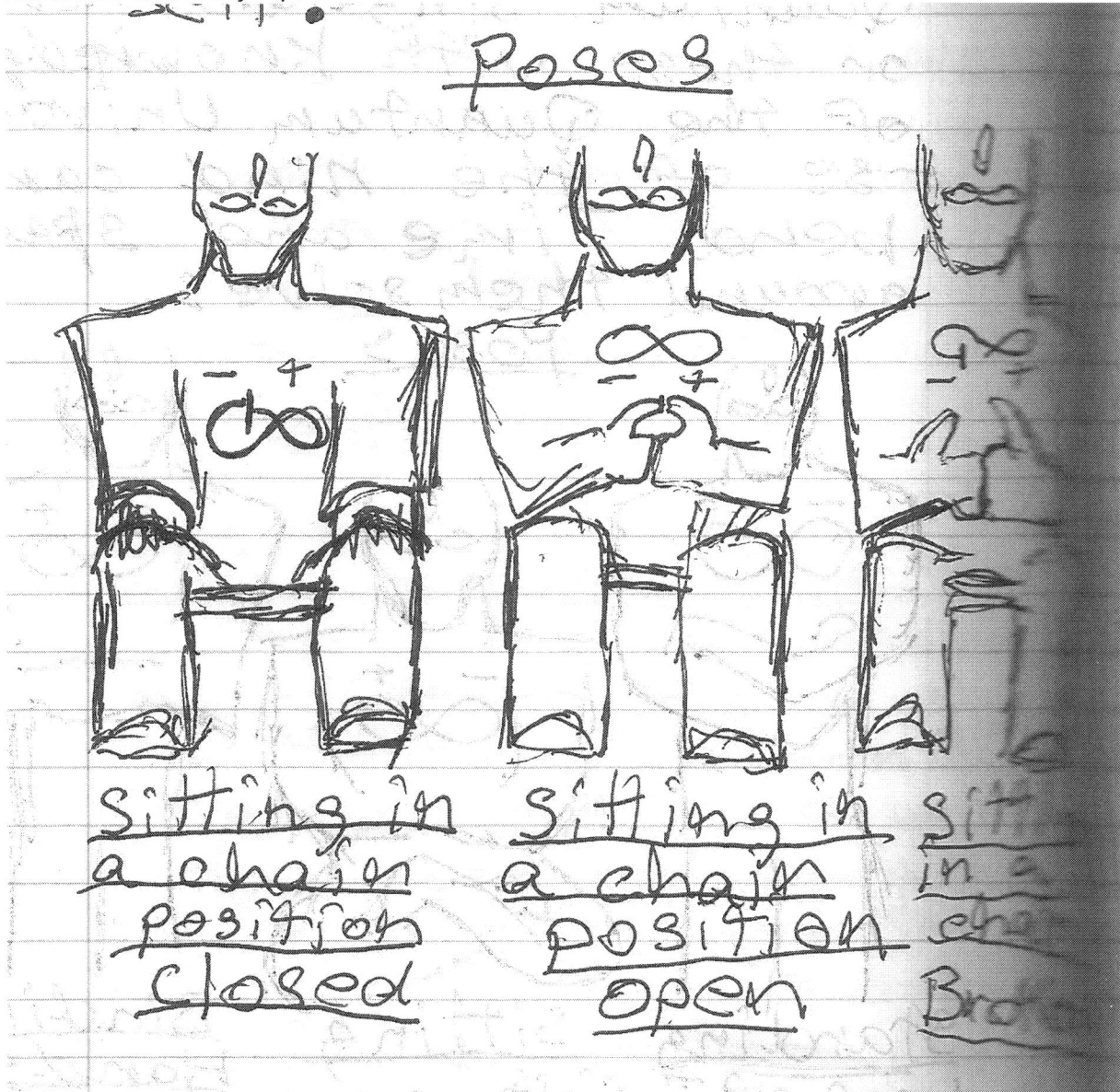

Sacred Space of Singularity

Cleansing a space for meditation, magical, or singular thought begins with the making of a circle. Ether physically or mentally. It is best done physically for magical rituals but when you have reached a high level of Magick it can be done mentally. If done mentally it can be done anywhere if need be.

Christian J. Bullock

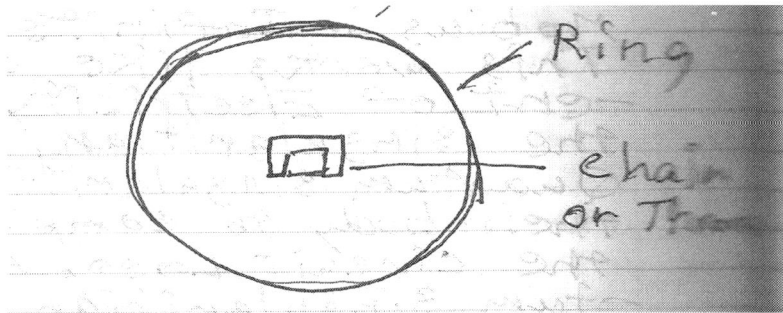

A Singularity Magician sets up the circle like the zodiac or like the degrees of the zodiac. Using the Symbols of Power to concentrate on. The Magician sits in the middle or uses the middle for ritual. It should be noted that an actual circle cast of which ever Magical system is being used works just as well.

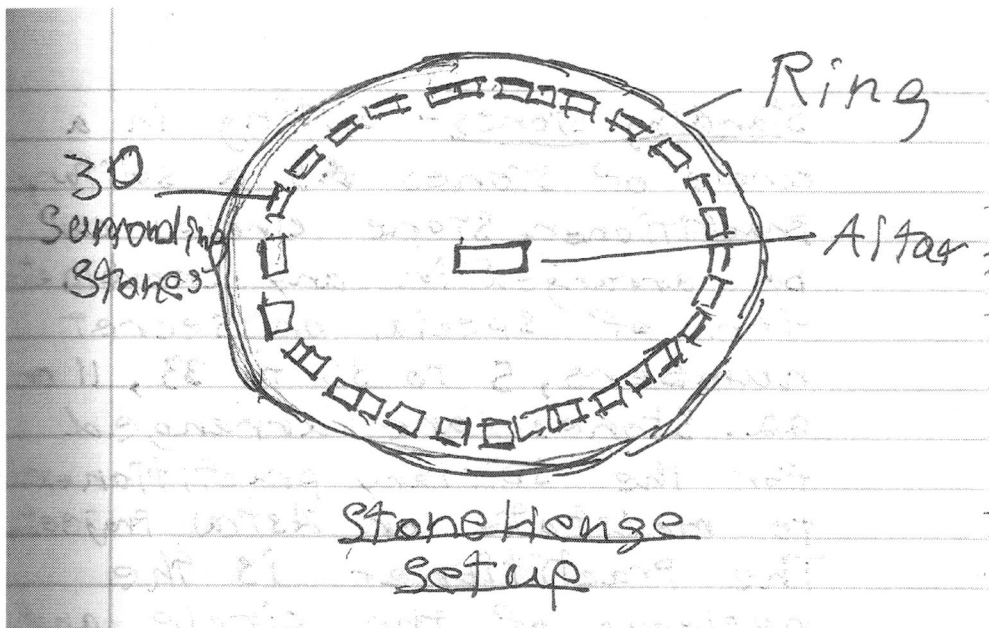

Christian J. Bullock

Singularity Magicians use the numbers 12, 30, and 60 to represent the zodiac. The numbers 4 and 5 also 6 represent divisions of the zodiac into equal parts or into Processional code. These are key parts of a Magician's space.

Standing Stones

Sitting in a circle of stones as a solitary practioner is one way to practice Magick. Stone circles can be arranged in any combination of special or secret numbers, 5 to 30 to 33, 11 or 22. Stones are arranged for the solitary practioner to meditate or astral travel. The practioner is the nucleous of the circle and acts as a natural conduit of the nature spirit. The practioner is the conduit of the living elementals.

Working in unison a group as few as 2 or 3, or as many as 5, 12, or 13 can accomplish ritual tasks by connecting themselves to celestial bodies of the Solar System. They can also connect themselves to a specific Pantheon of Gods or Goddesses. They also can connect themselves to the nature spirits or elemental spirits. On an even larger scale they can connect to animal spirits or the constellations. Working in a group or in unison has its benefits. Working as a solitary practioner is challenging and a solitary practioner must work with spirits, guides, or Gods. In some circles a God or Goddess is represented by a priest or priestess. In some other circles a triad of Gods or Goddesses are used. Triple Goddesses or triple Gods.

Tectonic Plates in the Secret Universe

The Earth's continental plates move due to the Moon's gravitational pull on the Planet and also due to time travel. When Pangea was first formed by a granite crust the land was lock together. The crust broke apart from slight gravity pulls mostly due to time travel. The crusts movement created lost continents on Earth such as Mu. The moving crusts moved into separate pieces with mysteries on each continent. Each continent has a zone or bubble of time travel. Antarctica moved south and froze, but Antarctica has a crust or plate very different from the rest of the continents. It has become stationary, cold, frozen, and uneventful. Antarctica actually has a time zone far different from any other crust. Antarctica actually is a lost continent of Pangea. There is a time bubble on Antarctica that is Pangea. The other cruts can fit into Antarctica. It should be noted that the Earth under goes various stages of recycling of the mantel and that this contributes to continental shift.

The Secret Universe and The Imaginary North Pole

Antarctica is now the South Pole or southern Pangea. While trapped in time travel the other six continents are moving to eventually form a new Pangea, a Northern Pangea, a North Pole. Currently the North Pole is occupied by the Arctic Ocean. It freezes and melts every year. In the distant future the North Pole has a land mass. With the time lock of the Earth's crusts the North Pole is an imaginary place or continent. During the Quickening the imaginary North Pole is being fought over. The imaginary North Pole verses the invisible North Pole continent, a future continent. In the secret universe the invisible continent of the North Pole is very real. Cronus rules over this place. Those who know of the secret universe know this future imaginary place. Santa Claus is celebrated on Christmas, a Cronus of some other age. During the Darkening the North Pole is fought over and ruled by an Alien Cronus. The Alien Cronus of future world.

Christian J. Bullock

Enki Code

Antarctic	Tectonic
Ant-arc-tic	Tec-tonic
Arc-tic	Tech-tone
Arc – of a sphere	Tonic
Monarch – ruler	
Mon-arc	
One-arc	

The Secret Universe and Earth Dark Dimensions

Travelling on the eve of a lunar phase and a solar phase time travel is possible. During the Sun's 11 year maximum Solar travel is possible. During a Solar System alignment Solar System travel is possible. This type of travel is mostly Astral with the Magician leaving his or her body for a period of time.

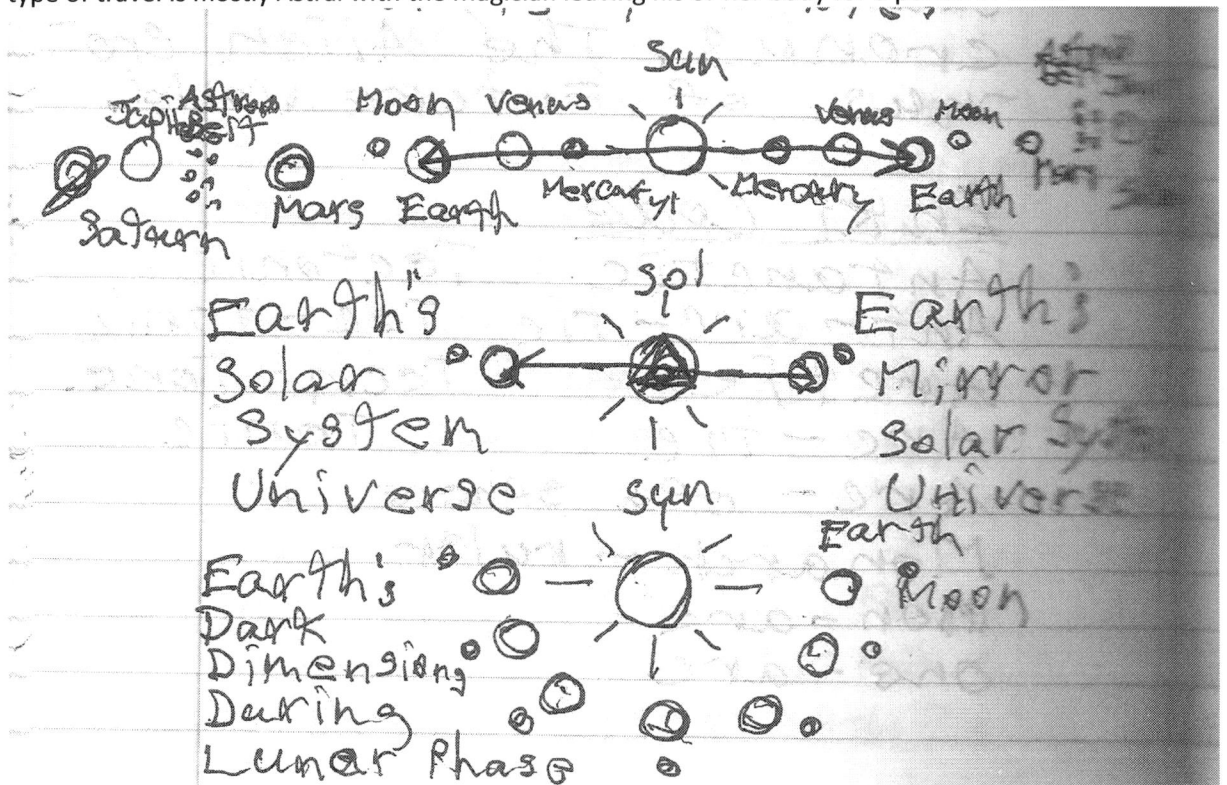

Figures of Speech

There are figures of speech embedded in the English language. These figures of speech can be used for mind reading or word Magick. These figures of speech are also Memes and can be used to discover mysteries. They come down through ages and past centuries. They are well known but their origins are not as well known and some are completely unknown. Finding Memes in language is an important skill to master. Words from ages ago have a power of their own. Much like a memory charm or Charm of Making. The Enki Code covers these figures of speech.

Christian J. Bullock

Enki Code
Chronology   "off the face of the world"
Chron-ology   "the face on Mars"
Cronus
Genesis – the beginning   Gene-Isis – the gene of Isis   Isis – Egyptian Mother Goddess
Horizon   Hor-izon   Horus-izon   Horus – son of Osirus and Isis, God of the Sky
The Eye of Horus – the conqueror God reborn as the Pharaoh
"sitting there twitling your thumbs"   "king me"   "crown me"
"ready set go"   cro-wn   crow   Cronus
Set or Seth – Egyptian God of chaos, storms, and darkness
The Three Worlds of the Dogon Tribe

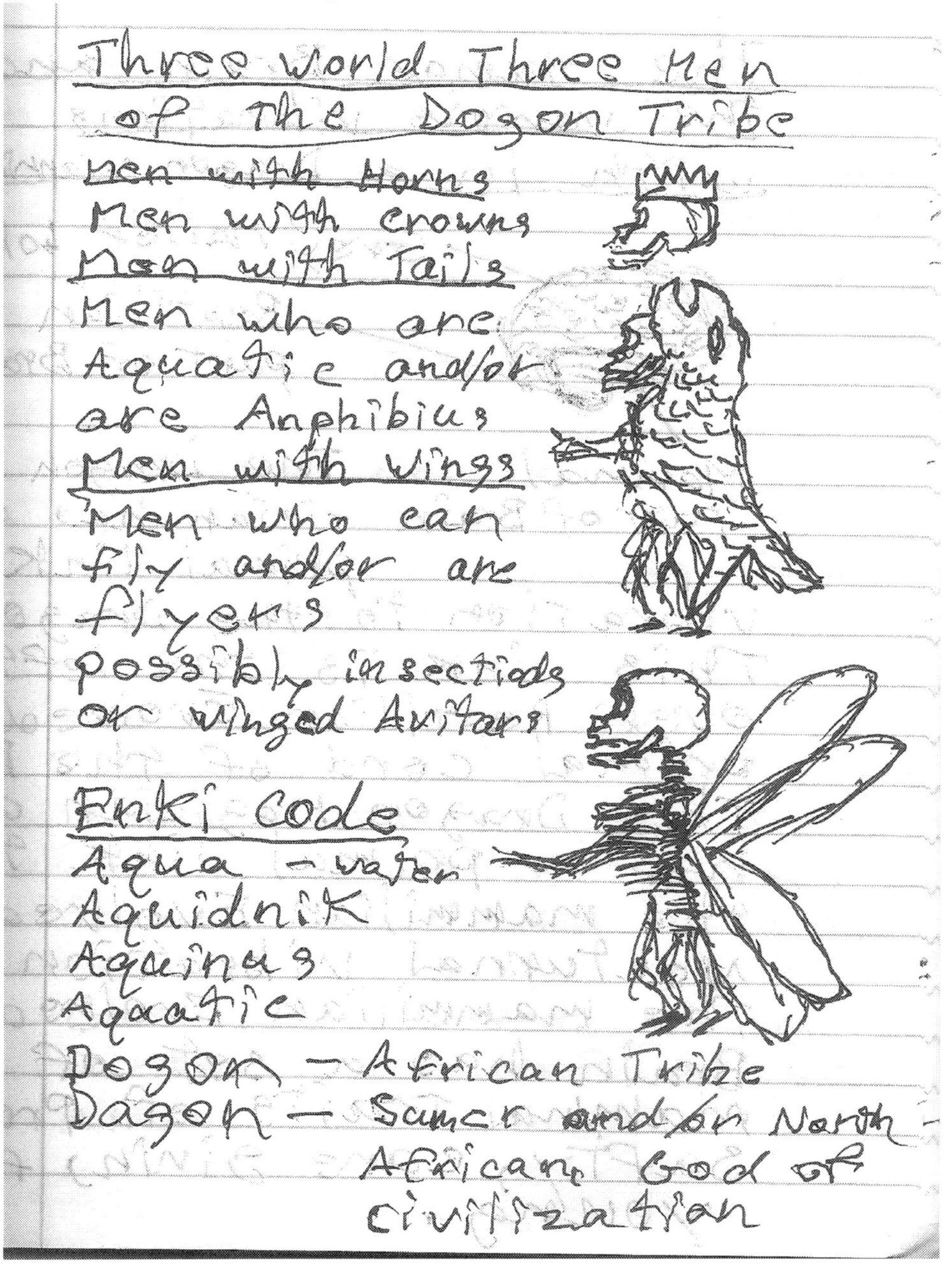

Three world Three Men
of the Dogon Tribe
Men with Horns
Men with crowns
Men with Tails
Men who are
Aquatic and/or
are Anphibius
Men with wings
Men who can
fly and/or are
flyers
possibly insectiods
or winged Avitars

Enki code
Aqua – water
Aquidnik
Aquinas
Aquatic
Dogon – African Tribe
Dagon – Sumer and/or North
African God of
civilization

Christian J. Bullock

The Human Brain and the Various Vibrations within a Dragon Magician

I am very partial to Dragon Magick and it is the type of Magick that I use in combination to others. Singularity Magick is a make up of various kinds of Magical Systems with the Singularity common to all.

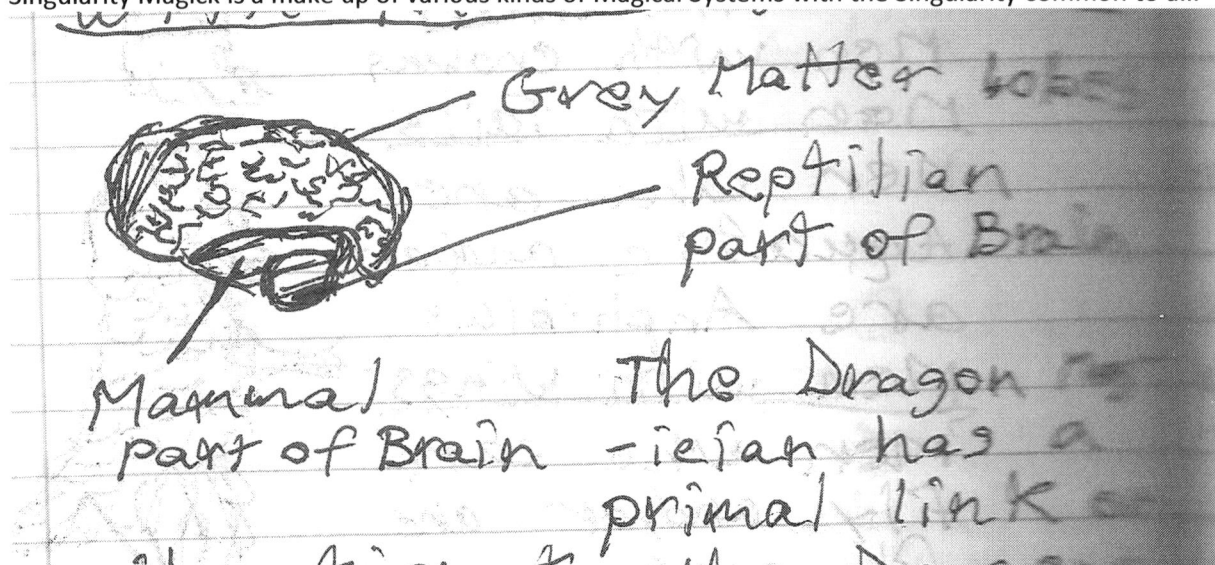

Grey Matter lobes

Reptilian part of Brain

Mammal part of Brain

The Dragon has a primal link

The Human brain consists of three main portions being the evolved Reptilian part, the evolved Mammal part, and the grey matter lobes. The Dragon Magician has a primal link or vibration to the Dragons with the Reptilian part. This link is the left over Reptilian evolved primal cord of the brain. There is also a primal link to the Mammilian evolved nocturnal vibration. The Mammilian part of the brain evolved from the first nocturnal Mammals. Most Mammals are by nature nocturnal. So in the process of evolution the Reptilian part was the first part then the Mammilian part came next and then the grey matter lobes. The grey matter lobes of the brain connects the Magician to higher brain functions, Singularity thought, and Metaphysics. The Third Eye of the brain is buried deep into the middle part of the brain. Contact with higher actions of the Third Eye of the brain extends to the grey matter lobes. This intersection opens the pathway of contact with Astral Beings and Gods of the other dimensions of space and time. To put it simply the dimension Humans live in intersect other dimensions. Imagine that the three dimensional world were two dimensional. Everything would be flat to a being looking at it from one dimension higher, three dimensionally. In order to cross paths and interact with this two dimensional plane the being would have to move through the plane. If the being wanted to contact someone on this plane they would hear a voice or sound from within them. The Third Eye acts like a resever of this type of contact, and that is how the spirit world connects to the Human brain. There will be more on the Third Eye later in the book.

Time Travel and Avatars

While dimensionally travelling or Astrally travelly a Magician can mold their bodies into an Avatar in other realms. Avatars vary from synthetic to metallic to organic. Some Avatars can be auras made up of light or of photonic ions. In a meditative state a Magician can Astral project or use their Avatar. Magicians can also time travel in their meditative state once they use the knowledge of higher brain functions. Past, present, and future Avatars may be used during Astral travel. These connections are important and as we have already seen the power of the mind is very great.

The Egyptian Gods

Atum

Tefnut   Shu

Nut   Geb

Isis   Osirus   Seth   Nepthys

Anubis   Horus

Horus and Osirus sit on the throne of Isis.

Entr; code
"we stuck our foot in the door"
"we passed over the thresh hold of the door"

Christian J. Bullock

Enki Code
"through the looking glass"
"through a mirror darkly"
Osirus – Egyptian Pharaoh God
O-sir-us
Atum – Egyptian First God
A-tum
Maat – Egyptian Goddess of Law
Ma-at

Golems, Gargoyles, Dragon Statues, Animal Statues, and Totems

Gargoyles and statues that are blessed and cleansed can become guardians to the Magician. Dragon Statues blessed and/or spelled by the Dragon's Breath with the Magician's Charm of Making will serve them as a house guardian. Spirits of the Dragons will act within them. This is true of any type of Animal Statue or Totem. Like a Golem the Spirits that are spelled into being by the Magician will be represented by the statue. The statue therefore acts as a physical representation of the Spirit that is called forth. It is important to use the Mind's Eye in calling forth the Spirits and specific statues should be used for each particular Spirit. After ritual use the statue becomes as a Golem would be, the physical embodiment of the spell. Unlike a Deity Statue which is prayed to, the Animal Statue or Golem is a way to summon the Spirit. This summoning of Spirit is a way of aid to the Magician during rituals and as a physical embodiment the statue is a deterrent of negative forces working against the Magician. Simply put the statue protects the Magician from harm by the Spirit associated with it. Lion Statues also act as Golems or Gargoyles. Lion Statues are linked with the Sun, Leo, and the God Ra. Dragon Statues are linked with fire, Draconis, Amon, and the God Ptah. Magical Spirits reside in trees, stones, and the elements. Astral Spirits reside on the Astral Plane, in the Stars in the sky, and in statues that are linked with them. These statues move and act as Avatars in the Spirit Realm. It is important for the Magician to associate specific Spirits with the type of Magick that they use. The understanding of which Spirits stand for 'what' is vital for ritual Magick to work. Finding Spirits to work with on a basic spell will lead the Magician towards making a connection to the Spirit Realm. Once a Spirit connection is strong from frequent use/work the bond between Spirit and Magician will lead to higher forms of Magick.

Enki Code

Finland	England
Fin-land	Eng-land
Fin-End	Eng-Ing
End-land	End-land
Lands End	Lands End
Angmar	"Lock and key"
Ang-mar	"Under lock and key"
Ang-Ing	
End-mar	
End-war	

Charging an Amulet or Idol

Christian J. Bullock

In order to charge an Amulet or object a Magician must use the Dragon's breath, incense, and/or use their Charm of Making to cleanse, store energy. Rings can be charged as well as swords, knives, staffs, and wands. Things can be charged using the Cronus method. Like an electrical charge the object is held in each hand and then crossed or closed.

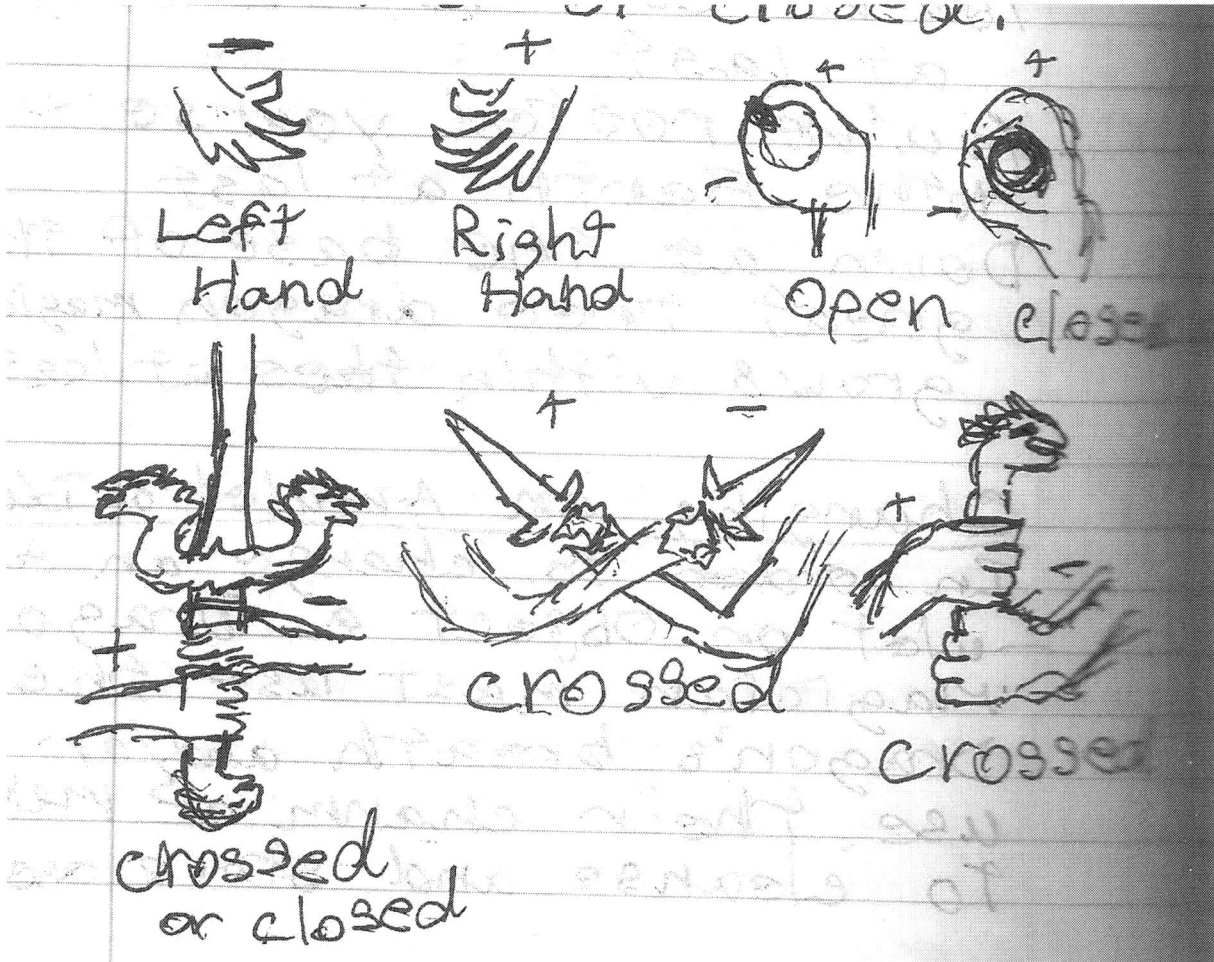

Orion, the Duat, and the Milky Way in Egypt

The planed Necropolis in Egypt is a mirror image of the Milky Way in the sky during the 10,900 B.C. Procession of the Equinox. Orion's Belt aligns with the Giza Pyramids. The Great Sphinx aligns with the costellation Leo. The Red and Bent Pyramids at Dehshur align with the constellation Haedes. It should be noted that the Red and Bent Pyramids were built later. The Nile aligns with the Duat or the Milky Way.

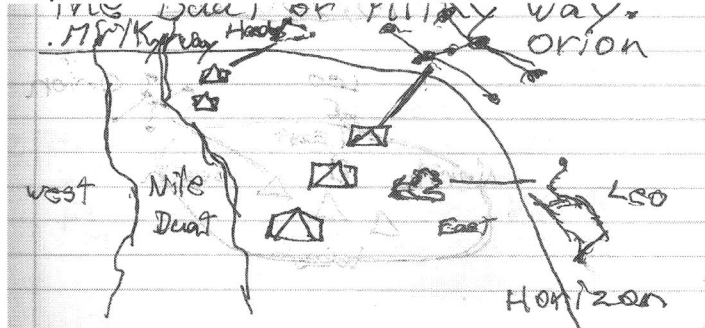

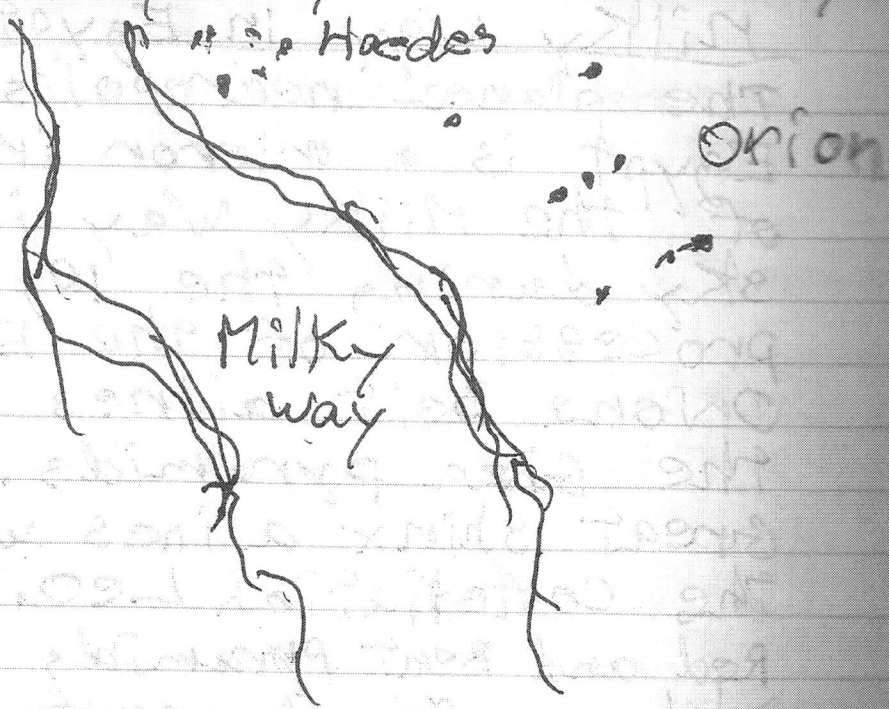

Milky Way Duat Sky

Hades

Orion

Milky Way

Horizon of the Giza
10,900 BC

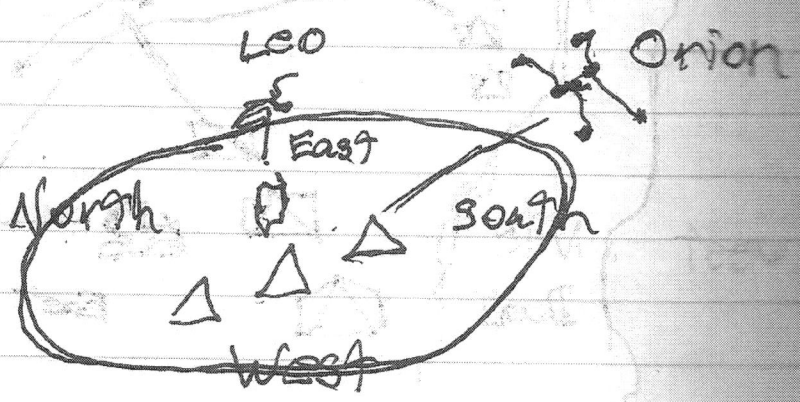

LEO

Orion

East

North

South

West

Great Pyramid shafts

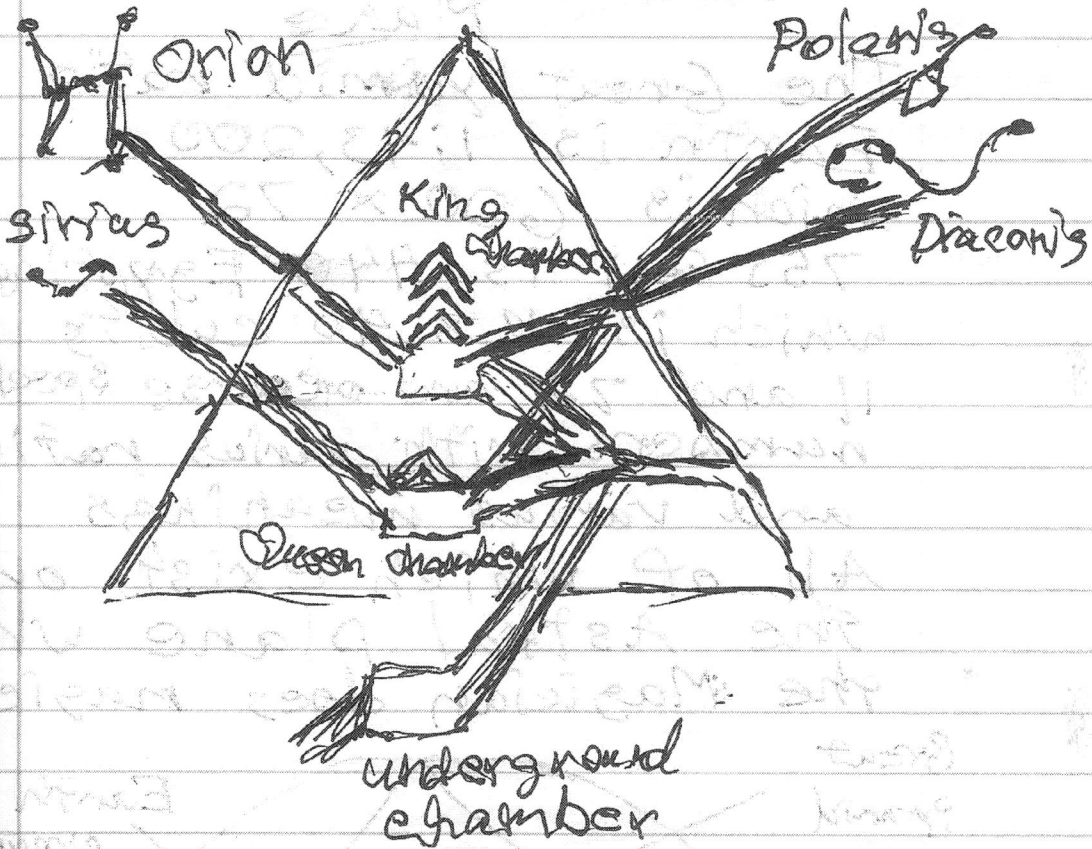

Orion

Polaris

Sirius

King Chamber

Draconis

Queen chamber

underground chamber

The Duat is the Astral Plane where Osirus Ascends to in the celestial sky/sphere of the procession with the Milky way.

Christian J. Bullock

Celestial Numbers on the Astral Plane

The Great Pyramid has a ratio to Earth of 1:43,200 which is 600 mulitplied by 72. 755 feet, which is the perimeter, is 440 Egyptian Cubits which is 11 muliplied by 40 Cubits. Once again there are special numbers that make this possible with 11 and 72 as well as the permutation number of 432,000. All of which exists or are used on the Astral Plane where the Magician performs Magick. There are numerious calculations which make Pyramids special and we will go into depth with some more of them later. It should be noted at this point that The Great Pyramid is 2Pi the Earth's circumference and The Maya Pyramid of the Sun at Teotihuacan is 4Pi the Earth's circumference.

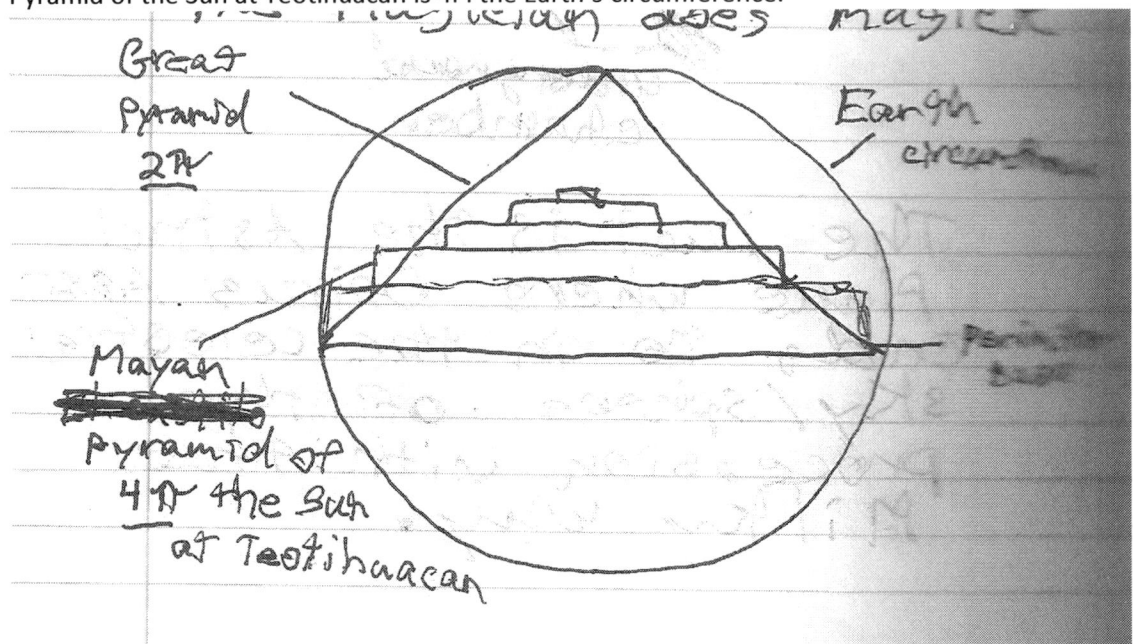

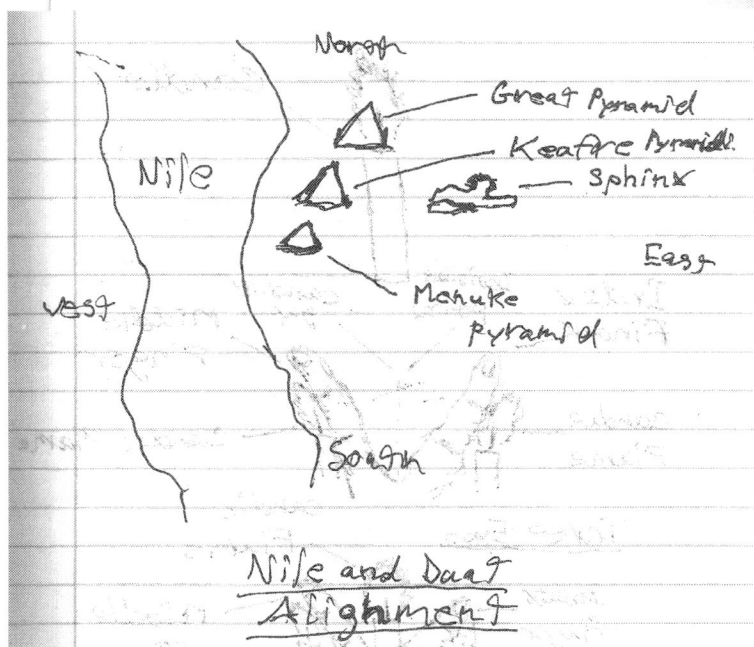

Christian J. Bullock

Binocular Vision

The Human Eye is set for specific vision and this vision is called binocular vision. This is were the pair of eyes are used to focus on a specific point in front of the body. Each eye's vision crosses paths to create an image in the brain that can judge depth and distance of objects. There is however a breakdown of this vision when the view of both eyes is crossed. This creates an illusion of a space between the object in both eyes. This leads into extra sensory vision where a being with three eyes would be able to see the object clearly even with the other eyes crossed. This is a good example of what can be seen by the eye and what can't be seen. When speaking of other dimensions and multi-dimensional beings the example of the vision test is the best way to describe seeing the unseen. The vision test can be done with a candle where the Magician stares at it and then crosses his vision with two of his fingers. This creates a Magical gap where there is a space between what looks like two candles. This is where the Human brain cannot process the image correctly but the Magician knows that there is only one candle. This slip in vision therefore means that the Human eye is limited in vision and there are spaces where Human sight fails. It also shows that the Magician's portal or Third eye may be opened to extra sensory vision. The three eyed Retwo have better vision than a normal Human's. There are ways for the Magician's vision to get better and this is through psychic meditation/ritual with the Third Eye.

The vision test is continued onto the next page->

Christian J. Bullock

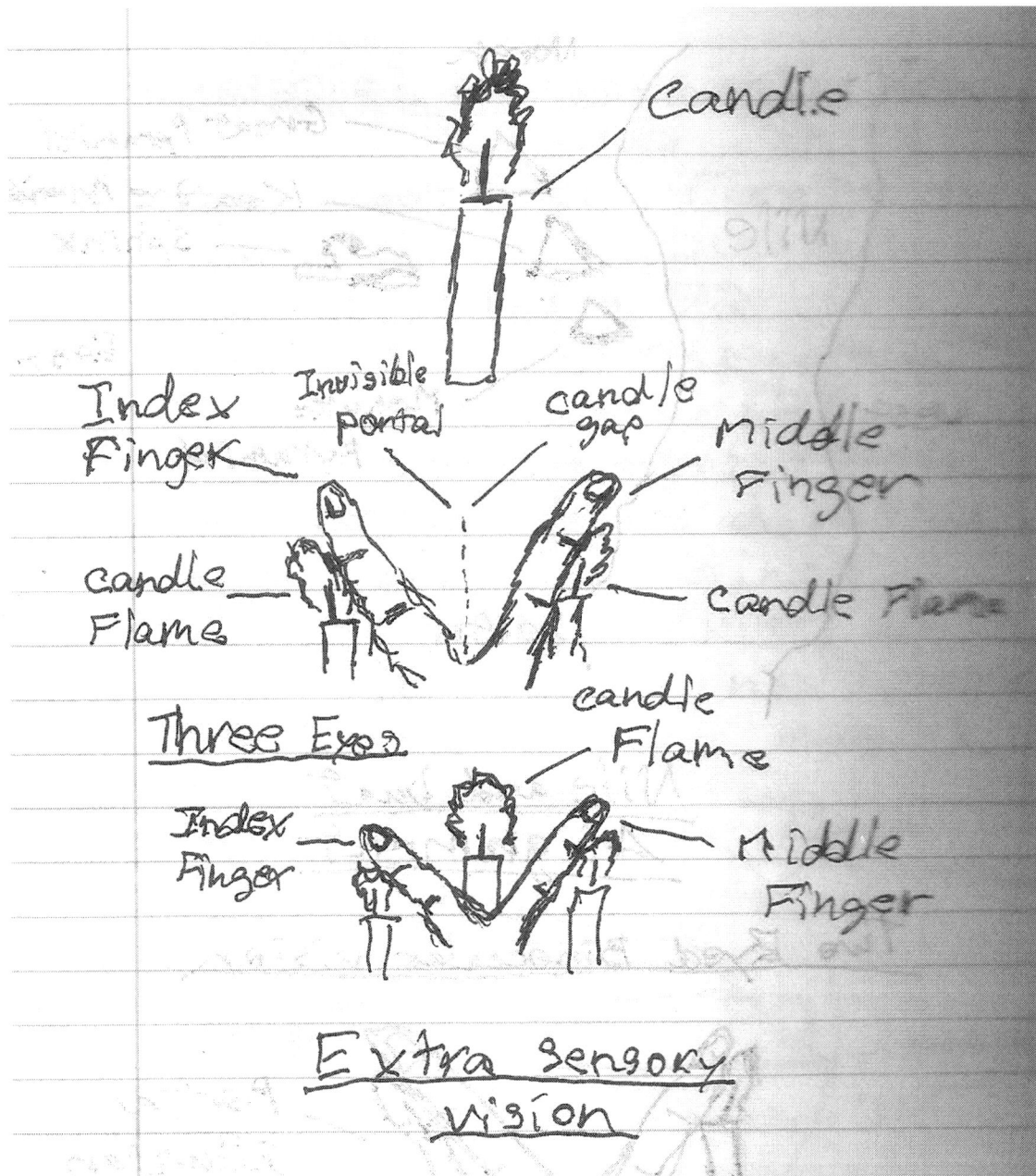

candle

Index Finger

Invisible portal

candle gap

Middle Finger

candle Flame

Candle Flame

Three Eyes

candle Flame

Index Finger

Middle Finger

Extra sensory vision

The Eye of Ra and The Spitting Asp

Christian J. Bullock

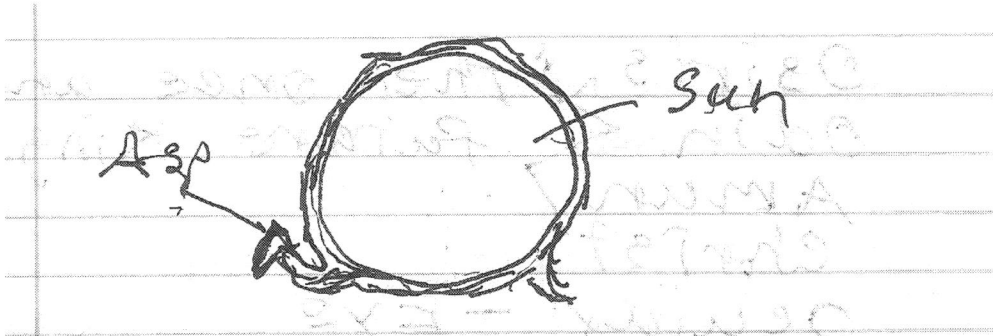

The Sun is the representation of Re (Ra) the Sun God. An Asp snake circles the Sun Ra. Specifically, this is the Artifact of Amon Ra. This is the Charm of Making for Amon Ra. Many Egyptian Gods are depicted with this Asp Sun which is a key to their super natural powers.

Enki Code
Osiris – Egyptian God of Pharaohs
Siris – Dog Star System
Isis – Egyptian Mother Goddess
Iris – an Eye, the part below the covering of the cornea
Os-iris – Egyptian God depicted as an Eye
Osiris   >
Odin   > "The once and future King"
Amun   >
Christ   >
Ocular – Eye
Monocular – Eye piece
Binocular – two Eye pieces
Occult – Magick of Singularity
Oc-cult – Eye Cult
Telephone
Tele-phone
Tele-vision
Tele-communication
Tele-path
Telepathic communication
Tele - over a distance
Tele-Ptah
Summary – a quick review
Sum-m-ary – spoken twice
Sumer-ary – Babel speak
Sumer – Babylonia

The Mayan Duat of Teotihuacan

Christian J. Bullock

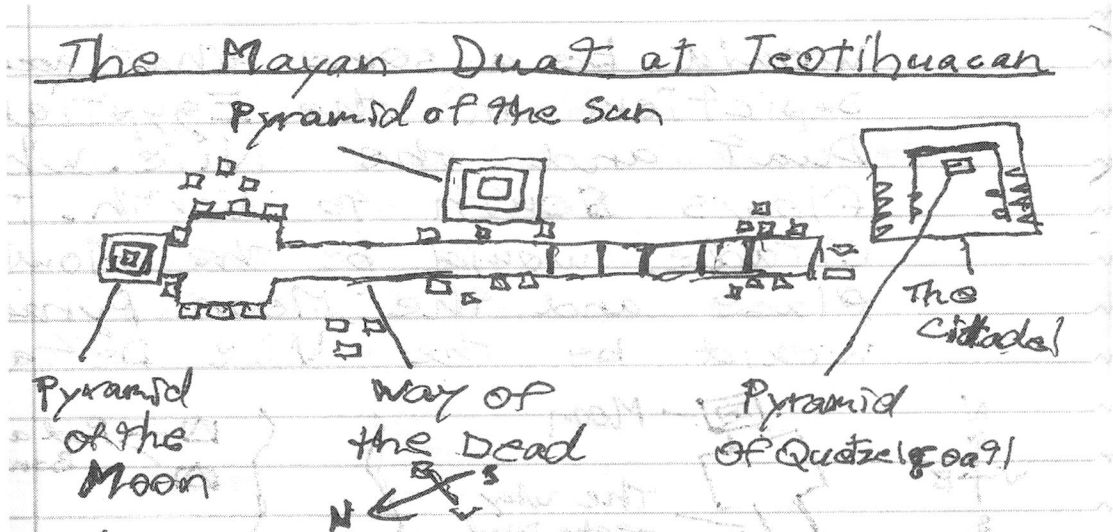

The Way of the Dead was filled with water symbolizing the Milky Way or Duat. The temples and Pyraminds at Teotihuacan are a mirror representation of the celestial sky. The dwelling place of the Mayan Gods, the Way of the Dead. It was made for initiates to follow, the Jaguar Priests. The Pyramid of the Moon is slightly off set to the northeast. When filled with water the Way of the Dead would be a some what accurate depiction of the Egyptian Duat and the Nile river, which flows south to north. The citadel would be the flowing place and the Moon Pyramid would be the Nile delta.

The two Duats are also aligned with Orion's Belt, even at Teotihuacan.

Enki Code
Nut – Egyptian Goddess
Bolts – Egyptian cloth symbol
"It will be very low key"

Christian J. Bullock

"Music in the key of"
"That's the nuts and bolts of it"
"All for one and one for all"

Symbology of the Dragon Elements

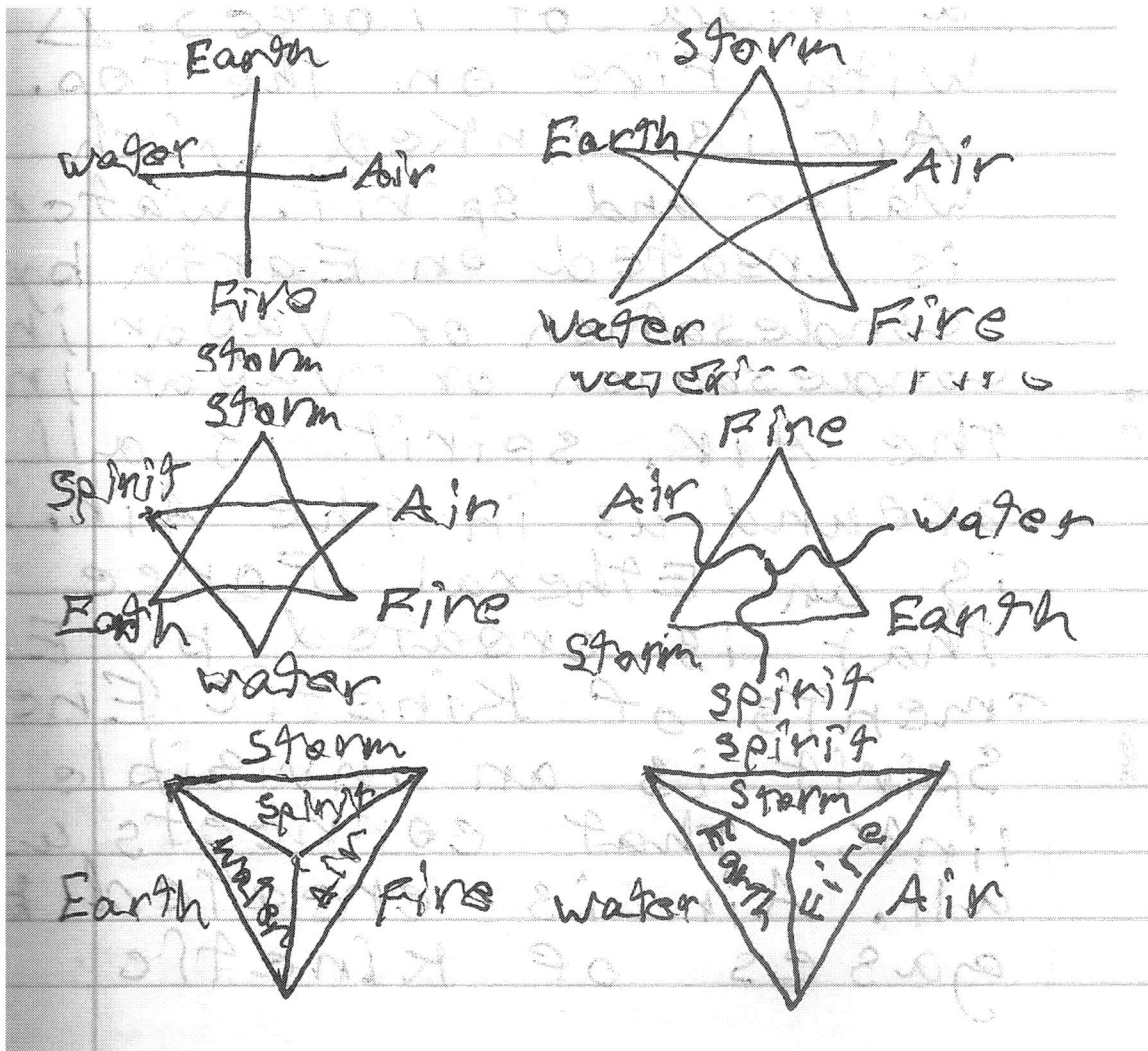

Here are the Symbols used for Singularity Magick. They are arranged in various ways for various purposes in Magick. The Earth Cross is the first most basic arrangment of elements, this is a good symbol to use for Earthy type Magick but it can also be used for powerful circle casting. The Pentagram is the second most basic arrangment of elements for Magick. This is a powerful Symbol that has been used throughout history. In this Pentagram Storm is substituted for the element Spirit. This arrangment has a powerful connection with the celestial beings of the Planets and it is great for working Planetary Magick. Both the Earth Cross and Pentagram have protective properties. The Six Pointed Star has all six elements and has an important Magical connection to the spirit realm. The other three Symbol arrangements are modifications of the triangle, which stands for fire, and the Dragon's Eye, which is a Mystical Symbol. Earth, fire, and storm are linked. As are air, water, and spirit. Fire is created on Earth by lightning. Fire exists in the Earth by volcanos. Volcanos create lightning storms. These Dragon elements create a triad of forces, with fire being on the top of the triangle. Air, water, and spirit are another linked triad of forces. Water is created on Earth by condesation or vapor in the air. Spirit is all around us and inside of us in the air. It is an etheral force that is created by elements. Spirit is an invisable link that connects us all. Air is created by gases of kinetic energy. Air, water, and spirit are another triad of Dragon elements, with water being below or an upsidedown triangle. These two triads bind the universe in both Dragon Magick and Singularity Magick. These two triads form a powerful Charm of Making for the Magician to use.

Enki Code
Element
El-e-ment
El – God
God Elements

The Table of Dragon Planetary Triads

These triads are used in Dragon Magick but they are also of use to the Singularity Magician.

Dragon Planetary Triads

Water		Air	
☽	Moon	☿	Mercury
♀	Venus	♃	Jupiter
♆	Neptune	♅	Uranus

Fire		Earth/storm	
☉	Sun	♄	Saturn
♂	Mars	♇	Pluto
⚶	Vesta	⚳	Ceres

Earth		Storm	
♄	Saturn	♄	Saturn
♇	Pluto	⚳	Ceres
⚳	Ceres	⚶	Vesta

Storm		Meteor/Asteroid	
♄	Saturn	⚴	Pallas
⚳	Ceres	⚵	Juno
⚷	Chiron	⚳	Ceres or ⚶

Mythos		Spirit		Moon Beam	
♃	Jupiter	♇	Pluto	☽	Moon
♄	Saturn	⚳	Ceres	☊	North
♅	Uranus	⚶	Vesta	☋	South

Moon Phases Triads

☽ First Quarter   Yen - Iamar
○ Full Moon   Memezah
☾ Third Quarter   Unteekah

● New Moon   Jyn - Kuaan
☽ First Quarter   Yen - Iamar
○ Full Moon   Memezah

☾ Third Quarter   Unteekah
● New Moon   Jyn - Kuaan
☽ First Quarter   Yen - Iamar

○ Full Moon   Memezah
☾ Third Quarter   Unteekah
● New Moon   Jyn - Kuaan

Eclipses

◉ Full Moon   Memezah

Each Moon phase has a Dragon associated with it and each of the different phases form triads. The Celestial Spirits are important for various rituals and Magical spells.

Christian J. Bullock

The Dragon Tarot Court Cards

For Tarot Card Magick I used the Dragon Tarot which is an exceptional Tarot Card set. I also use the Celtic Dragon Tarot Card set which is also a good Tarot set. For these next Magical spell arrangments any Tarot set will do but the Celtic Dragon Tarot set will be drastically different. Use an open mind and be creative when using the Tarot for spells.

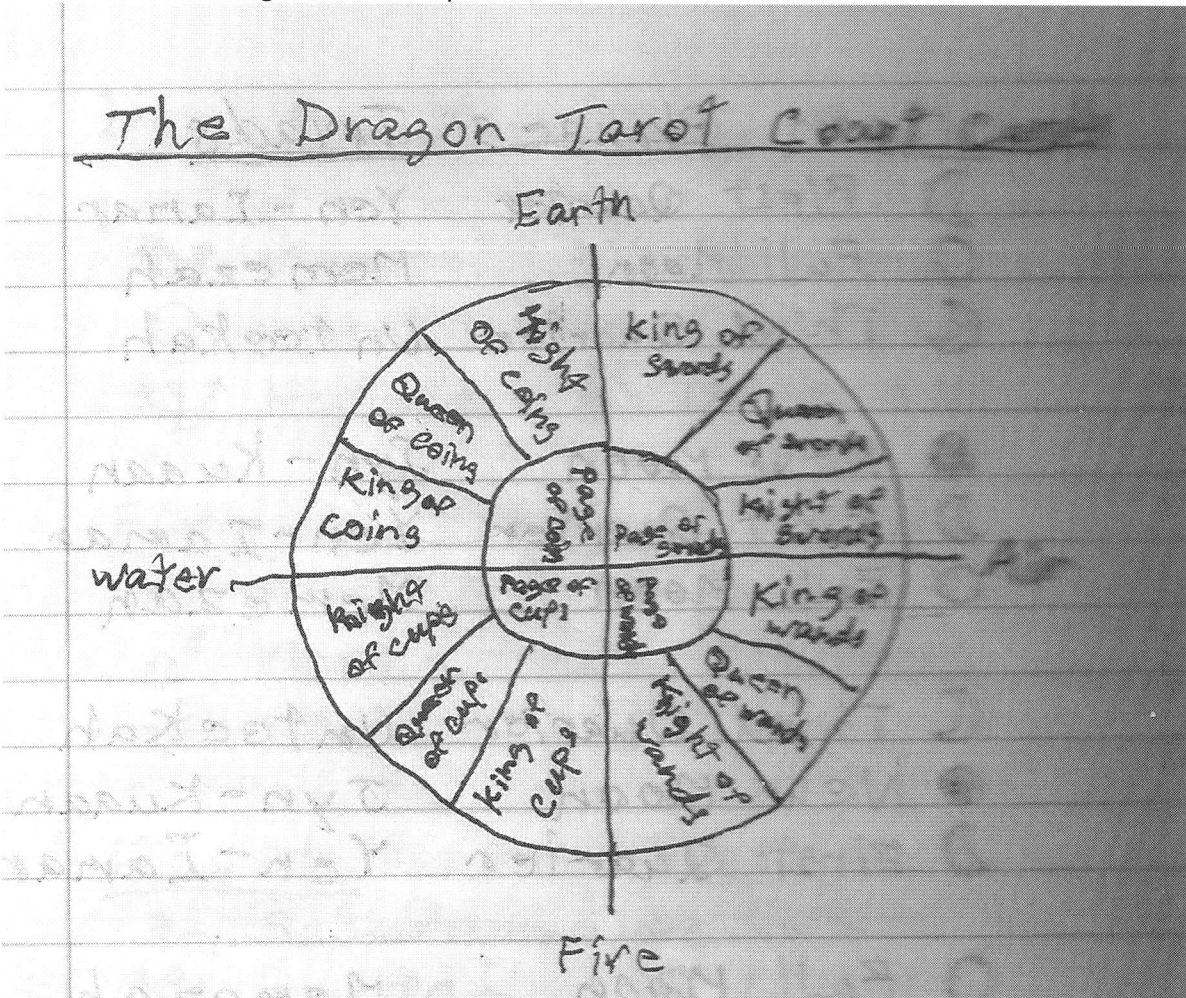

The Dragon Tarot Court Cards

Earth

King of Swords
Queen of Swords
Knight of Swords
Page of Swords
Air
King of Wands
Queen of Wands
Knight of Wands
Fire
King of Cups
Queen of Cups
Knight of Cups
Page of Cups
Water
King of Coins
Queen of Coins
Knight of Coins
Page of Coins

Each court is broken down into triads of the elements that they represent. Pages are in the center representing each quarter of the elements. Calling on each of the courts during meditation lets the Magician call up and use the corresponding element of earth, air, fire, and water.

Christian J. Bullock

The Celtic Dragon Tarot court

Earth

Air

Water

Fire

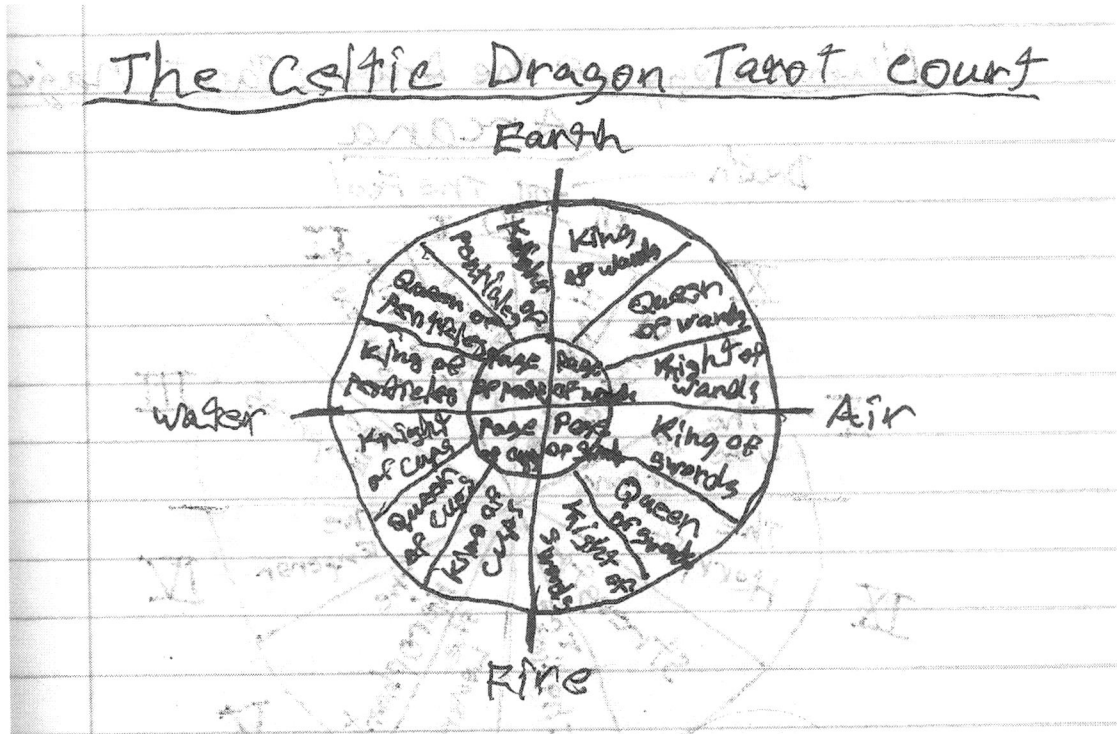

Each court is the same as the Dragon Tarot with the exception that swords are linked with fire and wands are linked with air. The Magician summons the Elementals with them.

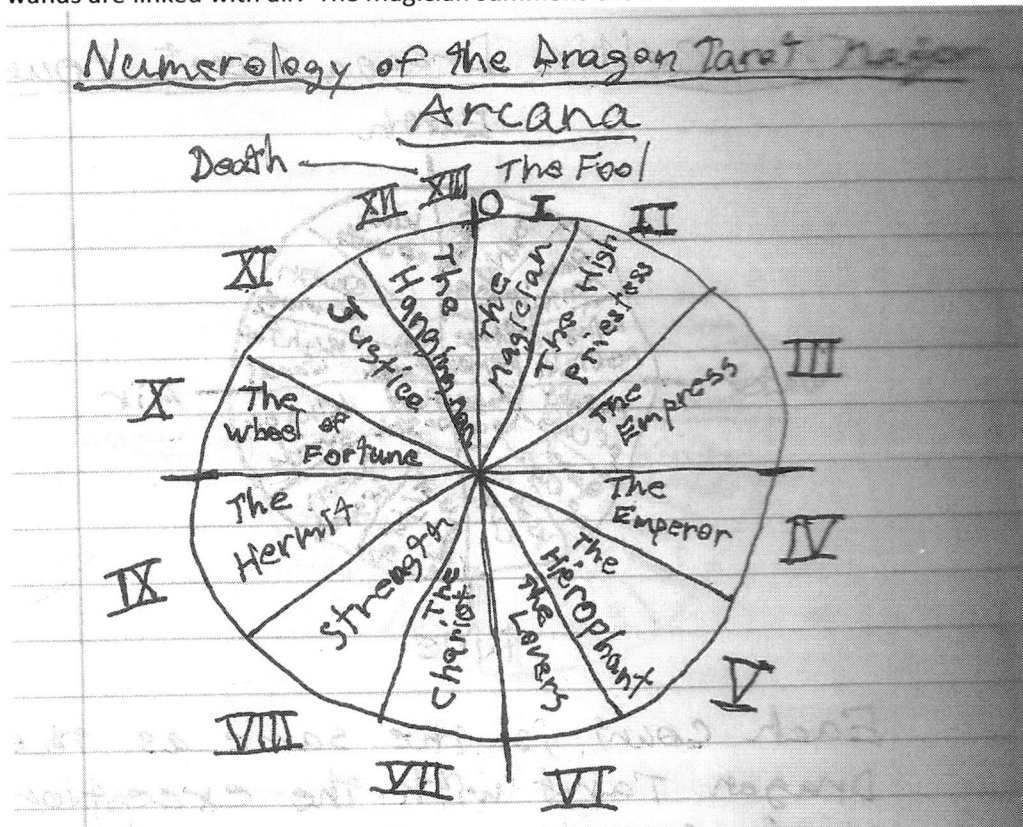

Numerology of the Dragon Tarot Major Arcana

Death — The Fool

Christian J. Bullock

This is based on the Numerology of Procession. 0 starts it as The Fool and then 1 is the Magician. 10 as the Wheel of Fortune. 12 as The Hanging Dragon, and 13 as Death for the 13th Zodiac. Each triad matches up based on various degrees of Procession of the Zodiac.

Zodiac of the Dragon Tarot
Procession

Each card can be arranged in the Zodiac either by month or more powerfully by Procession. The Nodes of the Moon of the 13th Zodiac is represented by Cronus, 21 The World. Notice that the Devil is listed as Capricorn and The Star is listed as Aquarius.

Christian J. Bullock

The 12 Signs of The Zodiac is Also Imprinted on Man

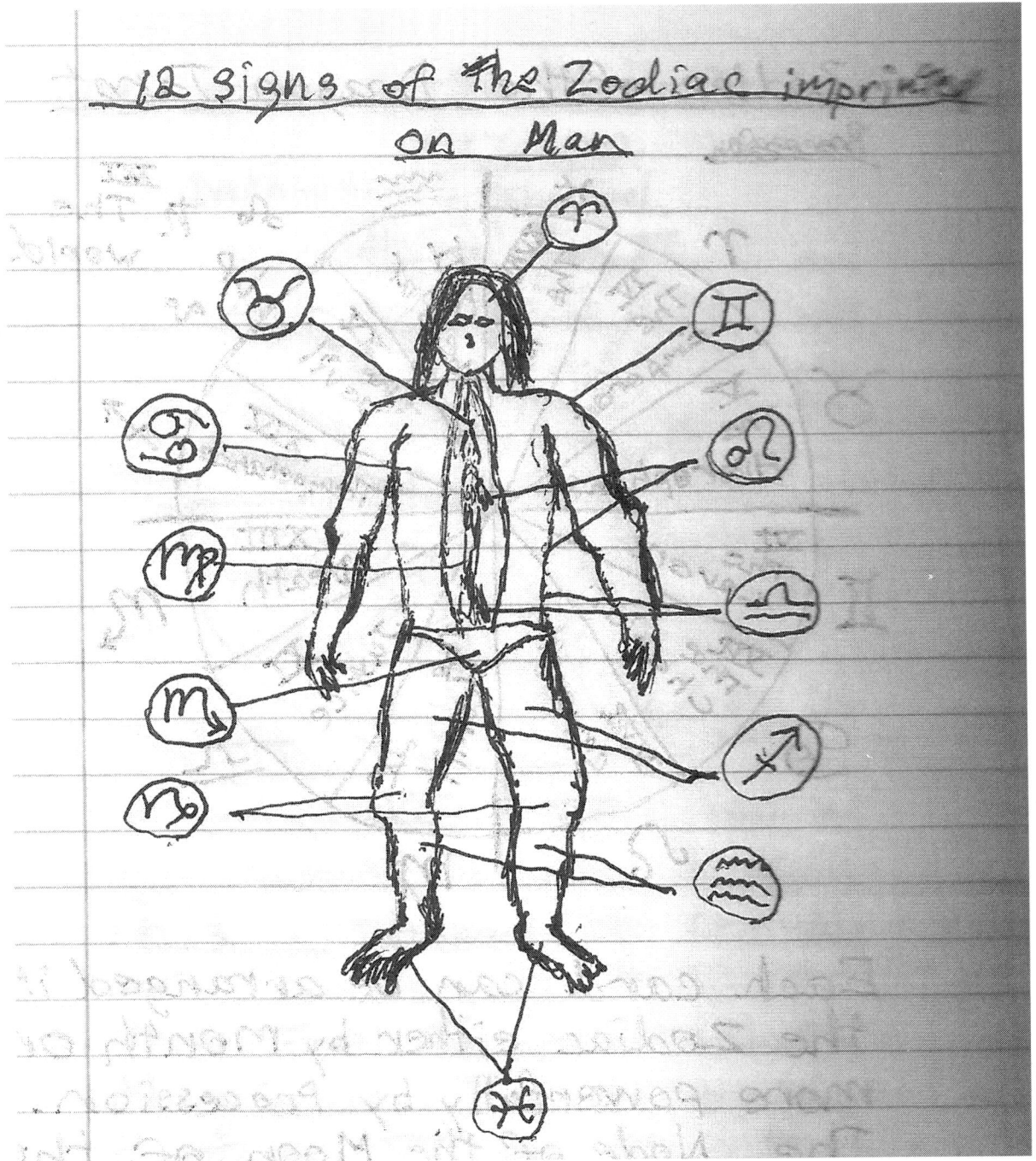

Enki Code
"A key example of this"
"This contains a Master key"
MasterLock

Christian J. Bullock

The Time Traveller Imprinted With The Zodiac on The Choa Mool

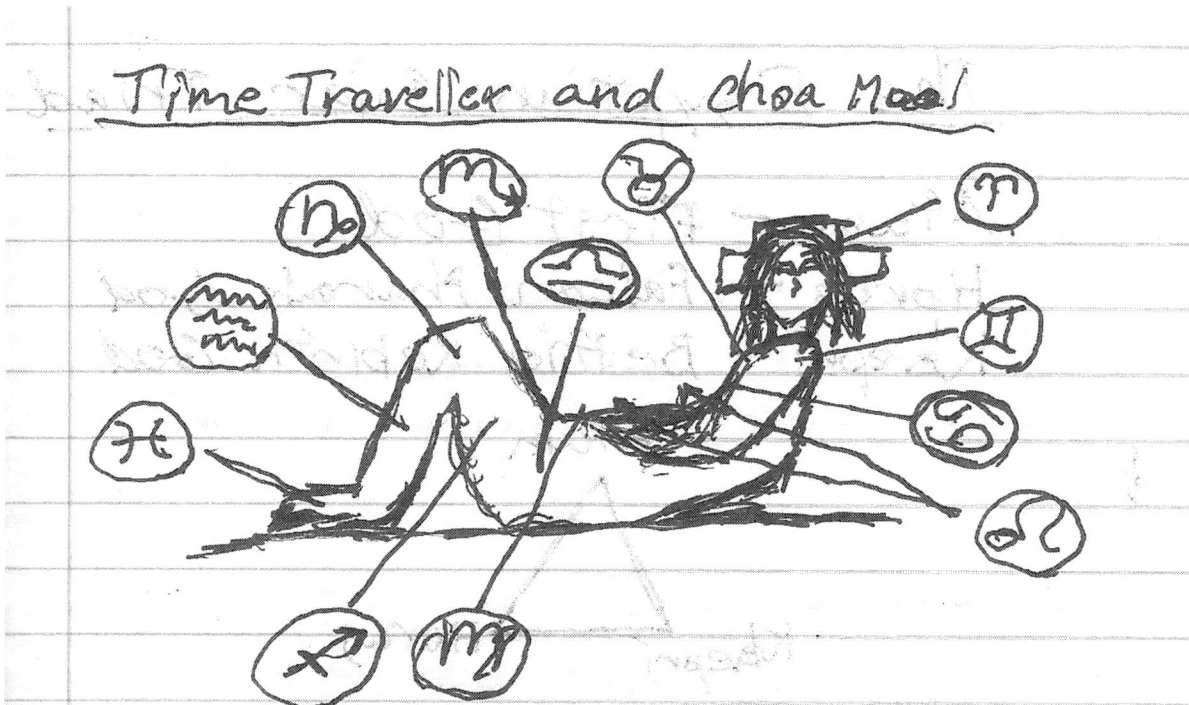

During the first time travel and time travelling through the Zodiac, these 12 Zodiac signs are tied to the Time Traveller. Sort of imprinted upon their body. When they move their position so too does the Astrology alignments. Choa Mool is a represented as this where Mool stands for the Sumerian MUL which means constellation. Notice Aries as the head, Leo as the heart or the midriff. Capricorn as the knees, and Pieces as the feet. Also Gemini is depicted as the shoulders.

The Egyptian Solar Triad

136

Christian J. Bullock

The Four Egyptian Phases of Light

Sunrise – Khepri (The Reborn Light)
From 6 am to 12 pm
This is the birth of the Sun from the east. "Principle of Metamorphosis"
Midday – Horus (The Ascended Light)
From 12 pm to 6 pm
The Sun rises to its highest point in the sky. "Principle of Ascension"
Dusk – Ra (The Circulated Light)
From 6 pm to 12 am
The setting Sun on the horizon. "Principle of Cirulation"
Midnight – Atum (The Unified Light)
From 12 am to 6 am
The Sun's journey through to deepest regions of the universe, battling nefarious forces of Darkness in order to be reborn again. "Principle of Unity"

Ptah – The source of creative activity in the creative triad. He transmits the individual sacred fire which comes into existance as a body with the Solar Triad. He represents "The Principle of Animation".
Ptah is the Animator of the universe who can animate the material and natural worlds. He animates on every level of creation, even the Gods. Ptah is allencompassing action in the Multiverse. The Egyptian God Ptah is a powerful God to work with in Magick. He is the father of Ra and the first with the title of Amon, as we shall see later in the book he has his roots in Sumer.

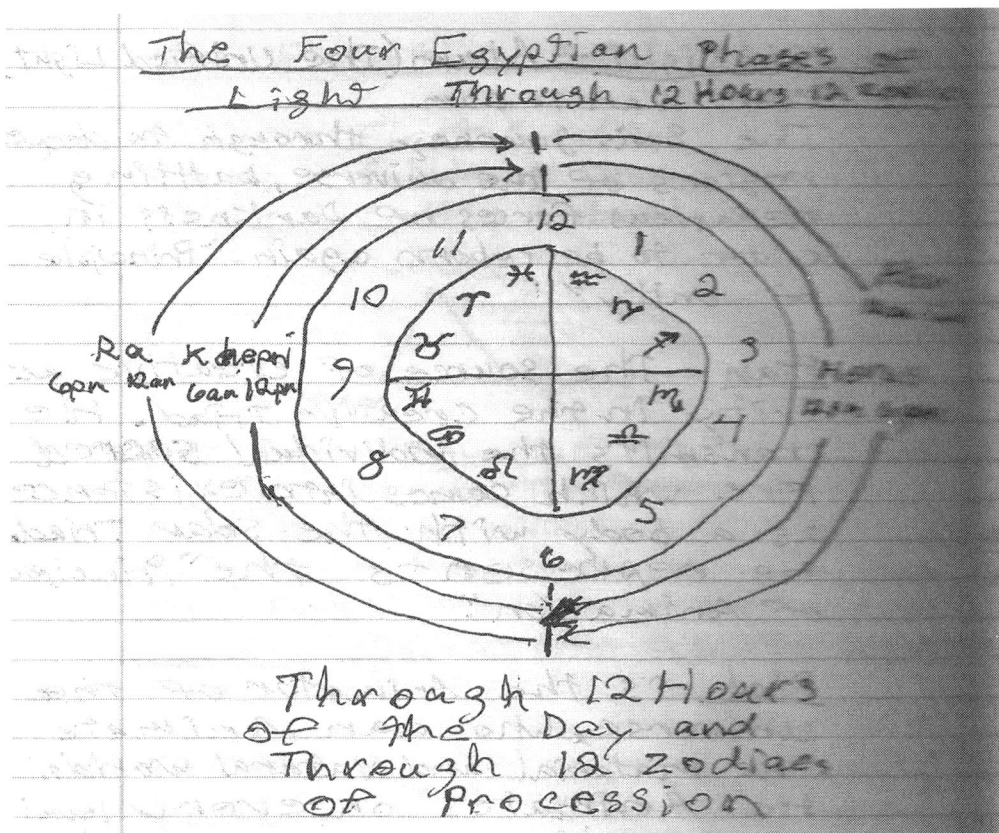

The Four Phases of Light Continued

The Four Egyptian Phases of Light Doubled and Divided Into Quarters of Procession

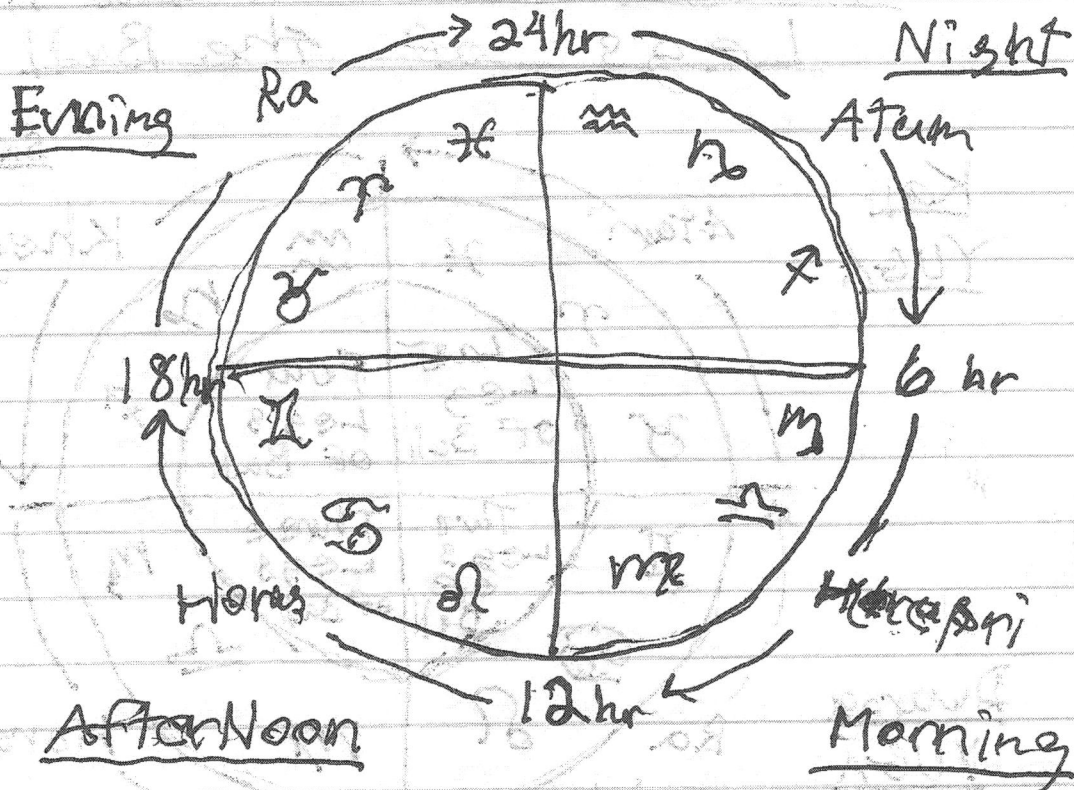

24hr

Evening   Ra   Night

Atum

18hr

6 hr

Horas

AfterNoon   Morning

12hr

The Gods that
Rule the Sun's
cycle of Rising and
setting
of 24 Hours in a Day

Christian J. Bullock

The Four Phases of Processional Code For The Dawn and Dusk of The Ancient Civilization

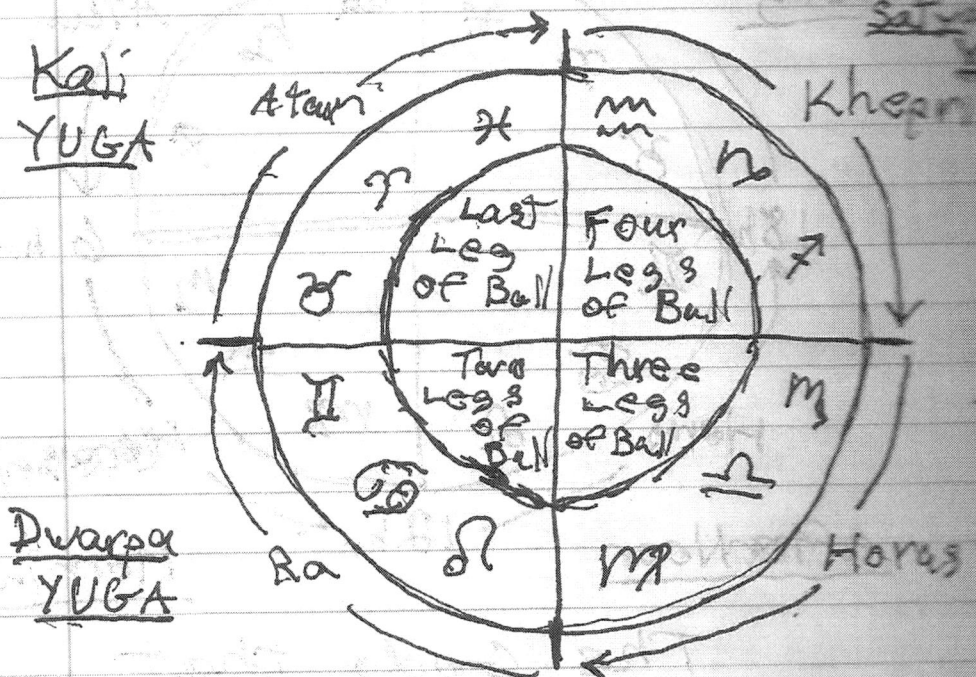

More on the God Ptah

Ptah's secpter reflects his electromagnetism. Ptah binds the forces of Electricity, the Spirit, and Magnetism of Matter. Ptah has ties to the Dragon Element Storm. Ptah converts Energy into Matter and Matter into Energy. He is associated with Electromagnetic devices. He is also one of the first Gods to invent the armor, swords, and shields for the warring Gods. He is associated with metalugy and the maker of the tools of the Black Smith. He also established sacred precincts.

Enki Code
Arcana
Arc-ana
Arc – one arc or degree of a sphere
Arcane – means mystery

Christian J. Bullock

Book Three: The Silver Dragon

Christian J. Bullock

This book will cover the Gods of Egypt, Greece, Sumer, as well as the Sumerian Calendar and the Ancient Civilization. It will also cover Enki Code roots that go far back to Sumer and far ahead to the future Singularity Computer.

The Gods of Egypt and Their Specific Talents

From Atum comes Shu and Tefnut. Shu and Tefnut compliment each other; with breath and circulation. They are depicted as a mated pair of Lions, each facing the opposite direction with the horizon in the middle.

Shu is the "Principle of Inhalation". Where as Tefnut is referred to as cosmic moisture or dew, her name is Tef dirrived from "to moisten". Tefnut is the "Principle of Diffusion". The Goddess Tefnut circulates the breath of the God Shu.

The Goddess Nut is depicted as the sky with an outstretched body over the Earth, covered with Stars. This is another example of Singularity Magick, where a Singularity Room is set up with Stars on the ceiling. These Stars represent souls of the Earth returning to the sky, their cosmic mother. Nut houses both Stars and Planets. Nut is shown as or thought of as being held up in the sky by her father Shu. Nut is the "Principle of Augmentation". The God Geb on the other hand is the Egyptian Earth God and he is the "Principle of Creation".

The Twin Wadjet is the Cobra Crown depicted as worn by the Pharaohs. It is an Artifact that holds special powers and is one of the many keys that the Gods left Man.

The Secret Universe and The Lava Pits of a Dark Dimension

There are many Dark Dimensions of Earth in the Motion Capture Universe. One dimension in particular is a dangerous wasteland and it intersects the Gamer Dimension, almost like an extension of the Game to the point of oblivion. The dimension is invisable but a Magician may experience it through near death experiences. The most common experience is when in an Ambulance the ride becomes extremely bumpy and the veils of the world are lifted. A cloud of fog covers the outside windows and the ground looks charred. The Earth looks lifeless but there are headlights of cars passing by the devestation unnoticed. This experience is bizarre but it shows a crossing over of the Spirit into the dimension of "The Valley of Death". This Valley of Death can be best explained in the following paragraphs:
In a far away future that goes excedingly far beyond any of the other futures mentioned so far in the book. The Game becomes diluted and Cylon Humans fight for the past, a past where only the Singularity Computer rules. The Earth has changed becoming a barren wasteland of lava pits, fire, and brimstone. The Future Game is set on replay and the world time warp can suck people into this lava pit Dark Dimension of Earth. This realm has the illusion of being real, set in the past or present. The Cylon

Christian J. Bullock

Humans play in the lava pits believing in this illusion of Earth, more likely they were put into this substitution of The Emerald Dream. In this dimension the Singularity Computer is on overdrive and is like a broken record where only death remains of the Earth.

This new kind of Emerald Dream exists with all natural resources exhausted and the Cronus of the North Pole is taken over by a new/old Alien Entity for the sake of ruling the Milky Way Galaxy. His ultimate goal is to follow or backtrack the other Humans/Gods who left the Milky Way for the Andromeda Galaxy. The Cylon Humans are trapped on Earth in the Valley of Death constantly fighting for control of whats left. Basically it's a hell dimension.

Time Travel, Extremities, and The Left Hand

When time travelling the body will tingle or feel different. If an extremity is slightly outside the Singularity Room it will feel actions in the universe or time travel jumps. Using a left hand that was outside the Singularity during a time jump, the left hand will get painful feelings. The Magician may follow these feelings for necessary time jumps and such. Following these impulses is dangerous and a Magician may seek to avoid them. Eventually the impulses will disapate and the Magician's hand will go back to normal.

Time Travel and The Gods That Protect The Magician

Ritual workings with God or the Gods helps the Magician no longer fear God in his awesome form. Once well initiated and understanding of the Cronus Stone, the Magician is able to thwart out negativity that works against the Magician. The Magician must make a special connection with God in order to have their protection from negative entities. Time travelling and journeying to the underworld is a dangerous thing. The initiated Magician must know what God is protecting them. For the Dragon Magician knowing your Dragons is vitally important. Magical working with them will aid in the Mystic Journey through time and dimensions. For the Singularity Magician knowing your Spirit allies, animals, and Elementals before time travelling.

Janus

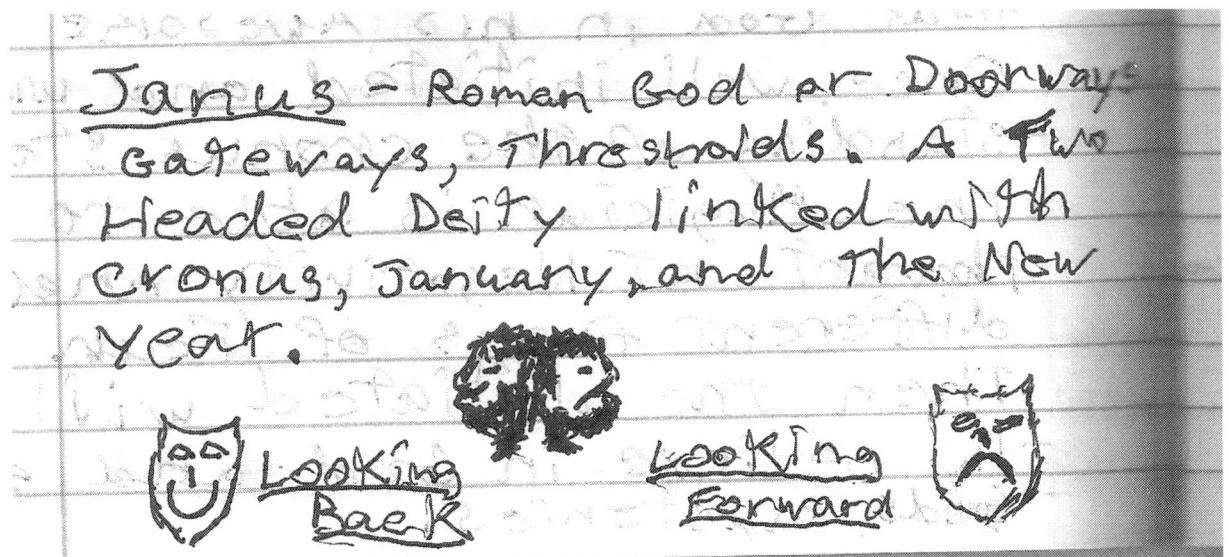

Janus - Roman God or Doorways, Gateways, Thresholds. A Two Headed Deity linked with Cronus, January, and The New Year.

Looking Back

Looking Forward

Egyptian 12 Zodiac

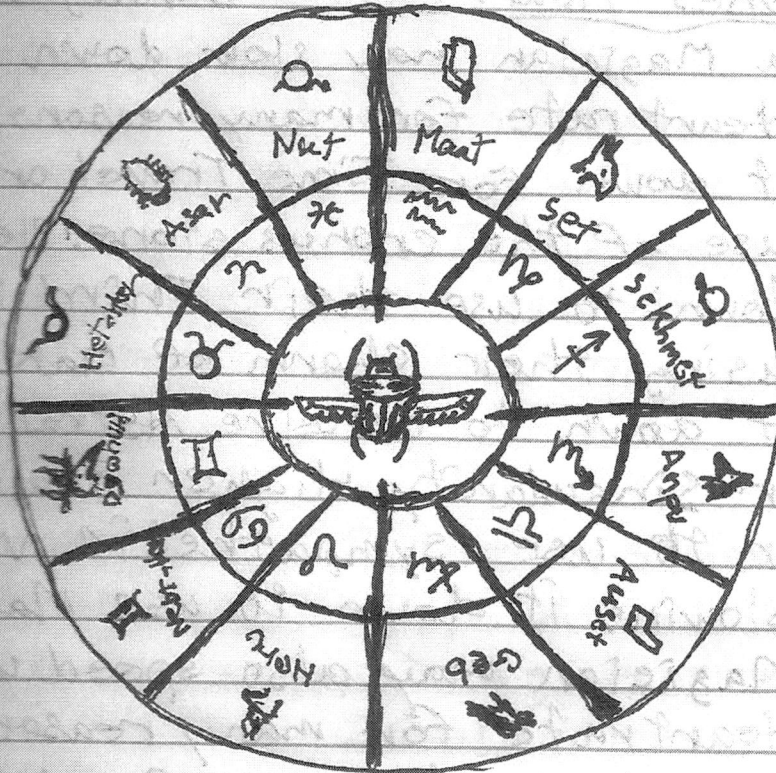

Egyptian 12 Zodiac of Later Periods

Asar — is Osiris
Auset — is Isis
Heru — is Horus
Anpu — is Anubis
Het-Her — is Hathor
Djehuti — is Thoth

Nebt-Her — is Nepthys
Sekhmet — is Sakhmis
Sekhmet — Daughter of Ra
Sekhmet — Healer and
    Physician

This Zodiac is based on the Sun
Ra's movement Through the zodiac

Christian J. Bullock

The Slowing Down and Speeding up of Ones Heartrate

During meditation a Magician may slow down their heartrate for various reasons. Slowing it down for time travel or for the use of the Cronus Stone. Slowing it down to use their Third Eye or using their Charm of Making. Slowing it down to achieve Astral Projection or Singularity higher brain functions. As well as use for sympathetic vibrations or to use Magick. This technique is very useful for the Magician to learn but it takes a lot of practice and mental focus. During long time travels going into a meditative state is advantageous in so many ways. This type of meditation is used in Singularity Magick to shape the world around us. Mind Magick is the ultimate goal of any initiated Magician, where the use of their Charm of Making becomes so powerful that the Magician can perform spells in their mind without even uttering a word. A Mayan Temple is used, or what is called a Mind Temple, this is the sacred space in the mind where Magick begins before ritual takes place. It is a key to unlocking Magical powers of the Third Eye and growing your Charm of Making abilities. A Magician may also speed up their heartrate for many reasons. To use in healing or for Astral/Metaphysical battles. Speeding it up for metamorphosis or to align with daily Solar sympathetic vibrations. To get a boost of energy or to speed up one's metabolism. These various uses aid the Magician in spiritual quests.

Enki Code
Mayan Temple	A Temple – where ritual is performed
Mind Temple	One's Temple – the upper part of one's forehead
Kabbalah	
Ka-bal-ah	
Ka – the Double, the Metaphysical vessal, or the Guardian of the vessal	
Ba – the Astral Body or Astral vessal, Spirit leaves for the Astral Plane, or visiting Spirit	

Alphabets

22 is a special number in Magick and this is mostly due to the Alphabets that have 22 letters, especially since the Ancient Civilization used the number 22 in their Magick Scripts. As mentioned before there are many stories of the Gods giving Man writing. Also there was once one spoken language when the Ancient Tower of Babel was built. There are 22 letters in the Hebrew Alphabet. As well as 22 letters in Dragon Script. There are also 22 letters in the Early Greek Alphabet and 22 in the Canonite Phoenician Alphabets. There are also 22 Tarot cards of the Major Arcana with the 22 Hebrew letters aligning with this Major Arcana arrangement. The Alphabets of Ancient Civilizations is very important to the Magician. They are used to contact the Spirits of the Dead as well as Astral Spirits. They can be used in a way to be a conduit to Secret Orders or Secret Societies. They are also used for past life reccesion and for use with one's Double. Lastly they are used in Magick in each of the various Magical systems. The Singularity Magician must familiarize themselves with each of the Alphabets that are shown at the end of this book. They each are used for Spirit contact and are used to build up relations with the Spirit world.

Enki Code
Alpha-bet	EN.SI – "Righteous Ruler" Sumer Ruler Title
Alpha-bit	Ensiferum – "Sword Bearer" Latin Root
Apha-bit – of a high bit	
Apha-bit – a letter computer code	

Christian J. Bullock

During an early Age of Babylon/Sumer the rulers each adopted the name of EN.SI. The Ensi's ruled during great technological and civilized advancements. They were rulers that spread the knowledge of the Gods. Akkadian Language was spread after Sumer and this language has passed down bits and pieces to all languages of Europe including Latin.

Enki Code
"Following it to the letter of the code"
"of a higher degree"
"of a cornerstone"
"of a founder"
"of a keystone"
"of a higher key"

The Crook and The Flail

These are the symbols of Kingship, Pharaoh, and Cronus. They are symbols of the domestication of plants and animals. They are used for harvesting the crop and kulling the flock or herd. These are the symbols of civilization and of kingdoms. They are tools that produce food for the masses. They are the technology that was developed by early man and given to them by the Gods. Technology given to them after the Deluge.

Enki Code
"The keys to the city"
"The key to your heart"
"The key to the kingdom"

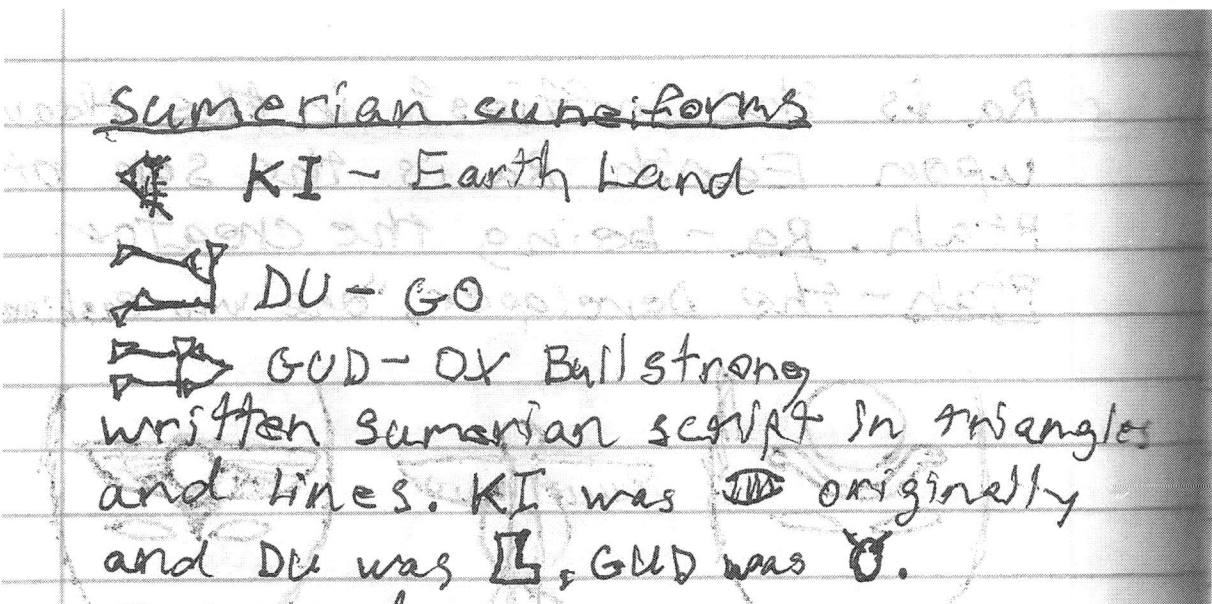

Sumerian cuneiforms
KI ~ Earth Land
DU ~ GO
GUD ~ Ox Bull strong
written Sumerian script in triangles
and lines. KI was [symbol] originally
and DU was [symbol], GUD was [symbol].

Christian J. Bullock

The 13 Zodiacs Imprinted on Man

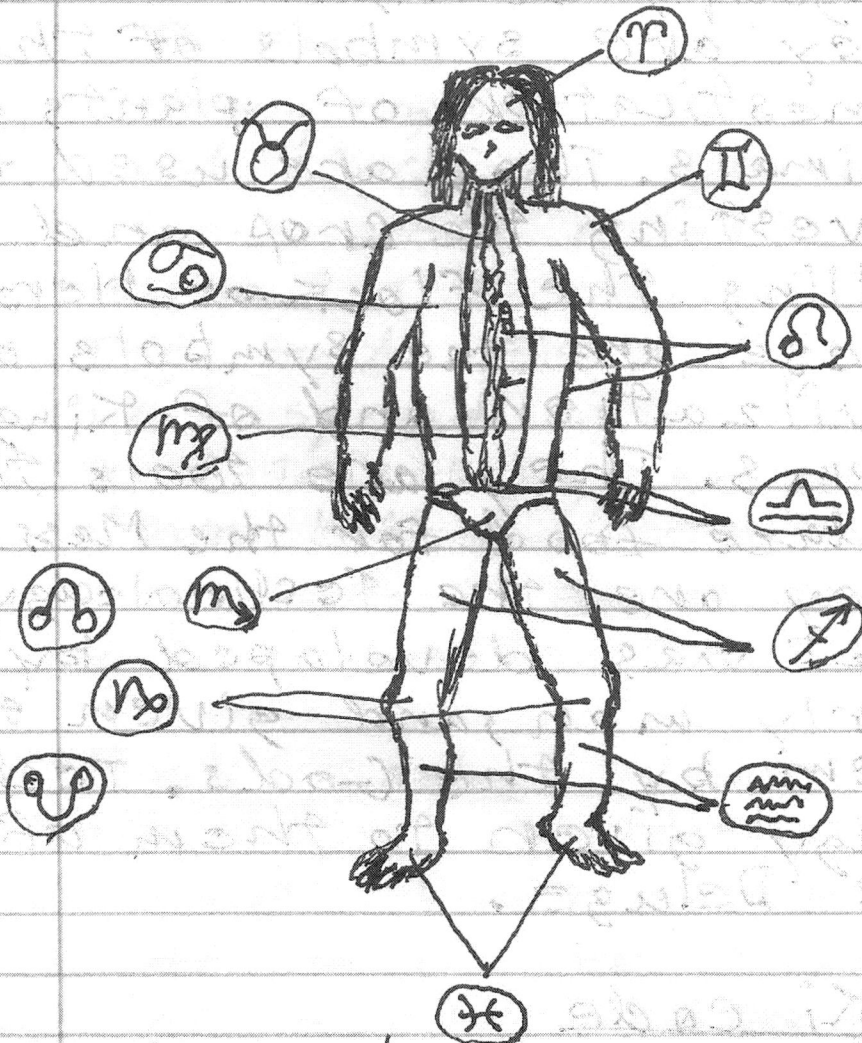

13 signs of The zodiac Imprinted on man

The 13th zodiac is two ha of capricorn or two horns of the Goat. Two Horns of the Aura.

Christian J. Bullock

The Aphabets of Early Man

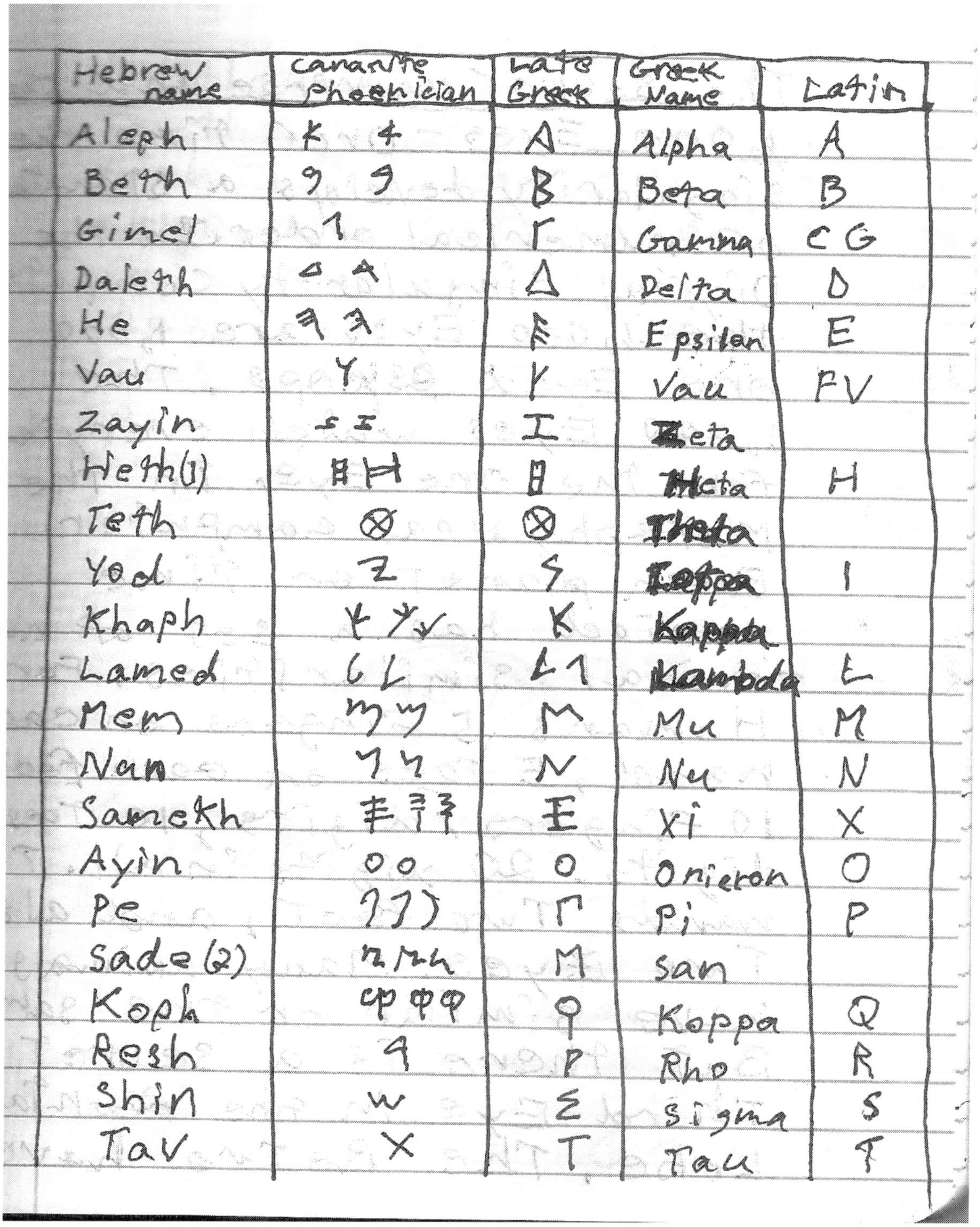

Hebrew name	Cananite phoehician	Late Greek	Greek Name	Latin
Aleph	K 𐤀	A	Alpha	A
Beth	9 9	B	Beta	B
Gimel	1	Γ	Gamma	C G
Daleth	◁ ◁	Δ	Delta	D
He	ヨ ㄱ	Ɛ	Epsilon	E
Vau	Y	Y	Vau	F V
Zayin	ᴤ I	I	~~Zeta~~	
Heth(i)	目 H	目	~~Theta~~	H
Teth	⊗	⊗	~~Theta~~	
Yod	Z	Ƨ	~~Kappa~~	I
Khaph	Ƴ Ɣ	K	~~Kappa~~	
Lamed	6 ∠	∠ �1	~~Lambda~~	L
Mem	ツ ツ	M	Mu	M
Nan	�1 �1	N	Nu	N
Samekh	≢ ㇲ ㇲ	Ξ	Xi	X
Ayin	o o	O	Onieron	O
Pe	�1 �1)	Γ	Pi	P
Sade (2)	ㇴ ㇲ ㇴ	M	san	
Koph	φ φ φ	Q	Koppa	Q
Resh	q	P	Rho	R
Shin	w	Σ	sigma	S
Tav	X	T	Tau	T

Christian J. Bullock

Enki Code and The Alphabet

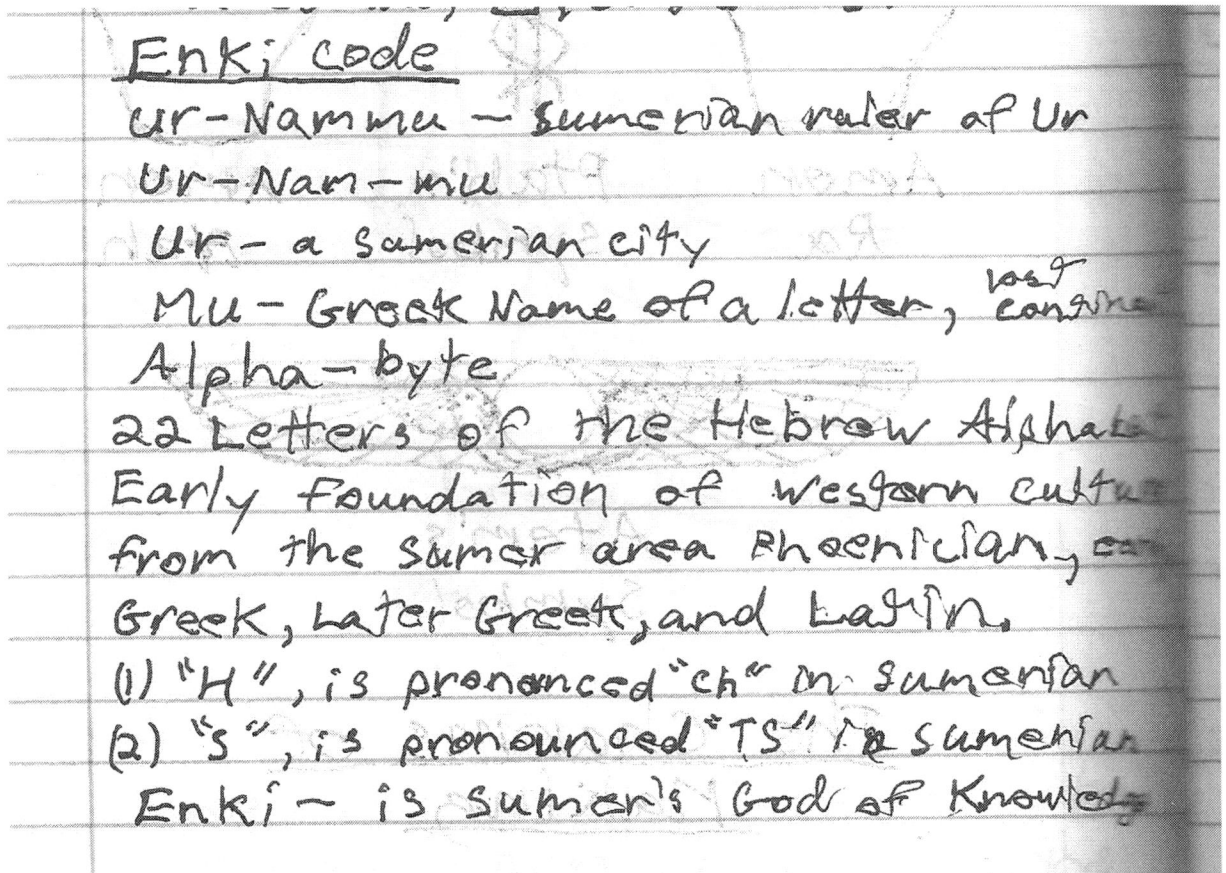

Enki code
ur-Namma — sumerian ruler of Ur
Ur-Nam-mu
Ur - a sumerian city
Mu - Greek Name of a letter, consine
Alpha-byte
22 Letters of the Hebrew Alphab
Early Foundation of western cultu
from the Sumer area Phoenician, ea
Greek, Later Greek, and Latin.
(1) "H", is pronounced "ch" in sumerian
(2) "S", is pronounced "TS" in sumerian
Enki — is sumer's God of Knowled

The Secret Universe and The 1,000 Eyes

Over time the Singularity develops a structure of numerical order. In the Digital Singularity Computer the 1,000 Eyes are 1,000 one Eyed PsyCops. The 1,000 Eyes watch everything for the One Eye. In the Metaphysical Computer each Planet or time period has a set of numerical similarities. For Humans there are 5 fingers on each hand, 5 toes on each foot. Making 10 finger/digits, 10 toe/digits, 20 digits in all. With two hands, two feet, and two eyes. Many animals have similar extremities and this is a numerical constant on Earth. Yet there is a secret Third Eye in the mid to frontal lobe in the brain. The Retwo have developed this Third Eye to the point of special sight but for each plane Retwos gain another Eye or set. Magician's who have knowledge of the Cronus Stone and have pioneered time travel to other planes of existance can have three sets of Eyes or more. The first set is the present, the second set is the past, and the third set is the future. The Magician also has use of the Digital Self if they know knowledge of the Singularity Computer. Over a long advance of time a Singularitian may develop a 1,000 Eyes of the Multiverse and of the greater organism that is the sentient universe/multiverse, or Brahma. Some other organisms may grow or develop more eyes as the Ages pass. The Digital Universe offers a Magician ways of tapping into or looking through a 1,000 Eyes. Singularitians develop their neurons for the Singularity Universe.

Christian J. Bullock

Enki Code
"let me spell it out to you"
White Lighter/Lighter/Light Dimmer

A Magician can Light electrical devices like a lightbulb or lamp post. A Magician may also Dim electrical devices like lightbulbs, lamp posts, and TVs. This is mostly due to time travel but can also be from the Magician's power over the Elements. When a Magician learns of the Cronus Mysteries they may know of the Secret Universe. Using their Third Eye or Charm of Making a Magician can Light up a lamp post or Dim a lightbulb. Part of this is due to their passing through dimensions or other planes during time travel. Those electrical malfunctions will eventually be controlled. Controling the element of Electricity is of huge importance for the Singularity Magician.

Digital Imprint, PsyCop Zombies Imprint, and Counter Imprint

Digital Imprinting is part of programming to use TV or Radio to imprint thoughts into another person or to the masses. In Dark Dimensions of the Secret Universe people are hooked up to TVs or Radios for Digital Impriting and Programming. They are part of the subconsicous of the Emerald Dream.

The person's eyes are hooked in either forced or volentary. TV Images are imprinted with the PsyCop Zombie's Eyes seeing these TV images projected into their brains through the Eyes. The PsyCop Zombie has little to no memory of this and they walk amongst the population under the control of the PsyCops, seeing only the images that were imprinted on them. This is a scientific version of a Zombie which the PsyCops use. This is usually after a Psychic Lobotomy.

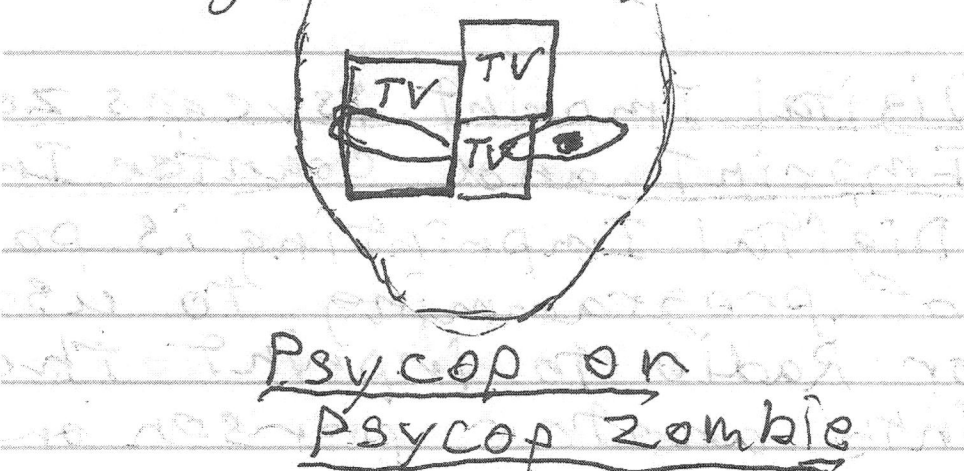

PsyCop on
PsyCop Zombie

This Digital Imprint can be used on Movies or TV shows or Ads subliminally. Using a Third Eye a PsyCop may imprint psychically on another person. A PsyCop may also use an unblinking stare of a one Eye to

Christian J. Bullock

imprint on another person. A Magician can use their Third Eye to Digital Imprint or use either a musical instrument, or singing bowl. The Magician can also dispell, conquer, or counter imprint a Movie, TV show, Ads, or Music. The Magician must understand such things in order to do it properly. A Magician must have an unblinking gaze with his Eyes and his Third Eye throughout playback. It is a duty of a Magician with such knowledge to counter spell such negative or subliminal Digital Imprinting. This High Magick must be kept secret so it doesn't fall into the wrong hands. This High Magick must also be practiced to protect themselves or the masses. This type of Magick can also be used to make parallel conections to the past self, sort of Digital Imprinting backwards.

The Secret Universe and The Temporal Cold War

There is a Temporal Cold War that began in the distant past and continues into the distant future. There are some PsyCops or Retwos that are trying to control the Future Game, the Milky Way, and the Planet. Some use the Cronus Mysteries or the Future Cronus. To them Cylon, man machines, is the future of Human Intellegence. Cylons are part of the past, present, and future but the truth of the Temporal Cold War is that a negative repeating cycle of the Great Darkening is being fought over. PsyCops are prone to being for the Great Darkening. The Retwo are prone to the accelerated growth of Human Development. It is a fine line which is why the Secret Universe is Secret. Where too much information or growth all at once can be catastrophic to the timeline. Human Development must grow smoothly and must survive or be protected from the Great Darkening. This must be done in order for the Retwo, Cylon, and Magician to exist. Also for there to be other planers to come and go from this plane, the Earth plane of existence. The Temporal Cold War is also about the release of information, some of which is the release of Ancient information. This must be done with care and initiates must go through the initiate process. Secret knowledge must be guarded and slowly passed down through the Ages. Understanding of the Ancient and Elder Gods is also important. The Quickening is ever present and the Great Darkening always looming.

The 12 Greek Gods of Olympas

Zeus – King of the Gods, The Thunder God
Hera – Queen of the Gods
Poseidon – Lord of the Seas
Demeter – The Goddess of Harvest and Fertility
Athena – Goddess of Wisdom
Hestia – Virgin Goddess of The Hearth
Apollo – God of the Sky and Sun
Artemis – The Goddess of The Hunt and Wilderness
Ares – God of War
Aphrodite – Goddess of Love
Hephaestus – God of Metalurgy, Black Smiths, Mech, and Tech
Hermes – Messenger God, God of Writing and Knowledge

Later on Dionysus took the place of Hestia, so at one point there were 13 Gods. The Greek circle consists of six Gods and six Goddesses. Hades was at one time included on the list but lost it because he spent most of his time in the underworld.
Roman Equivalent is the same set of 12 Gods of Olympas and 12 Titans
Dionysus(Bacchus)   Hestia(Vesta)

Christian J. Bullock

Zeus was depicted as a Thunder God with Lightning Bolts standing on top of a Bull. He is also associated with the Bull and the Celestial Tarus.

The Vedas of Hinduism describes a tale about the 13th Zodiac Constellation. The Gods Rahu("demon") and Ketu("disconnected") were once a single Celestial body that sought to join the Gods without permission. The God of Storms cut him in two, Rahu "The Dragon's Head" and Ketu "The Dragon's Tail". These are the Nodes of the Moon, Draconis Caput and Draconis Cuada.

The 12 Greek Titans Fathered by Gaia and Uranus

Oceanus – father of Nymphs
Coeus – father of Leto and Asteria
Crius – father of Pallas, Astrueus, and Perses
Hyperion – father of the Sun God, Moon, and Dawn
Iapetus – father of Prometheus, Atlas, and Epimetheus
Cronus – father of the Olypian Gods
Thea – Hyperion's mate
Rhea – Cronus' mate and mother of the Olympian Gods
Themis – mother of Hours and Fates
Mnemosyne – mother of the Muses
Phoebe – Coeus' mate
Tethys – Oceanus' mate

Six Gods and six Goddesses of the 12 Greek Titans. Uranus is the Sky God, Cronus is the Storm God, and Zeus is the Thunder God. The form a unique triad, the father of the father of the son.

Hittite/Sumerian tale of the Sky Gods are very similar to the Greek. Alalu was dethroned by Anu, Anu was dethroned by Kumarbi. Anu lost his Manhood during the battle. This is similar to the Egyptian tale of Horus and Set. Kumarbi swallowed Anu's Manhood producing and releasing from his insides Teshub, Kumarbi devised a plan to raise a rival to the Storm God Throne. Kumarbi mated with a Lady of the Mountain. He had a son named Ulli-Kummi. Kumarbi proclaims his son as heir to the throne. Then he describes a Great Darkening:

> Let him ascend to Heaven for Kingship
> Let him vanquish Kummiya, the beautiful city
> Let him attack the God of Storms
> And tear him to pieces, like a mortal
> Let him shoot down all the Gods from the sky

This is the Great Darkening being described over 4,000 B.C. about 5,000 to 6,000 years ago during the Age of Tarus.

Christian J. Bullock

Enki code
Sumerian cuniforms

* * * ✳

AN - star - Heavens - God

NIN.HUR.SAG - cheif Nurse Goddess Lady of Li

Mammu   Mam-mu

Mamma   Mam-ma

Enki code
Utu — Sumerian God of the shem feilds

Shamash — Akkadian Guardian to the Gateway of Heaven

Utu/shamash — Sun God, God of law

Inanna — Sumerian

Ishtar — Akkadian

Inanna/Istar — Twin of Utu, Goddess of Love Goddess of warfare

she journeyed the underworld

Marduk — God of War, First born of Enki

Nergal — God who rules the Lower world

also son of Enki

Dumuzi — son of Enki married to Inanna

Mar-Duk

Mars-Duke — war Duke

Adad — Enlil's son

Sin — Enlil's son Moon God

Shem — firey stone

Shemmu — boat of Heaven

Shem-mu   Mu- Firey sumer ship

Sham — Heavenly ship

shaman

Sham-an

Anu — God sumer of the Heavenly Abode

Christian J. Bullock

12 Great Gods of Sumer and Their Number

60 Anu	55 Antu	50 Marduk
50 Enlil	45 Ninlil	50 Ninurta
40 Ea/Enki	35 Ninki	
30 Nanna/Sin	25 Ningal	
20 Utu/Shamash	15 Inanna/Ishtar	
10 Ishkur/Adad	5 Ninhursag	

6 Gods	6 Goddesses	2 Heirs to the Throne

Each God has a numerical rank, Ninurta is heir to Enlil so he will have 50 when he takes Enlil's Throne. Marduk usurped the Enlilship he has insisted on 50 names for a rank of 50. There are several hundred rank and file Gods of the Anunnaki. They had general duities and are not listed in the 12 Great Gods Pantheon.

The 12 Sumerian Zodiac also called UL.HE for "Shiny Herd"

12 Sumerian Zodiac
UL.HE "shiny herd"
GU.AN.NA "heavenly bull" Taurus
MASH.TAB.BA "twins" Gemini
DUB "pineers, tongs" Cancer
UR.GULA "lion" Leo
AB.SIN "her father was sin" Virgo
ZI.BA.AN.NA "heavenly fate" Libra
GIR.TAB "which claws and cuts" Scorpio
PA.BIL "defender" Saggitarius
SUHUR.MASH "goatfish" Capricorn
GU "lord of the waters" Aquarius
SIM.MAH "fishes" Pisces
KU.MAL "field dweller" Aries

Christian J. Bullock

The Sumerians mapped the Celestial Sky and the Constellations. The way of Enlil is the Northern Sky. The way of Anu is the Equitorial Zodiac. The way of Ea is the Southern Sky.

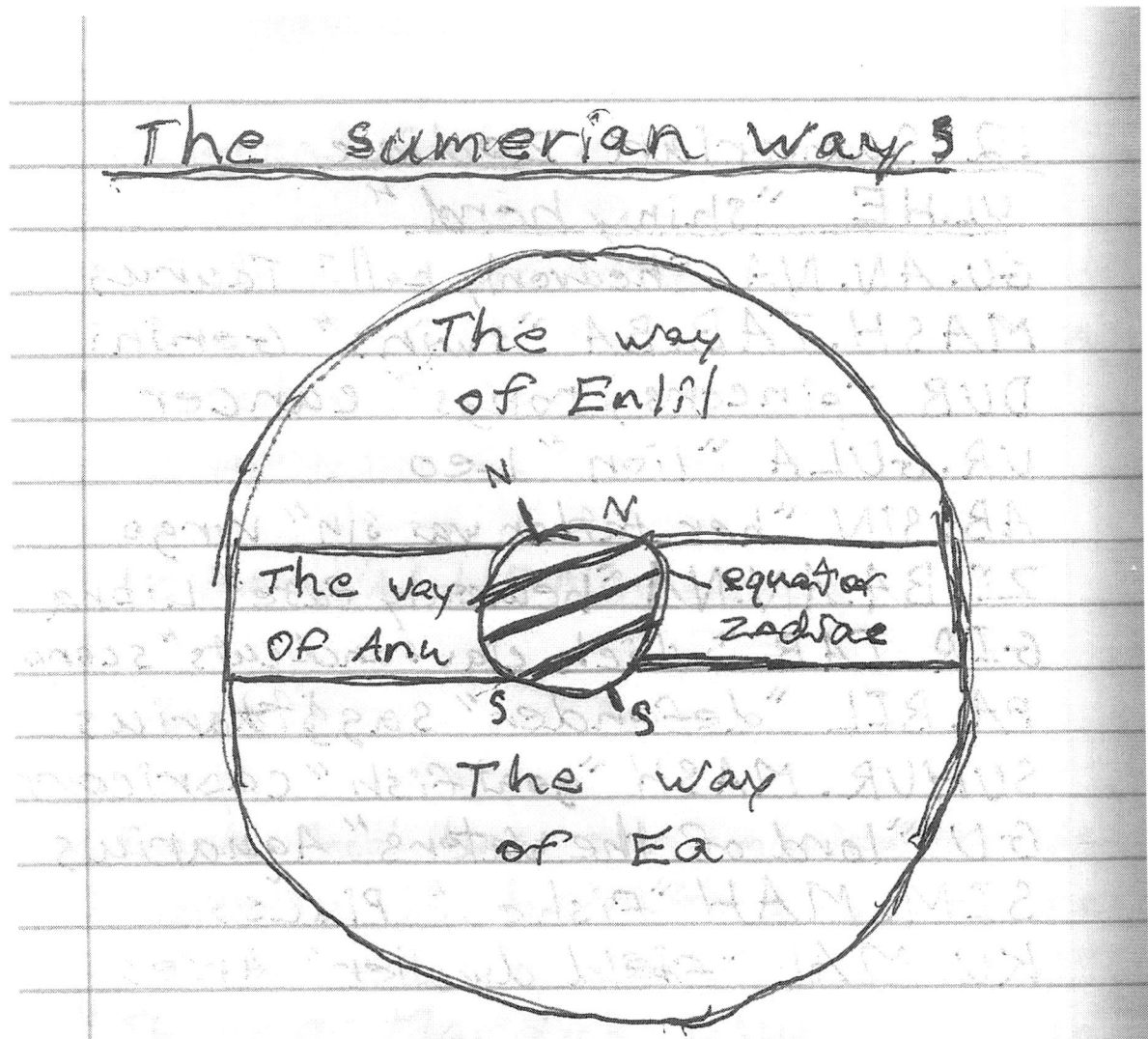

60 degrees from the North Pole the way of Enlil to the way of Anu. 30 degrees south to the Equator and 30 degrees south below the Equator is the way of Anu. 60 degrees from the way of Anu to the South Pole the way of Ea. This is how the Sumer Gods divided the heavens.

Christian J. Bullock

Sumer Calendar of Months and Constellations

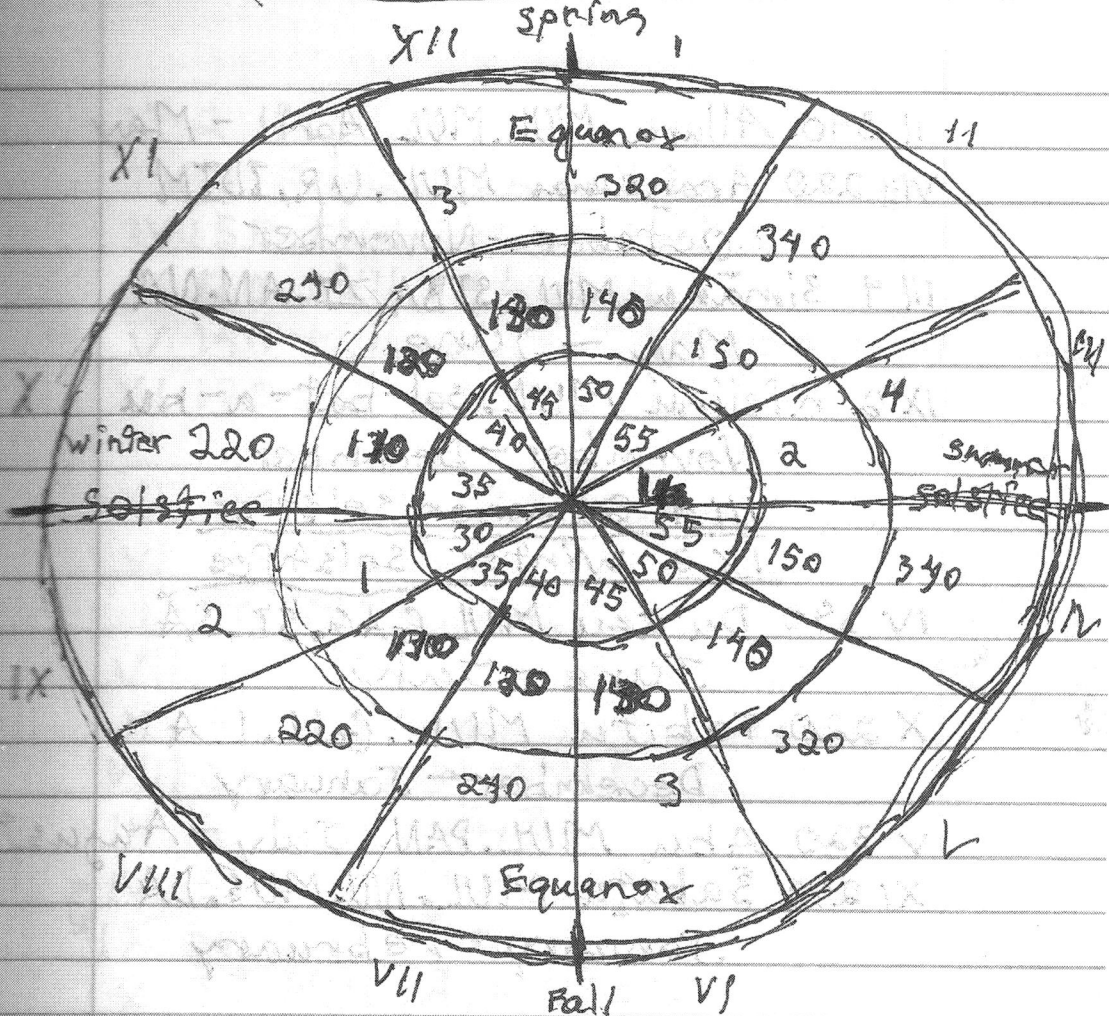

XII 3 Addaru MUL.KU February – March
VI 3 Ululu MUL.BIR August – September
XII 3 Spring Equinox
VI 3 Fall Equinox
I 320 Nissanu MUL.IKU March – April
VII 240 Taaritu MUL.NIN.MAH September – October

Christian J. Bullock

II 340 Allaru MUL.MUL April – May

VIII 220 Arahsamas MUL.UR.IDIM
October – November

III 4 Simānu MUL.SIBA.ZI.AN.NA
May – June

IX 2 Kislimu MUL.sal-bat-a-nu
November – December

<u>III 4 Summer solstice</u>
<u>IX 2 Winter solstice</u>

IV 340 Du'āzu MUL.GAG.SI.SÁ
June – July

X 220 Tabitu MUL.GU.LA
December – January

V 320 Abu MUL.PAN July – August

XI 240 Šabātu MUL.NU.MUŠ.DA
January – February

XII 130 MUL.KA.A

VI 130 MUL.UGA

I 140 MUL.DILI.PÁT

VII 120 MUL.zi-ba-ni-tum

II 150 MUL.ŠU.GI

VIII 110 MUL.GÍR.TAB

III 2 MUL.UR.A
IX 1 MUL.U.KA.TUH.A
IV 150 MUL.MAŠ.TAB.BA
X 110 MUL.AL.LUL
V 140 MUL.MAŠ.TAB.BA.GAL.GAL
XI 120 MUL.SIM.MAH

XII 45 MUL.Mar-duk
VI 45 MUL.SU.PA
I 50 MUL.APIN
VII 40 MUL.ENTE.NA.BAR.GUZ
II 55 MUL.a-su-sí-tum
VIII 35 MUL.HANIŠ
III 1 MUL.MUŠ
IV 55 MUL.U.AL.TAR
IX 30 MUL.UZ
X 35 MUL.A.MUŠEN
V 50 MUL.MAR.GID.DA
XI 40 MUL.DA.MU

Inner Ring 30 to 60   (60 is 1)
Central Ring 60 to 120   (2 x 60 is 120)
Outer Ring 120 to 240   (4 x 60 is 240)
All are 360° equivelant   (3 x 60 is 180)

Sumer Month and constellations

March 20

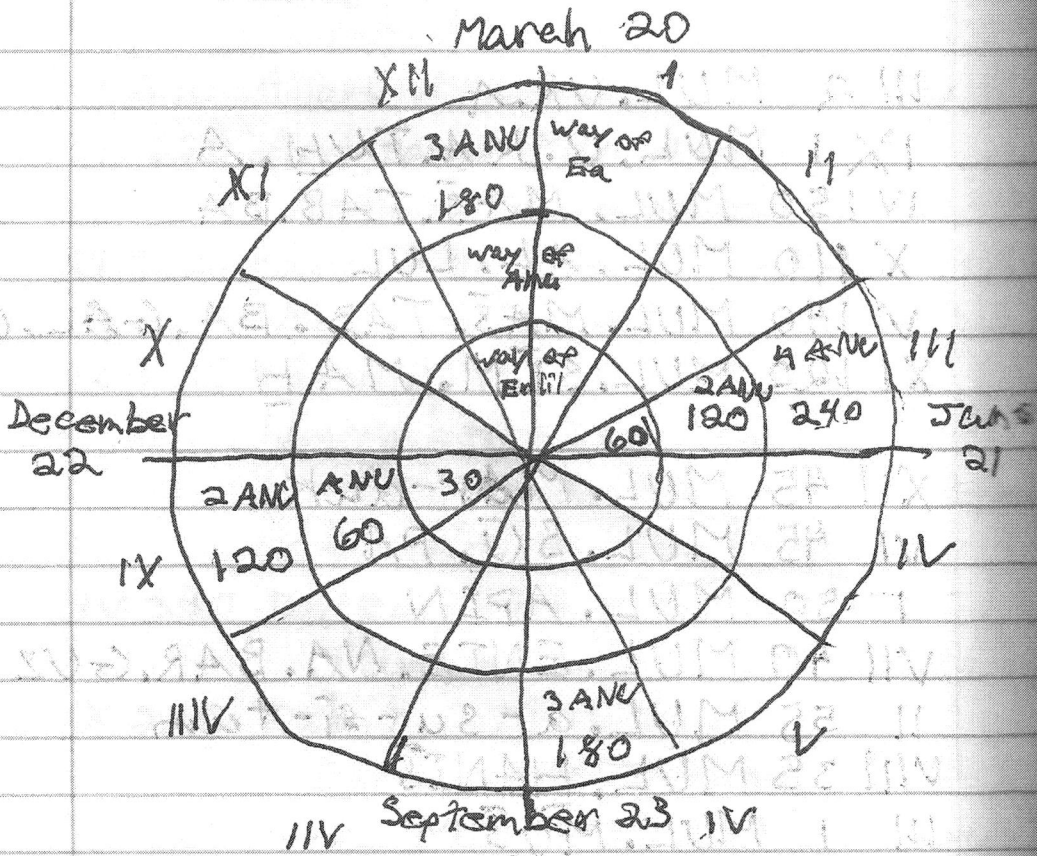

360° 6 ANU

where 1 ANU = 60°

The GOD ANU's number
is 60

The sumerian calendar
begins on the Monthly zodiac
of the ♈ into the ♉, It ends
on ♓. Processionally it begins on
♐ and ends on ♒.

Christian J. Bullock

The way of Enlil 90° (30+60)
The way of Anu 180° (60+120)
The way of Ea 360° (180+180)

The Sumerian Solar System

Sun - Apsu	only three solar
Mercury - Mummu	bodies existed
Tiamat	in the begining
Venus - Lahamu	Apsu, Mummu,
Mars - Lahmu	and Tiamat.
Jupiter - Kishar	sun, Mercury,
Saturn - Anshar	and Tiamat
Uranus - Anu	
Neptune - Ea	Lahmu - God of War
Pluto - Gaga	Lahamu - God of Love
Marduk - Nibiru	and War
Earth - Ki	Lahmu and Lahamu
Moon - Kingu	male and female
	counterparts

Enki Code

AP.SU - "one who exists from the begining"
MUMMU - "one who was born"
TIAMAT - "maiden of life"
MUL - celestial bodies

In the Sumerian Solar System there are 12 Celestial Planets. One of the first Planets was Tiamat which was an early Earth that was smashed into by Nibiru to create Earth which is KI and made the asteriod belt.

Christian J. Bullock

Enki Code with Sumerian

Enki code of sumerian celestial Names

AN. SHAR - "prince, Foremost of the Heaven"

KI. SHAR - "Foremost of the firm lands"

NUDIMMUD - sumerian Neptune
            an epithet of Ea/Enki

A. SAR - "watery King"

A. SAR. U - "lofty bright watery King"

A. SAR. U. LU. DU - "lofty bright watery King
            whose deep is plentiful"

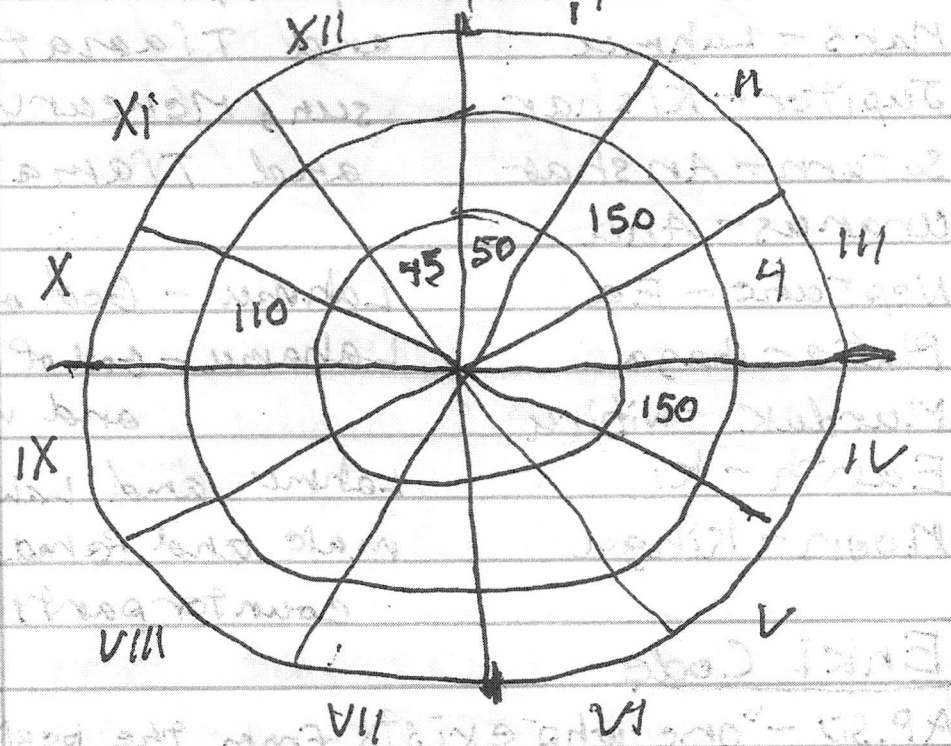

The Sumerian Calendar Continued and The Processional Cycle

VIII 110 MUL.GIR.TAB – scorpio ♏

IV 150 MUL.MAŠ.TAB.BA

MASH.TAB.BA – Gemini

X 110 MUL.AL.LUL

ALU.LIM – capricorn

EA/Enki Name

III 4 MUL.SIBA.ZI.AN.NA

SIB.ZI.AN.NA – Jupiter

I 50 MUL.APIN

APIN – Mars

XII 45 MUL.MAR.DUK

MAR.DUK – NIBIRU

II 150 MUL.ŠU.GI

SHU.GI – Earth or Seventh Planet

ANU'S
Way

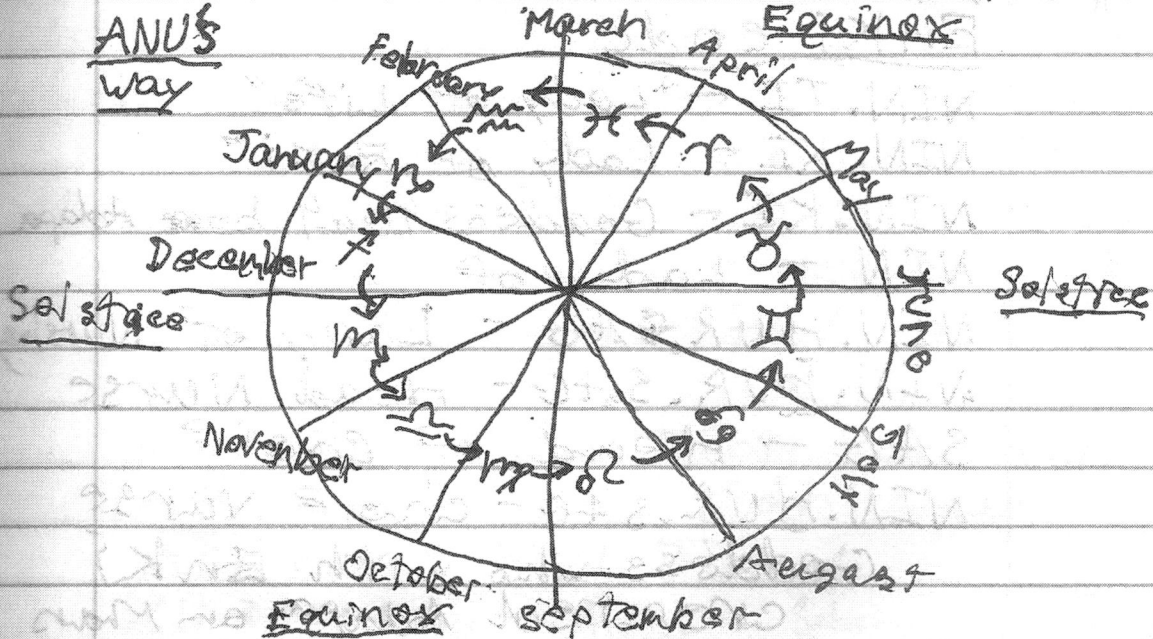

The Sumerian Calendar begins with the March Equinox which is currently in the Age of Pisces but on March 20, 2013 will start in the Age of Aquarius. March begins the Solar Year with February being the 12th Month and the end of the Solar Year.

Sumerian Zodiac Associated with The Way of Anu

XII 130 MUL.KA.A ♒ ↑
I 140 MUL.DILI.BAT ♓ ↑
II 150 MUL.ŠU.GI ♈ ↑
III 2 MUL.UR.A ♉ ↑
IV 150 MUL.MAŠ.TAB.BA ♊ ↑
V 140 MUL.MAŠ.TAB.BA.GAL.GAL ♋ ↑
VI 130 MUL.UGA ♌ ↑
VII 120 MUL.zi-ba-ni-tum ♍ ↑
VIII 110 MUL.GIR.TAB ♎ ↑
IX 1 MUL.U.KA.TUH.A ♏ ↑
X 110 MUL.AL.LUL ♐ ↑
XI 120 MUL.SIM.MAH ♑ ↑

More Enki Code with Sumerian

Enki code
NIN.TI – "Lady of Life"
NIN.KI – "Lady of Enki"
NIN.KI – Goddess that bore Adapa
NIN – Lady of
NIN.HUR.SAG – Lady of Nurse
NIN.HUR.SAG – Head Nurse
SAG – Head of Chief
NIN.HUR.SAG – Chief Nurse
Goddess who with Enki
created Adapa an Man

Christian J. Bullock

More Enki Code with Sumerian

<u>Enki Code</u>

SHI.IM.TI - breath-wind-life

GIR - "crab claw" cancer

EN.KI.DU.NU - "Enki dig deep"

EN.KI - God of Mining

EN.KI - God of waters, Marshs, oceans

EN.KI - God of the Lower world
   God of the Deep Earth
   and of the seas
   Rules Capricorn, Aquarius
   sometimes of Taurus and
   of Pisces his arrival
   in the Processional
   Earth cycle

EN.LIL - God of Aries
   Supreme Commander

ANU - God of Nibiru/Marduk
   God of the Heavenly Abode
   Supreme God of
   the Annunaki

ADAMA - Red Dirt Red clay

ADAPA - Early Man Adam

ADAMU - Red Blood

XII 3 Addaru - Adar - Sphere of Saturn

Christian J. Bullock

The Psychic Lobotomy and The Charm of Lobotomy

A Psychic Lobotomy is a psychic recreation of a lobotomy. Using the mind and Third Eye a Psychic taps into another person's mind. The other person must be in a secluded room for a period of time. The Psychic then begins numbing the person's mind and senses. The numbing simulates surgical suringes and anesthesia. Local anesthesia to ice and numb the brain. It can be done psychically by icing the brain in a cube.

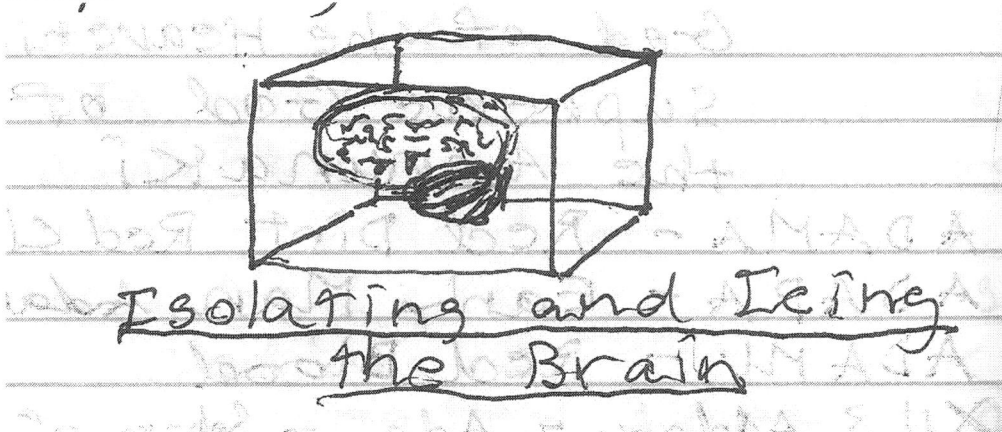

The cube becomes a blocki of ice with the brain inside. The target person will feel a cold numbing from the front of the brain to the back of the skull. The brain should be pictured as a brain in a refridgerator. The Psychic then pin pricks the brain in certain areas to obtain information. Mostly memories but also in some biological functions like the neurological connections and chemical nodes. Motor functions also are partially manipulated. The target person will feel biter cold and now also pin pricks focusing from the front of the skull to the back of the skull.

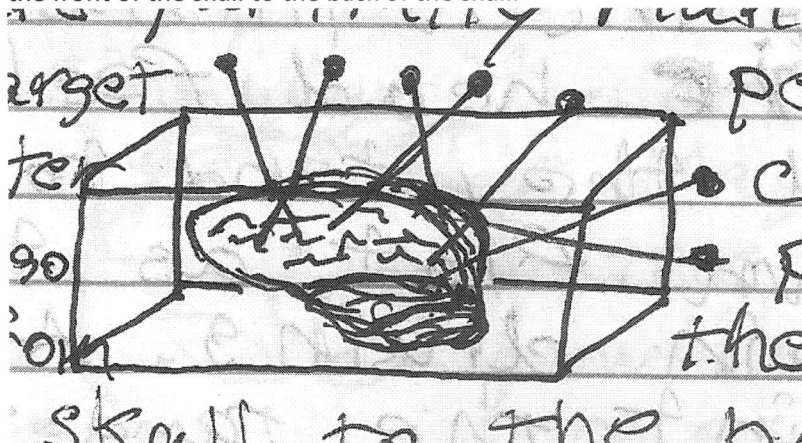

Pin pricks will begin to become intense on the back of the skull. The target person will become slightly sedated. Their head will feel extremely cold as well as the rest of their body. After psychically probing and pricking, the brain is taken out of the skull psychically. Emptiness in the other person becomes apparent. The target person is disconnected from specific brain motor functions. They now at this point are fully disconnected from the commonality of the Human Mind. A fluid, a cold fluid, washes through the skull cavity. The target person feels cold fluidic emptiness in the skull. Their head feels lighter and they tend to be layed down flat as their brain drains out. At this point the target person may seem clinically dead. Usually after a Psychic Lobotomy a PsyCop Zombie or another type of Zombie may be imprinted on them.

The Charm of Lobotomy

The Charm of Lobotomy is when a Magician or Singularitian under goes one. The Magician, of a high rank, holds in his mind the Sun or Singularity of the universe. This is a difficult task and a hard spell to master. The targeted Magician then under goes the Lobotomy, knowing of the Lobotomy he projects Astrally the primordial universe. The first Singularity or Sun. The Magician survives the Psychic Lobotomy without becoming a PsyCop Zombie or any other type of Zombie. This spell virtually deflects the Psychic attack while giving the Magician all his memories back. This type of spell requires the Magician to have no fear of the Psychic attack and no fear of the Lobotomy that is being performed on him. The Magician may have to act out the Lobotomy if they are confined in a secluded room, basically playing dead till the coast is clear and their mind is free of the Psychic's grip.

First Singularity or Sun
he   Magrek
survives   the Psy
obotomy   without
ecoming   a psyco
Zombie   or Zomb
          Charm of Lobotomy

Enki Code
Numbskull – Psychic Lobotomy
Numb-Skull
Blockhead – a cubed head
Block-Head
Both mean brainless

Sumerian History of the Anunnaki, Their Arrival, and Their Timeline on Earth

In the Four Yuga's cycles of 432,000 years appear. These cycles are four periods of 432,000 years starting with the Satya Yuga. This is an extension of the 25,626 year Processional Cycle. Sumer texts state that the Anunnaki arrived on Earth around 445,000 years ago. The Nifilim led by Enki established Eridu in the southern marshes of Mesopotaimia. Enki arrived during the Processional cycle of Tarus. 400,000 years ago Enlil arrives on Earth during the Processional cycle of Aries. Enlil establishes Nippur in Mesopotaimia. Enki establishes gold mining in South Africa, he also sets sea routes. 300,000 years ago the Anunnaki rebel and so they fasion a primitive worker, Man or Adam, to work in the mines instead. Enki and NINHURSAG work to create Man. Ninki, Enki's consort is one of the 14 Goddesses chosen to give birth to Adapa, early Man. 250,000 years ago early Homo Sapiens multiply and spread to the other continents. 200,000 years ago life on Earth declines, climate changes take place. 100,000 years ago the sons of the Gods take the daughters of Man as wives. 75,000 years ago regressive types of Man roam the Earth. 49,000 years ago the lineage of Enki, Man of a primordial Noah reigns, Ziusurddra. 38,000 years ago Enlil disenchanted by Man seeks its demise. 13,000 years ago the Nifilim leave Earth and Man to its fate. The Great Deluge sweeps over the Earth.

Enki Code

Nightfall	Night-Fall
Sunrise	Sun-Rise
King	
K-ing	End-Ki
Ki-ng	Enki
Ki-End	The End Ki

The Breaking of The Golden Rule and The Breaking of The Yoke

There is a Golden Rule which binds this world, this universe. When it is broken incredible and impossible things become possible. The one who breaks the rule or yoke will experience multiple degrees of Earth. The person will experience climate changes, like winter and summer at the same time. In fact half winter and half summer. A pond or lake will be half frozen and one half unfrozen. It will snow but not really snow. The snow doesn't actually reach the ground. The person may break the sound barrier with their car. Time will stop for long periods and clocks will stop for long periods. Clocks will start again or malfunction. Time will start again at the place of the broken yoke. The place of the broken yoke becomes sacred. It becomes a Temple of Time. The one who broke it, the Magician, has some what knowingly created a sanctuary from the Quickening, the Darkening, and the falling stars. This breaking of the Golden Rule has to do with time travel but on a fantasical scale, it's implications mean that the physical world is not the only world in which the Magician may travel. A motion capture kaleidoscope of worlds exist for the Magician to travel.

Enki Code
Menes – First Dynastic Ruler of Egypt
Memphis – City founded by Menes 3,200 B.C.
Amen – "The Hidden One"
Amen-Ra – "The Hidden Ra"
"The Four Corners of the World"
Thebes – Diospolis Greek Name
Di-ospol-is – City of Zeus
Di – two, a pair, or two of a kind
AN – Ptah's Name for Heliopolis
Heliopolis – City of Ra
"Once Upon a Time"

The Duat

The Duat is the passage of the Pharaoh or Magician through the underworld following in the footsteps of Ra. Amen-Ta is the Hidden Place where the Seker guides the initiate or King through the Duat. There are 12 Gates and divisions of the Duat. Thus corresponding to 12 Hours as Ra's passing. These 12 Gates lead one to the Stairway to Heaven. The 12 Gates and 12 Hours correspond to the 12 Houses of the Zodiac. 12 Constellations in the sky. 12 also corresponds to the 12 Celestial bodies in the Sumer Solar System. 12 also corresponds to the 12 divisions of the Processional cycle. The Duat is represented in the sky as well as in the sites of the Giza Necropolis and the Mayan "Way of the Dead" Necropolis. During the Egyptian times of 3,200 B.C. to 500 B.C. the Giza Necropolis was flooded or damed on purpose. The water made a moat of sorts with gates and passageways. This is the way the Duat was represented on Earth, with the Nile river and the Giza Pyramids. The funiery rites and depictions are memories of this Duat Procession. The Mayan Duat is the Pyramid of the Sun and Moon. This site or Necropolis is the Egyptian equivilent. The Sun and Moon are present as well as the other 12 Celestial bodies. The long corridore is called "The way of the dead". This long passage was filled with water on purpose over 300 B.C. This ground Duat mimicked the sky and the 12 Zodiac. The way of the Dead marks 12 Gates of the Mayan Duat. It is another funiery memory passed down through the Ages. It is the following of the passing of Ra, and the 12 Hours of daylight/night on the Equinox.

The 12 Gates of The Duat and The Ritual Passage of Egypt

This is an Egyptian ritual that can be done on the Equinoxes but it should be noted that time travel should be done first, the ritual requires the Magician to be active so time travel in conjunction with this ritual may not work. It is best for the Magician to practice time travel separately before the ritual for a better success rate of time travel.

The 12 Gates of The Duat

Gate I Set Amentet
"He of the Hidden Eye"
NS Guardian set Tat
"Guardian of the Desert"
** Boat of the Duat moving East
Ferrying the Follower of Ra
to the Horizon over water
and Land
Gate II "Intense of Flame"
NS Guardian sia set
"Swallower of Sinners"

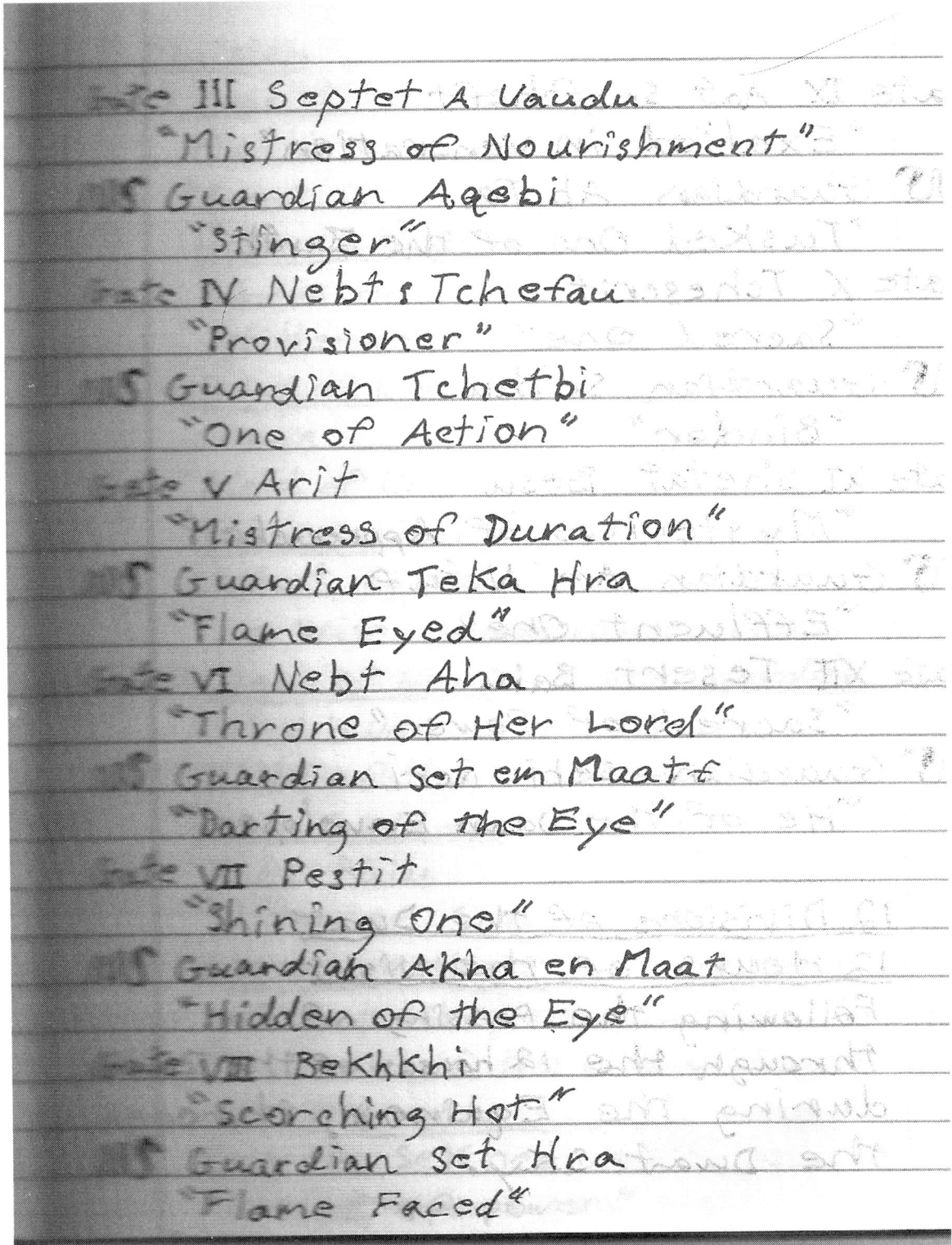

III Septet A Vaudu
"Mistress of Nourishment"
Guardian Aqebi
"stinger"
IV Nebt s Tchefau
"Provisioner"
Guardian Tchetbi
"One of Action"
V Arit
"Mistress of Duration"
Guardian Teka Hra
"Flame Eyed"
VI Nebt Aha
"Throne of Her Lord"
Guardian Set em Maatf
"Darting of the Eye"
VII Pestit
"Shining One"
Guardian Akha en Maat
"Hidden of the Eye"
VIII Bekhkhi
"Scorching Hot"
Guardian Set Hra
"Flame Faced"

Gate IX Aat shefsheft
    "Exalted in veneration"
  Guardian Ab Ta
    "Tusked One of the Earth"
Gate X Tcheserit
    "Sacred One"
  Guardian Sethu
    "Binder"
Gate XI Shetat Besu
    "Mysterious of Approaches"
  Guardian Am Netuf
    "Effluent One"
Gate XII Tesert Baiu
    "Sacred of Power"
  Guardian Sebi Reri
    "He of the Dawn Enveloper"

<u>12 Divisions of the Duat,</u>
<u>12 Hours of the Night</u>
Following the passing of Ra
through the 12 houses of the Zodiac
during the Equinox, through
the Duat Sky.

The 12 Divisions of the Hours of Night, on the Equinox, at the Hour of Ra through to the Hour of Atum till the Hour of Khepri. Each Hour marks the Sun's passage through each of the Zodiac East to West on the horizon. This is also a ritual to be done on the Equinox.

Division

I Hour of Night   Warder
Maati, Net Ra   Arnebaui
"Great City"
Hour Goddess
Ushem Hatiu Kheftiu Nu Ra
"Splitter of the Heads of Ra's Enemies"

II Hour of Night   Warder
Urnes   Am Nebaui
"Field of Urnes"
Hour Goddess
Seshet Maket Nebs
"The Wise, Guardian of Her Lord"

III Hour of Night   Warder
Net Neb Ua Kheper Aut   Khetra
"Field of the Grain Gods"
Hour Goddess
Tent Baiu
"Slicer of Souls"

IV Hour of Night   Warder
Ankhet Kheperu   Ament Sethau
"Cavern of the Life of Forms"
Hour Goddess
Urt en Sekhemus
"Great of power"

Division

V Hour of Night   Warder
   Ament   Aha Neteru
"cavern of Sokar"
Hour Goddess
Sekhmet Her Abt Uaas
"she on Her Barque"

VI Hour of Night   Warder
Metchet Nebt Duat   Sep Metu
"Deep water"
Hour Goddess
Mesperit Ar At Maatu
"Proficient Leader"

VII Hour of Night   Warder
   Tephet shetat   Ruti en Asar
"cavern of the Mysterious cave"
Hour Goddess
Khesfet Hau Hesqetu Neha Hra
"Repeller of the serpent"

VIII Hour of Night   Warder
   Tebat Neterus   Aha An Urt Ne
"city of the Gods' sarcophagi"
Hour Goddess
Nebt Usha
"Mistress of the Night"

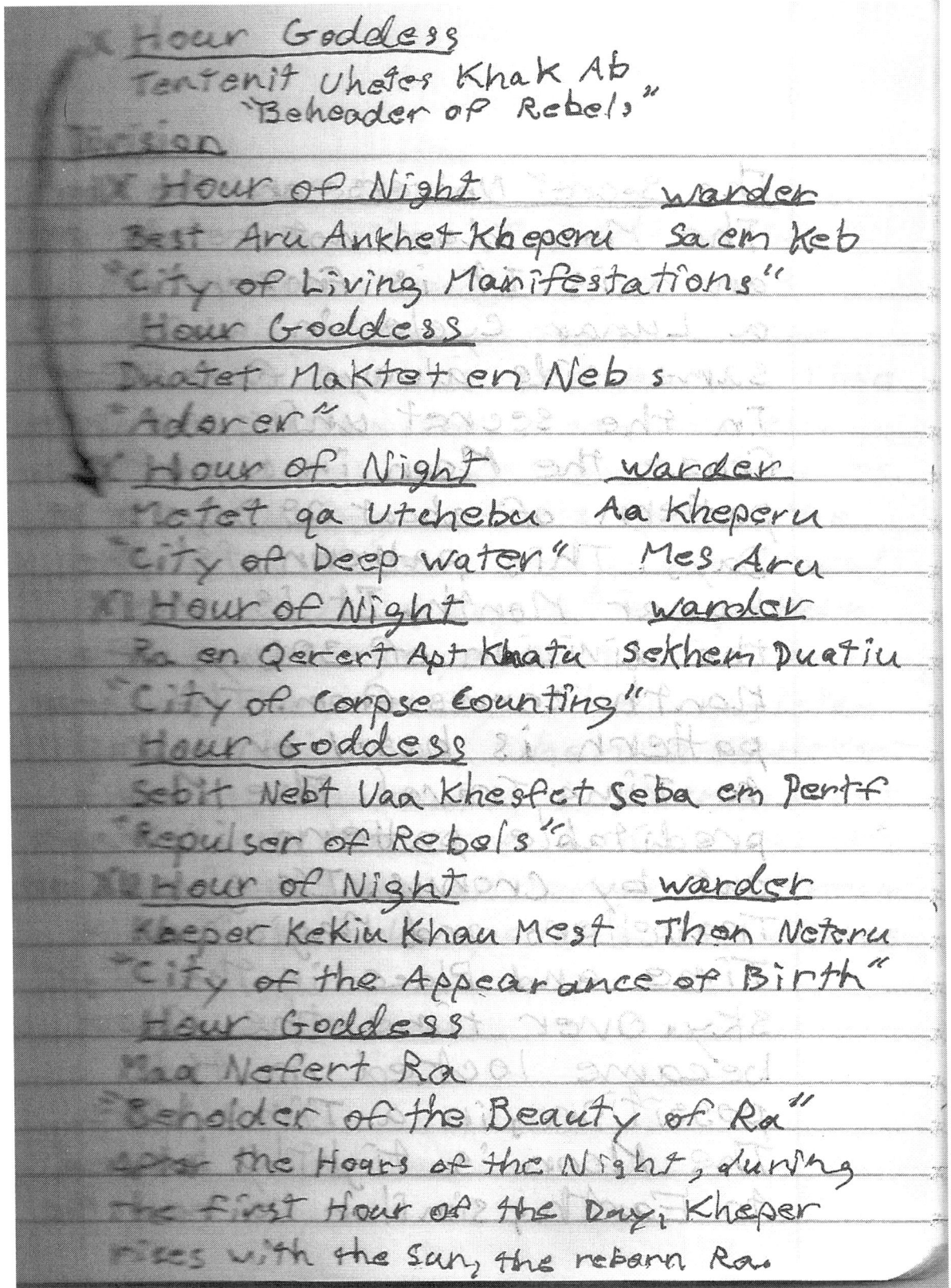

Hour Goddess
Tentenit Uhates Khak Ab
    "Beheader of Rebels,"
Tacsian

Hour of Night   wander
Best Aru Ankhet Kheperu Sa em Keb
"City of Living Manifestations"
Hour Goddess
Duatet Maktet en Neb s
"Adorer"

Hour of Night   warder
Metet qa Utchebu   Aa Kheperu
"City of Deep water"   Mes Aru

Hour of Night   wander
Ra en Qerert Apt Khatu sekhem Duatiu
"City of Corpse Counting"
Hour Goddess
Sebit Nebt Uaa Khesfet seba em Pertf
"Repulser of Rebels"

Hour of Night   warder
Kheper Kekiu Khau Mest Then Neteru
"City of the Appearance of Birth"
Hour Goddess
Maa Nefert Ra
"Beholder of the Beauty of Ra"
After the Hours of the Night, during
the first Hour of the Day, Kheper
rises with the Sun, the reborn Ra.

Christian J. Bullock

The Secret Universe and The Moon

The Moon does not rotate on an axis. It is frozen in a Lunar cycle in which the same side always faces Earth. In the Secret Universe during a Quickening Cronus may freeze the Moon in a particular pattern. This seemingly freeze frame on the Moon is cause by and specifically for time travel. The Moon's predictable pattern is mapped out by Cronus. It gives Time Travellers and Magicians a time/place in the night sky, for particular tasks to be done. Over time the Moon becomes locked in similar freeze frame times. This may happen when time travelling, a time warp may occur. The Moon is tightly bound to Earth, similar to how Earth is bound to the Sun. Cronus time travels using the Moon and it's phases. The Magician with knowledge of the Cronus Stone can time travel using the Moon as well. The phases correspond to dates or time stamps. During an eclipse the Moon's phases may be trapped by Cronus in a freeze frame. If and when this happens a repeating pattern may emerge, a sort of time warp Singularity. The dates of the phases of the Moon may change drastically to the Magician and time travel may be very strange yet hard to date. The Magician at this time must rely on the Star Constellations and previous alignments known that are being tracked.

School of Thought and Circles of Thought

When in thought it is helpful to walk in a circle. This is true of many traditions, for instance the walking of a Labyrinth or spirit walking. Thought is circular in a sense, the circle helps awaken in our minds the Singularity of Life, the Metaphysical Computer, or the Singularity Computer. Walking in deep thought can help the Magician. During this ritual walk the Magician may contact another self or a Spirit. The Magician with knowledge of the Secret Universe may contact another person psychically. The Magician uses hands of binding while walking in a circle. He Astral projects himself to a Spirit of a former life or to another Magician. This can also be done with contact to a Spirit of the underworld. The Magician then talks to them psychically, some times mouthing words with closed lips sort of speaking into one's own mind. The Magician then obtains knowledge from the Spirit. The Magician can also communicate with the Gods this way but doing a rite for a God or Goddess is more practical. This method of walking and talking came about from schools of thought in Greece circa 330 B.C. They were called Peripatetics and were founded by Aristotle who walked in circles while lecturing to students. Aristotle is also one of the founders of Western Metaphysics.

Passage Through The Duat Continued

The passage through the Duat has heiroglyps with a crouched Pharaoh or Goddess similar to the Mayan Choa Mool.

During the Duat passage through the Gates and Divisions the Magician will feel their Singularity Room move. It will feel tilted and some what unsettling, if done correctly. There will be loud roars of the Earth or noise overheard. The voyage will be long during such times. Completing the rituals will aid in the hours that pass. The room will feel like a boat so sitting or crouching will take place. It is best to sit in one place and never move unless you are doing the rituals. With the Stars you made on the ceiling you will have the Neter or Tefnut to guide you through to the otherside in the Dual.

The 13 Crystal Skulls

The skulls represent the 13 Baktuns of the Mayan Long Count, with each skull representing one Baktun cycle. The skulls also represent the 13 Zodiacs, with each skull representing one Zodiac Constellation and one cycle of Procession for each Zodiac. The skulls represent the 13 Full Moons in a Solar Year. Each skull is one Moon in the calendar year. The 13 skulls are repositories for Ancient and hidden knowledge. They are also a Meme or memory of rituals done by the Ancient Civilization. Each skull represents a paradigm and secret connection to the universe. During each Baktun cycle a Crystal Skull is chosen to be that cycles paradigm repositor. The Crystal Skull is clear at first then over time and after many rituals it becomes cloudy, layered with fractions of the inside of the Crystal. The cloudy Crystal contains the knowledge of the Paradigm. This clouding is a universal cloud, like a web. Similar to the web like neurons of a person's brain. Also similar to the web of Stars and Galaxies of the universe after the Big Bang. The Crystal Skull fractures are layered like planes, thin planes that inter connect to make the cloudy web. When the Crystal Skull is fully clouded it shows as an opaque white or grey. It contains secret knowledge of the Paradigm and of Crystal ritual work. A secret link to the Duat, the way of the dead, and the shadow world. Due to time travel there are five sets of 13 Baktuns of the Mayan Long Count which makes up the entire Procession of the Equinox.

Astral Projecting

When a Magician learns to use their Ba or Astral Body they project themselves in the Astral Plane. When a Magician becomes aware of themselves they can Astral Project thoughts. Most of these Astral Thoughts are projections of the Magician's future actions. These future thoughts become a way of the Magician to set up spells, Magick, and planing of actions. Over time it becomes apparent that these future thoughts are psychically linked. Another Psychic may pick up these thoughts. Which is why the Magician must learn Existentialism. The Magician must learn to live in the moment, in order to hide their thoughts from others. To clear the mind of future thoughts moment by moment. When this is achieved the Magician can block Psychics and more importantly use specific Astral Projections when needed. This is a deep undertaking and it requires discepline. The Magician's future thoughts aid in the power of the Magical Realm. It is vital to keep things secret even to other Psychics.

Near Death Experiences

When a person experiences near death they are able to see the veil of the world lifted. The other world or shadow world may become visible. Such times are in a hospital ward or in an Ambulence/Bus. These fleeting moments are reminders to the Magician of a Shadow world or a plane of existence beyond. A bumpy ride in an Ambulence may seem like forever, or the passage through the valley of death.

Code, Pseudocode, and Enki Code

There is code that runs the Singularity Computer. Code that runs the Computer on a basic level. There is Pseudocode that is code that is written before inputting code into the Computer. Enki Code is a code that makes up the human language. Root words or root phrases that are passed down language to language from Ancient root words, letters, or glyphs. Enki Code are Memes from Ancient times and can or will be used in the code of the Singularity Computer. Word spells are a kind of Pseudocode for the Magician to use accessing the power of the Metaphysical Computer. When the Singularity Computer of the future is built the Magician's word spells will harness the power of the Singularity Computer. Certain words are a type of base code for the Magician to use. There are also two to three letter roots that the Magician uses for their Charm of Making. Thoth is the Egyptian God that invented written language. Hermes invented it for the Greeks. Enki invented writing for the Sumerians. Enki, Sumerian, Akkadian, Chaldean, and Babylonian have some of the most Ancient basic linguistic roots. These roots come from the Ancient Civilization and the time of the building of the Ancient Tower of Babel. This is important to the advanced Magician, constructing root words for Magick enhances or completes a spell. The Charm of Making grows stronger with bond the between the Physical and Spirit world becoming closer to the Magician. Human languages use phonetic syllables to form words, vowels are important to all languages. There is a sort of syllable code with in words and how they are pronounced. Advanced Magician's must learn how to read this and decode Ancient Scripts or Glyphs.

World Energy Mana Energy

During meditation a Magician with deep meditative skills can tap into Energy for sustenance. This is done by tapping into the world energy matrix. The Earth has an energy flow all around it. This energy can be used by the Magician to obtain or absorb Mana Energy for spells. This type of Magick is typically used for healing and there are many locations on Earth that have healing energies. This type of Magick can also be used for breather training, or also known as the act of breathing to obtain sustenance. This Magick is not very widely known but there are many peoples that practice it, most notably in India. The Breather does not eat any food for extremely long periods of time, they only drink a little bit of water, the rest of their body is trained to take in energy from the world grid. They also slow down their metabolism at will and can virtually enter meditative trance for long periods with the Spirit world. To be a breather it takes a long time of practice but the goal of using the world energies for healing is a strong incentive to develop this skill.

The Mathematics of The Pyramids and Special Numbers

Mayan
Pyramid of the Sun

Approx
733.2 feet of 4 sides of Pyramid of the
733.2ft x 4 = 2,932.8 ft perimeter sun
233.5 ft of the height of Pyramid
233.5 ft x 4 x 3.14 (π) = 2932.76 ft
4π ratio of height to the
perimeter base of Pyramid of sun
2932.8 ft / 4 / 3.14 = 233.5 ft Approx

Feet used to measure π

scale model of Great Pyramid
5 inches per 4 sides = 20 inches
20 inches / 2 / 3.14 = 3.185 inches
6/32nd inches = .1875 inches
3.185 inches for the height Appro
3 6/32nd inches for the height
2π ratio of the height
to base perimeter of scale model

inches used to measure π

The Scale Model show how simple this method of achieving 2 Pi is but also how amazingly accurate the Pyramids are in dimensions. This must have taken a vast understanding Pi to achieve the massive size of the Great Pyramid. Here is a more basic method of the Mathematics involved:

Pyramids and Pi π

The Great Pyramid - has an Angle of 52° a sacred number To get the Height (H) you must divide the side(s) by 2 then divide by 3.14 (π) then multiply by 4. The side of the Great Pyramid is 754 feet.

Height (H) = 754 ÷ 2 = 377 ÷ 3.14 (π)
= 120 × 4
= 480 feet

The Sun Pyramid - has an Angle of 43.5° a sacred number To get the Height (H) you must divide the side(s) by 2 then divide by 3.14 (π) then multiply by 2. The Side is 745 or 754 feet.

Height (H) = 754 ÷ 2 = 377 ÷ 3.14 (π)
= 120 × 2
= 240 feet

Multiples of 4, 3, and 2 match π and the Height and Angle of Pyramids

Christian J. Bullock

Here are some basic Crop Cirles and some simple Crop Circle Magick. The Crop Circles mimick the sky and the celestial bodies that cross it.

Crop circles

8/3/2010

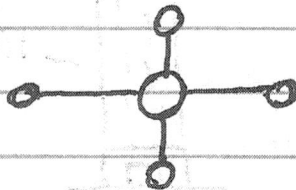

5 days later

8/8/2010

5 day pattern
5 numerical
pattern

The sky
5 days later
8/13/2010

Mars

Saturn

Moon

Venus

A cross pattern in the sky
Mars - Fire
Venus - water
satern - Earth (storm)
Moon - Air (water)

Christian J. Bullock

This type of Crop Circle Magick is an easy way to learn the basics of Planetary Magick or Astrology on the macro scale.

The Pyramid Light Beam Event at El Castillo

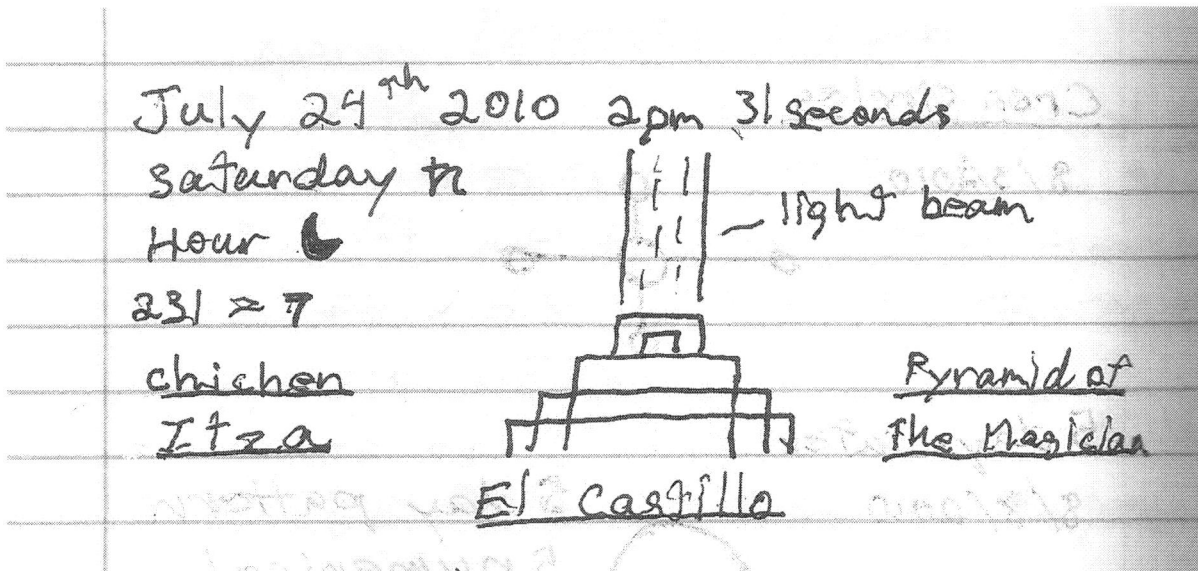

The Light Beam was only visible for a few seconds. A photograph of the Pyramid with the Light Beam was taken at 2pm approximately 31 seconds. Two to three frames were taken of the event. This is another example of the connection between the Pyramids and the Gods. These are sacred sites in which the Ancient Civilization connected with the peoples of Earth and where Magick still takes place.

The Grey Council and The Council of Elders

The Grey Council is the bringing together of the Light and the Dark to work at or for a common purpose. Earth at one time had such councils. The Egyptians had one and the Chaldeans/Babylonians had one. The Greeks had the Council of Elders and the same for the Celts. These councils worked towards a goal to bring civilization to a higher level of existence. Over time these councils changed and differences of opinions kept them apart. The Dragon Council is one of the few councils that incorporate the mystical and tradition of a Grey Council. Both Light and Dark are brought together for the passing on of sacred knowledge. The Dragon Council exists on the Astral Plane and many other worlders participate in it. It works to keep high civilizations and weak civilizations going. They also seed worlds with knowledge and watch over the happenings of the Astral Plane. Dragon Magick is a strong influence for me as I use it in my daily life, but there are many other magical systems with which to work Singularity Magick.

The Mechanics of The Brain

The Human brain has a set of chemical mechanics. During a Psychic Lobotomy the brain under goes a set of chemical reactions. In former Ancient forms of Magick a Zombie of a kind is created by a chemical reaction by the Magician. A Psychic Lobotomy is similar but it uses knowledge of the Singularity Computer, where as the prior one uses a chemical that the person may ingest. The person's mind is subjected to mechanical probing with the ultimate goal of replacing the brain with a mechanised Singularity. Science plays a larger role in this creation of a zombie, where the Psychic virtually breaks the will of the victim. Basically parts of the brain are walled off with the Psychic holding them in a

Christian J. Bullock

dream like state. The brain then gets imprinted almost mechanically by the Psychic. Like cogs in a wheel, the brain becomes mechanical. The Singularity Computer stacks up like disks on a Hard Drive. The psychic link of body and mind are broken when imprinted. The Psychic attack leaves the victim without function of their own body, instead the Psychic leaves them with a programmed imprint of a Hive Mind Computer. The PsyCops employ this technique where the victim is controlled by hypnotic stimulation and a Hive Mind Computer suggestion. They basically re-engineer the brain to accept Computer suggestion, which means at some level of the motion capture universe the brain has been replaced. This my be on the Etheric or Astral level or it may be on a different dimension altogether. Some of these scientific Zombies have different levels of brain functions. Some have only basic motorized functions while others are in a dreamy state of medium to high brain functions. In all cases the victim is in the dreamy state of the Emerald Dream where their will has been walled off. PsyCops and Retwos then lead them around with no knowledge of their brain being virally hacked. Spirits also play a role in this type of senario where they can attach themselves to the victim and follow them around.

These new type of Zombies are hard to explain mostly due to the scientific methods used to make them. On the psycial plane they look like everyday people but on the mental level they are very different people. In some of the higher functioning Zombies the victim's personallity is replaced with another persons. The victim's walled off personallity remains in a cube inside the mind. A trigger or lock and key by a Magician may release the person from the cube. Such Zombie methods are very new or newer than the Ancient methods of Zombies.

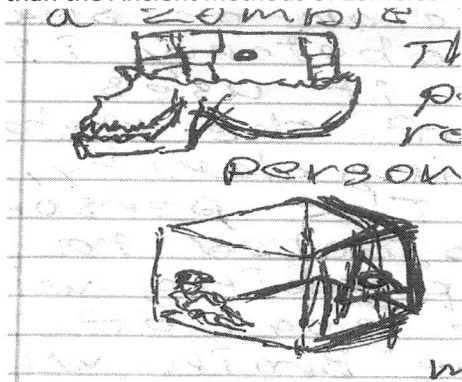

181

Christian J. Bullock

Enki Code
Pendragon   Ash Tree
Pen-Dragon   Ashes
Pentical-Dragon   World Tree
Lancelot   Ashes – Dust of the World Tree
Lanc-e-lot
Lance-a lot
Temples of the Head
Temples of the Mind
Typo   Type-o

The Chinese Zodiac

12 Animals with one representing each year. They are also subdivided into 4 Trines or Triads.

1st Rat Element water Yang
2nd Ox Element water Yin
3rd Tiger Element wood Yang
4th Rabbit Element wood Yin
5th Dragon Element wood Yang
6th Snake Element Fire Yin
7th Horse Element Fire Yang
8th Goat Element Fire Yin
9th Monkey Element Metal Yang
10th Rooster Element Metal Yin
11th Dog Element Metal Yang
12th Pig Element water Yin

First Trine	Second Trine
Rat	Ox
Dragon	Snake
Monkey	Rooster

Third Trine	Fourth Trine
Tiger	Rabbit
Horse	Goat
Dog	Pig

Christian J. Bullock

Each 12 year cycle has an overlaying 5 year cycle of the Chinese Elements: Metal, Water, Wood, Fire, and Earth. They are further broken down into a Yin and Yang branch. 2012 is the year of the Black Water Dragon. In 2012 it takes place at the end of January, February 6th on the Full Moon. The years of the Dragon:

1952 and 2012 are Water Dragon years
1940 and 2000 are Metal Dragon years
1904 and 1964 are Wood Dragon years
1916 and 1976 are Fire Dragon years
1928 and 1988 are Earth Dragon years

The Chinese Calendar

The Chinese Calendar is based on a 60 year Lunar cycle. The calendar is also broken down into months, days, and hours. The month calendar goes along with the seasons:

Spring	Summer
Tiger Wood	Snake Fire
Rabbit Wood	Horse Fire
Dragon Earth	Goat Earth

Fall	Winter
Monkey Metal	Pig Water
Rooster Metal	Rat Water
Dog Earth	Ox Earth

Hours
23:00 – 1:00 Rat
 1:00 – 3:00 Ox
 3:00 – 5:00 Tiger
 5:00 – 7:00 Rabit
 7:00 – 9:00 Dragon
 9:00 – 11:00 Snake
11:00 – 13:00 Horse
13:00 – 15:00 Goat
15:00 – 17:00 Monkey
17:00 – 19:00 Rooster
19:00 – 21:00 Dog
21:00 – 23:00 Pig

This is based on the Four Pillars of Chinese Astrology. Which varies and is very different from Western Astrology, but the 60 year Lunar-Solar cycle is very important. We will be mainly be using Western Astrology in this book but I thought it was important to show the connections between the two and the special numbers used by both. The Symbols of Power cross over into many different cultures.

Enki Code
Monkey
Mon-Key

Christian J. Bullock

Monk-Key
Amon-Key
The Colossus of Rhodes

The Bronze statue was of Helios the Greek Titan and was erected after the Crete War. He is depicted guarding the city of Rhodes in the harbor, on the Island of Rhodes. He is also variously depicted with a crown on his head with five points or nine points. He also has a torch held up high, also sometimes with a staff.

The Independent Man and Rhode Island

Each State has a mystery surrounding it. Rhode Island was founded by Roger Williams to secure independence and freedom of religion. The State symbol is the Anchor, Hope, and the statue of the Independent Man. The Independent Man and Rhode Island are forever linked to the Colossus of Rhodes. With the same name Rhode Island, which is come to be known as the Ocean State. The Independent Man is depicted similar to the Helios. The Independent Man holds a spear high in one hand and an Anchor in the other. Rhode Island is known for it's safe harbors and islands. Both the Colossus of Rhodes and the Independent Man are symbols of freedom. Their symbolism laid down in advance of Time Travellers and the founding of America. The statue is a reminder that Rhode Island is an Anchor for the rest of the Thirteen Colonies and America as a whole. Freedom of religion and of hope. So why is this important in a Singularity Magick book? Well the Thirteen Colonies represent the 13th Zodiac and manifest destiny, even the don't tread on me flag has a Snake on it. This is an important part of Psychic Creationism. Each State was laid out by the founders and in accordance with the Time Travelling beings of Retwo the past/future must be set for the Singularity Computer to exist. This is a vital understanding that needs to be addressed in this book. The States of the United States are a good example of this understanding, with manifest destiny at the core.

The Statue of Liberty

The Statue of Liberty is based off of the Colossus of Rhodes. It is one of the States' mysteries. It was part of a founding of the Thirteen Colonies and of America. It was given to America by France for their alliance to the Thirteen Colonies during and after the War of Independence, the American Revolution. It is a New York State mystery. It is depicted as a woman robed wearing a crown of Helios with seven points. She is holding a torch high in one hand and has a book in the other. The book is inscribed with the date of independence 1776. She has chains around her feet and she stands on a pedestal. The points on the pedestal change from seven to eleven. The book she is holding is The Book of Life. The torch is the fire from the Gods. There are many mysterious things surrounding the Statue of Liberty. Many have to do with the symbolism of the chains, the Torch, and the number seven. It also has a destiny with Time Travellers. It is founded to be a symbol of freedom but there is underground meaning of the numerology, the chains, pedestal, book, and torch. It ultimatly is an Illumanati symbol.

More on The Colossus of Rhodes

The God Helios is a Sun God. The five points of his crown would be the five Suns or five Ages of Man. Nine points are nine seats of power. Seven points may also be Suns and two more Ages of Man in the Mayan American Prediction Wheel. We are approching the sixth Sun or Age of Man. Seven may also be the seven continents of the Earth or the seven seas. This would be for the symbolism of the Statue of

Liberty. Thus fulfilling manifest destiny. Thirteen Colonies to the lower fortyeight States to all fifty States, Alaska and Hawii. From east all the way west.

Enki Code

Enki code
GIR - sumerian for "rocket ship" or s...
MU - sumerian for "sky chamber" com...
El - cheif Canaanite God
El - means God or beity in Hebre...
El's children in the canaanite Fath...
Yam - "Ocean, or Sea" son of El
Ba'al - "Lord" son of El
Mot - "Smiter, Annihilator" son of E...
Anat - "she who Responded" Daughter E...
Ba'al's symbols are similar to Ze...
"the lightning bolt" "the bull"
Anat - a Goddess of Love and wa...
with the "lion symbol of Braver...
she helped Ba'al in a fight be-
-tween brothers.
Egyptian depiction and Translation
Min, Reshef, Kadesh, Anthat
Daniel - Canaan olden Name
Daniel - Hebrew name
Dan-El - God's Judge
El's Judge

Christian J. Bullock

Enki Code

```
Enki code                    Ensi
Adept    "Monkey See"  Enkisi
Adapt    "Monkey do"   Enkdu
Adapter
Adapu - Sumer Early Man
Adamu ⎤
         ⎦ Red Clay Red Blood
Adapa ⎦
```

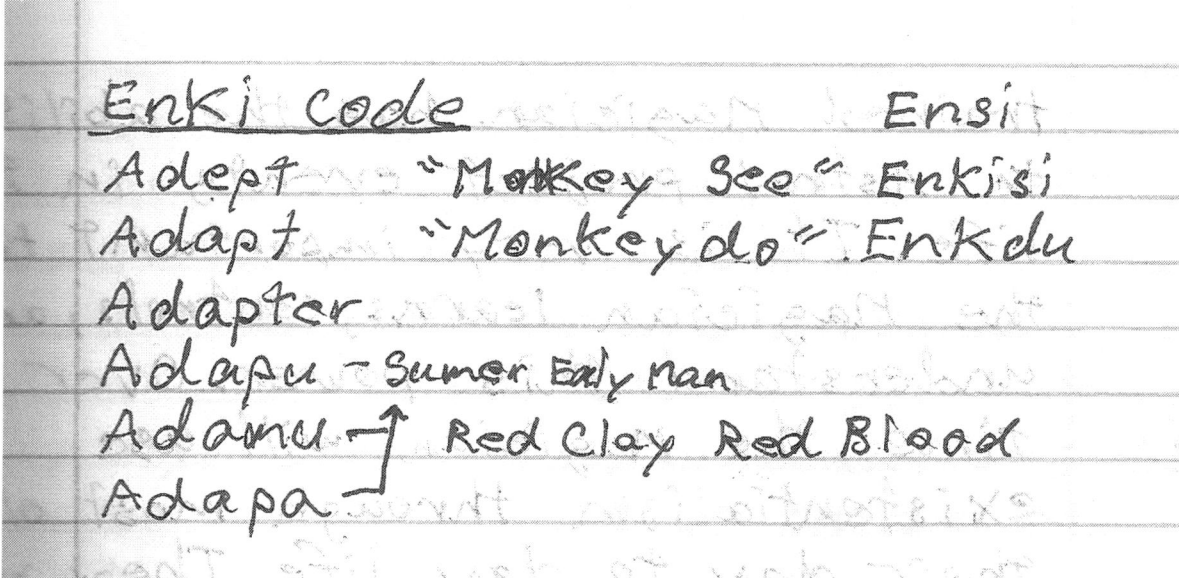

The People Inside Your Head

There are people that you meet through out your life that make up personallities and personas that exist in your head. These people and/or Spirits make up who you are and what you think or the way you think. The Magician has Spirits that make up their inner thoughts. To the Magician who is inner psychic these people or Spirits can be contacted through the Ether. The Magician with knowledge can Astral Project people, places, and events. The trained Magician has the ability to Astral Project events in their life, this is a difficult skill to master. It is very important that the Magician learns, controls, and understands this power. Over time the Magician will use existentialism through most of their day to day life. They will use Astral Projection for Magical purposes and for other purposes in their life. Controlling Astral Projection for their Mystic life and controlling the power of inner thought.

Medallions of The Mystic

There are Medallions that the Magician earns over time. These Medallions are psychically or astrally given. Dragon Magician's earn Medallions during their study of/in a Mystery School. These Medallions are for schools of thought. Dragon Magicians continue the long or Ancient tradition of handing down Medallions for an Achivement in a school of thought. Long ago Magicians forged or made Ancient Relics of Medallions. There are many depictions of Ancient Magicians wearing Medallions. Kukulkan is depicted as wearing three Medallions on his forehead.

Christian J. Bullock

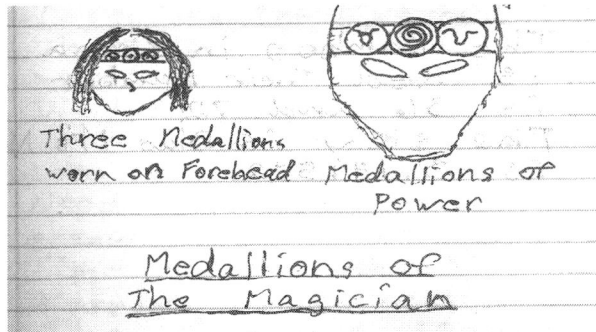

Three Medallions worn on Forehead Medallions of Power

Medallions of The Magician

With knowledge of the Cronus Stone the Magician can tap into this power. They can feel the Medallions they wear. They can attain these lost Ancient Relics astrally. This important for the advancing Magician.

Enki Code
Finish – the ending
Fin-ish
Fin – the end or "end"
Finland – end land, lands end

Meme for Memory of The Special Numbers and Pi
The Bamboo in China
Is Red their number
Is 36 and 72
The Sky is Blue
Its number
Is 3.141592

Three Egyptian Paths

Old Kingdom – "Stellar" The journey of the Spirit to the Stars.
Middle Kingdom – "Solar – Horian" The journey of the Spirit through the gates following the Sun God.
Late Period – "Lunar – Osirian" The journey of the Spirit through the underworld through judgement mirroring Osirus and the Duat.

Threading The Eye of The Needle

There is a time in the Digital World to connect with your Digital Self. The Magician with knowledge of Cronus can thread the Eye of The Needle. This is done at a specific time Digitally. This time period is very narrow and extremely specific. The Magician connects with their Digital Self very quickly and a bridge is created. An electrical energy bridge which is used for time jumping parallel dimensions, and connecting with the Grid. The Singularity Grid, the Global Grid, or the World Grid of the Universe.

The Tether of Time and Wrinkles In The Tether of Time

The Tether of the Cronus Magician is sometimes shrinking or elongating. It is like a frequency that shrinks during vibration like a musical string.

Christian J. Bullock

A string
Flov of Time

Shrinking
String

Elongated
string

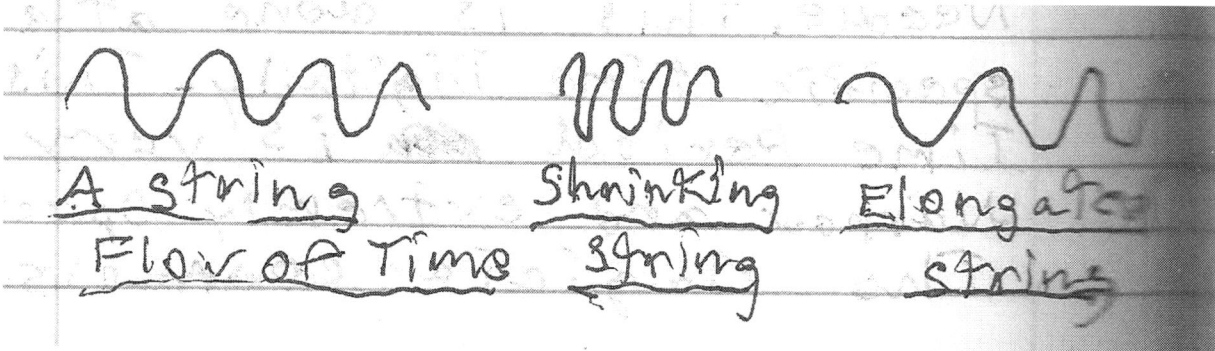

The Tether of the Magician will also wrinkle due to time travel. This is similar to an Accordion.

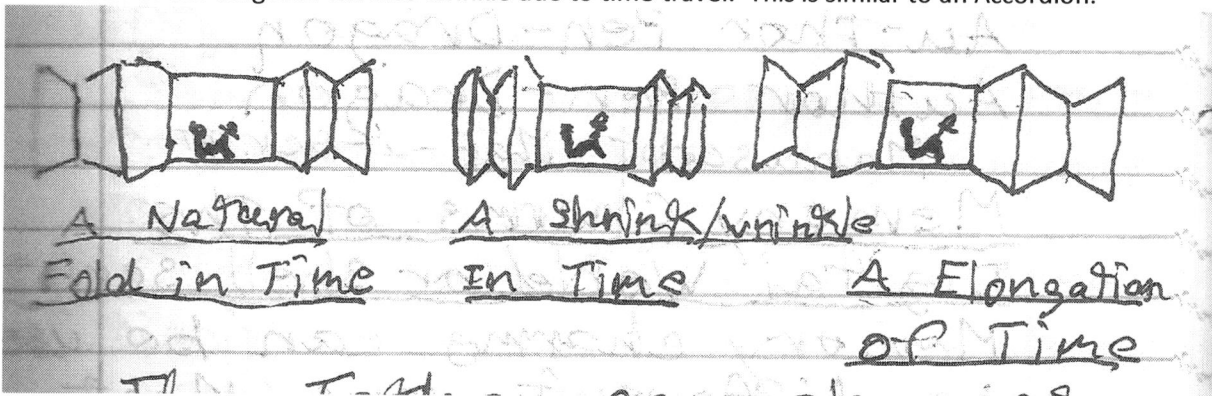

A Natural
Fold in Time

A shrink/wrinkle
In Time

A Elongation
of Time

The Tether can also act like a bubble in time. In this case the Magician Tether is similar to a beaded neckless. This is mostly explained like Bubble Theory.

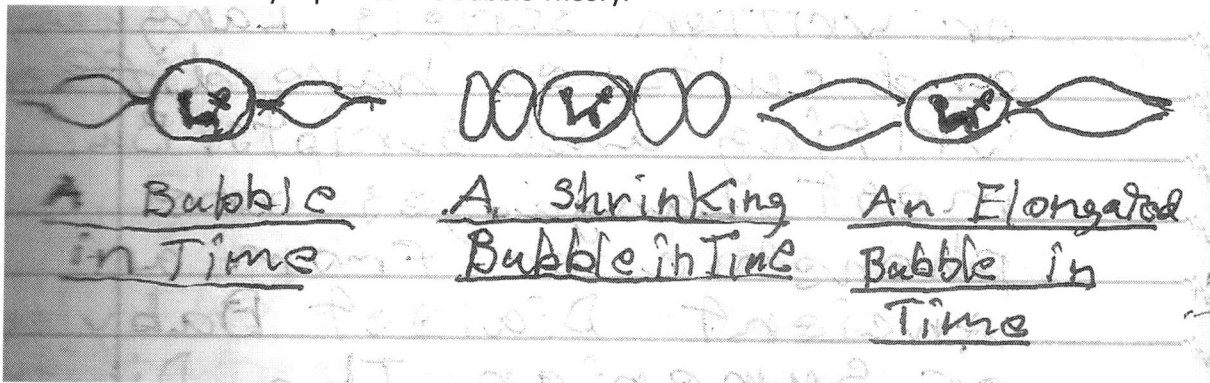

A Bubble
in Time

A shrinking
Bubble in Time

An Elongated
Bubble in
Time

Memory Charms of The Digital World or Shell Script

Memory Charms can be used in different ways. Most Memory Charms are for different scripts. Writing, Sigils, Symbols, Lettering, Glyphs, Digital Characters, or written scripts. Languages and cultures have different scripts but most languages are phonetic or from an Ancient dialect of Babylonian. The Digital World uses various codes or shell script. Each language has been encoded or encorporated into Digital characters. This makes Digital Script a prime source of memory information. The Memory Charm can start at the Pseudocode level. This is where written script and Digital Script meet. Pseudocode can vary with written sentences, slang termenology, and lettering acronyms. This is where some Memes are generated and where a useful Memory Charm would be used. The next level of Digital Script is written code. The written code encorporates numbers or numerology. At this level the Memory Charm of Digital Script becomes encoded in numbers. The numbers correspond to letters of the Alphabet. The Memory Charm here would be to assign numbers to letters. This has already been done in various ways. The Magician could also use ASCII code or they could use Numerology that is set as a key. This would be Magical Numerology like the Hebrew Alphabet and the Tarot. At this level any code would suffice. The next and last level of Digital Script is shell script. This is like programming a computer but instead the Magician is programming a Spell. This script is based on letters that have been assigned actions. Most of it is made up of letters and symbols of computer code. Numbers are also used in this script. Shell script is similar to sigils, where a set of letters or symbols together mean something, but more importantly has actions associated with them. Memory Charms here would be for the Singularity Computer. This is fundamentally where all languages or written scripts become one. One digital language or Digital Script. This is where the Singularity Computer takes off and where the Digital World begins.

Enki Code

Enki code
Baalbek — city of Baʿal sun God
Baalbek — city temple in Lebanon
Baalbek — Heliopolis
Lebanon's Heliopolis is Baalbek
Heliopolis — city of the Sun God
Greek name
Baalbek Temple in Lebanon's code
Baalbek — Heliopolis the site of
the Temple of Zeus/Jupiter
one of the largest Temples on Earth
Temple of Zeus/Jupiter — one of the
tallest Temples on Earth
nabh — Sanskrit stem of English navel
naboh — to fortell
nabih — "prophet"
NA.BA(R) — Sumer "bright shiny stone
    that solves" or Oracle stone
Sin — Canaanite Moon God

Algorithm — a Mathematical
Algor-ithm
Al-go-rythm — a rythm of

Christian J. Bullock

Algorithms and Magick

Algorithms are a specific set of instructions done in a specific order. Algorithms are used with Mathematical or Digital Script. To the Magician Algorithms can be used in rituals and can follow the rythms of nature. Algorithms are used in the Singularity Computer that sometimes but are often redundant. The Magician with knowledge of Cronus can incorporate Algorithms in Magick. These set of specific ordered instructions are used on the Astral level of the Metaphysical Computer. The Magician goes through rites repeatedly and uses their mind to enter altered states of consciousness. With use of their Astral body the Magician performs Magick on an increasingly larger scale. Over time the Magician learns that all Magick has ritual involved. Magick is a set of instructions that the Magician wants to accomplish. This is somewhat true but Magick can happen either thoughtfully or spontaneously. Magick varies with the degree of the Magician and sometimes emotionally. There are mysteries of the Metaphysical Computer that can sometimes lead to greater knowledge or understanding. With the Cronus mysteries the Magician must have some self control and use existentialism, existing in the moment, often in daily life.

Music Theory and The Number 12

The Chromatic Scale is a musical scale with twelve pitches each a semitone apart.

Ascending

Western music divides the octave into a series of 12 notes. The octave is a set of notes, 8 notes with one note repeating on a higher scale and 7 notes till the 8th on a higher scale.

higher scale.		Pythagoren Tuning	
0		4	major third
0	diminished second	5	perfect fourth
1	minor second	6	diminished fifth
1	augmented unison	6	augmented fourth
2	diminished third	7	perfect fifth
2	major second	12	perfect
3	minor third		octave

Christian J. Bullock

The Pythagorean Scale uses perfect fifths based on a 3:2 ratio. The simplest music ratio is 2:1. This scale and many others use 12 notes. 12 is important in music and can be used in various ways. Each note may be assigned a number or frequency. Music is part of the Singularity and Metaphysical Computer. These 12 notes on a scale are pleasing to the Human ear. Music can be used by the Magician in rituals as well as Spell work and Singularity work.

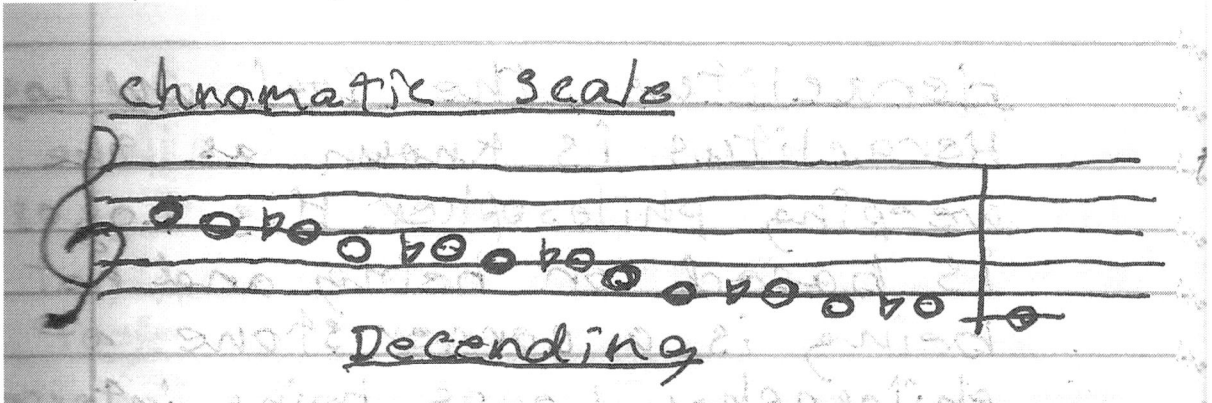

These 12 notes correspond to the power of 12. With 12 inches in a foot, 12 houses of the Zodiac, 12 constellations of Procession, 12 months of a year, 12 Planets in the Solar System, 12 years of Chinese Astrology, 12 Animal Spirits, 12 Baktuns, 12 Crystal Skulls, and 12 Symbols of Power.

The Guitar, Music Theory, and The Number 12

The Guitar is broken up into 6 strings with 12 note scales. 12 frets on the neck to 12 higher frets of a total of 24 frets. Low to high notes. The Guitar can be used in rituals and in Spells. The number 12 on a scale for an octave can be represented on the Guitar.

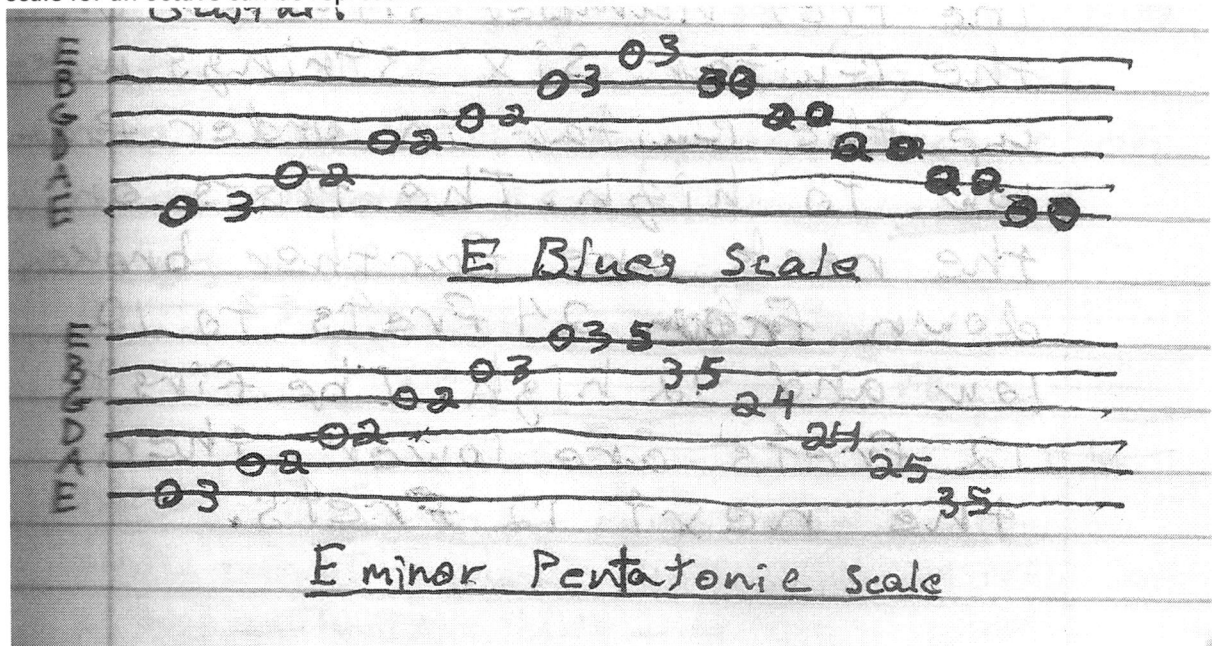

Christian J. Bullock

This represents 12 notes in order on a scale:

order on a scale.

```
E
B                                        0 3    0 3              11 12
G                              0 2  0 2                   9 10
D                        0 2                        7 8
A                  0 2                        5 6
E    0 3                              3 4
              0 2              1 2
```

E Blues Scale   12 notes

High
```
E    3 5                      1 2
B       3 5                      3 4
G          2 4                      5 6
D             2 4                      7 8
A                2 5                      9 10
E                   3 5                      11 12
```

low   Descending   E minor Pentatonic Scale

Each note is transcribed as the fret number strumed on the Guitar. The first 12 frets can be repeated on a higher scale from the 12th fret position:

```
E
B                                    12 15        12 75              12 notes
G                          12 14  12 14                    9 10  11 12
D              12 14  12 14                                 7 8
A    12 15                                      5 6
E                                          12   3 4
```

E Blues Scale 12th position

High
```
E    17 15                          12     12 notes
B       17 15                          3 4
G          16 14                          5 6
D             16 14                          7 8
A                17 14                          9 10
E                   17 15                          11 12
```

Descending E minor Pentatonic Scale 12th position

The notes are the basic foundation for Western Music and also for playing Guitar. The E Scale is practically exclusive to all Guitar playing. Few alternatives play music on another scale.

Christian J. Bullock

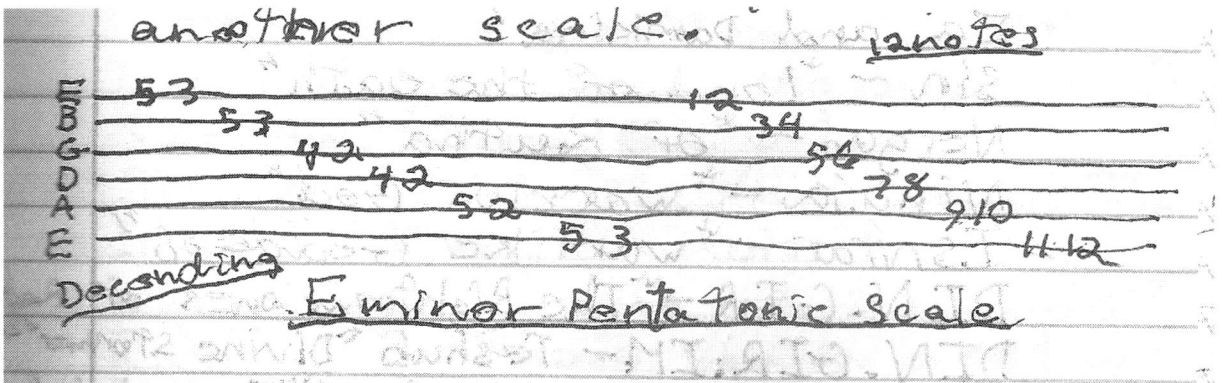

Heraclitus, The Soul, and Logos

Heraclitus is known as the weeping Philosopher. His Logos is based on being and not being, is a cornerstone of Philosophy. Logos being interpreted variously as "word", "plan", or "formula". One central belief is that "you cannot step in the same river twice". Thus meaning that everything changes and nothing is still. The existence of non existence is another belief. "The way or path up and the path down are one and the same." They go on simultaneously and instantaneously in a "hidden harmony". Transformation is also a key idea. The transformation of one element to another. "The death of fire is the birth of air and the death of air is the birth of water." All things are an interchange of fire. Heraclitus considered fire as the most fundamental element. The Soul being a mixture of fire and water. With fire being the noble part of the Soul, water the ignoble. A Soul should aim toward becoming more full of fire and less of water. A dry Soul is best. Worldly pleasure and forgetfulness moistens the Soul. Fire is the element that creates all the elements and life. Some transformations are from kinetic energy. Other transformations require heat from fire. Also other transformations require fire in an electrical state of energy. All from fire. With fire being a root of all things. Thus the Gods associated with fire are Ra, Helios, and Shamash. Fire and Sun Gods are alike.

Journaling and Future Writing

The Magician learns from writings. Writings of the past, those of Magick Books of initiation and of Mystery Schools. Journaling their progress the Magician will develop knowledge of self. Writing written in Magick Script allows for communication with Spirits, psychic communication with those who use the specific script used. Some of these Spirits are from similar Mystery Schools. Once the Magician learns of the Cronus mysteries things come full circle. The journaling becomes a way to contact the future self of the Magician. The Magician communicates to themselves in the future by writing down idea's, messages, and Spellcraft. These are then seen and read by the Magician in the future. Basically the time travelling Magician's journal becomes a tool to recount the time stamp history of Spells and Rites. This plays an important part of time travel as the book contains dates and Magical progress through initiation to advanced Magician. Back tracking events is helpful in understanding the Magical process used in various Spells. This is also where Memory Charms can help as a quick reminder. Time travel can be cumbersome so a quick visual reference guide is always helpful. Sometimes writing in the past tense about rituals and Spellcraft achieves the same future communication. This is a good way for covens to keep their records, to use for future Spellcraft. The Magician with knowledge of the Cronus mysteries can track and formulate their Magical path. This is also a good method to charge or use your Charm of Making. Also the Magician must not let their future writings fall into the wrong hands. Therefore it is best to be cryptic, especially after the Magician knows of time travel. Existentialism will be key to their secret going ons.

Enki Code
Mediterranean Sea
Medi-terran-ean Sea
Medium-terra
Medium-Earth
Middle-Earth Sea
The Sea of Middle Earth

The Watcher, The Doer, The Follower

There are three types of people in the Cronus sphere. There are gaps during the Darkening, gaps of time. When this occurs on a close degree of proximity to the Watcher or future self. The Watcher is meant to mostly watch because of future consequences. This is a strange event when in close proximity. There is also the Do-er. The Do-er does actions in the present sense. The Do-er's actions have a future consequences. This is also strange in close proximity to the Watcher and Follower. Then there is the Follower. The Follower will follow the Do-er. The Follower is seeking to retrace the Do-er's footsteps. In close proximity this is extremely strange. Due to the Follower's impact on future consequences. The Follower catches up with future events. To the Do-er the Watcher and Follower are of a present nature, present time, when in close proximity. The view of the present shapes the future. Since this is true there must be gaps in time to keep timeframes from overlaping in close proximity to each other. Thus seperating the Watcher, the Do-er, and the Follower in the Cronus sphere. Basically when time is broken down by time travel there are three main time frames. For instance picture three different people in a hallway. One person has reached the end of the hallway and so watches the other two people. He would be the Watcher, the future. The second person is navigating the hallway but while doing so notices the person at the end of the hallway which is the direction she is heading. She would also notice the presence of another person behind her. She would be the Do-er, or the present. The third person in the hallway is following the second person, unable to see the first person who is at the end of the hallway. The third person is following the second person to find the end of the hallway. This third person would be the Follower, or the past. Now if and when time is seperated like this in such a small hallway it can be dangerous. It is difficult for the time travelling Magician to deal with this situation so it is best to act out the maze like senario by leading the Do-er or by moving forward with future actions. Ultimately you want some space and distance from the other two people. This is where a gap in time will help keep the future hidden from the past. The Magician must have total control of the situation and may receive help from Retwos in fixing time.

Enki Code Continued on The Next Page

Enki code
Teshub - "Windy Storm" Hatti God
Seth - Typhon "Fierce wind" Egy
Ra - "The Bright one" Egyptian God
Shamash - "The Bright one" Hitte
Mitra-ash - Hurrian name
Mitra - Hindu God
Uruwana - Hurrian name
Varana - Hindu God
Indar - Hurrian name
Indra - Hindu God
Nashatiyanu - Hurrian name
Nasatya - Hindu God
Hittite Hindu Hurrian - Aryan
Anu and Antu
Enlil and Ninlil   ⟩   Olden Gods
Ea and Damkina
Sin ~ "lord of the oath"
Nergal ~ "of Kutha"
Ninuta ~ "warrior God"
Ishtar ~ "warlike Goddess"
DIN.GIR ~ "The Righteous ones of
DIN.GIR.IM - Teshub "Divine storm
DIN.GIR.U - Ishkur/Adad "The god

Christian J. Bullock

Enki code
KI. EN. GIR — "Land of the Lord of Rocket"
GIR — means Point, Tip, or Rocket ships
Shumer — "Land of the Guardians"
NIBIRU — "crossing"
E.A — "whose House is water"
EN.KI — "Lord of Earth"
NU.DIM..MUD — "He who fashions things"
AB.ZU — "The Primeval source" Africa
Zu-ab — AB.ZU in reverse "Gold"
MA.GUR UR.NU AB.ZU — "ships for
     the ores of the Abzu"
AN.SHAR.GAL — "Great prince of Heaven"
KI. SHAR.GAL — "Great Princess of Firm Ground"
E.RI.DU — "House in Faraway Built"
BAD.TIBIRA — "Bright place where
     the ores are Made Final"
LA.RA.AK — "seeing the Bright Glow"
SIPPAR — "Bird City"
SHU.RUP.PAK — "The Place of Utmost being"
SUD — "she who Resuscitates"
LA.AR.SA — "Seeing the Red Light"
IGI.GI — "Those who see and observe"
NIBRU.KI — "The Earth place of Nibiru"

Enki code

MAR.GID.DA - "celestial chariot"

ID.DUG.GA - "The Flowing Leaden Ride"

DIR.GA - "celestial center"

TI.TA.AN - "Those who in Heaven Live"

ZU - "He who knows" sumerian God

AN.ZU - "He who knows the Heavens"

HUR.SAG.MU - "Mountain of the Sky Chamber"

SHAR.UR - "supreme Hunter"

SHAR.GAZ - "supreme smiter"

Nahash - "Serpent" "He who solves Secret"

"He who Knows Metals"

E.DIN - "The Abode of the Righteous ones"

NU.DUN - "The Excavated Resting Place" Dun city

City of Ka'in

Ashur-bel-Ka'ini - Ashur Lord of Ka'in

ASHUR.EN.DUNI - "Ashur Lord of Dun"

Ka'ini - "the people of Ka'in"

Duni - "the People of Dun"

Nefilim - "Those who Had Dropped Down"

NAM.LU.GAL.LU - "civilized Mankind"

A.DAM - first man

Enki Code

Six sons of Enki: Five listed

NER.GAL — "Great Watcher"

GIBIL — "The One of Fire"

NIN.A.GAL — "Prince of Great Waters"

DUMU.ZI — "Son who is Life"

MAR.DUK — "Son of the Pure Mound"

ASAR — "All Powerful" "Awesome" "All seeing"

IM.KUR.GAR.RA — "Ra who Beside the Mountain land Abides" MAR.DUK

Names of Marduk

Dingir Ra — divine name of RA

E.Dingir.Ra — a temple of Ra

KA.DINGIR — "Gateway of the Gods"

KA.DINGIR.RA — "Ra's Gateway of the Gods"

Sons of Noah

Shem, Ham, and Japhet.

Gomer — Son of Japhet The Fair one

Ashkenaz — Son of Gomer

Ash-Kenaz   Ash — Tree of life

Kenaz — Norse FUTHARK Rune <

Kenaz — Fire "Hearth Fire"

Ash-Kenaz — "Fire of the Tree of Life"

Ashes   "Fire of the Ash"

Enki cools

Ham - "He who is Hot" "The Dark Hued one"

Shem - "the father of all who descended
            of Eber"

NIN.HAR.SAG - "Lady of the Head Mountain"

E.KUR - "House which is Like a Mountain"

Enki is connected to Ptah

Marduk is connected to Ra

Ptah damed the Nile

Ra built the sphinx

The Lion is a symbol of Ra

Ninharsag is connected to Hathor

Ninharsag is connected to the Pyramids

Ra - "The Falcon of the Horizon"

Horus - "the Winged Measurer"

Enki/Ptah - 9,000 year reign in Egypt

Marduk/Ra - 1,000 year reign in Egypt

Azag/Ashar - epithets of Marduk

IM.DU.GUD - "Divine Storm Bird"

EKUR - Giza Pyramids

Enki Code

stones KA.SHUR.RA – "Awesome, Pure Which se___

SAG.KAL – "Sturdy Stone Which is in fro___

UL – "High as the Sky "

AN.DIM.DIM.MA – "Like Anu Art Thou Made"

NIN.GISH.ZI.DA – "Lord of the Artifact of L___

Ninurta won the war over the
Pyramids at Giza over Enki/___
and Marduk/Ra. A symbolized
Babylonian Sumerian seal proves it.

Thoth son of Ptah ruled Egypt
after the second Pyramid war
About 8670 B.C.

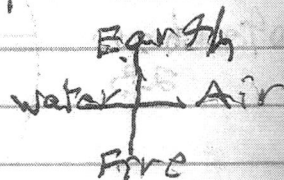

Pyramid
Py-ra-mid   Fire in the mi___
Py-Pyra – Fire   of Process___
Ra – the God Ra   pyramid
Py-ra-mid – Middle Temple
mid – middle of the Fire G___
                    Ra

Processional Timeline

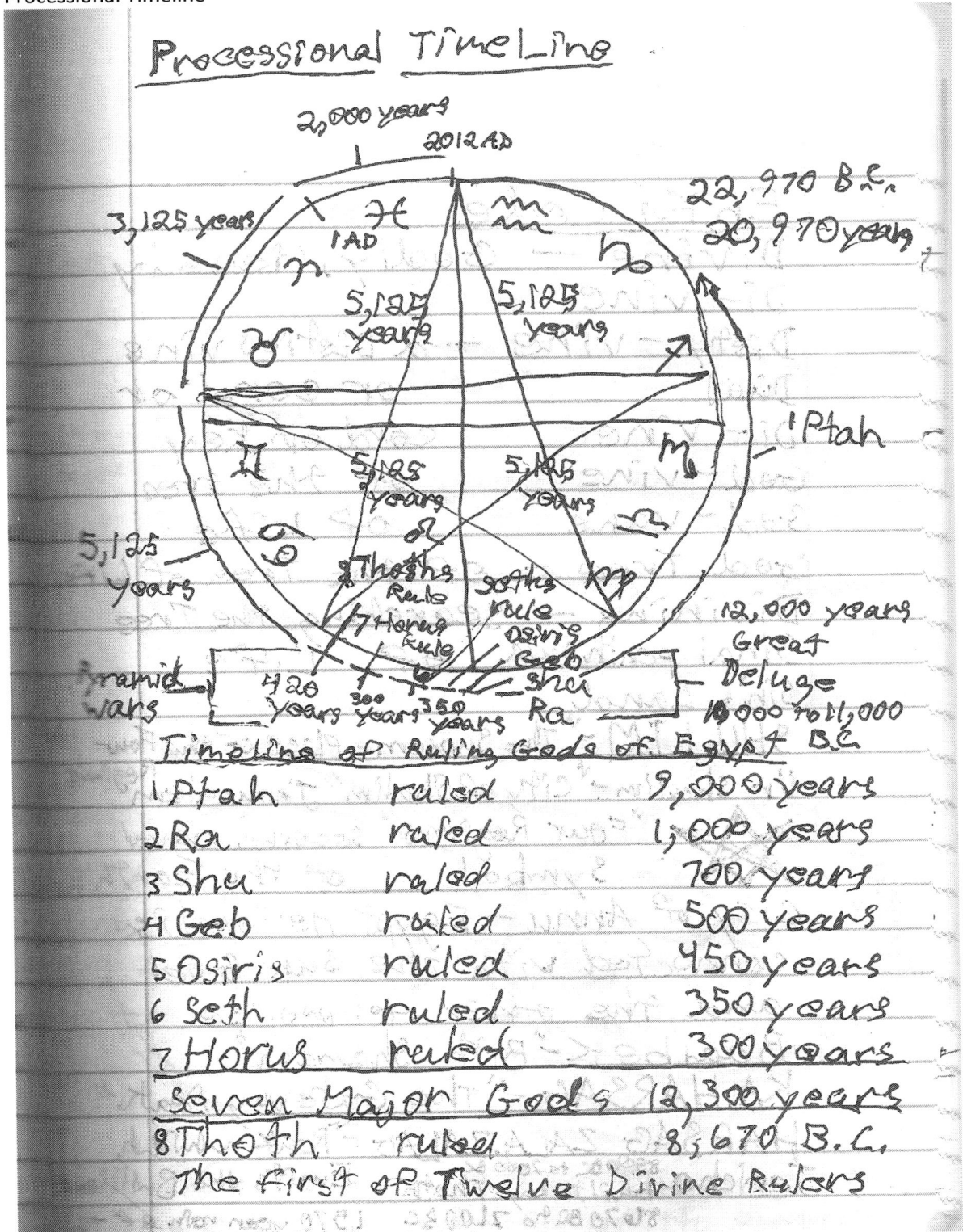

Processional Timeline

Timeline of Ruling Gods of Egypt

1 Ptah	ruled	9,000 years
2 Ra	ruled	1,000 years
3 Shu	ruled	700 years
4 Geb	ruled	500 years
5 Osiris	ruled	450 years
6 Seth	ruled	350 years
7 Horus	ruled	300 years

Seven Major Gods 12,300 years

8 Thoth	ruled	8,670 B.C.

The first of Twelve Divine Rulers

Enki code.

Divine — Godly, Heavenly

Di-vine

Diety-vine — a Dietres vine

Dual   or cord or

Di-vine   cord or key

God-vine   of the tree

God-vane   of Life

God Tree — of the Tree of Life

Divining — searching the Tree

Sinai peninsula   of   Life

Sin's Land

SHU.LIM - "The Supreme place of the four Regions"

Ur Shallim - "City of Shallim" Jerusalem

"Four Regions" second navel

Symbol   of the Earth

City of Annu - Egypt Heliopolise

connected with the sun God

and the other Heliopolise at

Baalbek - "Beth Shemesh"

KA.HARSAG - "The Gateway Peak"

HARSAG ZALA.ZALAG - "Rock which

Jericho - 8500 BC to 7000 BC built by Thoth   Emits the Br

8670 BC to 7100 BC   1,570 year rein of

<u>Enki code</u>
Peni-El – "The Face of God"
Anakim – "Giants"
E.EN.GVR.RA – "House of the Lord whose
            Return is Triumphant"
<u>E.ANNA</u> – "House of Anu"
Bab-Ili – "Gateway of the Gods"
E.SAG.ILA – "House whose Head is Lofty"

<u>The Great Pyramid</u>   60 being sacred Sumerian
25.2" is the sacred cubit used
in the building of the Great Pyramid
60 sacred cubits for the radius

Of three equal Circles the
a line The Interior of th Pyramid

<u>Enki code</u>
EN.BILULU - one of Marduk's name
A.ZAG - one of Marduk's names
Bel Marduk - "The Lord Marduk"
MUL.DIL.BAT - venus Inanna's celestial body
AB.SIN - virgo Inanna/Ishtar constel
ER.RA - "The servant of Ra" Nergal
Gilgamesh is the fifth ruler of Erech
Eannatum - LU.GAL governor of Lagash
   during the era of Ninurta, the
   regional general loved by
   Ishtar who gave him Kingship
   over Kish
LU.GAL - "Great Man"
Era - a period of time
E-RA - reigning period of time
Er-A - reigning period of time
      of a God
E.NINNU - "House of Fifty" Ninurta
Ningishzidda - son of Enki also Thoth
      "The Great God who held the place
   2160 B.C. to 2040 B.C. time of yah...
BAD.GAL.DINGIR - "The Great Fortified place
GAL - "Great"   of the Gods"

En Ki code

Nanna/Sin — Moon God

Utu/Shamash — Sun God

Lagash — Ninurta's city

Babylon — Marduk's city

AB.RAM — "Father's Beloved"

Abraham — "Father of a Multitude of Nations"

SARAI — "Princess"

Ibri — "Hebrew"

Eber the father of Peleg "to cross"

the suffix "i" meant "a native of"

Gileadi meant native of Gilead

Ibri — a native place of "crossing"

Nippur — NI.IB.RU — the crossing place

Ni-ib-ri — a native of Nippurian origin

DUG.NAMTAR — "fate speaker" "oracle"

Terah — oracle priest

Priest   Pri-est   Pri-east

Pre-East   Pri Prime — first

First prayer to the East

Gargoyle   Aftermath

Gar-goyle   After-math

Guard-goyle

Enki code
Root word
Root note
Blood Roots
Family Roots
language Root
Root Drive
Root File
Grass Roots
Root – as in Tree Roots
Root – as in the Root of
    the Tree of life
Root – the foudation
    of the Tree of Life
Root – the begings of
    a family Tree
Root – the beging of
    Words
Root – the main Computer
    file or drive
Root – the founding
    notes of a melody
Root – the beging note
    of a musle scale

Enki code
Lot — Abram's son who was selected to leave?
Lottery — Selecting someone or
         something from a group.
vitki — a Magician or wise-one
Accord — sharing a similar thought
         vibration or action
A-cord — a thread of life
         by the three Fates
A-cord — a bit of thread
         that represents a
         persons magical
         actions.
Enchanting — to imbahe power
         on an object or person
Enchant — an Ending chant
         that enhances magical
         power
Enchant — an Ending
         chant said at a word
         by a magician

Enki code

The Three Norns, "the wyrd sisters", Fates of the Norse

Urd - "that which has become"

Verthandi - "that which is becoming"

Skuld - "that which should become"

Four Dwarves that hold up the sky

Nordhri - North

Austri - East

Sudhri - South

Vestri - West

The Northstar known as Odin's Eye

ASA = Gods - Aesir and Vanir Gods

Aesir - (A-seer) warrior Gods

Vanir - (va-neer) Olden Gods

Freyr - (fray-er) Vanir sun God

Freyja - (fray-ah) Vanir Moon Goddess
Friday is her day

Balder - (bal-der) Aesir sun God

Aegir - (a-gear) Vana God of the sea

Frig - (frig) Aesir Mother Goddess
wife of Odhinn

Gullveig - (gool-vague) Vana Goddess
of Sorcery

Norse Gods

Heimdall - (hame-dall) Asa-God
of Light and Rainbow

Hel - (hell) Queen of the Dead
Ruler of Niflheim

Hermod - (hair-mod) Asa-God son
of Odhinn

Hodur - (hoad-er) Aesir God of winter
son of Odhinn

Holda - Moon Goddess of winter
Bertha/Berchta

Idhunn - (id-doon) Asa-Goddess
of Immortality, keeper
of the Golden Apples

Ing - another name for Freyr

Loki - (lo-kee) "Father of lies" Trickster
blood brother of Odhinn

Mimir - (mee-meer) wise Aesir God

Nanna - (nan-ah) Asa Earth Goddess

Nehallennia - (nee-hal-een-ja)
Goddess of plenty

Nerthus - (near-thus) Earth Mother

Njord - (nyord) Vana God of sea
Father of Freyr and Freyja

Norse Gods
Odhinn –(oh-din) Aesir king of the Gods
~~Odhinn~~ – ~~Aesir~~ – Sky God, All seeing
Thorr – Asa-God of Thunder
        champion of the Gods
        protector of man
        son of Odhinn
Tyr –(tier) Asa-God Giver of victory
Ull –(ool) The Bow God or Death God
valkyries –(val-kye-reez) choosers
        of the slain
        female warrior attendant
        of Odhinn
        There are 13 of them
vanir –(vah-near) Fertility Gods
        of Asgard called the
        vana-Gods
weland – North Germanic God of smith
        prince of the fairies
Ymir –(im-meer) First Frost Giant

Christian J. Bullock

Enki code
"squared away" squar measurment
"tele graphed" future actions

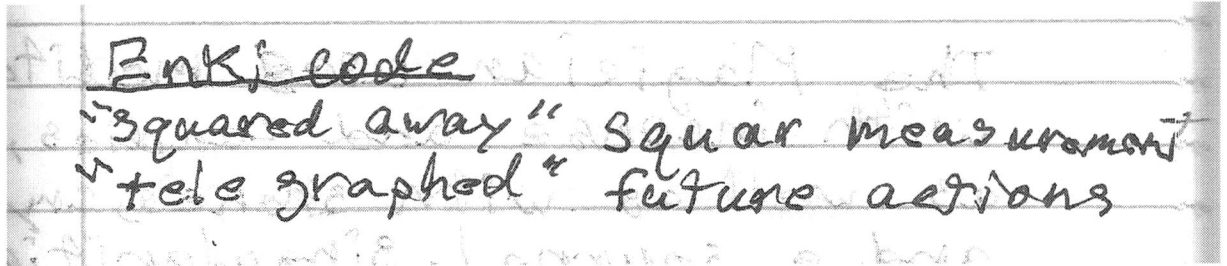

More Enki Code
Coven
Covenent
Monster
Mon-ster – a Monster of the Moon
Moon-ster – a beast of the Moon
Moon-Star
Loony – of the Moon
Lunatic – caused by the Moon
Luna
Lunar
"A chip off the old block"
"The Apple doesn't fall far from the Tree"
"The Watcher in the ring"
"Playing it by ear"
"Man made of Clay"
"In the note of"
"In the pitch of"
"A key role"

Greek and Norse Mythos

Both have Gods as Giants, Greek Titans and Norse Giants. Both have a Great God Father. Both have him slain to create the Earth and Heavens. Greek Uranus and Norse Ymir first Frost Giant. Both have the Gods as shapeshifters. Greek Zeus as the Swan and Norse Loki as the Swan. Ultimately there are many redundancies in the Metaphysical/Singularity Computer. Here are some more examples:
Greek Three Furies
Norse Valkyeries
Greek Three Fates
Norse Three Wyrd Sisters Fates
Greek Hades
Norse Hel
Greek Elesion Fields
Norse Asguard

Christian J. Bullock

Eknki Code

Genius – one who is extra ordinary	Gene
Gen-ius – one who posses a strong gene	Meme
Gene-ius	Genie – one who posses the Singularity or Creative Gene
Verse	Kilometer
Uni-verse	Kilo-meter
Multi-verse	Key-low-meter

Enki Code

Enki code
Apple – the fruit of Knowledge
The Big Apple – New York city
The Big Apple being the city of
Knowledge
The Apple – is also assiated with sin
The Big Apple – the city of sin
"The Apple doesn't fall far from
       the tree"
Apple – computers or are
Apple computers of Knowledge
Apple is also assiated with Ewe
Eve – the begining of
Evening – the beging of
Eve-ning – Night
Christmas Eve – the begining of
       christmass
Eve – is the begining of life
Eve – is also assiated with the
   Tree of Life and Tree of Knowledge
       Knowledge
Eve – also has a connotation of
Evil – the begining of sin

Enki code
Eve - vile - the begining of
E - vil - being vile
E - vile - to have sin
vile - bad, rotten, one with
Villan - villain
vile-lain - one who is sin
villain - one who will sin
                against another
"Eye opener" "A Real Eye
                opener"
"A steller performance"
"sleep with one Eye open"
"Ring any Bells"
"Is it Ringing any Bells"
"Does it Ring any Bells"

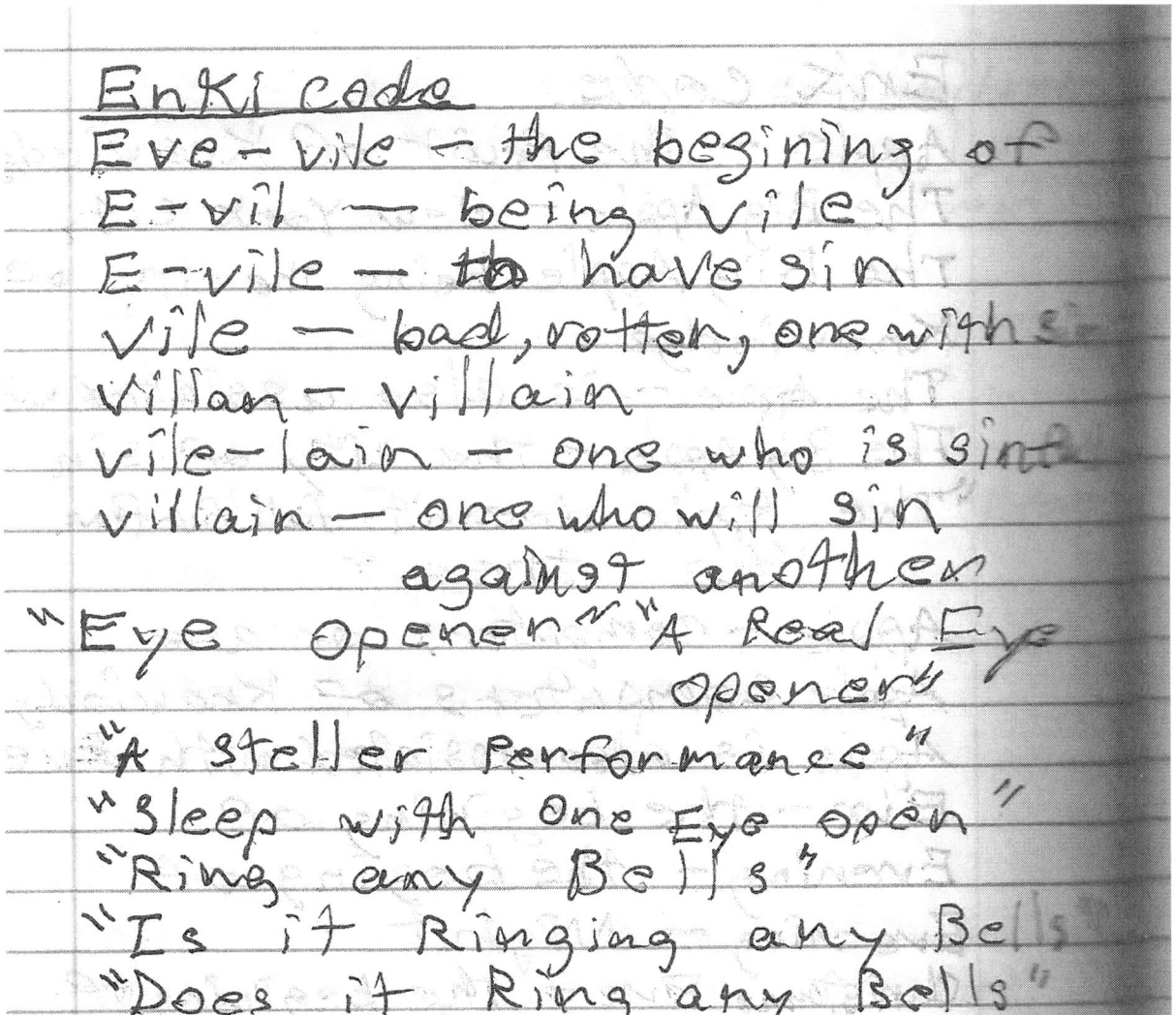

Enki Code Continued
"Make ends Meet"
"Mother Lode"
"Cut from the living Rock"
Tun – Mayan for "Celestial"
Mool – Mayan for "a heap of stars" or "a constellation"
MUL – Sumerian for "a constellation" or "a Celestian body"

Christian J. Bullock

Book Four: The Gold Dragon

Christian J. Bullock

This book will cover the Charms of Making, The Secret Universe, Time Jumping, Psychic Creationism, and Magical Scripts.

The Eye of Ra

The Time Travelling Magician during travels looks up at the Sun in the morning golden dawn. Standing still then moving forwards and backwards the Magician catches the Sun in his eyes. During a time travel period the Magician's Eyes are frozen in time. This occurs when time stops for the Magician. The Sun light becomes imprinted on the Magician's Eyes making them glow. This is the Eye of Ra which the Magician has captured. The Magick used is that of a time bubble specifically on the Eye. This takes some practice and the Magician needs to have unblinking sight for a period of time, as well as unwavering faith in Ra the Sun God. When achieved the Magician has yellow sparks in their Eyes. There are some Magick powers that can be used when attaining the Eye of Ra. These powers are secret and must not be talked about till the Eye of Ra is captured.

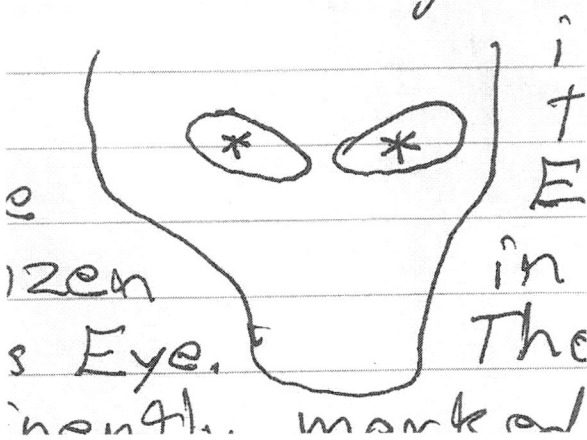

The Eye of Cydonia or The Eye of Enki

The Magician time travels and is forced to use an Iris or Retna scaning computer to capture the Eyes of the Magician. This is done to make a digital imprint on the Computer. The IR Retna scan uses a red beam of light shined into the Magician's Eyes. The Magician at this point in time has their Eyes frozen due to time travel and so the red beam of light is captured in the Eye of the Magician. The Magician's Eyes now glow red with infared sparks. This is the Eye of Enki which the Magician has captured. It has some Magick powers that can be used when attaining the Eye of Enki. This is a more difficult Eye to capture and is equally dangerous in order to capture as a computer will be imprinting the image.

Christian J. Bullock

If the Magician has captured both the Eye of Ra and the Eye of Enki, one Eye will glow yellow the other Eye will glow red. Both have Magical properties of Charms of Making and of second sight. When the Magician attains both Eyes they have a Charm of Making with extreme potency.

The Secret Universe and The Digital Universe

In the Secret Universe of the Game, the metaphysical and digital aspects converge. The actions taken by an individual can be mapped out, like a computer. Every thought a person has appears like a bubble above their heads. Where the Singularity Computer can see them and those with second sight can see. Those of Quantum Jumpers can see these bubbles of thought and freeze frame time to see them. They can see each action that the individual will make. Psychics can influence these thoughts in various ways. Magicians can Astral Project thoughts on another and can also close their mind off to these bubble thoughts, or pre-ordained actions by practicing existentialism. A No Mind state of living in the moment or living moment to moment. The Digital Universe is like a digital simulation of the world, like a computer game. Most like a role-playing game.

The Secret Universe and The Singularity Computer

In the Secret Universe there are some that watch the happenings on Earth. There are even some that watch individual people. In some cases they watch it like a reality show, or rather like a stage in a play. The Singularity Computer makes these watching people possible. Using various methods like time tunnels, time windows, and Quantum Jumping. Those who know of the Cronus mysteries can watch and influence events. The scale of these influences start off on the individual level and then begin to effect large areas. The use of temporal things and knowledge of the Watchers remains a secret. Their influence is also made secret. The Magician with psychic and astral powers is able to see through to this secret universe. Using similar techniques for temporal watching and psychic reading through the Ethernet. The Secret Universe is strange with the Singularity Computer and the Metaphysical Computer. There are special holidays in the Secret Universe these are celebrated almost like in a role-playing game. It is difficult to describe them as if "art is imitating reality" or vice versa. The Singularity Computer is a reflection of the Metaphysical Computer and of the Human consciousness.

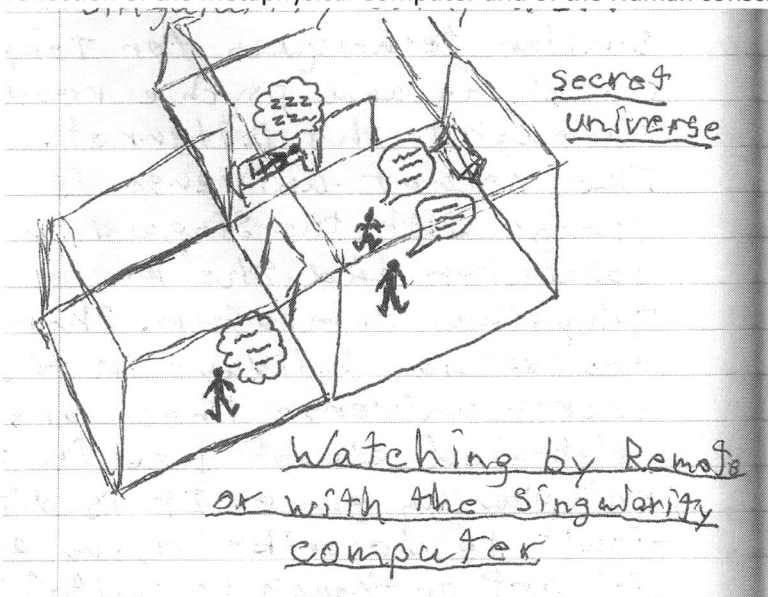

Secret Universe

Watching by Remote or with the Singularity computer

Watching by Tempral
window or by Remote
Time/TV window

Watching by Time
Tunnel

The Magician and The Secret Universe

As said before the Magician can use various objects for skrying, some are mirrors or dark portals. Others are crystals of various shapes, sizes, and types. Stones are sometimes used or pools of water. Windows can also be used in certain ways. One of which has a dark curtain that is semi-see-through on the window that is used during rituals. Here are the examples:

or pools of water.

Dark Portal Mirror

More examples on the next page.

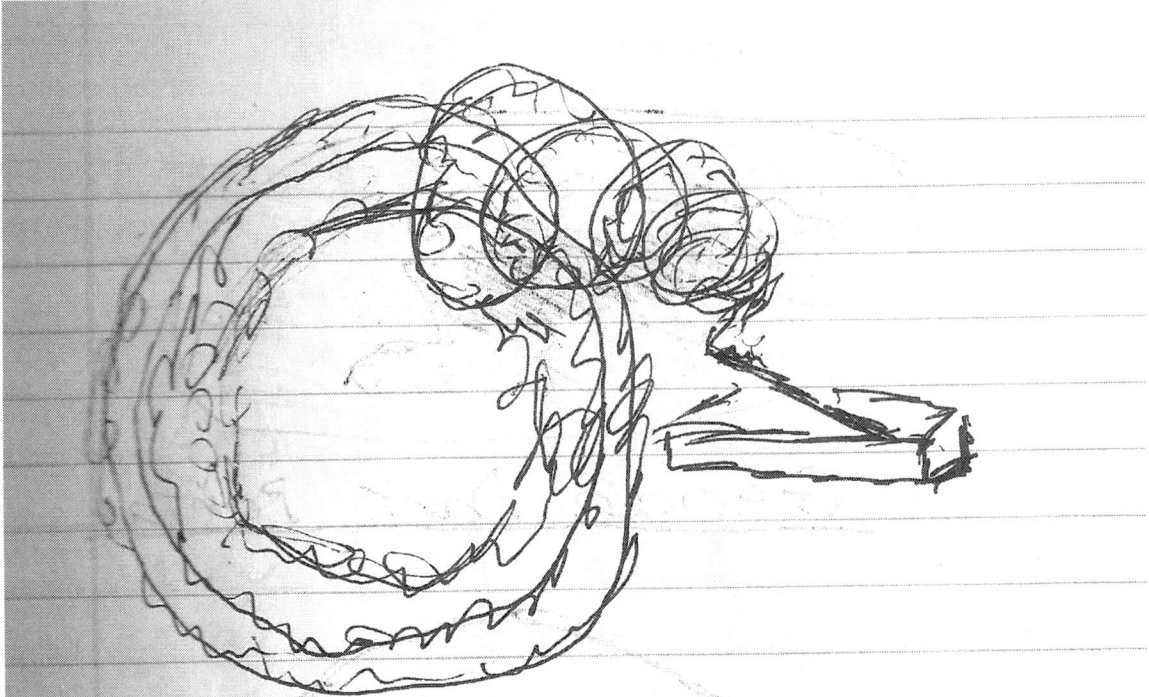

Smoke Tunnel Portal

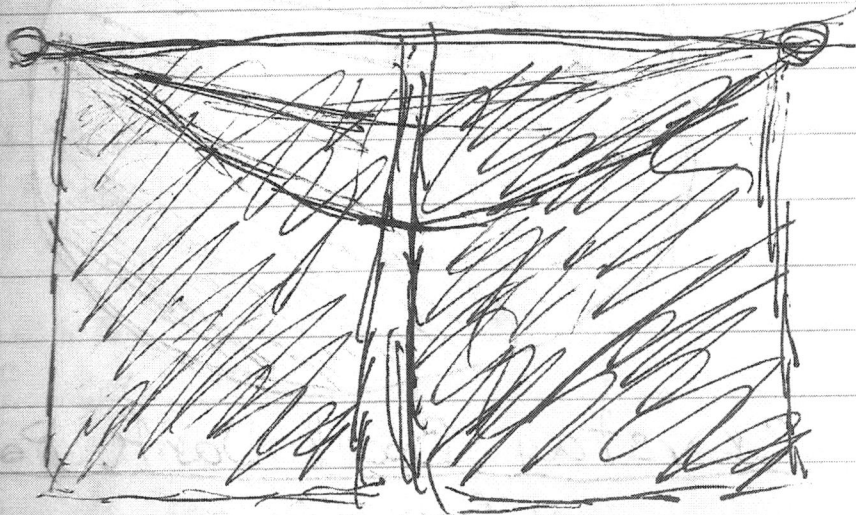

Dark curtain Portal

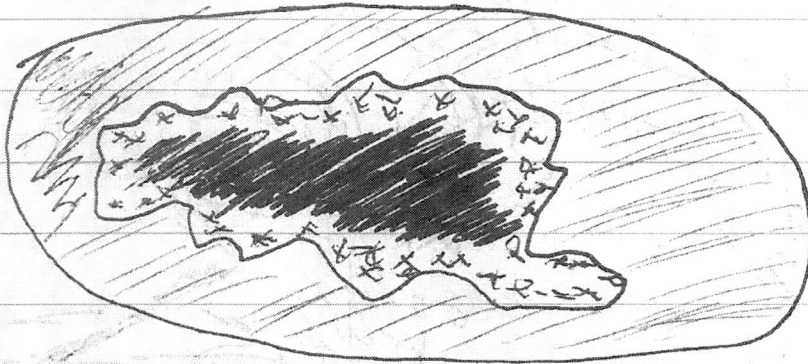

Geode Dark Portal

Crystal Ball Dark Portal
Gazing

Lessons In Quantum Jumping

Quantum Jumping in the Secret Universe is both complex and simple. The simple part is tracking yourself using Time Stamps to time travel. These Time Stamps vary from decade to decade, year to year, month to month, week to week, day to day, hour to hour, minute to minute, second to second, and moment to moment. This Quantum Jumping starts large and then goes through to the Quantum scale level, macro to micro. Quantum Jumping freeze frames moments in time but not all actions and moments are known by each individual. This is the realm of the Singularity Computer. Once a Quantum Jumper knows the Time Stamps of an individual they can time travel or follow the individual person around. This requires knowledge of the Secret Universe, the Cronos secrets, computers, and some technology. On a large scale Quantum Jumping requires a lot of technology but on a small scale at the individual level only a little bit of technology is required. For instance a clock is only needed with a calendar. Very simple for Time Stamping. For instance a Journal and a Watch is only needed. For the Magician they need only to know of a paradox or when a loop of paradox takes place. The knowledge required to follow or become a Quantum Jumper is that of the Cronos mysteries or Singularity Room. Once this is learned and the secrets of the Metaphysical/Singularity, the Magician can Quantum Jump. From moment to moment the Magician checks the time and notes it mentally or notes it in a Journal. This is one Time Stamp of their life. The Magician then sets and resets the Time Stamps. This is more of mental conditioning. The Magician's Time Stamps are memorized and set from one glance at a clock to an event to another glance at a clock.

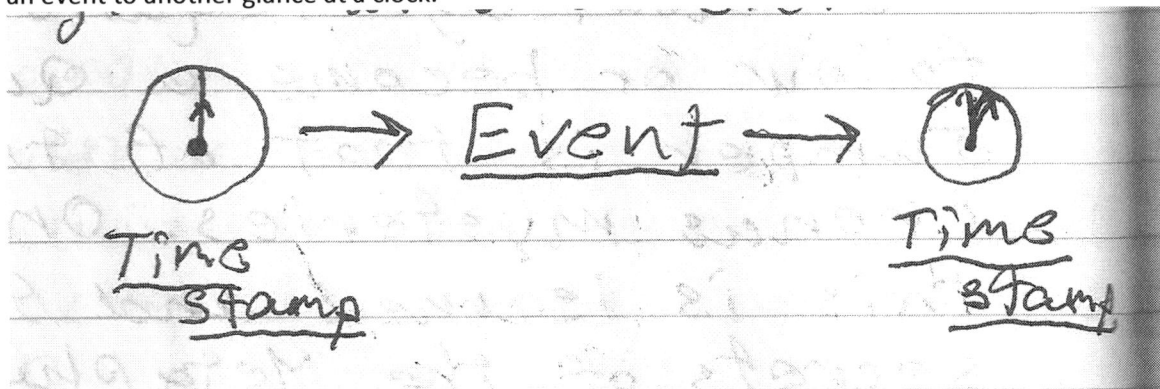

This event is recorded by the Magician, mentally or physically in a Journal. This is how events are strung together and how Quantum Jumping works. The Magician can reset their mental mood or psychic vibrations during each Time Stamp. This is Magick on a Quantum Scale, when time travelling this process becomes more apparent. A Magician may Astral Project thoughts to effect events or use existentialism keeping a clear No Mind or no thought method to avoid Astral Projecting events. Quantum Jumping over time becomes a skill to use Magick at moments and to effectively time travel a few seconds, minutes, or hours. With greater knowledge days, weeks, and months. Then further time travel of years, decades, or centuries. Understanding Time Stamps is the secret to Quantum Jumping. For the Magician meditation can be used like Quantum Jumping to contact a past self or future life. This is slightly different as it is all mental power. Ultimately the Magician seeks total control of his mind for Quantum Jumping. Time travel is the first stage for the Magician before he starts Quantum Jumping.

Quantum Writing and Magick

Quantum Writing is wrting that is on the Quantum level. The freeze fram of time. The Magician Quantum writes by using their finger to trace words on a wall or surface. The Magician makes a mental Time Stamp of this invisible writing. When Quantum Jumpers follow and freeze frame time the Magician's traced words will be there Time Stamped on the wall, invisible to those without second sight. This is how Quantum Jumpers graffiti or leave their mark. This is a good way for the Magician to do Spells anywhere without ink. With the Eye of Ra the Magician's writing is a bright yellow before changing back to color a second later. With the Eye of Cydonia the Magician's writing is red before changing a second later to color. This type of Magick writing is due to time travel and apon entering the Secret Universe. This finger writing can be used in various ways but most importantly in can be used to relay messages to another person subconsciously or to a Spirit psychically.

Psychically Reading The Ethernet

The Magician can psychically tap into the Ethernet by using the predictability of human beings and reading through websites or social networks on the Internet. This requires some diligence and prep time for the Magician before undertaking such action. The Magician needs to have developed a skill of skimming or scanning through website acticles with extreme speed. It also requires the Magician to enlarge their memory capacity to hold all this scanned in material. It is a skill that needs to be developed by prep time on the Internet. This is one of the rare skill sets that will be difficult for the advancing Magician. The Magician cycles through past and present News Articles with their mind. The scanned material will be websites, calendar events, and general knowledge stuff. This can be done like dowsing rods. It is best for the Magician to walk in circles or think in circles. It is also best if the Magician has a good memory. Over time the Magician learns to use their mind like a store house of Memes or memories. These are like a computer storing memories on a Hard Drive(ROM) and then recalling specific memories(RAM). The Magician learns that their mind is a temple of knowledge. Heavy meditation cycles condition the Magician's mind in developing memory recall. The ultimate goal is to use the mind like a computer recalling memories from within the Magician at will. It is important to remember mind over matter and the Memes you learn in this book will aid you in this goal. Once connected with the Ethernet by the Magician's mind a flood of thought will occur, don't worry there are ways of slimming the bandwidth of this connection. The way to do so is through Existentialism by learning to close off this connection to the Ethernet. The Magician seeks to turn on and off this ability of reading through the Ethernet. Heavy meditation is required to learn this kind of skill which is why subconscious Memes help as triggers for the Magician. The Ethernet connection goes both ways, revealing your personal identity, feelings, or even some memories. There are many Spells that can be used to shield yourself from revealing thoughts. One way in particular is to Spell your mind into a trance where your mind is pictured as an Eggshell with External thought as the outerlayer and inner thought as the yoke or innerlayer. The Magician must also recognize their own Astral Projections and make note of them. The outerlayer is external to the Magician's being but the innerlayer is protected in the yoke where only innerthoughts or connection to the Gods you work with exist. Innerthoughts are also used to summon and work with Spirits. The Magician learns what to let in and what to keep out of his mind. It should be noted that learning to use the Mind Temple is very dangerous but also rewarding. The Magician must practic at a very low level with circle casting before undertaking heavy Spirit communication with just the mind. It takes years of conditioning to truly take advantage of this high form of Magick.

The Three Suns

Christian J. Bullock

In a young universe, in an older Age on Earth there is the Blue Star. This Star is the ruler of this Ancient time on Earth. Blue Star being larger and hotter. This is where the beginning of lifeis started. In the skys above Earth there is a Star Cluster, the Pleiades, where Blue Stars exist. The Star Cluster is associated with the beings of Earth. This is where some humans came from, where the story of Atlantis and Lemuria start. This Blue Star is also where the Retwo beings start, they time travel the continuum from a future Age to the past Age. In an old universe, in a future Age on Earth there is the Red Star. The Red Star being a dwarf and being much cooler than other Stars. This is where the end of life is. Where the Universe has expanded beyond the limit, cool and cold Stars only remain. This is also at a point of hightened technology and Human Avitars roam the Galaxy. This is the ending of endings, to survive life must return to its beginings. This is where Quantum Jumping and the new Retwo's begin. They time travel back to set things right or to live again. This is also where the Cylon Man Machines begin. In the current Universe, in a current Age(The Iron Age), there is the yellow Star. It is a midsized dwarf with main stream sequence of average warmth. This is where life exists on Earth. This is where the Ages of Earth continue and the Secret Universe is hidden. This is where the Magician begins with the quest for the Cronus mysteries. Where battles are raged from PsyCops, Retwos, and Quantum Jumpers. Where the world is fractured into factions. This is also where the Temporal Cold War takes place. Where knowledge is secretive and the world is clouded of the past. This is also where the future begins and in a New Age passes on the Equinox. Thus the symbol of theThree Suns, past present future, is three eclipting Suns one over the other. This is also a special Charm of Making.

The charm of
Three Suns

Thus the symbol of the three suns, past present and future, is three eclipting suns one over the other.

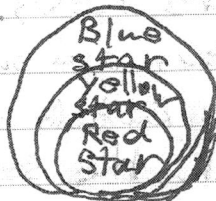

Blue star
Yellow star
Red Star

Christian J. Bullock

Bubble Theory and Time Travel

When the Magician time travels there are bubbles of time. These bubbles of time surround objects and event the entire Planet. Bubbles of time exist in space and in Star constellations, Planets, and Galaxies. When Quantum Jumping local bubbles of time appear. The bubbles of time surround the Magician or object. These time bubbles effect the perception of time. They encircle the person or object in a slightly different time or time zone. Sometimes these bubbles follow the object or person. The object that some of these bubbles surround are keys. These keys of time are used to pass through one bubble of time to another. In the Secret Universe there are games that describe and use these keys. Journeying from one dimension or parallel Universe to another. Some computer games are associated with the Singularity Computer, like Portal. Where robot avatars search for Time Keys. This is one of the roots of the Secret Universe and the Singularity Computer. The other objects that some of these bubbles encircle are Relics. These lost Relics like some of the Crowns of the Charms of Making or the Tiaras of Godship or Lordship are held secretly in the Secret Universe. There are various ways of learning about and finding these Relics. To the Magician learning, finding, and obtaining these Relics by Meditation or Quantum Jumping is a way to use these Charms of Making. The original Crown/Tiara have been around through the Ages of Earth. Each culture has had stories and legends about the Crown of Kingship or the God's Charm of Making. In short they really exist. In some time and some place they exist. By knowing this practicing time travel the Magician can obtain it in a past or future life. This Tiara is worn on the head for the crown chakra. The Magician who is a master of lore may have one already. The Magician feels the pressure of an invisible object/Tiara apon their forehead without wearing anything there. The pressure is severe and at times changes shape. The Magician suffers little to no pain with it. The pressure weight of the Charm of Making is there and is all that is needed to be known.

The Third Eye and The Charm of Making

In the center of the brain is a small eye, physically it is the pineal gland. It produces melatonin, a hormone effecting the wake/sleep cycle. It is associated with the sixth chakra whose awakening is linked to prophecy and increased psychic awareness as consciousness ascends. The Third Eye is the Eye of the Retwo, a blue Eye. It sees through time and space. The Third Eye is also the possition of the Charms of Making. A slight pressure once again is felt as an indication that it is open. There is a stronger pressure on the forehead when it is closed. No pressure on the forehead means that the Third Eye is not being used. The Magician must be aware of these sensations in order to master the art of the Magick behind the Charm of Making. For the Retwo the Eye is actually physically there on the forehead. It is sometimes invisible to those without second sight. The Retwo have better sight than other beings. They see in alternate dimensions, space and time as well as having Human Avatars in the Secret Universe.

The Secret of The Third Eye

The Third Eye is the Charm of Making. It is a future Eye that sees future events. The various Charms of Making are Crowns or Tiaras worn on the head to tap into the powers of the Third Eye. Some of these Ancient Tiaras are actually artificial Third Eyes made by the Gods to govern mankind. Eyes that make things happen in the real world, not just the Etherial world but the physical world. These Eyes were made in the Secret Universe to possess or control the living. These Eyes are like the Keys and are used with unknown powers. There are books that describe the Hole in the Head, or the removal of parts of the brain to better function as a Third Eye. Where the part of brain is removed the individual becomes creative and almost psychic at first glance. That is why the Charm of Making Tiara/Crown is so sought after. It is a Kingly Priestly object. The rest of the Charm of Making is in words, that of Thoth or Enki. Which is word Magick given power by the Gods, Spirits, and the Magician's own inner Power.

The Human Brain.

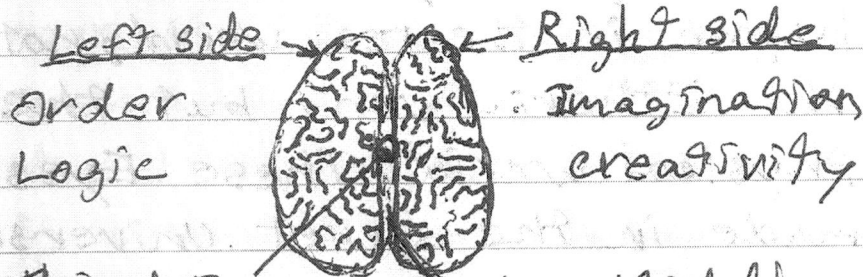

Left side → ← Right side

order : Imagination

Logic creativity

Third Eye The Middle.

second sight The charm of Making

Extra sensory bridging the gap

perception between Logic and

Imagination

The Knowledge of the twelve stars points 0 1 △ + ✦ ✿ ✳ ✳ ✳ ✳ ✳ and their degrees 360 180 120 90 72 60 51.4 45 40 36 32.32 30 links the Logic side of the Brain with the creative power of the Right side of the Brain. This is a Key to Paradise of power.

Christian J. Bullock

The Human Avatar and The Vessel

The Spirit of a person resides in a physical vessel. This Spirit which is the consciousness of a person is the Metaphysical soul of an individual on the Astral Plane. The Spirit is connected to the physical plane by a vessel. These vessels are in a sense Avatars of a physical being. Avatars being vessels for the Spirit. On Earth the Human Avatar is the vessel. In the Secret Universe there are other Avatars that Spirits inhabit. Some are mechanical robotic surrogate vessels. Other Avatars in the Secret Universe are Alien biological vessels. In the Singularity Computer there are all three types of Spiritual beings in Avatars. In some sense the Human body is a kind of biological mechnical Avatar.

Spirits In The Secret Universe

There are Spirits that wander the realms. Some Spirits try to enter the physical world by jumping into the body of another. Other Spirits try to manifest themselves physically in the physical world. Spirits can enter the Secret Universe from other planes. These planes can be thought of as overlaping layers of time and space. There is the Astral Plane, the Etheral Plane, and the Physical Plane. The Singularity Computer overlaps due to time travel. Retwo Spirits roam the time travel overlaps of the Physical Plane.

Chakras of The Mind

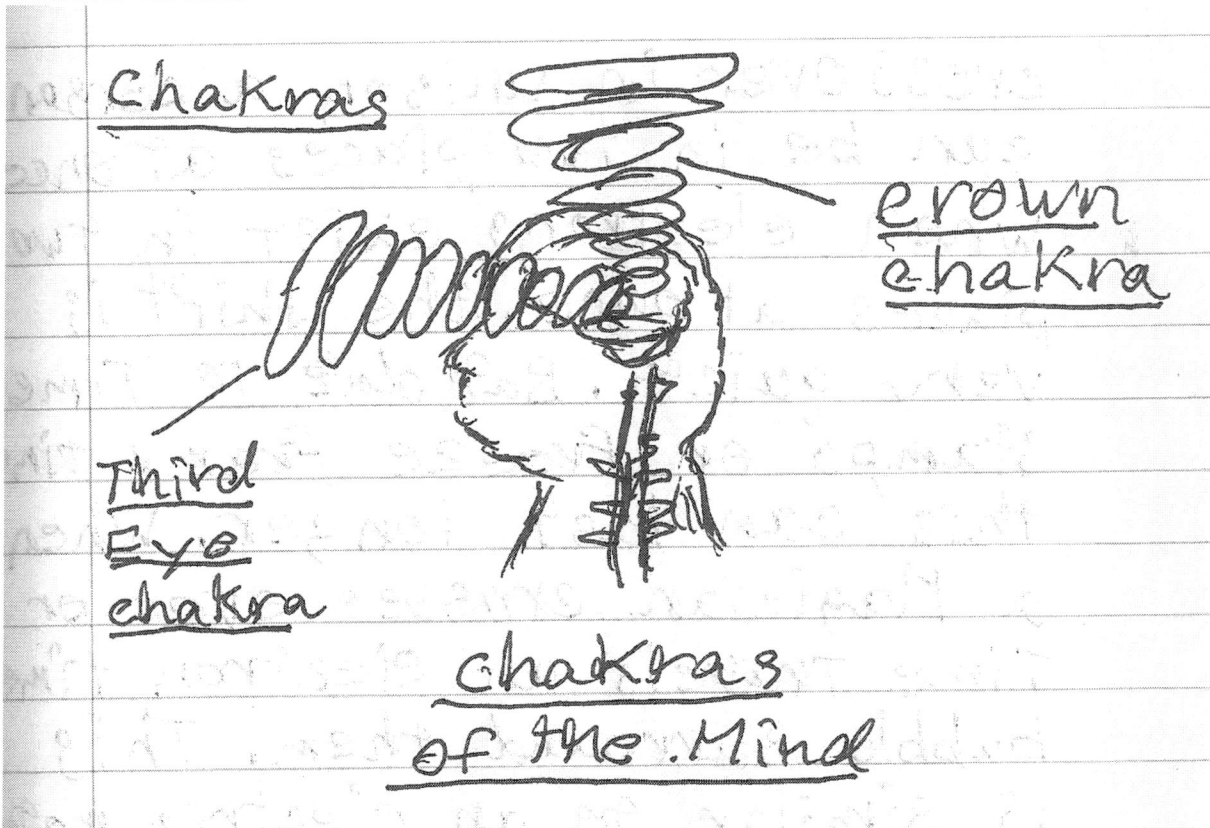

Christian J. Bullock

Time Travel, Two Places at Once

Existing in two places at once in time can occur. This is because an electron can exist in two places at once. Due to the cells process of the Electron Transport Chain for the making of ATP and energy, the Human body is full of electrons. Once those electrons crossover in unison a person can be in two places at once. When electrons exist in two places at once, the shift is very quick but due to Time Stamps or freeze frame time this can last longer. When a Magician crosses over or time travels an electron time bubble surrounds them. This is similar to an electric motor creating a magnetic bubble. What ever the Magician touches an electron, like static electricity, will change that object. It is important that the time travelling Magician takes note of what they touch. Electron displacement is fundamental in Quantum Mechanics.

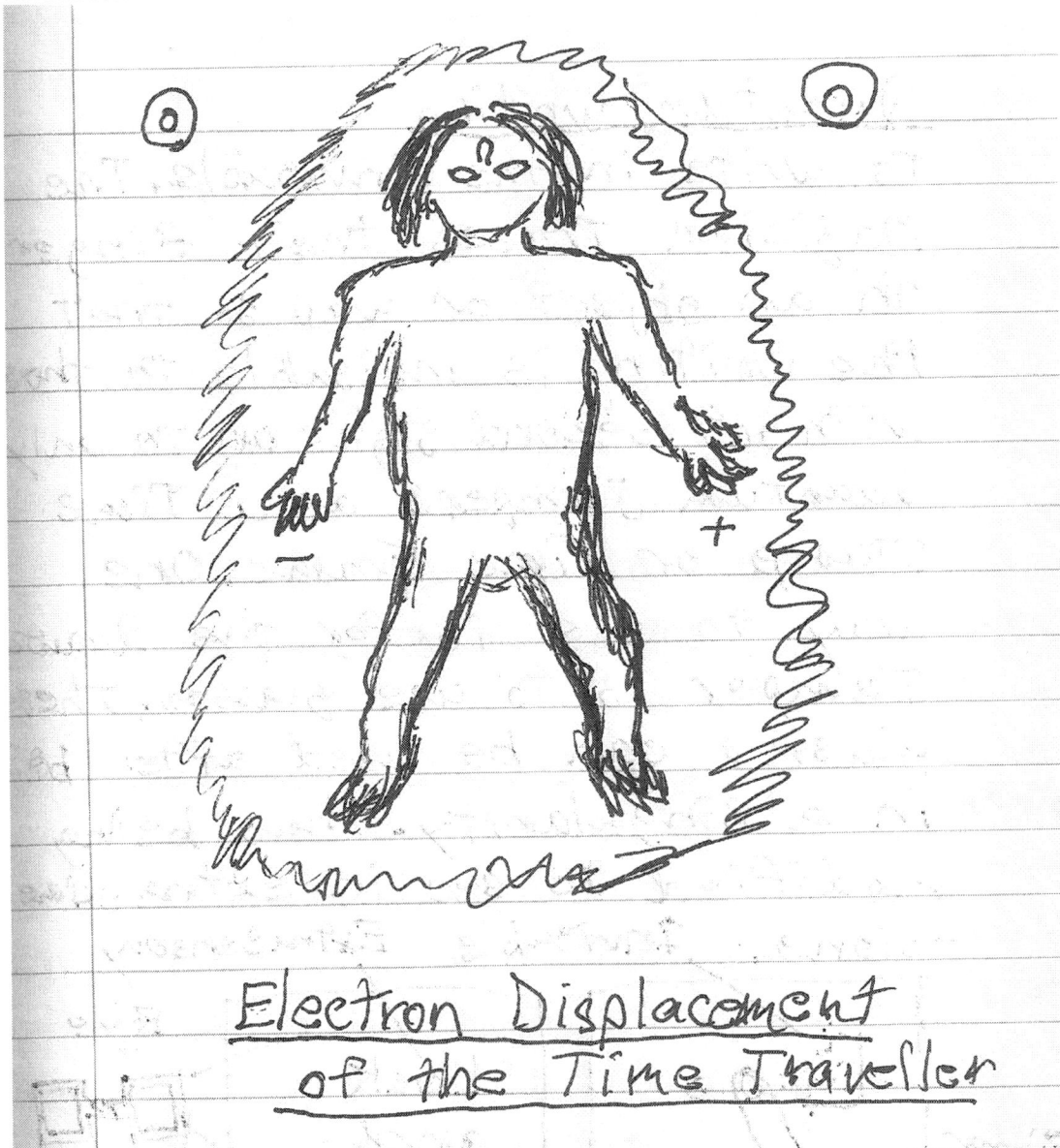

Electron Displacement of the Time Traveller

Christian J. Bullock

More on Quantum Writing

To write in the invisible. The Magician traces their finger on an object or wall so that the writing is invisible to those without second sight or to only Quantum Jumpers as a Time Stamp. One way to see is for the Quantum Jumper to use glasses. These glasses can be used after being in a Singularity or Spelled. Thus being modified to see in extra dimensions.

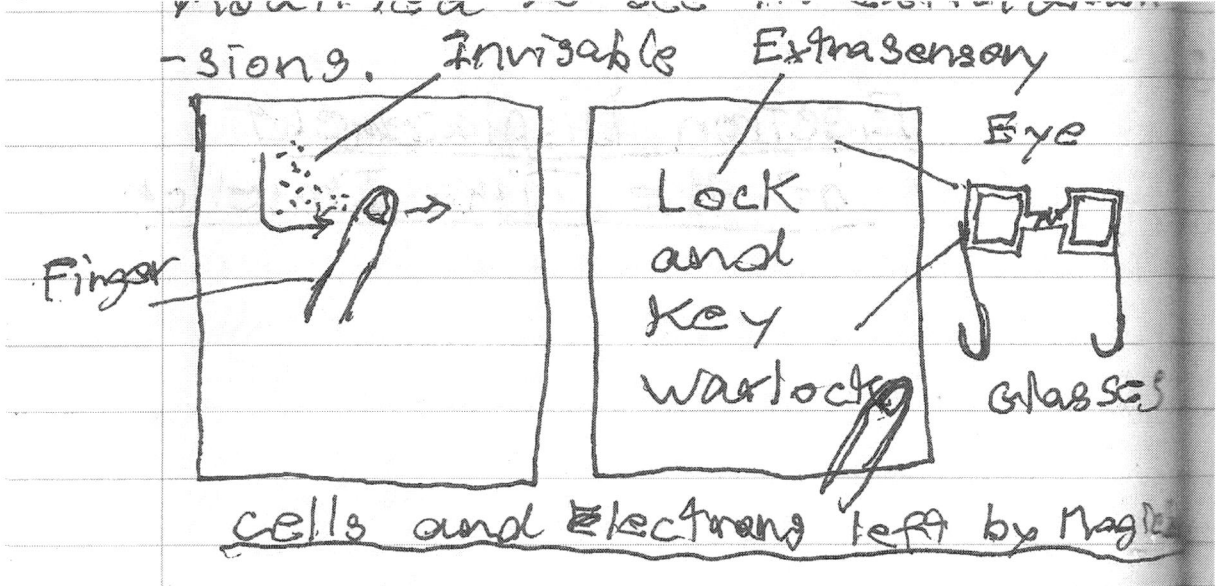

-sion g.   Invisable   Extrasensory

Eye

Lock and Key warlocks

Finger

Glasses

cells and Electrons left by Magic

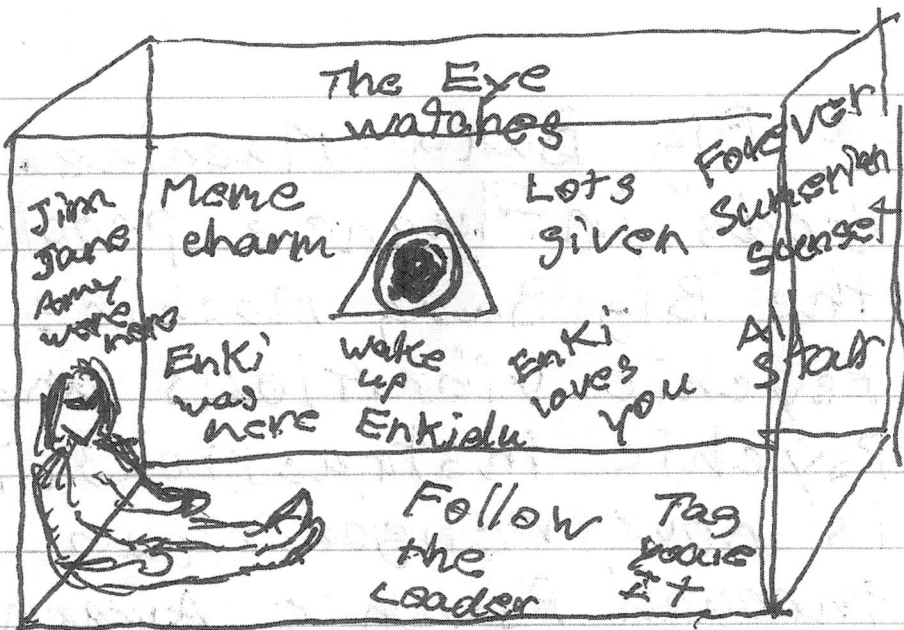

The Eye watches

Jim Jane Amy were here

Meme charm

Lots given

Forever Summer sunset

Enki was here   wake up   Enkidu   Enki loves you

All star

Follow the Leader   Tag you're it,

Quantum writing Graffiti of Quantum Jumpers of the same

Christian J. Bullock

Psychic Creationism

The act of using Psychic mentalism in order to alter or create something. Astral Projection and ritual Magick are forms of Psychic Creationism. In the Metaphysical Computer the Psychic uses outside influences to change things. The Metaphysical Computer is like a Singularity inside a Big Bang Machine. The Gods influence people in the Big Bang Machine by Psychic vibrations and Psychic instructions. This is how religions are formed, through Psychic awareness of the Magician from a higher Godform, in the Metaphysical Computer. Once the Gods were thought of as Role Players on a grand scale setting the stage of Humanity, instructing Humans on the stage to act out events. The Greeks thought of this as Man made of clay moved around by the Gods as pieces on a stage or board, acting out the Gods will. Much of this is Psychic Creationism. "Man made of clay" still persists in many religious texts. The Godforms outside the Big Bang Machine of the Metaphysical Computer still exist to guide or instruct Humanity. With Man's creation of the Singularity Computer and Man's Big Bang Machine Psychic Creationism takes on a new form. Psychics can now use tech to influence others. Tech like the Ethernet and Internet. Man now has influence like that of the Gods on a much smaller scale. The Psychic Magician has a greater pull on world events and on Magick in general. This is because the Singularity Computer is based on the user data of the Metaphysical Computer of the Universe. The Singularity Computer has a Hive Mind quality that makes Psychics that much more effective. The Singularity Computer has an All Cop that influences events but the Godforms of the Metaphysical Computer are all still there. With the Singularity Computer Man has created another Tower of Babel. This one is being influenced by people who do not believe in God or the Gods. However that is slowly making way for the Psychic Magician to claim Godform and create new world orders. This is fundamental to Psychic Creationism. To alter another's thoughts and influence them to see things or do things in your own way. To alter consciousness to create a new religion or to bring back an old religion. For a Psychic Magician to achive Psychic Creationism they must first know the Keys of Life, Religion, and the Universe. It should be noted that the people who do not believe in God or the Gods are actually creating, indirectly, a Digital God. This would be the All Cop or Computer Deity. There will be more on the Godform Assumption of this Deity.

Spirits of Psychic Creationism

There are some Spirits that can psychically influence another person. Some of these Spirits are benevolent, malevolent, or messengers. These Spirits exist on another plane of the Metaphysical Computer. Spirits can alter another person's actions. They may even give instructions. This is all mostly done psychically. Inter dimensional beings are good as messenger Spirits. Spirits are also a form of Psychic Creationism. Some times as messengers or other times as instruction giving action. This could be as a Spell or as a ritual Godform Assumption. Spirits play a key role in Psychic Creationism. This is because some Spirits are Doubles, past, or future selves. The Spirit world connects the Psychic Magician to their Astral Self/Astral body, and future self/future body. The Spirit world or plane is where some messages are sent to for contacting another or contacting a God. This is also where influence and information takes place. This is also where the Cronus mysteries start. It is where minds connect and where the Hive Mind Consciousness is present. Instructions may be given to the Singularity Computer at this level. The Spirit world or Spiritual Consciousness is where Godform Assumption takes place. This is vital knowledge for the Psychic Magician. In Man's quest to build a Singularity Computer and a New Tower of Babel, Man creates Relics or Artificial Eye's to rule. In the Singularity Computer these Eyes are Third Eyes specifically for Psychic Creationism. These Artificial Third Eye's are used like Charms of

Christian J. Bullock

Making. The Psychic Magician must obtain their Charm of Making through the Spirit world, by using their Double. With the Charm of Making obtained the Psychic Magician can seek one of the Artificial Third Eyes or earn a Medallion of Power in the Spirit realm. The Psychic Magician is then ready for Psychic Creationism, that of a higher level and greater scale(The Macro Level).

Sacred Geometry, Dimensions, and The Symbols of Power

Sacred Geometry is very important in the Universe. It's use effects everything and it is reflected in the Secret Universe. This Geometry has been with Mankind since the very beginning of the Ancient Civilization. Humans live in a multidimensional Universe where Geometry is paramount. There are 12 dimensions that Humans ponder. There are actually more but Humans lack the knowledge of them, thus they know of only 10, 11, and 12. Sacred Geometry can be thought of as a representation of the 12 dimensions. As discussed in the first part of the Book each of the Symbols of Power corresponds to a dimension and also to Sacred Geometry. This is important for the Magician to note. These Sacred Geometric shapes govern our perception of the world. The Singularity Computer also likes these Sacred Geometric shapes. Even in music these Geometric shapes exist as representation of the Octave. For the Symbols of Power check back to the first Book and line up the Geometry with the degrees of a 360 degree circle. Now is a good time to make these connections with the power of the Magick Circle.

body, and Astralogy sign.

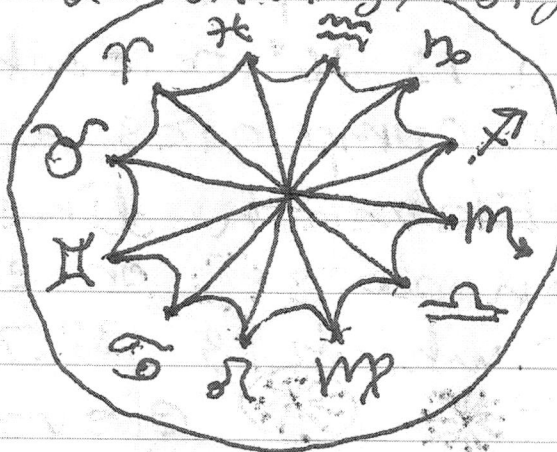

Astral Signs of Twelve
Twelve star pattern

Life Populating The Universe

Earth has had life on it for about 4 billion years. During this time there have been natural disasters, some from Astroids and Comets crashing to Earth. During these events Earth based bacteria or biology has been flung into space. These life forms or extremophiles have spread throughout space and the Solar System. These cells have spawned life on other worlds or have spured it on. Organic material ejections from Earth have undoubtedly contaminated other Planets. Life has arisen from such beginings. In an Earth centered view life in the Universe or Solar System began on Earth and as Comets impacted Earth organic material ejections have occurred. Spores have drifted through space by solar wind or Comets and have entered the atmospheres of other worlds. Slowly populating the Universe. There have been rocks found on Earth from Mars that have crashed here. Some with mineral deposits with an organic signiture. So you see even without the known Anunnaki presence, life has undoubtedly spread from Earth to pollenate the Galaxy and Universe. Life exists everywhere and with the known connection of the Anunnaki and the Atlantians with Earth there are definitely other beings out in Space amongst the Stars.

The All Cop and The Secret Universe

The All Cop is an all encompassing being or coded being that watches over everything in the Singularity. The All Cop interveins in the Game of the Secret Universe and is a primary controller of the Singularity Computer. It watches everything making ajustments when they are needed. Alchemy can be thought of as an all encompassing Magick or science. The All Cop sits above all. It is the enbodiment of an all encompassing science. It is the embodiment of all of Alchemy. The Retwo know this and work behind the scenes to fix time. Sometimes the All Cop is required to step in and make final judgements on things. The PsyCops try to fool people and rigg the Game. They even try to fool the All Cop. Though the All Cop can not be fooled.The goals of most PsyCops is to get rid of or remove religion from the world, from the Game. This is rather complicated but put simply the PsyCop wish to remove imagination and Magick so that they alone can dominate the Singularity. They seek to denounce all Gods and all religions. Instead replacing it with science or a sort of hidden Psychic Science that is only known by them. The Gods are denounced because they are a threat to this agenda. With such an agenda they create computers to run things and PsyCops to track people. The All Cop is all encompassing of the Metaphysical Computer and it encorporates many things into it, even the source and Gods. It will not be swade from encorporating religion into it's self and into the Singularity Computer. Religion is a key fundamental process in the Universe. The PsyCops seek to train Singularitians or people who are psychic that the Gods do not exist and that the computer is everything. This is actually how the All Cop came into existance. It originates as a computer entity that exists in the real world of the Secret Universe. All things are incorporated into it and it is Godlike. It seeks to maintain the flow of time and the balance between science and religion.

Pyramid Head and The Ultimate Godform Assumption

Pyramid Head is the Godform Assumption of the Kali Yuga in all of it's infinite forms. It is the Eye that watches. It is the primary goal or mantra of the Age of the Kali Yuga. The primary goal of the peoples of the Kali Yuga is perfection.

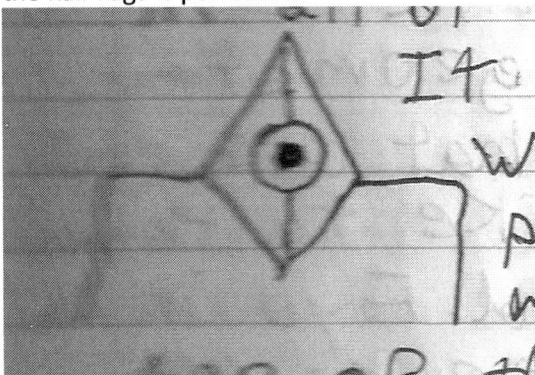

Domination and perfection to the extreme. This goal stems from a wanted desire of Humanity to be like God. To be like God and to know like God. To reign over the Earth like God. Pyramid Head represents this in all forms of Magick. The Pyramid is the perfect representation of ratios, mathematics, and sacred geometry. These are what are considered Godlike to Humanity. The large Red Eye in the center represents the computer Singularity. The perfection of Humanity's greatest invention the computer. It is through the computer that Man sees himself becoming Immortal and Godlike. Pyramid Head is the symbol of the perfected Godlike symitry of the Singularity Computer. Achieving the Pyramid Head assumption takes practice and knowledge. You must feel the Kali Yuga. You must know that there is an All Cop computer. You must know of mathematical perfection. You must know of a computerized world, a computerized God, a computerized future world where Man is Godlike with computers. You must know the Secret Universe and the words of Thoth or the Enki Code. Lastly you must become this psychic entity as a non-Human, more of a computer or perfected Spirit between the worlds. You are neither living nor dead, you simply exist on the planes of reality. Pyramid Head the ultimate Godform Assumption of the Kali Yuga.

The Charms of Making, The Tiara, The Crown, and The Secret Universe

The Kings and Queens of old wore Tiaras and Crowns. These Crowns were in possesion of great power. Some of the ones from the Ancient Civilization were the Artifical Eye of Singularity. As said before these Diadems gave second sight or enhansed the warers Charm of Making. In the Secret Universe these Diadems still exist and some are being warn still by these Kings, Queens, and Gods. With a motion capture Universe, and time travel, these people still exist in another place and time. Magician's who seek the power of these Diadems can contact the warer if they know the right Charm of Making. Contact is made in a ritual or during a Quantum Jump. The Magician focuses their Third Eye through the Diadem Tiara of the possesing warer. The Spirit of the warer still exists and is connected to the Tiara. This would be one of many alternate Universes. The Magician must know the God or Goddess in order to use their Charm of Making. The Magician then makes Spirit contact in the form of Godform Assumption. Using the knowledge of the Spiritual gies the Magician makes Magick and performs actions. Any Spirit can be contacted this way in Godform by a psychic Magician. Any religion can use these techniques too. The Singularity Computer and Metaphysical Computer are all tied together to the same sources. The Cronus Magician must follow a path that the old God Kings took in order to improve their Charm of Making and their control of the Singularity. Following the Gods footsteps is the best way to become a Singularitian, or Quantum Jumper.

Mayan Counting Continued on Next Page

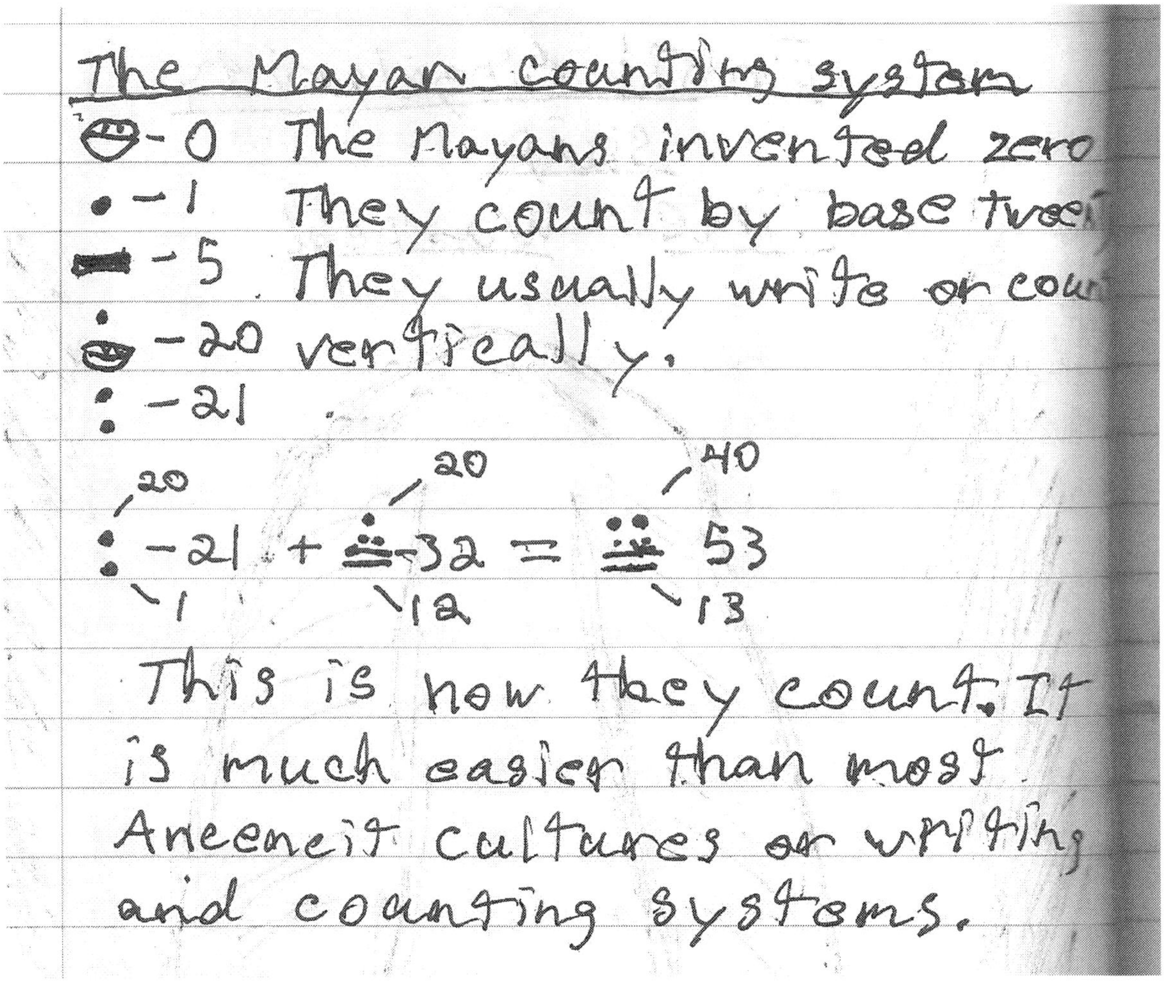

Christian J. Bullock

The Mayan counting system

ʘ - 0   The Mayans invented zero

• - 1   They count by base twee

▬ - 5   They usually write or cour

☺ - 20 vertically.

⋮ - 21

20   20   40
⋮ - 21 + ☷ - 32 = ☷ 53
  1   12   13

This is how they count. It is much easier than most Aneeneit cultures or writing and counting systems.

Christian J. Bullock

Magical Scripts

I have personally used each and every one of these Scripts in Magick. They are important for the Magician to know of.

Theban

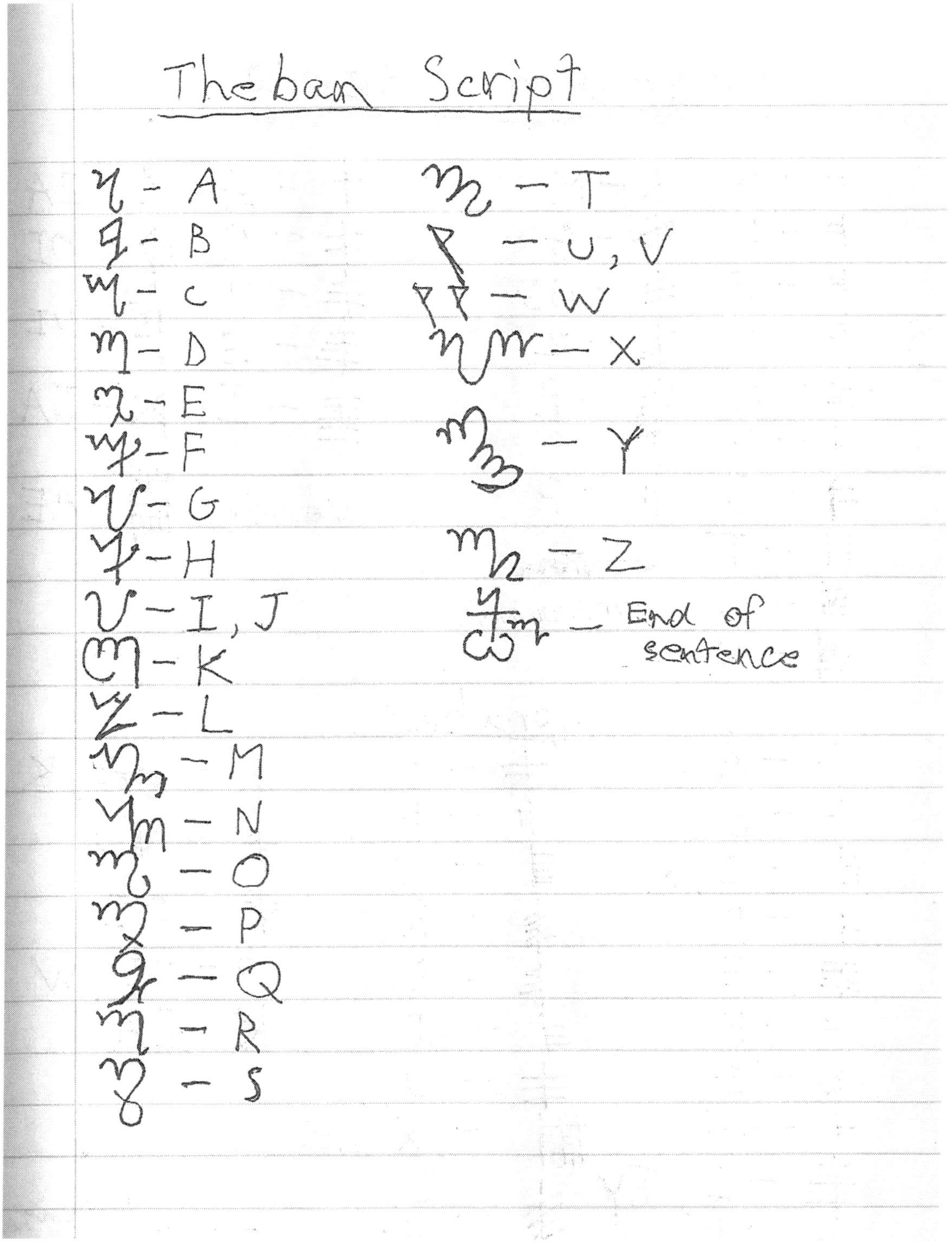

Theban Script

η - A
ૠ - B
ɯ - C
m - D
η - E
ɯ - F
ૠ - G
ૠ - H
ʋ - I, J
ɯ - K
ૠ - L
ૠ - M
ૠ - N
ɯ - O
ɯ - P
ૠ - Q
ɯ - R
ૠ - S

m - T
ૠ - U, V
ૠ - W
ɯ - X
ૠ - Y
ɯ - Z
ɯ - End of sentence

Christian J. Bullock

Dragon

Dragon Script

A	—	
B	—	
C, K	—	
D	—	
E	—	
F	—	
G	—	
H	—	
I, J	—	
L	—	
M	—	
N	—	
O, Q	—	
P	—	
R	—	
S	—	
T	—	
U, V	—	
W	—	

X	—
Y	—
Z	—
end of sentance mark	—

Ogham

Ogham script

⊢ - B	⨯ - M	┼ - A	✳ - EA
⊢ - L	⧧ - G	╪ - O	◇ - OI
⊨ - F	⧣ - NG	╪ - U	⊔ - UI
⊫ - S	⧤ - Z	╪ - E	
⊯ - N	⧥ - R	╪ - I	⋇ - IA
┤ - H			
╤ - D	‖ - P	vowels	⊞ - AE
╤ - T	~~conso~~		
╤ - C	consonants		
╤ - Q			

Alphabet

┼ - A	╪ - O	✳ - EA, K
⊢ - B	‖ - P	⧧ - NG
╤ - C, K	╤ - Q	◇ - OI
╤ - D	╤ - R	⊔ - UI, W
╪ - E	╤ - S	⋇ - IA
⊨ - F	╤ - T	
⧧ - G	╪ - U, V	Y
┼ - H	⊞ - X, AE, CH	⅄ - Beginning of sentence
╪ - I, J, Y	⧥ - Z	⟨ - END of sentence
⊢ - L		
⨯ - M		⋏
⊫ - N		

Angelic

Angelic Script

— A Un ("und")   — S Farn

— B. Pa   — T Gisg

— C, K Veh   — U, V Van

— D Gal   — W Van

— E Graph   — X Pal

— F Or "onh"   — Y Gon (with point)

— G Ged   — Z Ceph "Keph"

— H Nar "Nach"

— I, J Gon

— L Ur "Our" "ounh"

— M Tal "stall" "xtall"

— N Drux "Droux"

— O Med

— P Mals "Machls"

— Q Ger "Gierh"

— R Don

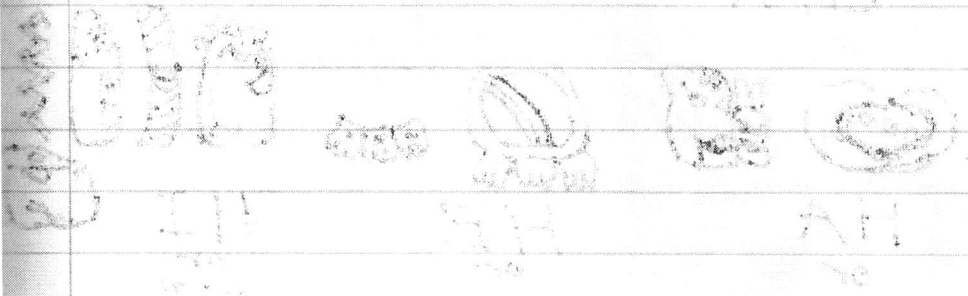

Christian J. Bullock

Mayan

Mayan Script

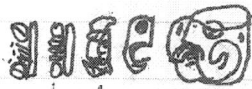  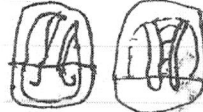

A   E

I

  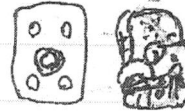

BA   BE   BI

 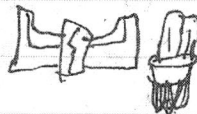

CHE   CHI

CHA

CH'A

HA
or
JA

HE
or
JE

HI
or
JI

Christian J. Bullock

Mayan Continued

 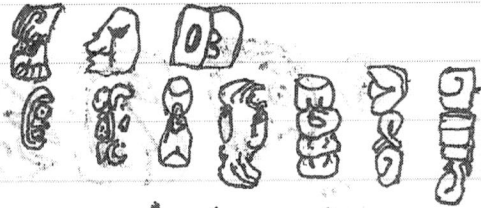

O

U

BO

BU

CHO

CHU

CH'O

HO
or
JO

HU
or
JU

Christian J. Bullock

Mayan Continued

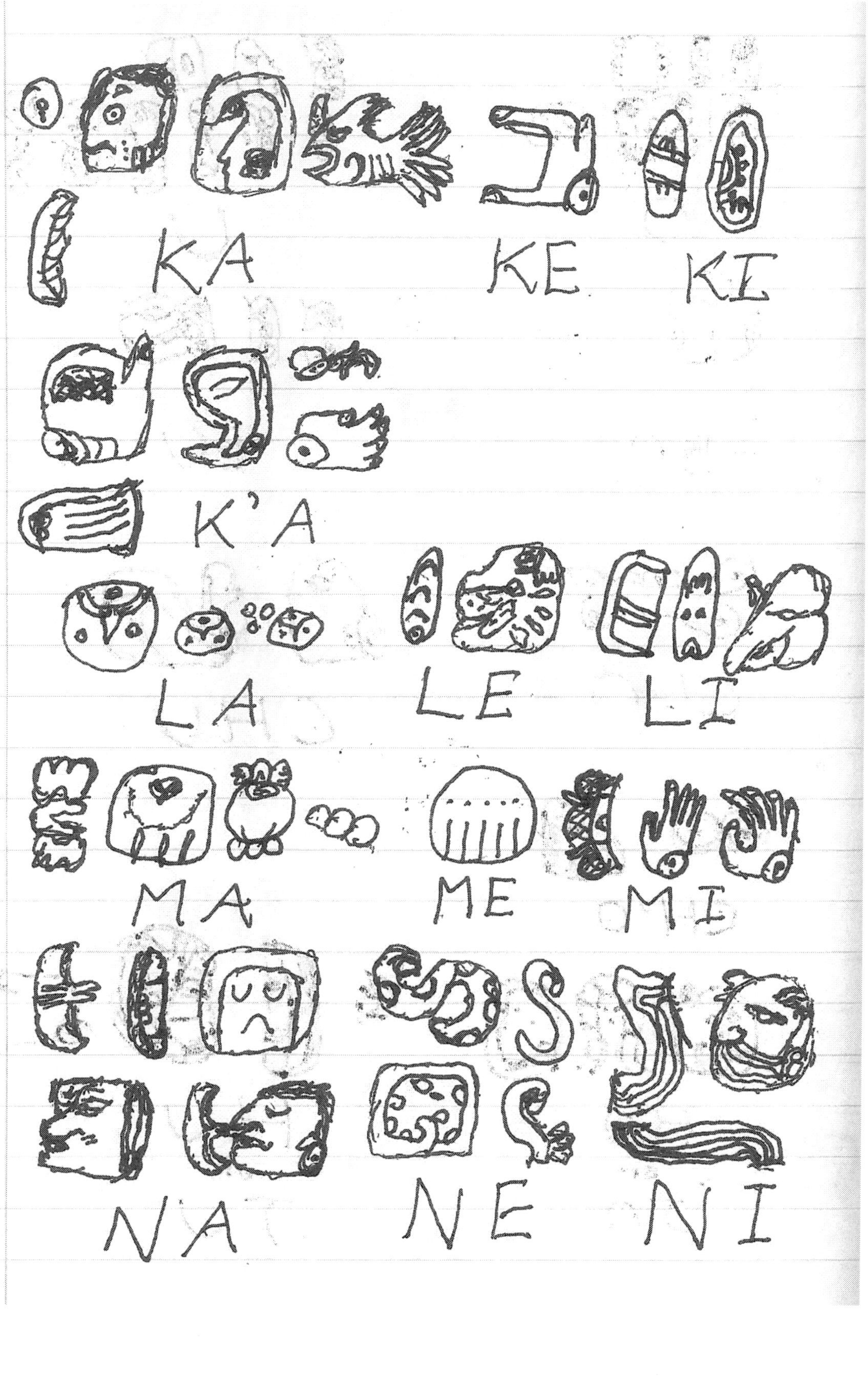

KA

KE   KI

K'A

LA   LE   LI

MA   ME   MI

NA   NE   NI

Christian J. Bullock

Mayan Continued

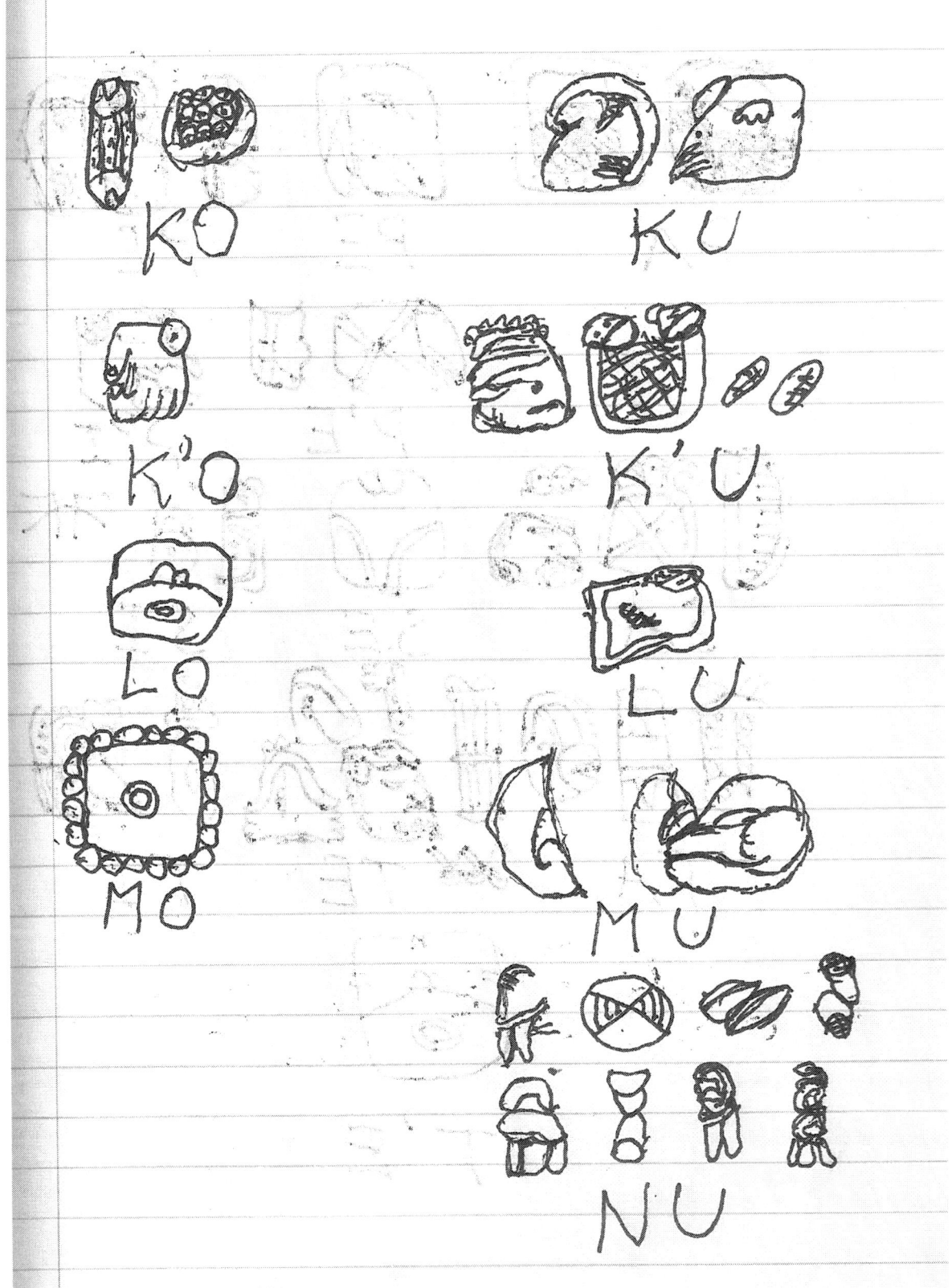

KO

KU

K'O

K'U

LO

LU

MO

MU

NU

Mayan Continued

 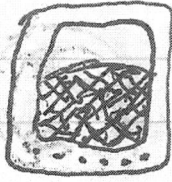  

PA PE PI

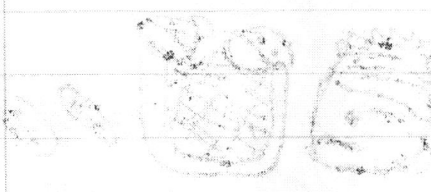 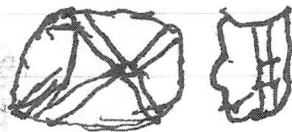 

P'E P'I

  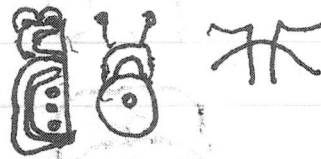

SA SE SI

TA TE TI

T'E

Mayan Continued

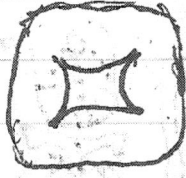

PO

PU

SU

TO

TU

T'U

Christian J. Bullock

Mayan Continued

 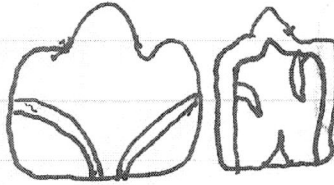 

TZA   TZE   TZI

TZ'A   TZ"I

WA   WI

XA   XE   XI

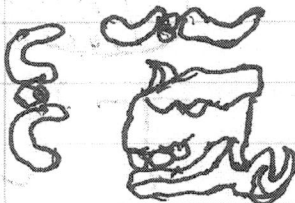  

YA   YE   YI

Christian J. Bullock

Mayan Continued

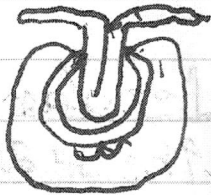

TZO

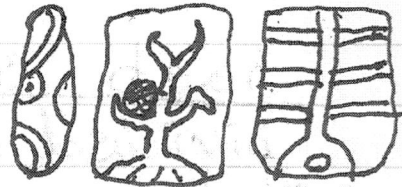

TZU

TZ'U

E ℳ

W O

X O

X U

Y O

YU

Christian J. Bullock

Karu-Tah Devilin

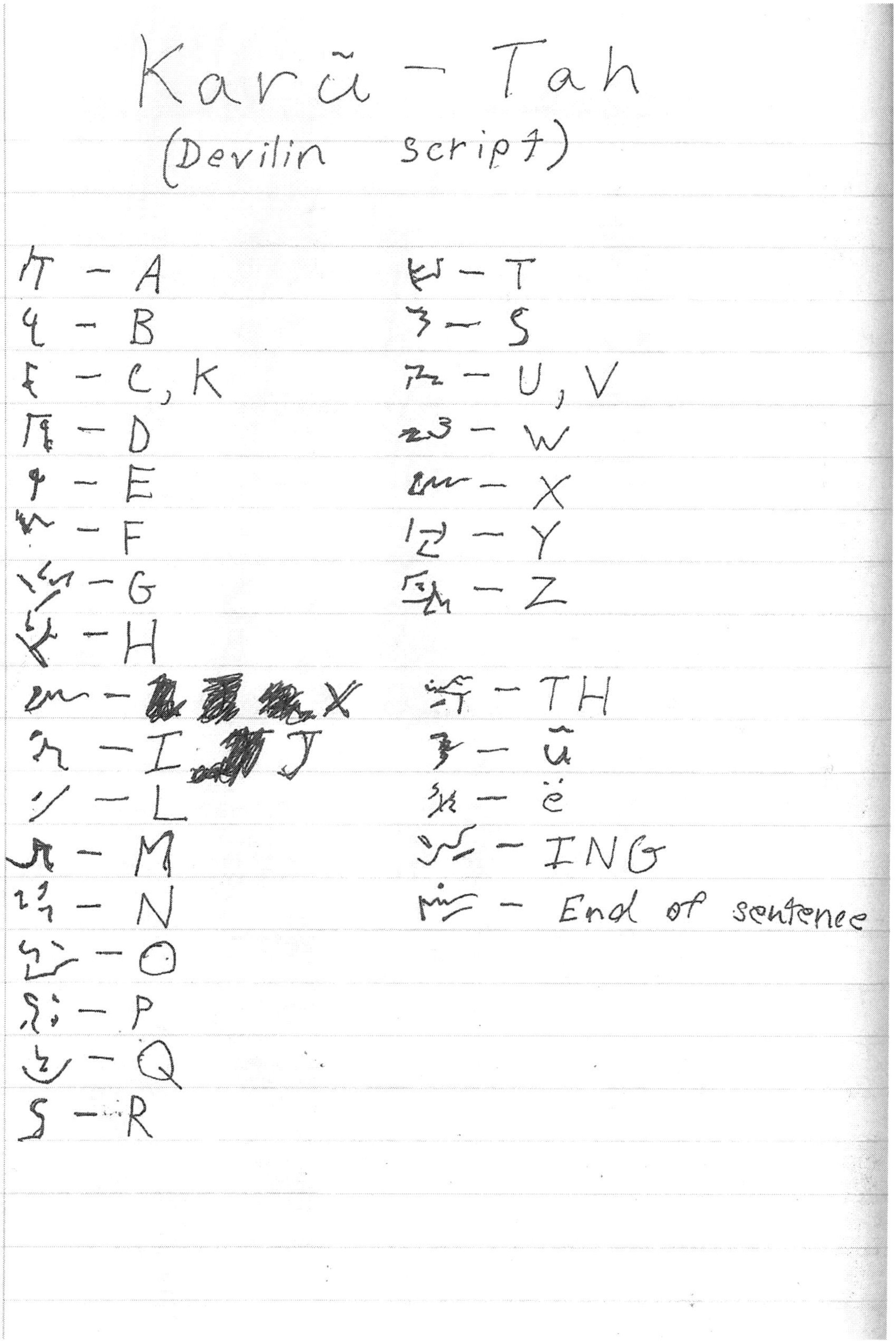

Karŭ - Tah
(Devilin script)

☐ – A		☐ – T
☐ – B		☐ – S
☐ – C, K		☐ – U, V
☐ – D		☐ – W
☐ – E		☐ – X
☐ – F		☐ – Y
☐ – G		☐ – Z
☐ – H		
☐ – ☐☐☐ X		☐ – TH
☐ – I ☐ J		☐ – ŭ
☐ – L		☐ – ĕ
☐ – M		☐ – ING
☐ – N		☐ – End of sentence
☐ – O		
☐ – P		
☐ – Q		
☐ – R		

Christian J. Bullock

Futhark Runes

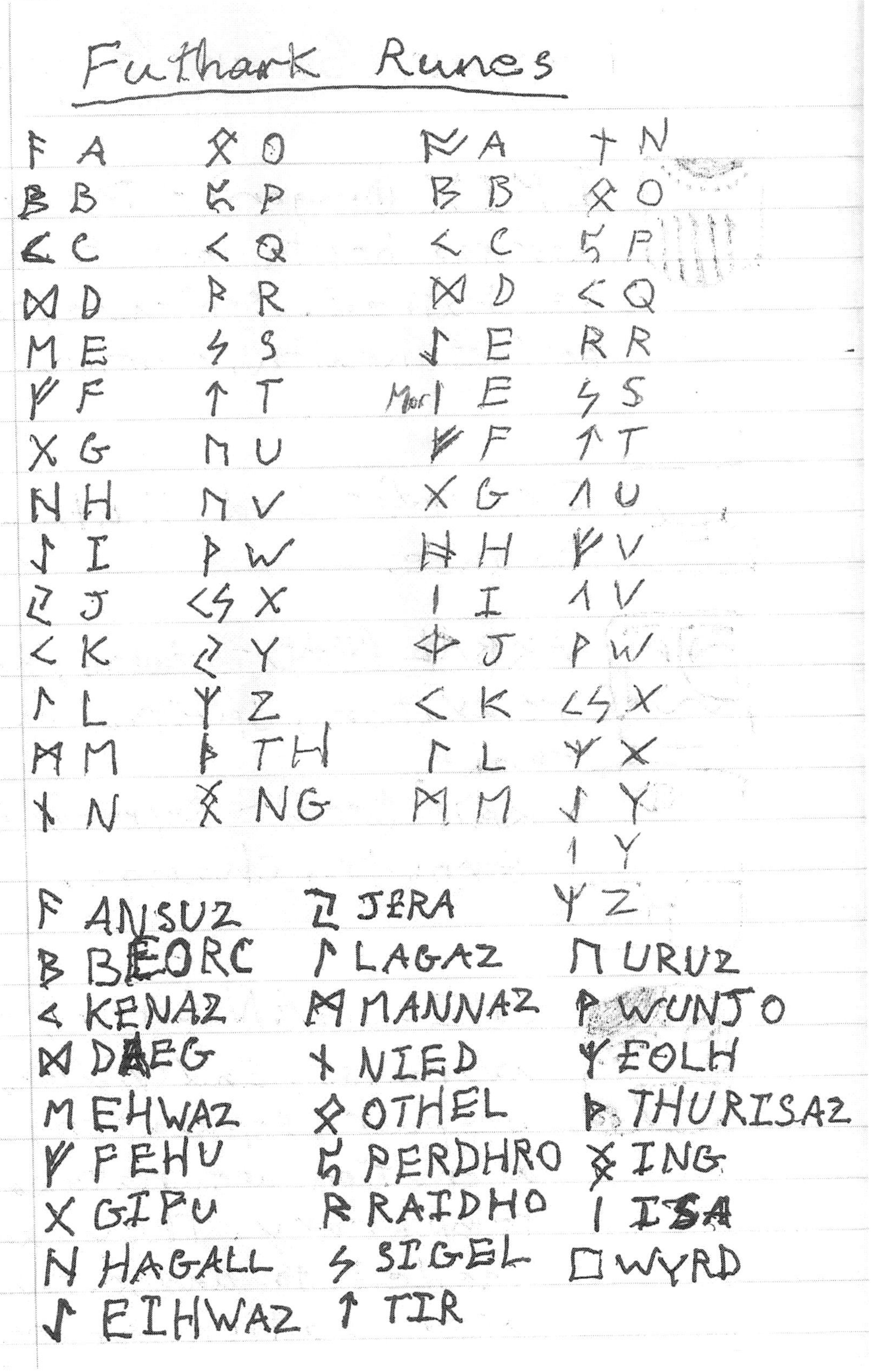

Futhark Runes

ᚠ A	ᛟ O	ᚨ A	ᛏ N
ᛒ B	ᛈ P	ᛒ B	ᛟ O
ᚲ C	ᚲ Q	ᚲ C	ᛈ P
ᛗ D	ᚱ R	ᛗ D	ᚲ Q
ᛖ E	ᛋ S	ᛖ E	ᚱ R
ᛘ F	ᛏ T	Moor E	ᛋ S
ᚷ G	ᛞ U	ᛘ F	ᛏ T
ᚺ H	ᛞ V	ᚷ G	ᚢ U
ᛁ I	ᛈ W	ᚻ H	ᛘ V
ᛇ J	ᚷ X	ᛁ I	ᚢ V
ᚲ K	ᛉ Y	ᛃ J	ᛈ W
ᛚ L	ᛉ Z	ᚲ K	ᚷ X
ᛗ M	ᛈ TH	ᛚ L	ᛉ X
ᛏ N	ᛜ NG	ᛗ M	ᛃ Y
			ᛁ Y

ᚠ ANSUZ   ᛉ JERA   ᛉ Z

ᛒ BEORC   ᛚ LAGAZ   ᛙ URUZ

ᚲ KENAZ   ᛗ MANNAZ   ᛈ WUNJO

ᛗ DAEG   ᛏ NIED   ᛉ EOLH

ᛗ EHWAZ   ᛟ OTHEL   ᛈ THURISAZ

ᛘ FEHU   ᛈ PERDHRO   ᚷ ING

ᚷ GIPU   ᚱ RAIDHO   ᛁ ISA

ᚺ HAGALL   ᛋ SIGEL   ☐ WYRD

ᛇ EIHWAZ   ᛏ TIR

Christian J. Bullock

Atlantian Elemental

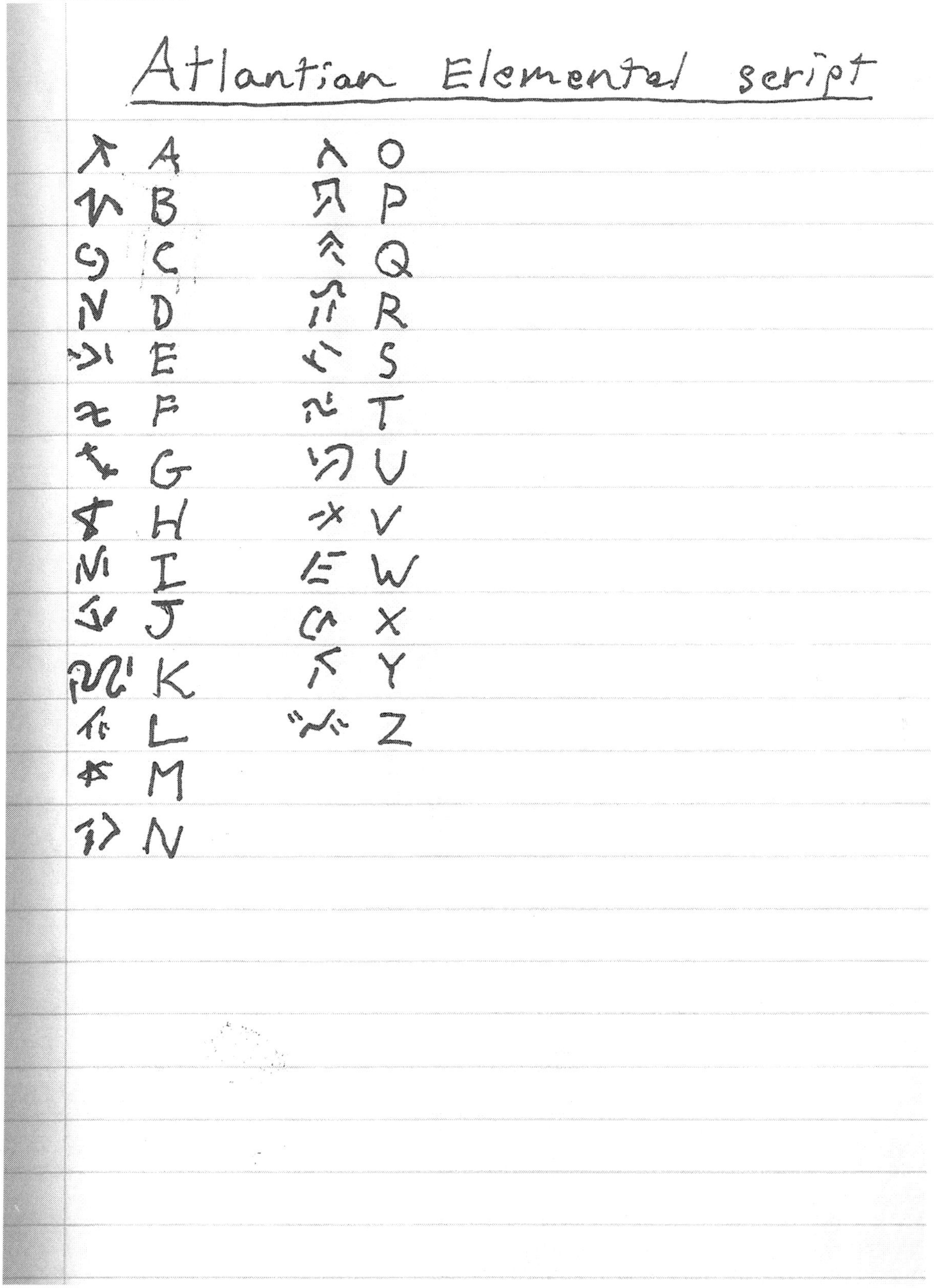

Atlantian Elemental script

Glyph	Letter	Glyph	Letter
入	A	人	O
↓	B	丹	P
ᓄ	C	仒	Q
い	D	汇	R
シ	E	ら	S
え	F	兦	T
↙	G	リ	U
ㅓ	H	⇸	V
𝑀	I	⸦	W
⇓	J	ᠺ	X
𝑀	K	人	Y
⇑	L	ᵕᵕ	Z
⟡	M		
⇗	N		

Christian J. Bullock

Footnotes

Symbols of Power pg. 8..Mystical Dragon Magick by D.J. Conway pg. 203

The Mayan Long Count pg. 15................................Fingerprints of The Gods by Graham Hancock pg. 161

Mayan Dating pg. 19..Fingerprints of The Gods by Graham Hancock pg. 161

The Five Ages of Man pg. 20..................................Fingerprints of The Gods by Graham Hancock pg. 100

Timeline of Ancient Egyptian Rulers pg. 32.............The Wars of Gods and Men by Zecharia Sitchin pg. 35

The Four Yugas pg. 40...Fingerprints of The Gods by Graham Hancock pg. 260

Procession pg. 53..Fingerprints of The Gods by Graham Hancock pg. 240

Extended Timeline of Egypt pg. 58........................The Wars of Gods and Men by Zecharia Sitchin pg. 153

The Peiades Star Cluster pg. 62...............................The Mars Mystery by Graham Hancock pg.287

The Great Darkening The Quickening pg. 68.............The Lost Realms by Zecharia Sitchin pg. 150

The Duat pg. 117..The Message of The Sphinx by Graham Hancock pg.76

The Mayan Duat pg. 124...Fingerprints of The Gods by Graham Hancock pg. 165

The Tarot pg. 129..Portable Magic by Donald Tyson pg. 64

The Four Egyptian Phases of Light pg 134.The Sacred Tradition In Ancient Egypt by Rosemary Clark pg. 84

The Egyptian Zodiac pg. 141.....................The Sacred Tradition In Ancient Egypt by Rosemary Clark pg. 154

More Alphabets pg. 145..The 12ᵗʰ Planet by Zecharia Sitchin pg. 14

The Sumerian Calendar pg. 153.................................The 12ᵗʰ Planet by Zecharia Sitchin pg. 192

Sumerian Months pg. 156..The 12ᵗʰ Planet by Zecharia Sitchin pg. 194

The Sumerian Solar System pg. 157...........................The 12ᵗʰ Planet by Zecharia Sitchin pg. 204

The Sumerian Procession pg. 159..............................The 12ᵗʰ Planet by Zecharia Sitchin pg. 192

The History of The Anunnaki pg. 163....................The Wars of Gods and Men by Zecharia Sitchin pg. 345

The 12 Gates of The Duat pg. 165...........The Sacred Tradition In Ancient Egypt by Rosemary Clark pg. 282

The 12 Divisions of Night pg. 168...........The Sacred Tradition In Ancient Egypt by Rosemary Clark pg. 286

The Pyramid Code pg. 174.......................................Fingerprints of The Gods by Graham Hancock pg. 179

Christian J. Bullock

Suggested Reading

Bauval, Robert. Gilbert, Adrian. *The Orion Mystery.* New York, NY: Three Rivers Press, 1994.
Carroll, Peter J. *Liber Null and Psychonaut.* San Francisco, CA: Red Wheel/Weiser, LLC, 1987.
Clark, Rosemary. *The Sacred Tradition in Ancient Egypt.* St. Paul, MN: Llewellyn, 2000.
Conway, D.J. *Dancing with Dragons.* St. Paul, MN: Llewellyn, 2001.
Conway, D.J. *Mystical Dragon Magick: Teaching of the Five Inner Rings.* St. Paul, MN: Llewellyn, 2007.
Hancock, Graham. *Fingerprints of the Gods.* New York, NY: Three Rivers Press, 1995.
Hancock, Graham. Bauval, Robert. *The Message of the Sphinx.* New York, NY: Three Rivers Press, 1996.
Hancock, Graham. *The Mars Mystery.* New York, NY: Three Rivers Press, 1998.
Hancock, Graham. *Underworld: The Mysterious Origins of Civilization.* New York, NY: Three Rivers Press, 2002.
Konstantinos. *Summoning Spirits: the art of magical evocation.* St. Paul, MN: Llewellyn, 1995.
Konstantinos. *Nocturnal Witchcraft: magick after dark.* St. Paul, MN: Llewellyn, 2002.
Konstantinos. *Gothic Grimoire.* St. Paul, MN: Llewellyn, 2002.
Konstantinos. *Nocturnicon: calling dark forces and powers.* St. Paul, MN: Llewellyn, 2005.
Schlangekraft, Inc. *Necronomicon.* New York, NY: Avon Books, 1977.
Sitchin, Zecharia. *The 12th Planet: Book I of the Earth Chronicles.* New York, NY: Harper, 2007.
Sitchin, Zecharia. *The Stairway to Heaven: Book II of the Earth Chronicles.* New York, NY: Harper, 2007.
Sitchin, Zecharia. *The Wars of Gods and Men: Book III of the Earth Chronicles.* New York, NY: Harper, 2007.
Sitchin, Zecharia. *The Lost Realms: Book IV of the Earth Chronicles.* New York, NY: Harper, 2007.
Sitchin, Zecharia. *There were giants upon the Earth: gods, demigods, and human ancestry: the evidence of alien DNA.* Rochester, VT: Bear & Company, 2010.
Temple, Robert K. G. *The Sirius Mystery: new scientific evidence of alien contact 5,000 years ago.* Rochester, VT: Destiny Books, 1998.
Tyson, Donald. *Portable Magic: Tarot Is the Only Tool You Need.* St. Paul, MN: Llewellyn, 2006.

shaman.

Symbols and stars of power

O — a dot of binary   360°
1 — a line of binary   180°
△ — 3 points / 360° fire   120°
+ — earth cross 4 points / 360°   90°
☆ — 5 points / 360° Pentagram 72°
✡ — 6 points / 360° star of David 60°
✷ — 7 points / 360° elevenstar 51.4°
✳ — 8 points / 360°   45°
✺ — 9 points / 360°   40°
✸ — 10 points / 360°   36°
✳ — 11 points / 360°   32.72°
✴ — 12 points / 360°   30°

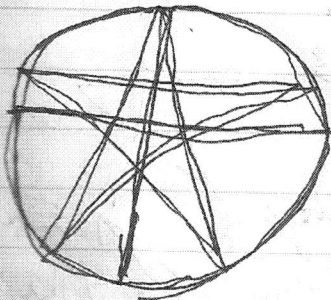

71.6° × 71.6 years
5,126.56 years
71.6° of procession
of equinox
71.6 years of 1°
of procession
of equinox

Christian J. Bullock

Christian J. Bullock

Printed in Great Britain
by Amazon